Fourth Workshop on Computational Models of Reference, Anaphora and Coreference (CRAC 2021)

Punta Cana, Dominican Republic
10-11 November 2021

ISBN: 978-1-7138-9176-5

Printed from e-media with permission by:

Curran Associates, Inc.
57 Morehouse Lane
Red Hook, NY 12571

Some format issues inherent in the e-media version may also appear in this print version.

Printed with permission by Curran Associates, Inc. (2024)

For permission requests, please contact the Association for Computational Linguistics at the address below.

Association for Computational Linguistics
209 N. Eighth Street
Stroudsburg, Pennsylvania 18360

Phone: 1-570-476-8006
Fax: 1-570-476-0860

acl@aclweb.org

Additional copies of this publication are available from:

Curran Associates, Inc.
57 Morehouse Lane
Red Hook, NY 12571 USA
Phone: 845-758-0400
Fax: 845-758-2633
Email: curran@proceedings.com
Web: www.proceedings.com

EMNLP 2021

Fourth Workshop on Computational Models of Reference, Anaphora and Coreference

Proceedings of the Workshop

November 10–11, 2021
Punta Cana, Dominican Republic

Message from the Program Chairs

This is the fourth edition of the Workshop on Computational Models of Reference, Anaphora and Coreference (CRAC). CRAC was first held in New Orleans three years ago in conjunction with NAACL HLT 2018. But the workshop series dates back to its predecessor, the Coreference Resolution Beyond OntoNotes (CORBON) that started in 2016, and have arguably become the primary forum for coreference researchers to present their latest results since the demise of the Discourse Anaphora and Anaphor Resolution Colloquium series in 2011. While CORBON focused on under-investigated coreference phenomena, CRAC has a broader scope, covering all cases of computational modeling of reference, anaphora, and coreference.

CRAC 2021 continued to attract a large number of very high quality papers. Specifically, we received 19 submissions which were rigorously reviewed by two to three program committee members. Based on their recommendations, we initially accepted 13 papers and conditionally accepted 3 papers. The three conditionally accepted papers were eventually accepted to the workshop after we made sure that the authors adequately addressed the reviewers' comments in the final camera-ready version. Overall, we were pleased with the large number of submissions as well as the quality of the accepted papers.

In 2021 we continued the two initiatives we started last year. First, with the goal of having a broad technical program, we introduced different paper categories. In addition to research papers, we welcomed survey papers, position papers, challenge papers, and demo papers. In each of these paper categories, authors were expected to report completed work. To encourage researchers to report work in progress and/or late-breaking results, we introduced another submission type, extended abstracts. Our second initiative involved recognizing outstanding research submitted to the workshop via a best paper award.

This is the first year where we have organized a joint CODI-CRAC shared task on modeling coreference in dialog. In addition, this year we have several EMNLP *findings* papers that are going to be presented at the workshop. This should allow researchers who did not participate in the workshop to disseminate their work to a smaller and more focused audience which should promote interesting discussions.

We are grateful to the following people, without whom we could not have assembled an interesting program for the workshop. First, we are indebted to our program committee members. This year we were able to recruit enough reviewers that the reviewing load was on an average of two papers per reviewer. All of them did the incredible job of completing their reviews in a short reviewing period. Second, we thank Ido Dagan for accepting our invitation to be this year's invited speaker. Ido will give a talk on *Modeling informational relations across multiple texts*. Third, we thank Massimo Poesio for agreeing to chair a plenary session that focuses on the topic of developing Universal Anaphora (UA), a unified, language-independent markup scheme that reflects common cross-linguistic understanding of reference-related phenomena. Motivated by Universal Dependencies, UA aims to facilitate referential analysis of the similarities and idiosyncrasies among typologically different languages, support comparative evaluation of anaphora resolution systems and enable comparative linguistic studies. Finally, we would like to thank the workshop participants for joining in.

We hope you will enjoy it as much as we do!

— Sameer Pradhan, Maciej Ogrodniczuk, Yulia Grishina, and Vincent Ng

Organizing Committee and Proceedings Editors:

Maciej Ogrodniczuk, Institute of Computer Science, Polish Academy of Sciences
Sameer Pradhan, University of Pennsylvania and cemantix.org
Massimo Poesio, Queen Mary University of London
Yulia Grishina, Amazon
Vincent Ng, University of Texas at Dallas

Program Committee:

Antonio Branco, University of Lisbon
Arie Cattan, Bar-Ilan University
Jackie Chi Kit Cheung, McGill University
Dan Cristea, Alexandru Ioan Cuza University of Iasi
Stephanie Dipper, Ruhr-University Bochum
Elisa Ferracane, Abridge
Yulia Grishina, Amazon
Christian Hardmeier, IT University of Copenhagen
Lars Hellan, Norwegian University of Science and Technology
Veronique Hoste, Ghent University
Yufang Hou, IBM
Mohit Iyyer, University of Massachusetts Amherst
Sobha Lalitha Devi, AU-KBC Research Center, Anna University of Chennai
Ekaterina Lapshinova-Koltunski, Saarland University
Sharid Loáiciga, University of Potsdam
Costanza Navaretta, University of Copenhagen
Anna Nedoluzhko, Charles University in Prague
Michal Novák, Charles University in Prague
Constantin Orasan, University of Surrey
Sameer Pradhan, University of Pennsylvania and cemantix
Marta Recasens, Google
Manfred Stede, University of Potsdam
Don Tuggener, Zurich University of Applied Sciences
Yannick Versley, Amazon
Bonnie Webber, University of Edinburgh
Juntao Yu, Queen Mary University of London
Yilun Zhu, Georgetown University
Heike Zinsmeister, University of Hamburg

Invited Speaker:

Ido Dagan, Bar-Ilan University, Israel

Table of Contents

Workshop Program

Wednesday, November 10, 2021

9:05–9:30 Session 1: Welcome

9:05–9:30 *The CODI-CRAC 2021 Shared Task on Anaphora, Bridging, and Discourse Deixis in Dialogue*
Sopan Khosla, Juntao Yu, Ramesh Manuvinakurike, Vincent Ng, Massimo Poesio, Michael Strube and Carolyn Rosé

9:30–10:30 Session 2: System Talks (part 1)

9:30–9:45 *Neural Anaphora Resolution in Dialogue*
Hideo Kobayashi, Shengjie Li and Vincent Ng

9:45–10:00 *Anaphora Resolution in Dialogue: Description of the DFKI-TalkingRobots System for the CODI-CRAC 2021 Shared-Task*
Tatiana Anikina, Cennet Oguz, Natalia Skachkova, Siyu Tao, Sharmila Upadhyaya and Ivana Kruijff-Korbayova

10:00–10:15 *The Pipeline Model for Resolution of Anaphoric Reference and Resolution of Entity Reference*
Hongjin Kim, Damrin Kim and Harksoo Kim

10:15–10:30 *An End-to-End Approach for Full Bridging Resolution*
Joseph Renner, Priyansh Trivedi, Gaurav Maheshwari, Rémi Gilleron and Pascal Denis

10:30–11:00 Coffee Break

11:00–11:15 Session 3: System Talks (part 2)

11:00–11:15 *Adapted End-to-End Coreference Resolution System for Anaphoric Identities in Dialogues*
Liyan Xu and Jinho D. Choi

11:15–11:45 Session 4: Analysis Papers

11:15–11:30 *Anaphora Resolution in Dialogue: Cross-Team Analysis of the DFKI-TalkingRobots Team Submissions for the CODI-CRAC 2021 Shared-Task*
Natalia Skachkova, Cennet Oguz, Tatiana Anikina, Siyu Tao, Sharmila Upadhyaya and Ivana Kruijff-Korbayova

11:30–11:45 *The CODI-CRAC 2021 Shared Task on Anaphora, Bridging, and Discourse Deixis Resolution in Dialogue: A Cross-Team Analysis*
Shengjie Li, Hideo Kobayashi and Vincent Ng

11:45–12:00 Session 5: Visioning and Discussion

Thursday, November 11, 2021

9:00–9:05	**Opening Remarks** Maciej Ogrodniczuk, Sameer Pradhan, Massimo Poesio, Yulia Grishina and Vincent Ng
9:05–10:30	**Paper Session 1**
9:05–9:20	*A Brief Survey and Comparative Study of Recent Development of Pronoun Coreference Resolution in English* Hongming Zhang, Xinran Zhao and Yangqiu Song
9:20–9:35	*Coreference Resolution for the Biomedical Domain: A Survey* Pengcheng Lu and Massimo Poesio
9:35–9:50	*FantasyCoref: Coreference Resolution on Fantasy Literature Through Omniscient Writer's Point of View* Sooyoun Han, Sumin Seo, Minji Kang, Jongin Kim, Nayoung Choi, Min Song and Jinho D. Choi
9:50–10:00	*(Findings) CDLM: Cross-Document Language Modeling* Avi Caciularu, Arman Cohan, Iz Beltagy, Matthew Peters, Arie Cattan and Ido Dagan
10:00–10:15	*DramaCoref: A Hybrid Coreference Resolution System for German Theater Plays* Janis Pagel and Nils Reiter
10:15–10:30	*A Hybrid Rule-Based and Neural Coreference Resolution System with an Evaluation on Dutch Literature* Andreas van Cranenburgh, Esther Ploeger, Frank van den Berg and Remi Thüss
10:30–11:00	**Coffee Break**
11:00–12:00	**Invited Talk**
	Modeling Informational Relations across Multiple Texts Ido Dagan
12:00–1:00	**Lunch Break**

Thursday, November 11, 2021 (continued)

13:00–14:30 Paper Session 2

13:00–13:10 *Lazy Low-Resource Coreference Resolution: a Study on Leveraging Black-Box Translation Tools*
Semere Kiros Bitew, Johannes Deleu, Chris Develder and Thomas Demeester

13:10–13:20 *(Findings) Collecting a Large-Scale Gender Bias Dataset for Coreference Resolution and Machine Translation*
Shahar Levy, Koren Lazar and Gabriel Stanovsky

13:20–13:30 *(Findings) Do UD Trees Match Mention Spans in Coreference Annotations?*
Martin Popel, Zdeněk Žabokrtský, Anna Nedoluzhko, Michal Novák and Daniel Zeman

13:30–13:40 *(Findings) End-to-end Neural Information Status Classification*
Yufang Hou

13:40–13:50 *Resources and Evaluations for Danish Entity Resolution*
Maria Barrett, Hieu Lam, Martin Wu, Ophélie Lacroix, Barbara Plank and Anders Søgaard

13:50–14:05 *CoreLM: Coreference-aware Language Model Fine-Tuning*
Nikolaos Stylianou and Ioannis Vlahavas

14:05–14:20 *Data Augmentation Methods for Anaphoric Zero Pronouns*
Abdulrahman Aloraini and Massimo Poesio

14:20–14:30 *Exploring Pre-Trained Transformers and Bilingual Transfer Learning for Arabic Coreference Resolution*
Bonan Min

14:30–14:45 Mini Break

Thursday, November 11, 2021 (continued)

14:45–14:55 Universal Anaphora Panel

14:45–14:55 *Introduction*
Massimo Poesio

14:55–15:05 *The Universal Anaphora Extension of the CoNLL-U Markup Scheme*
Anna Nedoluzhko, Martin Popel, Zdeněk Žabokrtský, Amir Zeldes and Dan Zeman

15:05–15:15 *The Universal Anaphora Scorer*
Juntao Yu

15:15–15:25 *The CODI/CRAC Shared Task on Anaphora Resolution in Dialogue*
Sopan Khosla, Juntao Yu, Ramesh Manuvinakurike, Vincent Ng, Massimo Poesio, Michael Strube and Carolyn Rosé

15:25–15:45 Discussion

15:45–16:15 Best Paper Session

15:45–16:00 *Event and Entity Coreference using Trees to Encode Uncertainty in Joint Decisions*
Nishant Yadav, Nicholas Monath, Rico Angell and Andrew McCallum

16:00–16:15 *On Generalization in Coreference Resolution*
Shubham Toshniwal, Patrick Xia, Sam Wiseman, Karen Livescu and Kevin Gimpel

16:15–16:45 Coffee Break

Thursday, November 11, 2021 (continued)

16:45–17:50 Paper Session 3

16:45–17:00 *Improving Span Representation for Domain-adapted Coreference Resolution*
Nupoor Gandhi, Anjalie Field and Yulia Tsvetkov

17:00–17:15 *Coreference by Appearance: Visually Grounded Event Coreference Resolution*
Liming Wang, Shengyu Feng, Xudong Lin, Manling Li, Heng Ji and Shih-Fu Chang

17:15–17:30 *Anatomy of OntoGUM—Adapting GUM to the OntoNotes Scheme to Evaluate Robustness of SOTA Coreference Algorithms*
Yilun Zhu, Sameer Pradhan and Amir Zeldes

17:30–17:40 *Understanding Mention Detector-Linker Interaction in Neural Coreference Resolution*
Zhaofeng Wu and Matt Gardner

17:40–17:50 *(Findings) Coreference-aware Surprisal Predicts Brain Response*
Evan Jaffe, Byung-Doh Oh and William Schuler

17:50–18:00 Closing Remarks
Maciej Ogrodniczuk, Sameer Pradhan, Massimo Poesio, Yulia Grishina and Vincent Ng

A Brief Survey and Comparative Study of Recent Development of Pronoun Coreference Resolution in English

Hongming Zhang, Xinran Zhao, Yangqiu Song
Department of Computer Science, HKUST
hzhangal@cse.ust.hk, xzhaoar@connect.ust.hk, yqsong@cse.ust.hk

Abstract

Pronoun Coreference Resolution (PCR) is the task of resolving pronominal expressions to all mentions they refer to. Compared with the general coreference resolution task, the main challenge of PCR is the coreference relation prediction rather than the mention detection. As one important natural language understanding (NLU) component, pronoun resolution is crucial for many downstream tasks and still challenging for existing models, which motivates us to survey existing approaches and think about how to do better. In this survey, we first introduce representative datasets and models for the ordinary pronoun coreference resolution task. Then we focus on recent progress on hard pronoun coreference resolution problems (e.g., Winograd Schema Challenge) to analyze how well current models can understand commonsense. We conduct extensive experiments to show that even though current models are achieving good performance on the standard evaluation set, they are still not ready to be used in real applications (e.g., all SOTA models struggle on correctly resolving pronouns to infrequent objects). All experiment codes will be available upon acceptance.

1 Introduction

The question of how human beings resolve pronouns[1] has long been of interest to both linguistic and natural language processing (NLP) communities, for the reason that a pronoun itself only having weak semantic meaning brings challenges to natural language understanding. To explore solutions for that question, pronoun coreference resolution (PCR) (Hobbs, 1978) was proposed.[2] As a challenging yet vital natural language understanding task, pronoun coreference resolution is to find the correct reference for a given pronominal anaphor in the context and has been shown to be useful for a series of downstream tasks, such as machine translation (Mitkov et al., 1995; Lapshinova-Koltunski et al., 2018), summarization (Steinberger et al., 2007), and dialog systems (Strube and Müller, 2003).

Type	# Pairs	F1 (no mention)	F1 (mention)
NP-NP	25,828	0.690	0.768
NP-P	43,883	0.667	0.707
P-P	41,741	0.754	0.763
Overall	111,452	0.705	0.742

Table 1: The performance of the End-to-end model on the CoNLL-2012 shared task coreference resolution dataset. The model's performances of different coreference types are reported separately.

To investigate the difference between PCR and the general coreference resolution task, which tries to identify not only the coreference relations between noun phrases (NP) and pronouns (P) but also potential coreference relations between noun phrases or coreference relations between pronouns, we conduct experiments with one recent breakthrough model (i.e., End-to-end model (Lee et al., 2017)) on the CoNLL-2012 shard task (Pradhan et al., 2012) under two settings: one without the gold mention and one with the gold mention. In the 'without gold mention' setting, models are required to first identify spans from the documents as the mentions and then predict the coreference relations among these mentions. As a comparison, if gold

[1] Some pronouns may refer to non-nominal antecedents. For example, the pronoun "it" in "It is too cold in the Winter here" does not refer to any real object (Kolhatkar et al., 2018). But in this survey, we only focus on pronouns that refer to nominal antecedents.

[2] PCR is also known as anaphora resolution (Versley et al., 2016). Previous studies (Ng, 2005; Zhang et al., 2019c) mainly focus on three kinds of pronouns: third personal pronoun (e.g., *she, her, he, him, them, they, it*), possessive pronoun (e.g., *his, hers, its, their, theirs*), and demonstrative pronoun (e.g., *this, that, these, those*). The first and second personal pronouns are typically not considered as they often refer to the current speakers, which are normally out of the conversation or document. Besides that, conventional PCR works (Ng, 2005; Zhang et al., 2019b,c) mostly focusing on identifying coreference relations between pronouns and noun phrases rather than coreference relation between pronouns.

Proceedings of the 4th Workshop on Computational Models of Reference, Anaphora and Coreference (CRAC 2021), pages 1–11
Punta Cana, Dominican Republic, November 10–11, 2021.

mentions are provided, models only need to predict the coreference relations (i.e., the task of distinguishing between referential and non-referential instances is ignored). From the results in Table 1, we can see that, without the gold mention, the model performs well on P-P coreference relations, while not as well on the other two kinds of relations. However, if gold mentions are provided, the model can achieve very good performance on the NP-NP coreference relations. Compared with other kinds of coreference relations, no matter whether the gold mention is provided or not, resolving pronouns to noun phrases is always the most challenging one.

The correct resolution of pronouns typically requires reasoning over both linguistic knowledge (e.g., 'they' typically refers to plural objects[3]) and commonsense knowledge (e.g., in sentence "The fish ate the worm, it was hungry.", 'it' refers to 'fish' because hungry things tend to eat rather than be eaten.). Considering that the ordinary PCR task evaluates the inference over both types of knowledge at the same time, the performance on ordinary PCR tasks cannot clearly reflect models' performance regarding different knowledge types. To address this problem, the Winograd Schema Challenge (WSC) (Levesque et al., 2012) task is proposed. The influence of all commonly used linguistic knowledge is avoided during the creation of WSC such that WSC can be used to reflect how current PCR models can understand commonsense knowledge. In Section 2 and 3, we introduce the progress and remaining challenges on the ordinary PCR and WSC tasks respectively. After that, we introduce other PCR tasks that are developed for different research purposes in Section 4. In the end, we conclude this survey with Section 5. The contribution of this survey is three-fold: (1) we broadly introduce available PCR tasks, datasets, and models; (2) We summarize the main contribution of recent models; (3) We conduct experiments to analyze the limitations of current models, which can help the community think about how to better solve PCR in the future.

2 Ordinary PCR

Ordinary pronoun coreference resolution tasks are often defined over formal textual corpus (e.g., newspaper) and the annotation is usually conducted by domain experts or linguists. The PCR task can be formally defined as follows. Given a text D, which contains a pronoun p, the goal is to identify all the mentions that p refers to. We denote the correct mentions p refers to as $c \in \mathcal{C}$, where $\mathcal{C}$ is the correct mention set. Similarly, each candidate span is denoted as $s \in \mathcal{S}$, where $\mathcal{S}$ is the set of all candidate spans. Note that in the case where no golden mentions are provided, all possible spans in D are used to form $\mathcal{S}$. The task is thus to identify $\mathcal{C}$ out of $\mathcal{S}$. In the rest of this section, we introduce the widely used datasets as well as the progress and limitation of current approaches.

2.1 Datasets

Throughout the years, researchers in the NLP community have devoted great efforts to developing high-quality coreference resolution datasets[4] and we introduce representative ones as follows:

1. **MUC**: MUC-6 (Grishman and Sundheim, 1996) and MUC-7 (Chinchor, 1998), which were developed for the 6th and 7th message understanding conferences respectively, are the earliest coreference resolution datasets. They are focusing on English news articles and are relatively small compared with modern datasets.

2. **ACE**: The ACE dataset (Doddington et al., 2004) was proposed as part of the Automatic Content Extraction program. Compared with MUC datasets, ACE extends the corpus domain from news to other domains like telephonic speeches and broadcast conversations.

3. **CoNLL shared tasks**: CoNLL-2011 (Pradhan et al., 2011) and CoNLL-2012 (Pradhan et al., 2012) shared tasks were proposed to evaluate models' abilities of resolving unrestricted coreference resolution. Among these two, CoNLL-2011 only contains annotations in English and CoNLL-2012 extends the coverage to multiple other languages (i.e., Chinese and Arabic). Compared with MUC and ACE, CoNLL shared tasks have a much larger scale. Moreover, as CoNLL-2012 shared tasks provide clear training, dev, and test set separation as well as the official evaluation tool, it is the most widely

[3]One exception is the entities that are related to organizations. For example, "they" can refer to "the company" (Hardmeier et al., 2018). Another exception is to prevent generic masculine, where "they" can refer to singular entity in gender-neutral language.

[4]Some datasets (e.g., CoNLL-2012 shared task) are originally designed for the general coreference resolution task. Nonetheless, we can easily convert them into a PCR task.

used evaluation benchmark for the coreference resolution task.

4. **WikiCoref**: Recently, a new coreference dataset WikiCoref (Ghaddar and Langlais, 2016) was proposed as a supplementary of CoNLL shared tasks. Different from CoNLL, where most of the corpus is from the newswire, WikiCoref directly annotates Wikipedia pages, which provides a new way to evaluate models' performances in the out-of-domain setting.

5. **Crowd-sourced Coref**: Poesio et al. (2019) leveraged a crowd-sourced game to collect 2.2 million annotations about 108,000 coreference relations, which makes it one of the largest coreference datasets. Moreover, their annotations also include ambiguous coreference relations.

2.2 Methods

In this subsection, we introduce representative models for the ordinary PCR task. We first briefly introduce conventional approaches that rely on human-designed rules or features and then introduce the end-to-end model, which is a groundbreaking model for solving coreference resolution tasks. After that, we briefly introduce a few recent improvements over the end-to-end model.

2.2.1 Rule and Feature Based Methods

Before the deep learning era, human-designed rules (Hobbs, 1978; Raghunathan et al., 2010), knowledge (Ponzetto and Strube, 2006; Versley et al., 2016), and features (Ng, 2005; Wiseman et al., 2016) dominated the general coreference resolution and PCR tasks. Some rules and features are crucial for correctly resolving pronouns (Lee et al., 2013). For example, 'he' typically refers to males and 'she' typically refers to females; 'it' typically refers to singular objects and 'them' typically refers to plural objects. The performances of these methods heavily rely on the coverage and quality of the manually defined rules and features. Based on these designed features (Bengtson and Roth, 2008), a few more advanced machine learning models were applied to the coreference resolution task. For example, instead of identifying coreference relation pair-wisely, (Clark and Manning, 2015) proposes an entity-centric coreference system that can learn an effective policy for building coreference chains incrementally. Besides that, a novel model was also proposed to predict coreference relations with a deep reinforcement learning framework (Clark and Manning, 2016). Moreover, heuristic rules based on linguistic knowledge can also be incorporated into constraints for machine learning models (Chang et al., 2013).

2.2.2 End-to-end Model

Leveraging human-designed rules or features can help accurately resolve some pronouns, but it is hard to manually design rules to cover all cases. To solve this problem, an end-to-end deep model (Lee et al., 2017) was proposed. Different from other machine learning-based methods, it does not use any human-defined rules, yet achieves surprisingly good performance. Specifically, the end-to-end model first leverages the combination of Bidirectional LSTM and inner-attention modules to encode local context and generate representations for all potential mentions. After that, a standard feed-forward neural network is used to predict the coreference relations. Experiment results show that the proposed model is simple yet effective. Its success proves that current deep models are capable of capturing rich contextual information, which is crucial for resolving coreference relations.

2.2.3 Further Improvements

Recently, on top of the end-to-end model, a few improved works were proposed to address different limitations of the original end-to-end model[5]:

1. **Higher-order Information**: One limitation of the original end-to-end model is that all predictions are based on pairs, which is not sufficient for capturing higher-order coreference relations. To fix this issue, a differentiable approximation module was proposed in (Lee et al., 2018) to provide the higher-order coreference resolution inference ability (i.e., leveraging the coreference cluster to better predict the coreference relations). Moreover, this work first incorporates ELMo (Peters et al., 2018), a kind of deep contextualized word representations, as part of the word representation, which is proven very effective.

2. **Structured Knowledge**: Another limitation of the end-to-end model is that its success heavily relies on the quality and coverage of the training data. However, in real applications, it is labor-intensive and almost impossible to annotate a large-scale dataset to contain all scenar-

[5]These models once achieved better performance either on the general coreference resolution task or the PCR task.

Model	Third Personal (18,147)			Possessive (6,843)			Demonstrative (546)			Overall (25,536)		
	P	R	F1	P	R	F1	P	R	F1	P	R	F1
Deterministic (Raghunathan et al., 2010)	25.5	58.9	35.6	22.9	64.3	33.8	3.4	5.7	4.2	23.4	57.0	33.4
Statistical (Clark and Manning, 2015)	25.8	62.1	36.5	28.9	64.9	40.0	9.8	6.3	7.6	25.4	59.3	36.5
Deep-RL (Clark and Manning, 2016)	78.6	63.9	70.5	73.3	68.9	71.0	3.7	2.9	5.5	76.4	61.2	68.0
End-to-end (Lee et al., 2017)	70.7	77.8	74.1	75.6	74.0	74.8	37.8	71.7	49.5	68.3	76.4	72.1
+ KG (Zhang et al., 2019c)	80.0	75.6	77.7	81.7	72.2	76.7	50.8	**64.6**	**56.9**	77.9	74.0	75.9
+ SpanBERT (Joshi et al., 2020)	**82.4**	**80.5**	**81.5**	**83.9**	**81.0**	**82.4**	**52.0**	61.5	56.4	**82.2**	**80.2**	**81.2**

Table 2: Performances of different models on the CoNLL-2012 shared task. Precision (P), recall (R), and the F1 score are reported. Numbers of different types of pronouns in the test set are shown in the brackets. Best models are indicated with the **bold** font.

Model	Training data	Test data CoNLL	i2b2
End-to-end	CoNLL	72.1	75.2
	i2b2	20.0	92.3
+ KG	CoNLL	75.9	80.9
	i2b2	42.7	95.2
+ SpanBERT	CoNLL	79.6	40.8
	i2b2	28.5	80.5

Table 3: Models' performance (in F1 score) in cross-domain setting on different training/test data.

ios. To solve this problem, two works (Zhang et al., 2019b,c) were proposed to inject external structured knowledge into the end-to-end model. Among these two, (Zhang et al., 2019b) requires converting external knowledge into features while (Zhang et al., 2019c) directly uses external knowledge in the format of triplets.

3. **Stronger Language Representation Models**: Recently, along with the fast development of language representation models, a few works (Kantor and Globerson, 2019; Joshi et al., 2020) have been trying to replace the encoding layer of the original end-to-end model with more powerful language representation models. SpanBERT (Joshi et al., 2020) replaces ELMo with SpanBERT and boosts the performance by 6.6 F1 over the general coreference resolution task.

2.3 Performances and Analysis

We follow the experimental setting of (Zhang et al., 2019c) and test the performance[6] of representative models (Raghunathan et al., 2010; Clark and Manning, 2015, 2016; Lee et al., 2017; Zhang et al., 2019c; Joshi et al., 2020) on the CoNLL-2012 dataset (Pradhan et al., 2012). The experiment setting (both detection the mentions and resolving the coreference relations) and evaluation metric are the same as these previous works on CoNLL-2012. From the results in Table 2, we can observe that with the help of the end-to-end model and further modifications, the community has made great progress on the standard evaluation set. For example, the end-to-end model achieves an F1 score over 70 and adding external knowledge (either in a structured way or a representation way) further boost the performance. Among all pronoun types, all models perform better on third personal and possessive pronouns, and relatively poorly on demonstrative ones. This is mainly because of the imbalanced distribution of the dataset (i.e., third personal and possessive pronouns appear much more than demonstrative ones).

2.3.1 Cross-domain Performance

To investigate whether current PCR models are good enough to be used in real applications, which can be out of the training domain, we conduct experiments on the cross-domain setting. In detail, we select two different PCR datasets from different domains (i.e., CoNLL (Pradhan et al., 2012) from news and i2b2 (Uzuner et al., 2012) from the medical domain) and try to train the model on one dataset and test it on the other. We conduct experiments with three best-performing models and show the results in Table 3, from which we can see that all models[7] perform significantly worse if they

[6]We use the released codes of different models along with their default hyper-parameters to finish the experiments. For the end2end model, we also include ELMo (Peters et al., 2018) as part of the representation and achieve better performance than the original one in Table 1.

[7]SpanBERT performs poorly on i2b2 when it is not trained on it. The reason can be that the medical corpus is too different from the pre-trained corpus of SpanBERT and we use the default hyper-parameters, which might not be the best ones. Since the main contribution of SpanBERT is helping models to identify the mention spans, in our setting focusing on reference detection, such improvement is not necessary

Model	Object Type	P	R	F1
End-to-End	Infrequent	66.5	73.8	70.0
	Frequent	73.0	83.3	77.8
+ KG	Infrequent	77.9	72.5	75.1
	Frequent	78.0	77.7	77.9
+ SpanBERT	Infrequent	71.3	72.4	71.9
	Frequent	83.3	85.3	84.3

Table 4: Influence of the frequency.

are used across domains (i.e., when the domains of training and test data are different). Compared with the baseline method, adding explicit knowledge can help achieve slightly better performance in the cross-domain setting because its training objective allows models to learn to selectively use suitable knowledge rather than just fitting the training data.

2.3.2 Influence of Frequency

To further analyze the performance of existing models, we split the pronouns based on the frequency of the objects they refer to. If an object appears more than ten times in the whole dataset, we denote it as a frequent object. Otherwise, we denote it as an infrequent object. As a result, we collect 1,095 frequent and 470,232 infrequent objects, whose average frequencies are 36.2 and 1.46 respectively. We report the performance of best-performing models on infrequent and frequent objects separately in Table 4. In general, all models perform better on frequent objects because they appear more in the training data. Another interesting observation is that, even though adding external KG and a stronger language representation model can both boost the performance, their improvements come from different types of objects. For example, the main contribution of adding KG is on infrequent objects because even though they are less frequent in the training data, they can still be covered by some external knowledge. As a comparison, using a strong language representation model mainly benefits the frequent objects because it has a stronger ability to fit the training data. This observation is consistent with our previous observations that adding external KG has more effect on those relatively rare pronouns (i.e., demonstrative pronouns).

3 Hard PCR

As aforementioned, the correct resolution of pronouns requires the inference over both linguistic knowledge and commonsense knowledge. To clearly reflect how models can resolve pronouns

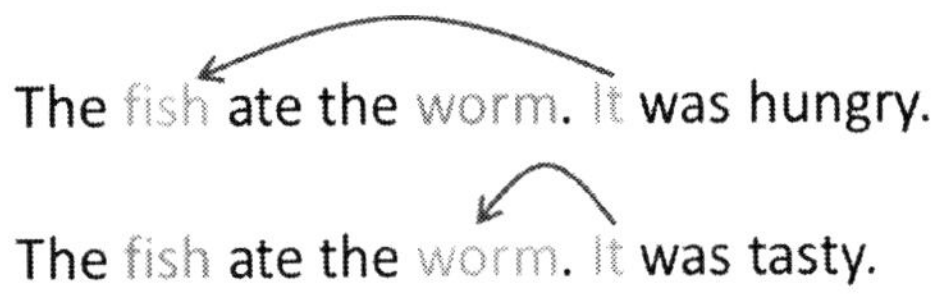

Figure 1: WSC question examples.

that require the inference over commonsense knowledge, the hard PCR task was proposed. As Winograd Schema Challenge (WSC) is one of the most popular hard PCR tasks, we use the task definition in WSC to define the hard PCR task. For each question q, a sentence s is given, which contains a pronoun p and two candidates n_1, n_2. The task is to find out which of the candidates p refers to. Different from the ordinary PCR task, the influence of all commonly observed features (e.g., gender or plurality) are removed via careful expert design. In WSC, all questions are paired up such that questions in each pair have only minor differences (mostly one-word difference), but the answers are reversed. One pair of the WSC instances is shown in Figure 1. Solving these questions typically requires the support of complex commonsense knowledge. For example, human beings can know that the pronoun 'it' in the first sentence refers to 'fish' while the one in the second sentence refers to 'worm' because 'hungry' is a common property of something eating while 'tasty' is a common property of something being eaten. Without the support of such commonsense knowledge, answering these questions becomes challenging because both the fish and worm can be hungry or tasty by themselves.

3.1 Datasets

We introduce datasets as follows:

1. **Winograd Schema Challenge**: Among all the hard pronoun coreference resolution tasks, WSC is among the most popular ones. In total, WSC has 273 questions[8]. Its small size determines that it cannot be used to train a good supervised model and can only be used as the evaluation set.

2. **Definite Pronoun Resolution**: Another hard pronoun coreference resolution dataset

[8]The latest version of WSC has 284 questions, but as all the following works are evaluated based on the 273-question version, we still use the 273-question version in this survey.

is the definite pronoun resolution dataset (DPR)[9] (Rahman and Ng, 2012). Different from WSC, DPR leveraged undergraduates rather than experts to create the dataset. In total, DPR collected 1,886 questions, which is a slightly larger scale than the official WSC. However, as DPR can not guarantee that all DPR questions follow the strict design guideline of WSC, questions in DPR are relatively simpler.

3. **WinoGrande**: One common problem of WSC and DPR is their small scales. To create a larger scale dataset, WinoGrande (Sakaguchi et al., 2020) was proposed. By leveraging annotators from Amazon Mechanical Turk, WinoGrande collected 53 thousand WSC-like questions. Moreover, to make sure of the dataset quality, WinoGrande applied a bias reduction algorithm to filter out examples that may contain annotation bias. Experimental results prove that WinoGrande is much more challenging than the original WSC because the SOTA models on WSC only achieve 51% accuracy on WinoGrande, which is similar to the random guess.

4. **KnowRef**: KnowRef (Emami et al., 2019), similar to WinoGrande, also aimed at creating a larger scale WSC dataset but with a different approach. Instead of using crowd-sourcing + adversarial filtering framework, KnowRef tried to extract WSC-like questions from raw sentences. As a result, KnowRef collected eight thousand WSC-like questions.

3.2 Methods

In this subsection, we introduce existing approaches for the hard PCR task. As the majority of the methods are evaluated based on WSC, all the discussion and analysis are based on their performance on WSC.

3.2.1 Reasoning with Structured Knowledge

At first, people tried to leverage different commonsense knowledge resources to solve WSC questions in an explainable way. For example, Liu et al. (2016) first leveraged the commonsense triplets from ConceptNet (Liu and Singh, 2004) to train the word embeddings and then applied the embeddings to solve the WSC task. Knowledge hunter (Emami et al., 2018) proposed to leverage search engines (e.g., Google) to acquire needed commonsense knowledge. It first searched WSC questions in search engines and then used the returned searching results to solve WSC questions. SP-10K (Zhang et al., 2019a) conducted experiments to show that selectional preference (SP) knowledge such as human beings are more likely to eat 'food' rather than 'rock' can also be helpful for solving WSC questions. Last but not least, ASER (Zhang et al., 2020) tried to use knowledge about eventualities (e.g., 'being hungry' can cause 'eat food') to solve WSC questions. In general, structured commonsense knowledge can help solve one-third of the WSC questions, but their overall performance is limited due to their low coverage. There are mainly two reasons: (1) coverage of existing commonsense resources are not large enough; (2) lack of a principled way to use structured knowledge for NLP tasks. Current methods (Emami et al., 2018; Zhang et al., 2019a, 2020) mostly rely on string match. However, for many WSC questions, it is hard to find supportive knowledge in such way.

3.2.2 Language Representation Models

Another approach is leveraging language models to solve WSC questions (Trinh and Le, 2018), where each WSC question is first converted into two sentences by replacing the target pronoun with the two candidates respectively and then the language models can be employed to compute the probability of both sentences. The sentence with a higher probability will be selected as the final prediction. As this method does not require any string match, it can make prediction for all WSC questions and achieve better overall performance. Recently, a more advanced transformer-based language model GPT-2 (Radford et al., 2019) achieved better performance due to its stronger language representation ability. The success of language models demonstrates that rich commonsense knowledge can be indeed encoded within language models implicitly. Another interesting finding about these language model based approaches is that they proposed two settings to predict the probability: (1) Full: use the probability of the whole sentence as the final prediction; (2) Partial: only consider the probability of the partial sentence after the target pronoun. Experiments show that the partial model always outperforms the full model. One explanation is that the influence of the imbalanced distribution of candidate words is relieved by only considering the sentence probability after them. Such observation also explains why GPT-2 can outperform unsuper-

[9] This dataset is also referred to as WSCR in some works.

	Methods	Correct	Wrong	NA	A_p	A_o
Unsupervised	Random Guess	137	136	0	50.2%	50.2%
	Knowledge Hunting (Emami et al., 2018)	119	79	75	60.1%	57.3%
	SP (Human) (Zhang et al., 2019a)	15	0	258	**100%**	52.7%
	SP (PP) (Zhang et al., 2019a)	50	26	197	65.8%	54.4%
	ASER (String Match) (Zhang et al., 2020)	63	27	183	70.0%	56.6%
	LM (Single) (Trinh and Le, 2018)	149	124	0	54.5%	54.5%
	LM (Ensemble) (Trinh and Le, 2018)	168	105	0	61.5%	61.5%
	GPT-2 (Radford et al., 2019)	193	80	0	70.7%	70.7%
Finetuning	BERT (Devlin et al., 2019) +ASER (Zhang et al., 2020)	177	96	0	64.5%	64.5%
	BERT (Devlin et al., 2019) +DPR (Rahman and Ng, 2012)	195	78	0	71.4%	71.4%
	BERT (Devlin et al., 2019) +WinoGrande (Sakaguchi et al., 2020)	210	63	0	76.9%	76.9%
	RoBERTa (Liu et al., 2019) +DRP (Rahman and Ng, 2012)	227	46	0	83.1%	83.1%
	RoBERTa (Liu et al., 2019) +WinoGrande (Sakaguchi et al., 2020)	246	27	0	90.1%	**90.1%**
Human Beings	Original (Levesque et al., 2012)	252	21	0	92.1%	92.1%
	Recent (Sakaguchi et al., 2020)	264	9	0	96.5%	96.5%

Table 5: Performances of different models on the 273-question version WSC. *NA* means that the model cannot give a prediction, A_p means the accuracy of predict examples without *NA* examples. And A_o the overall accuracy of all examples (i.e., Correct, Wrong, and *NA* examples)

vised BERT on WSC because models based on BERT, which relies on predicting the probability of candidate words, cannot get rid of such noise.

3.2.3 Fine-tuning Representation Models

Last but not least, we introduce current best-performing models on the WSC task, which fine-tunes pre-trained language representation models (e.g., BERT (Devlin et al., 2019) or RoBERTa (Liu et al., 2019)) with a similar dataset (e.g., DPR (Rahman and Ng, 2012) or WinoGrande (Sakaguchi et al., 2020)). CorefBERT (Ye et al., 2020), in addition, introduced a new pre-training task that requires models to predict mention references. This idea of fine-tuning was originally proposed by (Kocijan et al., 2019), which first converts the original WSC task into a token prediction task and then selects the candidate with higher probability as the final prediction. In general, the stronger the language models and the larger the fine-tuning datasets are, the better the model can perform on the WSC task.

3.3 Performances and Analysis

To clearly understand the progress we have made on solving hard PCR problems, we show the performance of all models on Winograd Schema challenge in Table 5. From the results, we can make the following observations:

1. Even though methods that leverage structured knowledge can provide explainable solutions to WSC questions, their performance is typically limited by their low coverage.
2. Different from them, language model based methods represent knowledge contained in human language with an implicit approach, and thus do not have the matching issue and achieve better overall performance.
3. In general, fine-tuning pre-trained language representation models (e.g., BERT and RoBERTa) with similar datasets (e.g., DPR and WinoGrande) achieve the current SOTA performances and two observations can be made: (1) The stronger the pre-trained model, the better the performance. This observation shows that current language representation models can indeed cover commonsense knowledge and along with the increase of their representation ability (e.g., deeper model or larger pre-training corpus like RoBERTa), more commonsense knowledge can be effectively represented. (2) The larger the fine-tuning dataset, the better the performance. This is probably because the knowledge about some WSC questions is only covered by WinoGrande but not in DPR.

To investigate the reason behind WinoGrande's success, we divide WinoGrande into subsets based on the instances' relevance towards WSC. Assuming that the instance set of WinoGrande and WSC are $\mathcal{I}_{WG}$ and $\mathcal{I}_{WSC}$ respectively, for each instance $i \in \mathcal{I}_{WG}$, we design its relevance score as follows:

$$R_{WSC}(i) = Max(\frac{O^2(i,i')}{L(i) \cdot L(i')}, i' \in \mathcal{I}_{WSC}), \quad (1)$$

L.R. \ Rel.	High (13,466)	Medium (13,466)	Low (13,466)	Overall (40,398)
1e-6	87.81%	85.63%	84.95%	**88.89%**
2e-6	87.46%	87.81%	50.53%	**90.32%**
5e-6	87.10%	86.74%	50.17%	**91.76%**
1e-5 (default)	**87.81%**	85.66%	84.94%	87.46%
2e-5	53.04%	51.25%	52.33%	**84.58%**
5e-5	51.97%	50.09%	51.97%	**55.56%**
1e-4	**53.75%**	53.05%	52.69%	51.06%
Average	72.71%	71.46%	61.08%	**78.51%**

Table 6: Performance of fine-tuning RoBERTa with different learning rates and three subsets of WinoGrande split by their instances' relevance towards the original WSC. L.R. means learning rate and Rel. means relevance to WSC data. Numbers of instances are shown in brackets. Best performed datasets for each learning rate is indicated with the **bold** font.

where $O(i, i')$ is the unigram co-occurrence of i and i' and $L()$ is the instance length. We use the released code and dataset to conduct the experiments and follow all hyper-parameters as the original paper (Sakaguchi et al., 2020) except the batch size[10].

From the results in Table 6, we can observe that: (1) The most relevant instances contribute the most to the success. In some learning rate settings, it performs similar to or even better than the overall set; (2) Less relevant instances also help, which shows that current fine-tuning approach is not just fitting the data but also learning some underneath knowledge about solving the task from the data; (3) The model can be sensitive to the hyper-parameters (i.e., learning rate). Different subsets have different best hyper-parameters and the learning process can easily fail with a bad hyper-parameter choice. To achieve a good performance on a fixed dataset like WSC, we can tune the hyper-parameters. But to create a reliable PCR system we can rely on in real life, we probably need a more robust model.

4 Other PCR Tasks

Besides the ordinary and hard PCR tasks, PCR is also an important research topic for many special purposes (e.g., gender bias) or in some special settings (e.g., Visual-aware PCR). In this section, we briefly introduce these tasks:

1. **PCR in the Medical Domain**: I2b2 (Uzuner et al., 2012) is a dataset that focuses on identifying coreference relations in electronic medical records. As reported in (Zhang et al., 2019c), the training set of I2b2 contains 2,024 third personal pronouns, 685 possessive pronouns, and 270 demonstrative pronouns. Its test set contains 1,244 third personal pronouns, 367 possessive pronouns, and 166 demonstrative pronouns. As a dataset in a relatively narrow domain, the usage of domain knowledge becomes important. As shown in (Zhang et al., 2019c), i2b2 can be used as an additional dataset to evaluate models' cross-domain abilities.

2. **PCR for Machine Translation**: ParCor (Guillou et al., 2014) and ParCorFull (Lapshinova-Koltunski et al., 2018) are datasets focusing on PCR in parallel multi-lingual datasets, which can be used in downstream machine translation tasks. Different from other PCR works, it focuses on how to leverage the PCR results for better translation rather than how to solve the PCR problem.

3. **PCR for Chatbots**: CIC (Chen and Choi, 2016) is a dataset focusing on identifying coreference relations in multi-party conversations. Compared with the ordinary PCR tasks, which are mostly annotated on formal textual data (e.g., newswire), identifying coreference relation in conversation is more challenging.

4. **PCR for Studying Gender Bias**: Nowadays, gender bias has been a hot research topic in the NLP community (Rudinger et al., 2018; Zhao et al., 2018). WinoGender (Rudinger et al., 2018) is among the most popular works. The setting of WinoGender is similar to the setting of WSC (Levesque et al., 2012), where each sentence contains one target pronoun and two candidate noun phrases and the models are required to select the correct antecedent from the two candidates. But the purpose is different. WSC aims at evaluating models' abilities to understand commonsense knowledge, while WinoGender aims at evaluating how well models can predict without the influence of gender bias. The experiments show that some gender bias (e.g., 'he' is more likely to be predicted to be the doctor rather than the nurse by the machine) indeed exists in pre-trained language representation models. Such observation is astonishing and motivates the community to think about how to minimize the influence of such gender bias.

[10]The original batch size is 16 and our batch size is 4 due to the GPU memory limitation, so the experimental result is slightly different from the one reported in the original paper.

5. **Visual-aware PCR**: Recently, a visual-aware PCR dataset (Yu et al., 2019), which evaluates how well models can ground pronouns to visual objects, was proposed. Similar to CIC (Chen and Choi, 2016), visual-aware PCR also focuses on pronouns in daily dialogue, where the language usage is informal and a lot of background knowledge can be missing. For example, if one speaker refers to something both speakers can see, they may directly use a pronoun rather than introduce it first. In such a case, a pronoun may refer to not mentioned objects in the conversation. As analyzed in the original paper, 15% of pronouns in conversations refer to not mentioned objects and for them, leveraging the visual context information becomes crucial. As shown in (Kottur et al., 2018), grounding pronouns to the visual objects can significantly help the model to better understand the dialog and generate the better response, which further proves that visual-aware PCR is an important research topic to explore.

5 Conclusion

In this paper, we survey the progress on the pronoun coreference resolution (PCR) task, and analyze the improvement and limitations of existing approaches. Experiments and analysis on both the ordinary and hard PCR tasks demonstrate that even though we have made great progress according to the main evaluation metric, the PCR task is still far away from being solved. For example, all best-performing ordinary PCR models struggle on the cross-domain setting as well as infrequent objects. Also, even though fine-tuning pre-trained language representation models can achieve near-human performance on WSC, it can be sensitive to the hyper-parameters. All codes will be released to encourage the research on the PCR task.

Acknowledgements

This paper was supported by Early Career Scheme (ECS, No. 26206717), General Research Fund (GRF, No. 16211520), and Research Impact Fund (RIF, No. R6020-19) from the Research Grants Council (RGC) of Hong Kong.

References

Eric Bengtson and Dan Roth. 2008. Understanding the value of features for coreference resolution. In *Proceedings of EMNLP 2008*, pages 294–303.

Kai-Wei Chang, Rajhans Samdani, and Dan Roth. 2013. A constrained latent variable model for coreference resolution. In *Proceedings of EMNLP 2013*, pages 601–612.

Yu-Hsin Chen and Jinho D. Choi. 2016. Character identification on multiparty conversation: Identifying mentions of characters in TV shows. In *Proceedings of SIGDIAL 2016*, pages 90–100.

Nancy A Chinchor. 1998. Overview of muc-7/met-2. In *the Seventh Message Understanding Conference(MUC7)*.

Kevin Clark and Christopher D. Manning. 2015. Entity-centric coreference resolution with model stacking. In *Proceedings of ACL 2015*, pages 1405–1415.

Kevin Clark and Christopher D. Manning. 2016. Deep reinforcement learning for mention-ranking coreference models. In *Proceedings of EMNLP 2016*, pages 2256–2262.

Jacob Devlin, Ming-Wei Chang, Kenton Lee, and Kristina Toutanova. 2019. BERT: pre-training of deep bidirectional transformers for language understanding. In *Proceedings of NAACL-HLT 2019*, pages 4171–4186.

George R. Doddington, Alexis Mitchell, Mark A. Przybocki, Lance A. Ramshaw, Stephanie M. Strassel, and Ralph M. Weischedel. 2004. The automatic content extraction (ACE) program - tasks, data, and evaluation. In *Proceedings of LREC 2004*.

Ali Emami, Noelia De La Cruz, Adam Trischler, Kaheer Suleman, and Jackie Chi Kit Cheung. 2018. A knowledge hunting framework for common sense reasoning. In *Proceedings of EMNLP 2018*, pages 1949–1958.

Ali Emami, Paul Trichelair, Adam Trischler, Kaheer Suleman, Hannes Schulz, and Jackie Chi Kit Cheung. 2019. The knowref coreference corpus: Removing gender and number cues for difficult pronominal anaphora resolution. In *Proceedings of ACL 2019*, pages 3952–3961.

Abbas Ghaddar and Philippe Langlais. 2016. Wikicoref: An english coreference-annotated corpus of wikipedia articles. In *Proceedings of LREC 2016*.

Ralph Grishman and Beth Sundheim. 1996. Message understanding conference- 6: A brief history. In *Proceedings of COLING 1996*, pages 466–471.

Liane Guillou, Christian Hardmeier, Aaron Smith, Jörg Tiedemann, and Bonnie L. Webber. 2014. Parcor 1.0: A parallel pronoun-coreference corpus to support statistical MT. In *Proceedings of LREC 2014*, pages 3191–3198.

Christian Hardmeier, Luca Bevacqua, Sharid Loáiciga, and Hannah Rohde. 2018. Forms of anaphoric reference to organisational named entities: Hoping to widen appeal, they diversified. In *Proceedings of the Seventh Named Entities Workshop*, pages 36–40.

Jerry R Hobbs. 1978. Resolving pronoun references. *Lingua*, 44(4):311–338.

Mandar Joshi, Danqi Chen, Yinhan Liu, Daniel S. Weld, Luke Zettlemoyer, and Omer Levy. 2020. Spanbert: Improving pre-training by representing and predicting spans. *Trans. Assoc. Comput. Linguistics*, 8:64–77.

Ben Kantor and Amir Globerson. 2019. Coreference resolution with entity equalization. In *Proceedings of ACL 2019*, pages 673–677.

Vid Kocijan, Ana-Maria Cretu, Oana-Maria Camburu, Yordan Yordanov, and Thomas Lukasiewicz. 2019. A surprisingly robust trick for the winograd schema challenge. In *Proceedings of ACL 2019*, pages 4837–4842.

Varada Kolhatkar, Adam Roussel, Stefanie Dipper, and Heike Zinsmeister. 2018. Survey: Anaphora with non-nominal antecedents in computational linguistics: a Survey. *Computational Linguistics*, 44(3):547–612.

Satwik Kottur, José M. F. Moura, Devi Parikh, Dhruv Batra, and Marcus Rohrbach. 2018. Visual coreference resolution in visual dialog using neural module networks. In *Proceedings of ECCV 2018*, pages 160–178.

Ekaterina Lapshinova-Koltunski, Christian Hardmeier, and Pauline Krielke. 2018. ParCorFull: a parallel corpus annotated with full coreference. In *Proceedings of LREC 2018*.

Heeyoung Lee, Angel X. Chang, Yves Peirsman, Nathanael Chambers, Mihai Surdeanu, and Dan Jurafsky. 2013. Deterministic coreference resolution based on entity-centric, precision-ranked rules. *Computational Linguistics*, 39(4):885–916.

Kenton Lee, Luheng He, Mike Lewis, and Luke Zettlemoyer. 2017. End-to-end neural coreference resolution. In *Proceedings of EMNLP 2017*, pages 188–197.

Kenton Lee, Luheng He, and Luke Zettlemoyer. 2018. Higher-order coreference resolution with coarse-to-fine inference. In *Proceedings of NAACL-HLT 2018*, pages 687–692.

Hector Levesque, Ernest Davis, and Leora Morgenstern. 2012. The winograd schema challenge. In *Proceeedings of KRR 2012*.

Hugo Liu and Push Singh. 2004. Conceptnet—a practical commonsense reasoning tool-kit. *BT technology journal*, 22(4):211–226.

Quan Liu, Hui Jiang, Zhen-Hua Ling, Xiaodan Zhu, Si Wei, and Yu Hu. 2016. Commonsense knowledge enhanced embeddings for solving pronoun disambiguation problems in winograd schema challenge. *arXiv preprint arXiv:1611.04146*.

Yinhan Liu, Myle Ott, Naman Goyal, Jingfei Du, Mandar Joshi, Danqi Chen, Omer Levy, Mike Lewis, Luke Zettlemoyer, and Veselin Stoyanov. 2019. Roberta: A robustly optimized BERT pretraining approach. *CoRR*, abs/1907.11692.

Ruslan Mitkov et al. 1995. Anaphora resolution in machine translation. In *TMMT*.

Vincent Ng. 2005. Supervised ranking for pronoun resolution: Some recent improvements. In *Proceedings of AAAI 2005*, pages 1081–1086.

Matthew E. Peters, Mark Neumann, Mohit Iyyer, Matt Gardner, Christopher Clark, Kenton Lee, and Luke Zettlemoyer. 2018. Deep contextualized word representations. In *Proceedings of NAACL-HLT 2018*, pages 2227–2237.

Massimo Poesio, Jon Chamberlain, Silviu Paun, Juntao Yu, Alexandra Uma, and Udo Kruschwitz. 2019. A crowdsourced corpus of multiple judgments and disagreement on anaphoric interpretation. In *Proceedings of NAACL-HLT 2019*, pages 1778–1789.

Simone Paolo Ponzetto and Michael Strube. 2006. Exploiting semantic role labeling, WordNet and Wikipedia for coreference resolution. In *Proceedings of NAACL-HLT 2006*, pages 192–199.

Sameer Pradhan, Alessandro Moschitti, Nianwen Xue, Olga Uryupina, and Yuchen Zhang. 2012. Conll-2012 shared task: Modeling multilingual unrestricted coreference in ontonotes. In *Proceedings of CoNLL 2012*, pages 1–40.

Sameer Pradhan, Lance A. Ramshaw, Mitchell P. Marcus, Martha Palmer, Ralph M. Weischedel, and Nianwen Xue. 2011. Conll-2011 shared task: Modeling unrestricted coreference in ontonotes. In *Proceedings of CoNLL 2011*, pages 1–27.

Alec Radford, Jeff Wu, Rewon Child, David Luan, Dario Amodei, and Ilya Sutskever. 2019. Language models are unsupervised multitask learners. *OpenAI Blog*, 1(8):9.

Karthik Raghunathan, Heeyoung Lee, Sudarshan Rangarajan, Nate Chambers, Mihai Surdeanu, Dan Jurafsky, and Christopher D. Manning. 2010. A multipass sieve for coreference resolution. In *Proceedings of EMNLP 2010*.

Altaf Rahman and Vincent Ng. 2012. Resolving complex cases of definite pronouns: The winograd schema challenge. In *Proceedings of EMNLP-CoNLL 2012*, pages 777–789.

Rachel Rudinger, Jason Naradowsky, Brian Leonard, and Benjamin Van Durme. 2018. Gender bias in coreference resolution. In *Proceedings of the 2018 Conference of the North American Chapter of the Association for Computational Linguistics: Human Language Technologies, NAACL-HLT, New Orleans, Louisiana, USA, June 1-6, 2018, Volume 2 (Short Papers)*, pages 8–14.

Keisuke Sakaguchi, Ronan Le Bras, Chandra Bhagavatula, and Yejin Choi. 2020. WINOGRANDE: an adversarial winograd schema challenge at scale. In *Proceedings of AAAI 2020*.

Josef Steinberger, Massimo Poesio, Mijail A Kabadjov, and Karel Jevzek. 2007. Two uses of anaphora resolution in summarization. *Information Processing & Management*.

Michael Strube and Christoph Müller. 2003. A machine learning approach to pronoun resolution in spoken dialogue. In *Proceedings of ACL 2003*, pages 168–175.

Trieu H. Trinh and Quoc V. Le. 2018. A simple method for commonsense reasoning. *CoRR*, abs/1806.02847.

Ozlem Uzuner, Andreea Bodnari, Shuying Shen, Tyler Forbush, John Pestian, and Brett R South. 2012. Evaluating the state of the art in coreference resolution for electronic medical records. *J. Am. Medical Informatics Assoc.*, 19(5):786–791.

Yannick Versley, Massimo Poesio, and Simone Ponzetto. 2016. *Using Lexical and Encyclopedic Knowledge*, pages 393–429. Springer Berlin Heidelberg, Berlin, Heidelberg.

Sam Wiseman, Alexander M. Rush, and Stuart M. Shieber. 2016. Learning global features for coreference resolution. In *Proceedings of NAACL-HLT 2016*, pages 994–1004.

Deming Ye, Yankai Lin, Jiaju Du, Zhenghao Liu, Peng Li, Maosong Sun, and Zhiyuan Liu. 2020. Coreferential reasoning learning for language representation. In *Proceedings of EMNLP 2020*.

Xintong Yu, Hongming Zhang, Yangqiu Song, Yan Song, and Changshui Zhang. 2019. What you see is what you get: Visual pronoun coreference resolution in dialogues. In *Proceedings of EMNLP-IJCNLP 2019*, pages 5122–5131.

Hongming Zhang, Hantian Ding, and Yangqiu Song. 2019a. SP-10K: A large-scale evaluation set for selectional preference acquisition. In *Proceedings of ACL 2019*, pages 722–731.

Hongming Zhang, Xin Liu, Haojie Pan, Yangqiu Song, and Cane Wing-Ki Leung. 2020. ASER: A large-scale eventuality knowledge graph. In *Proceedings of WWW 2020*, pages 201–211.

Hongming Zhang, Yan Song, and Yangqiu Song. 2019b. Incorporating context and external knowledge for pronoun coreference resolution. In *Proceedings of NAACL-HLT 2019*, pages 872–881.

Hongming Zhang, Yan Song, Yangqiu Song, and Dong Yu. 2019c. Knowledge-aware pronoun coreference resolution. In *Proceedings of ACL 2019*, pages 867–876.

Jieyu Zhao, Tianlu Wang, Mark Yatskar, Vicente Ordonez, and Kai-Wei Chang. 2018. Gender bias in coreference resolution: Evaluation and debiasing methods. In *Proceedings of NAACL-HLT 2018*, pages 15–20.

Coreference Resolution for the Biomedical Domain: A Survey

Pengcheng Lu and **Massimo Poesio**
School of Electronical Engineering and Computer Science
Queen Mary University of London, United Kingdom
{pengcheng.lu, m.poesio}@qmul.ac.uk

Abstract

Issues with coreference resolution are one of the most frequently mentioned challenges for information extraction from the biomedical literature. Thus, the biomedical genre has long been the second most researched genre for coreference resolution after the news domain, and the subject of a great deal of research for NLP in general. In recent years this interest has grown enormously leading to the development of a number of substantial datasets, of domain-specific contextual language models, and of several architectures. In this paper we review the state-of-the-art of coreference in the biomedical domain with a particular attention on these most recent developments.

1 Introduction

Coreference resolution is the process of identifying entities in a text and finding all mentions that refer to the same entities. It is a fundamental and challenging NLP task, supporting downstream tasks such as information extraction and question answering.

In the biomedical domain, issues with coreference resolution are one of the most frequently mentioned challenges for information extraction from the biomedical literature (Castano et al. 2002, Miwa et al. 2012). Biomedical coreference resolution has become an essential task to support the discovery of complex information by identifying coreference links in biomedical texts.

In recent years in particular, biomedical coreference resolution has attracted a great deal of attention due both to its great potential for application, and to its theoretical interest e.g., as an application of knowledge embeddings and entity linking. Several biomedical coreference corpora have been made available, especially for protein coreference which is a supporting task for BioNLP 2011 shared task (Nguyen et al., 2011).

Biomedical coreference is quite different from the general domain coreference, such as different

Example a) It must be noted, however, that the alphaA/BKO mice also lack the HSPB2 gene product and the contribution of this protein to normal lens morphology and functions should not be overlooked.

Example b) However, comprehensive assessment of the Rb/E2f1 double-null rescued retina revealed a differentiation defect in cholinergic starburst amacrine cells (SACs). Recent breakthroughs have revealed that these interneurons are critical for direction selectivity and developmentally important rhythmic bursts ...... SAC ...... these retinal neurons ......

Figure 1: Examples of coreference relations in the CRAFT-CR dataset. The mentions marked red are coreferent.

markable types. Therefore, domain-specific knowledge is important for bridging the gap. Figure 1 shows two examples of biomedical coreference in the CRAFT-CR dataset (Cohen et al., 2017). In example a), the mention *this protein* refers to the antecedent *the HSPB2 gene product*. To understand the coreference relation, we need the background knowledge that proteins are fundamental encoded by genes. In example b), to correctly resolve the coreference relation between these different biomedical entities, the biomedical-domain knowledge that *cholinergic starburst amacrine cell* is a kind of *interneuron* and belongs to *retinal neuron* are required.

A large number of coreference models for the biomedical domain have already been proposed, from rule-based models (Castano et al. 2002, Kim and Park 2004, Lin and Liang 2004, Nguyen et al. 2012, Miwa et al. 2012, Kilicoglu and Demner-Fushman 2016, Li et al. 2018), machine learning-

Proceedings of the 4th Workshop on Computational Models of Reference, Anaphora and Coreference (CRAC 2021), pages 12–23
Punta Cana, Dominican Republic, November 10–11, 2021.

based models (Yang et al. 2004, Torii and Vijay-Shanker 2005, Su et al. 2008, Gasperin 2009, Kim et al. 2011) to recent deep learning-based models (Trieu et al. 2018, Trieu et al. 2019, Li et al. 2021). These models usually integrate biomedical specific information, typically specific rules, pre-trained embeddings and features.

This paper reviews and analyses coreference datasets and models for the biomedical domain, as well as recent biomedical language representation models which can enhance coreference models with domain-specific knowledge. In addition, we conduct experiments to evaluate the ability of these language represetation models for biomedical coreference task.

The structure of this paper is as follows. In Section 2 we briefly provide some background on coreference resolution in the general domain. Section 3 reviews the main datasets used to study biomedical coreference. Overviews of biomedical language representation models and biomedical coreference models are provided in Sections 4 and 5, respectively. Section 6 introduces the methodology of comparing the biomedical language representation models for coreference. Section 7 presents the evaluation results including the performance of previous models and our experiments, and Section 8 concludes.

2 Background

Coreference resolution in the general domain has a long history of being studied from early heuristic-based and rule-based approaches to recent learning-based approaches.

Lee et al. (2017) proposed the first end-to-end neural coreference resolution model which uses LSTM encoder. Based on the end-to-end model, many extensions to the model have been proposed. BERT and SpanBERT were proposed to replace the LSTM encoder and achieved better performance on OntoNotes dataset (Joshi et al. 2019, Joshi et al. 2020). Wu et al. (2020) adapted question-answering framework on coreference resolution, and achieved the state-of-the-art result with 83.1% F1 score on OntoNotes dataset. Ye et al. (2020) proposed a novel language representation model CorefBERT, which can capture the coreferential relations in context.

However, these general coreference systems do not work well in the biomedical domain due to the lack of domain knowledge. For example, the end-to-end model (Lee et al., 2017) only achieved 33.85% and 61.25% F1 scores on CRAFT-CR and BioNLP datasets respectively (Trieu et al., 2018), but achieved 68.8% F1 score on OntoNotes dataset (Hovy et al., 2006), which covers multiple genres, such as newswire, broadcast news and web data.

3 Biomedical Coreference Datasets

Several biomedical datasets with coreference annotations exist, but different document selection criteria, annotation schemes, domains and coreference types were used. The best known include:

MEDSTRACT (Pustejovsky et al., 2002) is a corpus consisting of MEDLINE abstracts with coreference annotation. It is mainly concerned with two forms of anaphora: pronominal and sortal (definite noun phrase) anaphora. This corpus adapted the MUC-7 annotation scheme (Hirschman, 1997); in addition, semantic types from UMLS (Bodenreider, 2004) were also annotated.

FlySlip (Gasperin et al., 2007) contains anaphoric links among noun phrases, including coreferent and associative relations. Different from MEDSTRACT, full-text biomedical articles were annotated in this corpus. FlySlip was annotated according to a domain-specific annotation scheme.

GENIA-MedCo (Su et al., 2008) is a coreferentially annotated version of the GENIA corpus (Kim et al., 2003), which in turn consists of 1999 MEDLINE abstracts. This corpus follows the MUC-7 annotation scheme, but adds more linguistic based relations.

DrugNerAR (Segura-Bedmar et al., 2010) was created to study anaphoric expressions in the task of extracting drug-drug interactions in pharmacological literature. This corpus consists of 49 full-text from the DrugBank database, which contains 4900 drug entries.

BioNLP-ST'11 COREF (Nguyen et al., 2011) was created in support of one of the tasks of the BioNLP 2011 shared task, focusing on finding anaphoric protein references, and based on the observation that one of major difficulties in event extraction is coreference resolution. This corpus was derived from three resources: MedCo coreference annotation (Su et al., 2008), Genia event annotation (Kim et al., 2008), and Genia Treebank (Tateisi et al., 2005).

HANAPIN (Batista-Navarro and Ananiadou, 2011) is comprised of 20 full-text articles from biochemistry literature. In addition to nominal and

Dataset	Document Type	Annotation Scheme	Domain	Coreference type	Semantic type of markables	Relation Type	Publicly Available
MEDSTRACT	100 MEDLINE abstracts	MUC-7	molecular biology	pronoun, sortal	UMLS semantic types	pairwise coreference	Yes
FlySlip	5 full-text articles	domain-specific	fruit fly genomics	noun phrase	genetic entities	coreference chain	Yes
GENIA-MedCo	1999 MEDLINE abstracts	MUC-7	transcription factors in human blood cells	pronoun, noun phrase	GENIA Ontology types	pairwise coreference	Yes
DrugNerAR	49 full articles	MUC-7	drug-drug interactions	pronoun, noun phrase	drugs	pairwise coreference	Yes
BioNLP 11 COREF	1210 MEDLINE abstracts	BioNLP	molecular biology	pronoun, noun phrase	protein names	pairwise coreference	Yes
HANAPIN	20 full-text articles	MedCo	marine natural products chemistry	pronoun, sortal, numerical, abbreviation	chemical compounds, organisms, drug effects, diseases, drug targets	coreference chain	Yes
CRAFT-CR	97 full texts articles	OntoNotes	mouse genomics	pronoun, noun phrase, verb, event, Nominal premodifiers	all types	coreference chain	Yes

Table 1: Comparison of biomedical datasets with coreferent annotations.

pronominal anaphora, this corpus also annotated abbreviation/acronyms and numerical anaphora.

CRAFT-CR (Cohen et al., 2017) consists of 97 full-text biomedical journal articles. Similar to the general domain, this corpus was annotated with coreferent chains in full-text articles, while most other biomedical coreference datasets focuse on annotating the pairwise coreference relation between an anaphor and its antecedent. In addition, all coreference expressions were annotated regardless of semantic type.

These datasets are summarized in Table 1.

4 Biomedical Language Representation Models

The news domain and the biomedical domain are different in a number of respects, such as markable types. Some authors have argued that biomedical domain knowledge is the key to bridging the gap (Choi et al., 2014), and that therefore, incorporating biomedical specific representation is beneficial for resolving coreferring expressions in the biomedical domain. In this section, we will give a brief introduction to biomedical language representation models.

4.1 Pre-training on biomedical corpora

Following the success of large-scale pre-training language models (PLMs) in the general domain, several biomedical-domain PLMs have been developed in recent years by pre-training on large-scale biomedical corpora.

Most biomedical PLMs conduct continual pre-training of the general domain PLMs and still use vocabulary trained on the general domain text. BioBERT (Lee et al., 2020) is the first transformer-based biomedical PLM, pre-trained on PubMed abstracts and PubMed Central full-text articles. ClinicalBERT and Bio_ClinicalBERT (Alsentzer et al., 2019) are pre-trained on MIMIC-III Clinical Notes, whereas BlueBERT (Peng et al., 2019) uses both PubMed and MIMIC-III for pre-training. All these models are pre-trained based on general BERT, except Bio_ClinicalBERT which is initialized from BioBERT.

In addition to initializing from general BERT, some biomedical PLMs are directly pre-trained on biomedical text from scratch and use domain-specific custom vocabulary. SciBERT (Beltagy et al., 2019) is pre-trained on biomedical and computer science papers from scratch and achieved good performance on many scientific NLP tasks. PubMedBERT (Gu et al., 2020) and BioELECTRA (raj Kanakarajan et al., 2021) are both pre-trained on PubMed abstract and PubMed Central full text articles, but the latter adopts ELECTRA architecture (Clark et al., 2019). BioMegatron (Shin et al., 2020) is a large-scale model based on Megatron (Shoeybi et al., 2019) architecture. It also investigated the effect of vocabulary and corpora domain on the performance of biomedical tasks.

4.2 Integrating biomedical knowledge bases

Although the biomedical PLMs, such as BioBERT, have achieved good performance on many biomedical tasks, however, these models can be further enhanced by integrating biomedical knowledge bases, such as UMLS (Bodenreider, 2004).

Several models enhance biomedical PLMs by integrating synonym knowledge from UMLS. Each mention in the biomedical text can be linked to a Concept Unique Identifier (CUI) in UMLS, and each CUI has a synonym set. SAPBERT (Liu et al., 2021), UMLSBERT (Michalopoulos et al., 2021) and BIOSYN (Sung et al., 2020) further pre-trained PubMedBERT, Bio_Clinical BERT and BioBERT on UMLS synonyms, using multi-similarity loss, multi-label loss and synonym marginalization algorithm respectively.

In addition to synonym knowledge, Clinical KB-BERT (Hao et al., 2020) injects UMLS relation knowledge into BioBERT. Whereas CODER (Yuan et al., 2020) learns both synonym and relation knowledge based on PubMedBERT or mBERT (Devlin et al., 2019) via contrastive learning. Also, some research focus on fusing the UMLS entity embeddings with contextual embeddings to improve biomedical PLMs (He et al., 2020; Fei et al., 2021; Yuan et al., 2021).

This paper selected some of the models above to evaluate the ability of biomedical-specific representation for biomedical coreference task, detailed in Section 6.

5 Coreference Models for the Biomedical Domain

5.1 Rule-based models

Early approaches to biomedical coreference resolution are primarily rule-based. These models rely on syntactic parsers to extract hand-crafted features and rules.

Nguyen et al. (2012) implemented a protein coreference system that makes use of syntactic information from the parser output, and protein-indicated information. The results showed that domain-specific semantic information is important for coreference resolution. Miwa et al. (2012) developed a rule-based coreference system, as a part of the EventMine event extraction system. A set of rules was developed based on syntactic trees and predicate-argument structures. The system achieved 55.9% F1 score on BioNLP 2011 protein coreference task. Kilicoglu and Demner-Fushman (2016) developed a new corpus of structured drug labels and proposed a general framework based on a smorgasbord architecture for fine-grained biomedical coreference resolution. The framework adopted different strategies for each coreference type and mention type, and combined them to reach desired performance, like selecting dishes from a smorgasbord. Li et al. (2018) presented two methods for bio-entity coreference resolution: a rule-based method and a recurrent neural network (RNN) model. The rule-based model created a set of syntactic rules or semantic constraints for coreference and achieved a state-of-the-art performance with 62.0% F1 score on BioNLP 2011 protein coreference task.

These rule-based models mostly designed rules for specific type of coreference relation and even specific corpus, which limits the scope of the resolution.

5.2 Machine learning-based models

In the early years, due to the lack of publicly available annotated corpora, researchers have to annotate their own corpora for developing machine learning approaches (Yang et al., 2004, Torii and Vijay-Shanker, 2005, Su et al., 2008, Gasperin, 2009).

After the BioNLP 2011 protein coreference dataset was made publicly available, several machine learning-based models were developed for this task. Kim et al. (2011) adapted a general coreference system Reconcile (Stoyanov et al., 2010) for the biomedical domain by modifying several components to biomedical texts. It trained two separate classifiers for detecting anaphora and antecedent mentions.

In addition to using machine learning-based methods only, several models adopted hydrid approach, i.e., combining both machine learning-based and rule-based methods. D'Souza and Ng (2012) proposed a hybrid approach that used a classifier with syntactic path-based features. It investigated five different learning-based methods, and a rule-based approach for anaphora resolution. This model achieved a superior performance than previous either rule-based or learning-based models on BioNLP 2011 protein coreference task. Li et al. (2014) later also used a hybrid approach, adopting the rule-based method or the machine learning method for three types of anaphora. As the method of D'Souza and Ng (2012), they also used different rules for different types of anaphora. The system achieved better performance with 68.6% F1 score than previous methods on BioNLP 2011 protein coreference development data.

	BioNLP	**CRAFT**
Training set (docs)	800	60
Development set (docs)	150	7
Test set (docs)	260	30
Avg. sent. per doc	9.2	312.4
Avg. words per doc	258.0	8181.0

Table 2: Statistics of BioNLP and CRAFT.

5.3 Deep learning-based models

In recent years, much effort has been made on using deep learning methods for biomedical coreference.

Trieu et al. (2018) applied general domain end-to-end neural coreference resolution system (Lee et al., 2017) to biomedical text, integrating the domain specific features to enhance the system. The model was evaluated on BioNLP 2011 protein coreference dataset and CRAFT-CR dataset. The results indicated that in-domain embeddings and domain-specific features helped improve the performance. Then, Trieu et al. (2019) proposed a system to address the challenge of coreference resolution in the full-text articles in the CRAFT-CR dataset. The model also applied end-to-end system (Lee et al., 2017), but enhanced the system by utilizing a syntax-based mention filtering method and replacing LSTM with BERT. This model achieved better performance on the CRAFT-CR dataset.

Different from the models above, Li et al. (2021) integrated external knowledge to enhance the neural coreference system for biomedical texts. A knowledge attention module was developed to select the most related and helpful knowledge triplets. This model achieved the state-of-the-art perfor-

Classification			Model	dev			test		
rule-based	machine learning	deep learning		R	P	F1	R	P	F1
	✓		Reconcile (Kim et al., 2011)	26.7	74.0	39.3	22.2	73.3	34.1
✓			(Nguyen et al., 2012)	57.8	67.8	62.4	52.5	50.2	51.3
✓			EventMine (Miwa et al., 2012)	53.5	69.8	60.5	50.4	62.7	55.9
✓	✓		(D'Souza and Ng, 2012)	59.9	77.1	67.4	55.6	67.2	60.9
✓	✓		(Li et al., 2014)	69.8	67.5	68.6	-	-	-
✓			Simple system (Choi et al., 2016)	64.4	63.4	63.9	50.0	46.3	48.1
✓			(Kilicoglu and Demner-Fushman, 2016)	63.2	72.4	67.5	-	-	-
✓			(Li et al., 2018)-rule	68.8	76.0	**72.2**	60.2	63.8	62.0
		✓	(Li et al., 2018)-neural	60.4	61.9	61.2	54.9	58.0	56.4
		✓	E2E_MetaMap (Trieu et al., 2018)	56.7	71.7	63.1	47.5	55.6	51.2
		✓	KB-attention (Li et al., 2021)	63.4	68.1	65.6	69.4	69.6	**69.5**

Table 3: Performance of biomedical coreference models on BioNLP 2011 protein correference development and test sets.

mance on the BioNLP 2011 protein coreference dataset and CRAFT-CR dataset.

6 Comparing the Biomedical Language Representation Models for Coreference

In Section 4, we introduced a series of biomedical language representation models. To investigate the ability of these models for biomedical coreference task, we conduct experiments to evaluate these models on CRAFT-CR dataset.

6.1 Baseline model

We employ the higher-order coreference model (Lee et al., 2018) as the baseline model, but use different pre-trained language models with BERT architecture to replace LSTM encoder.

The goal is to learn a distribution $P(y_i)$ over possible antecedents $Y(i)$ for each span i:

$$P(y_i) = \frac{e^{s(i,y_i)}}{\sum_{y' \in Y(i)} e^{s(i,y')}} \quad (1)$$

where $s(i,j)$ is a pairwise score for a coreference link between span i and span j. The pairwise score is computed by the mention score of i, the mention score of j, and two kinds of joint compatibility scores of i and j:

$$s(i,j) = s_m(i) + s_m(j) + s_c(i,j) + s_a(i,j) \quad (2)$$

The mention score and joint compatibility scores are computed using span representation g_i and g_j from bidirectional LSTMs:

$$s_m(i) = \mathit{FFNN}_m(g_i) \quad (3)$$

$$s_c(i,j) = g_i^T W_c \, g_j \quad (4)$$

$$s_a(i,j) = \mathit{FFNN}_a([g_i, g_j, g_i \circ g_j, \phi(i,j)]) \quad (5)$$

where *FFNN*$(\cdot)$ represents a feed-forward neural network, W_c is a learned weight matrix, $\circ$ denotes element-wise product, and $\phi(i,j)$ represents speaker and metadata features.

6.2 Applying pre-trained language models

We apply two types of PLM to replace LSTM encoder respectively:

Biomedical PLMs: to enhance the baseline model with biomedical domain knowledge, several biomedical PLMs are selected, including models pre-training on biomedical corpora or integrating biomedical knowledge bases.

SpanBERT: since SpanBERT (Joshi et al., 2020) is a state-of-the-art coreference resolution model in the general domain, we also evaluate SpanBERT and general BERT (Joshi et al., 2019) on biomedical coreference.

Since CRAFT-CR is a more challenging biomedical coreference dataset consisting of full-text articles, we choose CRAFT-CR to fine-tune and evaluate these models. The details are introduced in Section 7.2.

7 Results

In this section, we first present the performance achieved by previous biomedical coreference models decribed in Section 5. Then we describe our experiment and report the results.

7.1 Results by datasets

Recent biomedical coreference models are mostly evaluated on BioNLP 2011 protein coreference

Model	B^3	BLANC	CEAFE	CEAFM	LEA	MUC	Avg.
E2E_MetaMap (Trieu et al., 2018)	36.4	46.5	33.1	41.0	32.4	51.8	40.2
BERT_filter (Trieu et al., 2019)	44.0	48.9	39.8	49.0	40.0	57.0	46.4
KB-attention (Li et al., 2021)	54.9	63.1	48.6	59.4	51.3	64.5	**57.0**

Table 4: F1 scores of biomedical coreference models on CRAFT-CR test set.

Model	B^3	BLANC	CEAFE	CEAFM	LEA	MUC	Avg.
BioBERT	41.67	42.39	32.44	45.15	39.00	53.66	42.38
SciBERT	25.66	28.30	16.76	30.34	22.67	40.70	27.41
Bio_ClinicalBERT	38.19	36.91	30.11	41.56	35.57	48.22	38.43
PubMedBERT	34.96	33.14	25.49	38.49	32.32	47.02	35.24
UMLSBERT	27.53	26.95	19.95	31.40	24.95	39.80	28.43
Clinical KB-BERT	44.56	44.99	37.25	48.29	41.67	55.17	45.32
BERT_base	32.96	31.36	22.58	36.25	30.73	44.34	33.04
SpanBERT_base	47.05	46.30	39.90	51.27	44.36	57.69	**47.76**

Table 5: F1 scores of different PLMs combined with c2f-coref model on CRAFT-CR test set.

dataset[1] and CRAFT-CR dataset[2], of which the statistics are shown in Table 2. The performance on the two datasets are summarized and analysed respectively as follows.

Table 3 shows the performance of different biomedical coreference models on BioNLP 2011 protein coreference development and test sets. These models are evaluated using the scorer provided by the BioNLP shared task organisers. As shown in Table 3, KB-attention (Li et al., 2021) achieved the best performance of 69.5% F1 score on the test set of BioNLP. This indicates that integrating external biomedical knowledge base can further enhance the coreference models for the biomedical domain. In addition, compared with deep learning-based models, some rule-based (Kilicoglu and Demner-Fushman 2016, Li et al. 2018) or hybrid models (D'Souza and Ng 2012, Li et al. 2014) still achieved favorable performance.

Table 4 shows the F1 scores of different biomedical coreference models on CRAFT-CR test set. We can see that the best performance is also achieved by KB-attention (Li et al., 2021), showing the advantage of fine-grained knowledge base integration. However, the results on CRAFT-CR are overall lower than those on BioNLP. The possible reason is that CRAFT-CR consists of full-text articles, hence the length of documents in CRAFT-CR is much greater. This makes CRAFT-CR more challenging than BioNLP dataset which comprises abstracts only.

7.2 Experiments

7.2.1 Experimental setup

We conduct experiment using following models:

- **biomedical PLMs+c2f-coref**: we refer to the higher-order coreference model (Lee et al., 2018) as *c2f-coref*. We build the c2f-coref system on top of different biomedical PLMs respectively, including BioBERT, SciBERT, Bio_ClinicalBERT, PubMedBERT, UMLSBERT, and Clinical KB-BERT. Among these models, UMLSBERT and Clinical KB-BERT integrate external biomedical knowledge base, i.e., UMLS, while other models are pre-trained on large-scale biomedical datasets.

- **BERT_base+c2f-coref** (Joshi et al., 2019): the c2f-coref system on top of BERT representation.

- **SpanBERT_base+c2f-coref** (Joshi et al., 2020): the c2f-coref system on top of SpanBERT_base, which pre-trained span representations to better represent and predict spans of text.

We run these models on the CRAFT-CR dataset of latest released version 4.0.1[3]. CRAFT-CR con-

[1] http://2011.bionlp-st.org/home/protein-gene-coreference-task

[2] https://github.com/UCDenver-ccp/craft-shared-tasks

[3] https://github.com/UCDenver-ccp/CRAFT/releases/tag/v4.0.1

Model	Evaluation script	Programming language	Time cost	MUC	B^3	CEAFE	Avg.
SpanBERT_base +c2f-coref	CoNLL scorer 9.0	Perl	about 1.5h	48.67	8.61	18.90	25.39
	CoVal script	Python	about 30s	55.99	43.97	40.01	46.66
	CRAFT evaluation script	Clojure	about 20m	57.69	47.05	39.90	48.21

Table 6: F1 scores of SpanBERT_base+c2f-coref on CRAFT-CR test set using different evaluation scripts.

sists of 97 full-text journal articles from PMC. As shown in Table 2, 60 documents are used for fine-tuning these models.

These models are fine-tuned using learning rate of 1×10^{-5} for PLMs parameters and 2×10^{-4} for task parameters with Adam optimizer, a dropout of 0.3, and `max_training_len` of 384 for SpanBERT_base and 128 for other PLMs respectively. For SciBERT and PubMedBERT, we use the specific domain vocabulary, while general BERT vocabulary is used for other models.

For evaluation, we calculate F1 scores on six common metrics including B^3, BLANC, CEAFE, CEAFM, LEA and MUC using the official evaluation script[4] provided by the CRAFT shared task organizers, which is also used by previous models (Trieu et al. 2018, Trieu et al. 2019, Li et al. 2021).

7.2.2 Results

The F1 scores of different PLMs combined with c2f-coref model on the CRAFT-CR test set are shown in Table 5. We can see that SpanBERT_base achieved the best performance of 47.76% F1 score, even without biomedical domain pre-training. This proves the powerful ability of SpanBERT on coreference resolution task.

In addition, biomedical PLMs outperform BERT_base on CRAFT-CR, except SciBERT (Beltagy et al., 2019) and UMLSBERT (Michalopoulos et al., 2021), which shows that biomedical domain knowledge can generally benefit coreference models for the biomedical domain. Moreover, Clinical KB-BERT (Hao et al., 2020), which is initialized from BioBERT (Lee et al., 2020), achieved better performance than other biomedical PLMs, indicating that biomedical PLMs can be further enhanced by integrating external biomedical knowledge bases. However, SciBERT performs worse than BERT_base on the CRAFT-CR dataset, although pre-trained on scientific texts and achieved better performance than BERT_base on some other scientific NLP tasks such as NER, as reported in Beltagy et al. (2019). One possible reason is that the pre-training corpora of SciBERT contain a number of computer science articles, which is unlikely to be beneficial for biomedical tasks.

Among these biomedical PLMs, SciBERT (Beltagy et al., 2019) and PubMedBERT (Gu et al., 2020) are pre-trained on domain-specific text from scratch, while others conduct continual pre-training based on the general domain. Although Gu et al. (2020) shows that domain-specific pre-training from scratch outperforms continual pre-training from general-domain language models, the results of our experiment are the opposite. Presumably the reason is that CRAFT-CR annotated all semantic type markables and covered a wider range of coreferences, so pre-training on the general domain is also beneficial.

7.2.3 Results using different evaluation scripts

Apart from the official evaluation script provided by CRAFT shared task organizers, we also used two other evaluation scripts, i.e., CoNLL scorer 9.0 and the CoVal script, to evaluate these models for comparing the differences between these evaluation scripts on the CRAFT-CR dataset. CoNLL scorer 9.0[5] is a modified version of the original reference coreference scorer (Pradhan et al., 2014) used for CoNLL-2011/2012 shared tasks. It added an optional partial mention matching scheme and handling for discontinuous mentions, i.e., mentions composed of non-contiguous tokens. The CoVal script[6] is a python coreference scorer for both CoNLL and ARRAU datasets (Uryupina et al., 2020).

The results of three different evaluation scripts for SpanBERT_base+c2f-coref model on CRAFT-CR test set are shown in Table 6. The F1 scores of MUC, B^3 and CEAFE metrics as well as the averaged value are provided. As shown in Table 6, a strange phenomenon is that the results of CoNLL

[4] `https://github.com/UCDenver-ccp/craft-shared-tasks`

[5] `https://github.com/bill-baumgartner/reference-coreference-scorers`

[6] `https://github.com/ns-moosavi/coval`

scorer 9.0 are much lower than those of the other two evaluation scripts, especially on the B^3 and CEAFE metrics. The reason of that is not clear and needs further analysis. Whereas, the results of the CoVal script and CRAFT official evaluation script are close, although the scores of the latter are a little higher.

In addition to the F1 scores, the time cost of the three evaluation scripts are quiet different. The CoNLL scorer 9.0 took about one and a half hours, while the CoVal script only needed about 30 seconds for evaluation.

8 Conclusion

In this paper, we review and analyse the progress of biomedical coreference datasets, biomedical language representation models and coreference models for the biomedical domain. Biomedical coreference is an essential but challenging task. Some efforts have been made in this field, but there is still a much room for improvement. The experiments which we conducted indicate biomedical domain knowledge from either pre-training on biomedical texts or integrating biomedical knowledge bases can enhance coreference models for the biomedical domain.

Acknowledgements

This research was supported in part by the China Scholarship Council, and the DALI project, ERC Grant 695662.

References

Emily Alsentzer, John Murphy, William Boag, Wei-Hung Weng, Di Jindi, Tristan Naumann, and Matthew McDermott. 2019. Publicly available clinical bert embeddings. In *Proceedings of the 2nd Clinical Natural Language Processing Workshop*, pages 72–78.

Riza Theresa Batista-Navarro and Sophia Ananiadou. 2011. Building a coreference-annotated corpus from the domain of biochemistry. In *Proceedings of BioNLP 2011 Workshop*, pages 83–91.

Iz Beltagy, Kyle Lo, and Arman Cohan. 2019. Scibert: A pretrained language model for scientific text. In *Proceedings of the 2019 Conference on Empirical Methods in Natural Language Processing and the 9th International Joint Conference on Natural Language Processing (EMNLP-IJCNLP)*, pages 3615–3620.

Olivier Bodenreider. 2004. The unified medical language system (umls): integrating biomedical terminology. *Nucleic acids research*, 32(suppl_1):D267–D270.

José Castano, Jason Zhang, and James Pustejovsky. 2002. Anaphora resolution in biomedical literature.

Miji Choi, Karin Verspoor, and Justin Zobel. 2014. Evaluation of coreference resolution for biomedical text. In *MedIR@ SIGIR*.

Miji Choi, Justin Zobel, and Karin Verspoor. 2016. A categorical analysis of coreference resolution errors in biomedical texts. *Journal of biomedical informatics*, 60:309–318.

Kevin Clark, Minh-Thang Luong, Quoc V Le, and Christopher D Manning. 2019. Electra: Pre-training text encoders as discriminators rather than generators. In *International Conference on Learning Representations*.

K Bretonnel Cohen, Arrick Lanfranchi, Miji Joo-young Choi, Michael Bada, William A Baumgartner, Natalya Panteleyeva, Karin Verspoor, Martha Palmer, and Lawrence E Hunter. 2017. Coreference annotation and resolution in the colorado richly annotated full text (craft) corpus of biomedical journal articles. *BMC bioinformatics*, 18(1):1–14.

Jacob Devlin, Ming-Wei Chang, Kenton Lee, and Kristina Toutanova. 2019. Bert: Pre-training of deep bidirectional transformers for language understanding. In *Proceedings of the 2019 Conference of the North American Chapter of the Association for Computational Linguistics: Human Language Technologies, Volume 1 (Long and Short Papers)*, pages 4171–4186.

Jennifer D'Souza and Vincent Ng. 2012. Anaphora resolution in biomedical literature: a hybrid approach. In *Proceedings of the ACM Conference on Bioinformatics, Computational Biology and Biomedicine*, pages 113–122.

Hao Fei, Yafeng Ren, Yue Zhang, Donghong Ji, and Xiaohui Liang. 2021. Enriching contextualized language model from knowledge graph for biomedical information extraction. *Briefings in Bioinformatics*, 22(3):bbaa110.

Caroline Gasperin, Nikiforos Karamanis, and Ruth Seal. 2007. Annotation of anaphoric relations in biomedical full-text articles using a domain-relevant scheme. In *Proceedings of DAARC*, volume 2007. Citeseer.

Caroline V Gasperin. 2009. Statistical anaphora resolution in biomedical texts. Technical report, University of Cambridge, Computer Laboratory.

Yu Gu, Robert Tinn, Hao Cheng, Michael Lucas, Naoto Usuyama, Xiaodong Liu, Tristan Naumann,

Jianfeng Gao, and Hoifung Poon. 2020. Domain-specific language model pretraining for biomedical natural language processing. *arXiv preprint arXiv:2007.15779*.

Boran Hao, Henghui Zhu, and Ioannis Paschalidis. 2020. Enhancing clinical bert embedding using a biomedical knowledge base. In *Proceedings of the 28th international conference on computational linguistics*, pages 657–661.

Bin He, Di Zhou, Jinghui Xiao, Xin Jiang, Qun Liu, Nicholas Jing Yuan, and Tong Xu. 2020. Integrating graph contextualized knowledge into pre-trained language models. In *Proceedings of the 2020 Conference on Empirical Methods in Natural Language Processing: Findings*, pages 2281–2290.

Lynette Hirschman. 1997. Muc-7 coreference task definition, version 3.0. *Proceedings of MUC-7, 1997*.

Eduard Hovy, Mitch Marcus, Martha Palmer, Lance Ramshaw, and Ralph Weischedel. 2006. Ontonotes: the 90% solution. In *Proceedings of the human language technology conference of the NAACL, Companion Volume: Short Papers*, pages 57–60.

Mandar Joshi, Danqi Chen, Yinhan Liu, Daniel S Weld, Luke Zettlemoyer, and Omer Levy. 2020. Spanbert: Improving pre-training by representing and predicting spans. *Transactions of the Association for Computational Linguistics*, 8:64–77.

Mandar Joshi, Omer Levy, Luke Zettlemoyer, and Daniel S Weld. 2019. Bert for coreference resolution: Baselines and analysis. In *Proceedings of the 2019 Conference on Empirical Methods in Natural Language Processing and the 9th International Joint Conference on Natural Language Processing (EMNLP-IJCNLP)*, pages 5803–5808.

Halil Kilicoglu and Dina Demner-Fushman. 2016. Bioscores: A smorgasbord architecture for coreference resolution in biomedical text. *PloS one*, 11(3):e0148538.

J-D Kim, Tomoko Ohta, Yuka Tateisi, and Jun'ichi Tsujii. 2003. Genia corpus—a semantically annotated corpus for bio-textmining. *Bioinformatics*, 19(suppl_1):i180–i182.

Jin-Dong Kim, Tomoko Ohta, and Jun'ichi Tsujii. 2008. Corpus annotation for mining biomedical events from literature. *BMC bioinformatics*, 9(1):1–25.

Jung-Jae Kim and Jong C Park. 2004. Bioar: Anaphora resolution for relating protein names to proteome database entries. In *Proceedings of the Conference on Reference Resolution and Its Applications*, pages 79–86.

Youngjun Kim, Ellen Riloff, and Nathan Gilbert. 2011. The taming of reconcile as a biomedical coreference resolver. In *Proceedings of BioNLP Shared Task 2011 Workshop*, pages 89–93.

Jinhyuk Lee, Wonjin Yoon, Sungdong Kim, Donghyeon Kim, Sunkyu Kim, Chan Ho So, and Jaewoo Kang. 2020. Biobert: a pre-trained biomedical language representation model for biomedical text mining. *Bioinformatics*, 36(4):1234–1240.

Kenton Lee, Luheng He, Mike Lewis, and Luke Zettlemoyer. 2017. End-to-end neural coreference resolution. In *Proceedings of the 2017 Conference on Empirical Methods in Natural Language Processing*, pages 188–197.

Kenton Lee, Luheng He, and Luke Zettlemoyer. 2018. Higher-order coreference resolution with coarse-to-fine inference. In *Proceedings of the 2018 Conference of the North American Chapter of the Association for Computational Linguistics: Human Language Technologies, Volume 2 (Short Papers)*, pages 687–692.

Chen Li, Zhiqiang Rao, Qinghua Zheng, and Xiangrong Zhang. 2018. A set of domain rules and a deep network for protein coreference resolution. *Database*, 2018.

Lishuang Li, Liuke Jin, Zhenchao Jiang, Jing Zhang, and Degen Huang. 2014. Coreference resolution in biomedical texts. In *2014 IEEE International Conference on Bioinformatics and Biomedicine (BIBM)*, pages 12–14. IEEE.

Y Li, X Ma, X Zhou, P Cheng, K He, and C Li. 2021. Knowledge enhanced lstm for coreference resolution on biomedical texts. *Bioinformatics (Oxford, England)*.

Yu-Hsiang Lin and Tyne Liang. 2004. Pronominal and sortal anaphora resolution for biomedical literature. In *Proceedings of the 16th Conference on Computational Linguistics and Speech Processing*, pages 101–109.

Fangyu Liu, Ehsan Shareghi, Zaiqiao Meng, Marco Basaldella, and Nigel Collier. 2021. Self-alignment pretraining for biomedical entity representations. In *Proceedings of the 2021 Conference of the North American Chapter of the Association for Computational Linguistics: Human Language Technologies*, pages 4228–4238.

George Michalopoulos, Yuanxin Wang, Hussam Kaka, Helen Chen, and Alexander Wong. 2021. Umlsbert: Clinical domain knowledge augmentation of contextual embeddings using the unified medical language system metathesaurus. In *Proceedings of the 2021 Conference of the North American Chapter of the Association for Computational Linguistics: Human Language Technologies*, pages 1744–1753.

Makoto Miwa, Paul Thompson, and Sophia Ananiadou. 2012. Boosting automatic event extraction from the literature using domain adaptation and coreference resolution. *Bioinformatics*, 28(13):1759–1765.

Ngan Nguyen, Jin-Dong Kim, Makoto Miwa, Takuya Matsuzaki, and Junichi Tsujii. 2012. Improving protein coreference resolution by simple semantic classification. *BMC bioinformatics*, 13(1):1–12.

Ngan Nguyen, Jin-Dong Kim, and Jun'ichi Tsujii. 2011. Overview of the protein coreference task in bionlp shared task 2011. In *Proceedings of the BioNLP Shared Task 2011 Workshop*, pages 74–82. Citeseer.

Yifan Peng, Shankai Yan, and Zhiyong Lu. 2019. Transfer learning in biomedical natural language processing: An evaluation of bert and elmo on ten benchmarking datasets. In *Proceedings of the 18th BioNLP Workshop and Shared Task*, pages 58–65.

Sameer Pradhan, Xiaoqiang Luo, Marta Recasens, Eduard Hovy, Vincent Ng, and Michael Strube. 2014. Scoring coreference partitions of predicted mentions: A reference implementation. In *Proceedings of the conference. Association for Computational Linguistics. Meeting*, volume 2014, page 30. NIH Public Access.

James Pustejovsky, José Castano, Roser Sauri, Jason Zhang, and Wei Luo. 2002. Medstract: creating large-scale information servers from biomedical texts. In *Proceedings of the ACL-02 workshop on Natural language processing in the biomedical domain*, pages 85–92.

Kamal raj Kanakarajan, Bhuvana Kundumani, and Malaikannan Sankarasubbu. 2021. Bioelectra: Pretrained biomedical text encoder using discriminators. In *Proceedings of the 20th Workshop on Biomedical Language Processing*, pages 143–154.

Isabel Segura-Bedmar, Mario Crespo, César de Pablo-Sánchez, and Paloma Martínez. 2010. Resolving anaphoras for the extraction of drug-drug interactions in pharmacological documents. In *BMC bioinformatics*, volume 11, pages 1–9. BioMed Central.

Hoo-Chang Shin, Yang Zhang, Evelina Bakhturina, Raul Puri, Mostofa Patwary, Mohammad Shoeybi, and Raghav Mani. 2020. Bio-megatron: Larger biomedical domain language model. In *Proceedings of the 2020 Conference on Empirical Methods in Natural Language Processing (EMNLP)*, pages 4700–4706.

Mohammad Shoeybi, Mostofa Patwary, Raul Puri, Patrick LeGresley, Jared Casper, and Bryan Catanzaro. 2019. Megatron-lm: Training multi-billion parameter language models using model parallelism. *arXiv preprint arXiv:1909.08053*.

Veselin Stoyanov, Claire Cardie, Nathan Gilbert, Ellen Riloff, David Buttler, and David Hysom. 2010. Coreference resolution with reconcile. In *Proceedings of the ACL 2010 Conference Short Papers*, pages 156–161.

Jian Su, Xiaofeng Yang, Huaqing Hong, Yuka Tateisi, and Jun'ichi Tsujii. 2008. Coreference resolution in biomedical texts: a machine learning approach. In *Dagstuhl Seminar Proceedings*. Schloss Dagstuhl-Leibniz-Zentrum für Informatik.

Mujeen Sung, Hwisang Jeon, Jinhyuk Lee, and Jaewoo Kang. 2020. Biomedical entity representations with synonym marginalization. In *Proceedings of the 58th Annual Meeting of the Association for Computational Linguistics*, pages 3641–3650.

Yuka Tateisi, Akane Yakushiji, Tomoko Ohta, and Jun'ichi Tsujii. 2005. Syntax annotation for the genia corpus. In *Companion Volume to the Proceedings of Conference including Posters/Demos and tutorial abstracts*.

Manabu Torii and K Vijay-Shanker. 2005. Anaphora resolution of demonstrative noun phrases in medline abstracts. In *Proceedings of*, pages 332–339.

Hai-Long Trieu, Anh-Khoa Duong Nguyen, Nhung Nguyen, Makoto Miwa, Hiroya Takamura, and Sophia Ananiadou. 2019. Coreference resolution in full text articles with bert and syntax-based mention filtering. In *Proceedings of The 5th Workshop on BioNLP Open Shared Tasks*, pages 196–205.

Hai Long Trieu, Nhung TH Nguyen, Makoto Miwa, and Sophia Ananiadou. 2018. Investigating domain-specific information for neural coreference resolution on biomedical texts. In *Proceedings of the BioNLP 2018 workshop*, pages 183–188.

Olga Uryupina, Ron Artstein, Antonella Bristot, Federica Cavicchio, Francesca Delogu, Kepa J Rodriguez, and Massimo Poesio. 2020. Annotating a broad range of anaphoric phenomena, in a variety of genres: the arrau corpus. *Natural Language Engineering*, 26(1):95–128.

Wei Wu, Fei Wang, Arianna Yuan, Fei Wu, and Jiwei Li. 2020. Corefqa: Coreference resolution as query-based span prediction. In *Proceedings of the 58th Annual Meeting of the Association for Computational Linguistics*, pages 6953–6963.

Xiaofeng Yang, Jian Su, Guodong Zhou, and Chew Lim Tan. 2004. An np-cluster based approach to coreference resolution. In *COLING 2004: Proceedings of the 20th International Conference on Computational Linguistics*, pages 226–232.

Deming Ye, Yankai Lin, Jiaju Du, Zhenghao Liu, Peng Li, Maosong Sun, and Zhiyuan Liu. 2020. Coreferential reasoning learning for language representation. In *Proceedings of the 2020 Conference on Empirical Methods in Natural Language Processing (EMNLP)*, pages 7170–7186.

Zheng Yuan, Yijia Liu, Chuanqi Tan, Songfang Huang, and Fei Huang. 2021. Improving biomedical pretrained language models with knowledge. In *Proceedings of the 20th Workshop on Biomedical Language Processing*, pages 180–190.

Zheng Yuan, Zhengyun Zhao, and Sheng Yu. 2020. Coder: Knowledge infused cross-lingual medical term embedding for term normalization. *arXiv preprint arXiv:2011.02947*.

FantasyCoref: Coreference Resolution on Fantasy Literature Through Omniscient Writer's Point of View

♠Sooyoun Han, ♠Sumin Seo, ♠Minji Kang, ♠Jongin Kim
♠Nayoung Choi, ♣Min Song, ◇Jinho D. Choi
♠Department of Digital Analytics, Yonsei University, Seoul, South Korea
♣Department of Library and Information Science, Yonsei University, Seoul, South Korea
◇Department of Computer Science, Emory University, Atlanta, GA, USA
{honeycello, soominn20, codenavy94, jongin.kim}@yonsei.ac.kr
{skdudenql11, min.song}@yonsei.ac.kr, jinho.choi@emory.edu

Abstract

This paper presents a new corpus and annotation guideline for a novel coreference resolution task on fictional texts, and analyzes its unique characteristics. *FantasyCoref* contains 211 stories of *Grimms' Fairy Tales* and 3 other fantasy literature annotated in the omniscient writer's point of view (OWV) to handle distinctive aspects in this genre. This task is more challenging than general coreference resolution in two ways. First, documents in our corpus are 2.5 times longer than the ones in OntoNotes, raising a new layer of difficulty in resolving long-distant referents. Second, annotation of literary styles and concepts raise several issues which are not sufficiently addressed in the existing annotation guidelines. Hence, considerations on such issues and the concept of OWV are necessary to achieve high inter-annotator agreement (IAA) in coreference resolution of fictional texts. We carefully conduct annotation tasks in four stages to ensure the quality of our annotation. As a result, a high IAA score of 87% is achieved using the standard coreference evaluation metric. Finally, state-of-the-art coreference resolution approaches are evaluated on our corpus. After training with our annotated dataset, there was a 2.59% and 3.06% improvement over the model trained on the OntoNotes dataset. Also, we observe that the portion of errors specific to fictional texts declines after the training.

1 Introduction

Coreference resolution is a core NLP task to link all mentions that refer to the same entity together in a document (Pradhan et al., 2011, 2012). A few coreference datasets have been created for several genres (Hovy et al., 2006; Li et al., 2016; Zhou and Choi, 2018); however, coreference resolution on literary texts has been comparatively underexplored. This may be due to the nature of this entertainment genre being not as important. Nonetheless, with the latest advancement in neural-based coreference systems (Lee et al., 2018; Joshi et al., 2020; Wu et al., 2020), the scope of this task is getting broader and likely emerges as a key component to teach children how to read in education applications (Hill et al., 2016) or to conduct engaging conversations in chatbots.

Unlike non-fictional texts, referents in literary texts can be interpreted quite differently, depending on which point of view that the annotator takes (e.g., which character's point of view, which part of the story that the reader is at). This unique property in literature is more frequently noticeable in the fantasy genre.

For instance, in the famous story *Snow White*, the *evil queen* disguises herself as an *old woman* and gives Snow White a poisonous apple. From Snow White's point of view, she does not know that the *old woman* is her *step-mother* at this point, but the writer knows it. Moreover, the three mentions, *evil queen*, *old woman*, and *step-mother*, all refer to the same entity but appear differently, which can be confusing even in the reader's point of view before one finishes reading the entire story.

To accomplish the main purpose of coreference resolution, language understanding, this issue of inconsistent interpretation needs to be addressed with specific guidelines. Distinguished from most of previous work, this study conducts coreference annotation in the omniscient writer's point of view, which can reflect the author's intention of how the text should be understood, and therefore, is proper for reading comprehension.

Also, OntoNotes, the most widely known coreference dataset (Hovy et al., 2006), does not ana-

Proceedings of the 4th Workshop on Computational Models of Reference, Anaphora and Coreference (CRAC 2021), pages 24–35
Punta Cana, Dominican Republic, November 10–11, 2021.

lyze this issue in its guidelines. Moreover, previous studies of coreference resolution on literary texts (Bamman et al., 2020; Roesiger et al., 2018; Yoder et al., 2021) present only limited analyses on dynamic issues that occur in fictional texts (e.g., asymmetry of knowledge, comprehensive physical or status change in entities).

The lack of a high-quality dataset in terms of size and consistency is the major hindrance in this task. This inspires us to create a new coreference corpus on literature and evaluate a state-of-the-art coreference system on this genre to confirm the feasibility of this research. Contributions of this work are as follows:

- We analyze a full range of coreference annotation related properties observed in fictional texts (especially, fantasy texts) and present the corresponding guidelines for this genre (Section 2).
- We create the corpus called *FantasyCoref*, comprising of 211 stories in *Grimms' Fairy Tales*, two stories from *The Arabian Nights*, and *Alice's Adventures in Wonderland* with coreference annotation that shows high inter-annotator agreement (Section 3).
- We evaluate a state-of-the-art coreference system on *FantasyCoref* (Section 4), and give error analysis specific to fictional texts, depicting limitations of the current system on this genre. We also show how the training the system on our dataset brings change to the error distributions (Section 5).

To the best of our knowledge, this is the first publicly available corpus that provides full coreference annotation on fantasy literature. We believe that this work will lead a new perspective of coreference resolution on this unexplored domain.[1]

2 Annotation

The source materials used for our coreference annotation are *Household Tales by Brothers Grimm by Jacob Grimm and Wilhelm Grimm* (*Grimms' Fairy Tales*; henceforth, `GFT`), which consists of 211 stories[2]. Three additional fantasy texts (henceforth, `AFT`) have also been annotated to be used as a separate test set. `AFT` includes *The Story of Aladdin* and *The Story of Ali Baba and the Forty Thieves* from *The Arabian Nights: Their Best-known Tales by Nora Archibald Smith and Kate Douglas*[3] with *Alice's Adventures in Wonderland by Lewis Carroll*[4]. All sources are available on the Project Gutenberg. The materials consist solely of fantasy texts, from which literary-specific characteristics such as metamorphoses of a character, metaphorical expressions, and asymmetry of knowledge are abundantly found. Meanwhile, these features hardly appear in non-fictional contexts, and thus, the existing corpora (which mostly choose non-fictions as their materials) have paid less attention to these literary features.

2.1 Annotation Process

A group of three linguists is formed for this project, who use an open source tool called CorefAnnotator (Reiter, 2018) to create our *FantasyCoref* corpus. Our annotation guidelines are largely based on the OntoNotes Coreference Guidelines 7.0 (Hovy et al., 2006), while referring to other studies on literary texts (Bamman et al., 2020; Roesiger et al., 2018) to consider the characteristics of the genre. The referents are annotated with the omniscient writer's point of view. Furthermore, while defining coreference relations, we adopt the entity-cluster view, which is also adopted by the CoNLL shared tasks (Pradhan et al., 2011, 2012). This view indicates that two or more mentions are non-hierarchically grouped into the same entity cluster (Cranenburgh, van, 2019).

2.2 Annotation Guidelines

Several annotation issues specific to fictional texts, which have not yet been addressed or developed into concrete guidelines in the previous studies, are outlined under the following four categories. Examples from `GFT` and the percentage of corresponding stories are shown in Table 1.

The table not only shows the issue percentage of `GFT` stories, but also that of 100 documents sampled from the OntoNotes corpus. The samples are chosen with a stratified sampling method to have homogeneous distribution of the entire genres included in the dataset (i.e., news, conversational telephone speech, weblogs, usenet newsgroups,

[1] All our resources including the FantasyCoref corpus are publicly available through our open source project: `https://github.com/emorynlp/FantasyCoref`

[2] `https://www.gutenberg.org/ebooks/5314`

[3] `https://www.gutenberg.org/ebooks/20916`

[4] `https://www.gutenberg.org/ebooks/11`

Issue	Annotation Examples	Issue % (FantasyCoref)	Issue % (OntoNotes)
Asymmetry of Knowledge	[*Cinderella*] They never once thought of [Cinderella]$_x$, and believed that [she]$_x$ was sitting at home in the dirt, picking lentils out of (...) He waited until [her]$_x$ father came, and said to him, "[The stranger-maiden]$_x$ has escaped from me, and I believe [she]$_x$ has climbed up the pear-tree.	36.4% (78/214)	2.0% (2/100)
Changes in Entities	[*The Frog-King or Iron Henry*] "How [the silly frog]$_x$ does talk!" (...) But when [he]$_x$ fell down [he]$_x$ was no frog but a King's son with beautiful (...) the way [the King's son]$_x$ heard a cracking behind [him]$_x$ (...).	24.8% (53/214)	1.0% (1/100)
Foretelling or Wishes	[*Jorinda and Joringel*] At last he dreamt one night that he found [a blood-red flower]$_x$, (...) He sought until the ninth day, and then, early in the morning, he found [the blood-red flower]$_x$.	7.0% (15/214)	1.0% (1/100)
Lexical Variations	[*The Wonderful Musician*] "(...) I will fetch hither [a good companion]$_x$ for myself." Then he took [his fiddle]$_x$ from his back, and played (...).	23.4% (50/214)	35.0% (35/100)

Table 1: Annotation issues, their corresponding examples from Grimms' Fairy Tales, and the proportion of documents from FantasyCoref and OntoNotes, respectively, in which each issue has been found.

broadcast, and talk shows). The comparison between the two corpora shows that several issues are dominantly specific to fictional texts. Moreover, although OntoNotes shows higher proportion on *Lexical Variations*, lexical variety found in non-fictions often differ from those in fictions. While lexical variations in non-fictional texts such as news (e.g, *Iran - the city, the Ford - the company*) are relatively easy to assume from world-knowledge, this may not be the case for literary contexts: The linkage among metaphorical expressions and paraphrases need to be indirectly assumed from utterances and actions of characters, which may be far more complicated and confusing in coreference resolution tasks. Hence, it can be said that the existing guideline does not provide sufficient information on these literary-specific issues. We believe the following guidelines are highly necessary to achieve fine-quality annotation of literary texts. More examples and explanations of the issue categories are provided in Appendix A.

Asymmetry of Knowledge This occurs when the knowledge is shared differently (a) between the reader and the characters or (b) between characters or when (c) the reader's knowledge changes throughout the plot (e.g., a plot-twist) (Bamman et al., 2020). Furthermore, we elaborate this issue by categorizing it into *deception (lie, disguise)*, *mistaking*, *secret* and *a plot-twist*. In these cases, we follow the omniscient writer's point of view.

Changes in Entities In literary texts, changes often take place in the development of entities (e.g., transformations or changes in the status of a character). While this phenomenon has been addressed in the previous literature (Roesiger et al., 2018), they have not suggested a specific guideline for such. When there exist separate mentions referring to a human-character, an animal, an object, or a place before and after changes, we group them under a single entity as long as they hold the same identity throughout the story.

Foretelling or Wishes One of the characteristics of literature is that characters often face a prophecy, curse or dream, and what has been foretold becomes reality. This is parallel to cases where a character's wish is granted and an entity that has been wished for is realized. In this case, we link the first appearance of an entity in the foretelling (or wishes) to its following real-world counterparts.

Lexical Variations Literary texts frequently make use of lexical variations or paraphrases (Roesiger et al., 2018). Hence, a character or a noun phrase is often repetitively referred to as various expressions. We group these anaphoric (e.g., the dragon = monster) or metaphoric expressions (e.g., three girls = gifts) under a single entity.

2.3 Inter-Annotator Agreement

To ensure the quality of our annotation, the standard coreference evaluation metrics, MUC (Vilain et al., 1995), B^3 (Bagga and Baldwin, 1998), and $CEAF_{\phi_4}$ (Luo, 2005), are used to estimate inter-annotator agreement (IAA). The Kappa score (Cohen, 1960) is considered the standard method of evaluating IAA in NLP tasks; however, it evaluates IAA in a pair-wise fashion, while coreference resolution assigns a markable to a coreference chain. Therefore, to avoid the Kappa score over-penalizing the wrongly assigned markable (He, 2007), we used the aforementioned metrics instead.

The agreement scores are calculated in four stages. First three stages were on GFT and the last stage was on AFT. In each stage, the annotators have been divided into three groups consisting of two annotators (i.e., first group of annotator 1 and 2, second group of annotator 1 and 3, third group of annotator 2 and 3), and each group worked independently on two random stories. Then, sets of scores calculated by the three groups are averaged into the final score for each stage. Table 2 shows the IAA scores in three stages. After the third stage, a high IAA score of 87% is achieved. The score of the last stage is similar with the third stage's even though the it used stories other than *Grimm Stories*.

Stage	MUC	B^3	$CEAF_{\phi_4}$	Avg-F1
1	90.34	84.48	74.21	83.01
2	92.25	86.70	73.62	84.19
3	91.72	86.87	**82.54**	**87.04**
4	**92.62**	**87.14**	78.45	86.07

Table 2: Inter-annotator agreement scores measured by the evaluation metrics, MUC, B^3, and $CEAF_{\phi_4}$, in three stages and the averaged score for each stage.

3 Corpus

3.1 Corpus Overview

FantasyCoref is a novel dataset of 367,891 tokens comprising of GFT and AFT, and is publicly available. The statistical information of our corpus is shown in Table 3.

	Average per document		Total	
	GFT	AFT	GFT	AFT
# of sentences	57	327	12,128	980
# of tokens	1,614	9,115	340,546	27,345
# of entities	28	116	5,829	347
# of mentions	270	1,529	56,968	4,587
# of mentions per entity	9	14	-	-

Table 3: Basic statistics of FantasyCoref.

3.2 Corpus Analytics

FantasyCoref is larger than the other existing public coreference resolution corpus on literary texts in English: LitBank (Bamman et al., 2019, 2020). *FantasyCoref* covers all types of noun phrases while LitBank annotates only six subsets of entity types (people, facilities, locations, geo-political entities, organizations and vehicles).

Compared with other benchmark datasets such as OntoNotes (Hovy et al., 2006), *FantasyCoref* shows a larger number of tokens per document. Regarding this characteristic, we calculated the average distance between mentions by the number of tokens between a mention and its antecedent within a single entity. *FantasyCoref*'s average distance between consecutive mentions and spread(distance between the first mention and the last mention within the same entity) are longer than OntoNotes'.

On the qualitative side, *FantasyCoref* presents a new perspective of coreference resolution by introducing an omniscient writer's point of view to the corpus which can handle multiple perspectives between timelines and characters that exist in literature. Furthermore, *FantasyCoref* consists of fantasy texts, which include various situations such as metamorphoses of characters and prophecies becoming to reality. Such issues make coreference resolution more complex compared to the other genre of the literature.

	# of tokens	# of docs	# tokens per document
FantasyCoref	370K	214	1,700
OntoNotes	1,600K	2,384	700
LitBank	210K	100	2,100

Table 4: Comparison between FantasyCoref and other coreference resolution corpora. Tokens per document are rounded to the nearest ten.

	Antecedent Distance		Spread	
	Fantasy Coref	Onto Notes	Fantasy Coref	Onto Notes
mean	57	48	484	171
std	191	112	823	280
min	1	1	1	1
median	13	14	186	46
max	7,086	4,362	11,010	4,876

Table 5: Comparison of mention distance between FantasyCoref and OntoNotes.

4 Experiment

4.1 Model

We use the state-of-the-art NLP model, Emory Language and Information Toolkit (ELIT) (Xu and Choi, 2020), to examine how well the existing coreference resolution model accounts for our annotated corpus, *FantasyCoref*. We experiment on end-to-end coreference systems with and without higher-order inference (HOI) approaches implemented in ELIT: attended antecedent (`AA`), entity equalization (`EE`), span clustering (`SC`), and cluster merging (`CM`).

The end-to-end coreference system is based on *c2f-coref* model (Lee et al., 2018) and SpanBERT (Joshi et al., 2020), and we adopt the "*independent*" splitting variant for long documents introduced by Joshi et al. (2019). The higher-order inference is a widely adapted method for global optimization of coreference links. Both `AA` and `EE` refines mention representation by aggregating its antecedents' information. While `AA` uses the distribution over antecedents from the span-ranking process as attention mechanism for refinement, `EE` aggregates all mentions in the cluster thus equalizing all representations of mentions in the same cluster. `SC` also refines mention representation from spans in cluster where it belongs, but differs from `EE` that it constructs the actual clusters from true predicted entities. `CM` ranks antecedents by sequentially merging entity clusters (see Xu and Choi (2020) for more details).

Both the OntoNotes model, which is trained on OntoNotes dataset, and our model, which is trained on `GFT`, are evaluated on the test set.

4.2 Data Processing

Development and test set are chosen from 211 stories (10 stories each) in `GFT` using stratified sampling method so that the train/dev/test set could have homogeneous distributions in terms of number of sentences, tokens, entities, mentions, and number of issues in Table 1. The rest of the stories (171 stories) are used as a train set to train our model. Note that all stories in `AFT` are only used as a separate test set to evaluate the generalization ability of our model on additional fictional texts.

Furthermore, in the case of the dev/test set, additional partitioned version is constructed to reduce the number of tokens to be similar to that of the OntoNotes dataset (467 tokens). The purpose is to compare the models' performance on both long and short version of the dataset, as it is widely known that the performance of coreference resolution on long documents is relatively poor. The partitioning process was done towards preserving the original entity chain. Each story is partitioned by finding the case where the sum of the number of entities in each partition is minimum so that the original entity chains are not cut in the middle and the partitioning does not produce extra number of entities in each partition. In addition, the stories were not partitioned in the middle of pair quotation marks to avoid starting or ending the partition in the middle of one's utterance. The train set is not partitioned, since feeding the model as many sentences as it can handle would be more desirable to learn coreferent links between distant mention pairs.

For brevity, the original versions and the partitioned versions of the dev/test set are referred to as follows for the rest of the paper:

- split 1: the original version of the `GFT` dev/test set
- split 2: the partitioned version of the `GFT` dev/test set
- split 3: the partitioned version of the `AFT` test set (We do not evaluate our model on the original version of `AFT` because we encounter a memory issue due to their large number of tokens, averaging to 9199).

The statistical information of the train/dev/test set and the comparison before and after partitioning is shown in Table 6.

			# of tokens per doc	# of docs
GFT	train	original	1,611	171
	dev	original (split 1)	1,652	20
		partitioned (split 2)	525	63
	test	original (split 1)	1,601	20
		partitioned (split 2)	525	61
AFT	test	original	9,119	3
		partitioned (split 3)	516	53

Table 6: Statistics of the train/dev/test set and before and after partitioning

split 1	MUC			B^3			$CEAF_{\phi_4}$				
	P	R	F1	P	R	F1	P	R	F1	Avg. F1	Avg-M
SpanBERT + AA (OntoNotes model)	81.02	86.61	83.72	66.76	69.72	69.21	58.13	**66.16**	61.89	71.27	-
SpanBERT (Ours)	84.47	86.01	85.23	**70.86**	72.69	**71.76**	**67.28**	62.09	**64.58**	**73.86**	**73.21 (±0.60)**
+ AA	83.90	86.19	85.03	69.16	69.67	69.41	66.23	59.10	62.46	72.30	71.74 (±0.56)
+ EE	**84.90**	62.83	72.21	70.22	44.46	54.45	63.56	34.80	44.98	57.21	56.94 (±0.29)
+ SC	83.70	86.24	84.95	70.42	71.29	70.85	65.87	60.78	63.22	73.01	72.62 (±0.39)
+ CM	82.87	**88.04**	**85.38**	66.79	**76.28**	71.22	66.60	62.41	64.44	73.68	73.18 (±0.37)

split 2	MUC			B^3			$CEAF_{\phi_4}$				
	P	R	F1	P	R	F1	P	R	F1	Avg. F1	Avg-M
SpanBERT (OntoNotes model)	81.01	87.82	84.27	69.17	75.21	72.06	64.96	65.31	65.13	73.82	-
SpanBERT (Ours)	83.64	87.92	85.73	71.15	77.69	74.28	72.97	62.20	67.15	75.52	75.11 (±0.66)
+ AA	83.33	86.69	84.98	71.88	75.22	73.51	70.82	62.53	66.42	74.97	74.77 (±0.22)
+ EE	**84.04**	87.72	85.84	**74.60**	75.80	**75.19**	72.37	**67.07**	**69.62**	**76.88**	**76.55 (±0.37)**
+ SC	83.78	87.06	85.39	71.90	76.58	74.17	71.55	60.70	65.68	75.08	74.92 (±0.13)
+ CM	83.83	**88.05**	**85.89**	72.06	**78.04**	74.93	**72.98**	62.11	67.11	75.98	75.49 (±0.35)

split 3	MUC			B^3			$CEAF_{\phi_4}$				
	P	R	F1	P	R	F1	P	R	F1	Avg. F1	Avg-M
SpanBERT + SC (OntoNotes model)	87.12	**87.68**	87.40	77.39	**78.80**	**78.09**	68.45	55.02	61.00	75.50	-
SpanBERT (Ours)	88.64	82.94	85.69	76.78	72.44	74.55	**73.21**	48.66	58.47	72.90	-
+ EE	**88.66**	86.39	**87.51**	**79.86**	73.93	76.78	55.19	**73.76**	**63.14**	**75.81**	-

Table 7: The best performance result of different approaches on *FantasyCoref*, measured by the standard coreference evaluation metrics, MUC, B^3, and $CEAF_{\phi_4}$. The main evaluation metric is the averaged F1 of the three metrics. (P: Precision, R: Recall, Avg-M : the mean of Avg-F1 and the standard deviation from three developments)

4.3 Experiment Details

The experiment is comprised of three parts:

1. (for every approaches in Section 4.1) we take the best performing model on the GFT split 1 dev set and compare the result with the OntoNotes model on the GFT split 1 test set.
2. (for every approaches) we take the best performing model on the GFT split 2 dev set and compare the result with the OntoNotes model on the GFT split 2 test set.
3. We take the best performing model from part 1 and 2 and compare the result with the OntoNotes model on the AFT split 3 test set.

4.4 Results

Table 7 shows the results of the OntoNotes model and our model evaluated on the GFT test set (split 1, split 2) and the AFT test set (split 3). For the OntoNotes model, only the result of the best model among the five approaches are reported. In the case of our model, we report the mean scores and the standard deviations after three repeated developments for precise measurement.

The effect of training the model on GFT dataset is clear, when comparing the performance of the OntoNotes model with ours, for both split 1 and 2. The Avg-F1 score improves 2.59% (71.27% to 73.86%) and 3.06% (73.82% to 76.88%) for split 1 and 2, respectively. It can be interpreted that the model captures and learns the characteristics of coreferent links specific in fictional texts. In fact, we observe that the error types specific to fictional texts decreases after fine-tuning, which will be discussed in more detail in Section 5.

SpanBERT with entity equalization (EE; HOI suggested by Kantor and Globerson (2019)) shows a considerable performance difference in split 1 and 2 (Table 7). According to the published code of EE[5], the number of candidate spans is limited to

[5] https://github.com/lxucs/coref-ee

300 for the reason that the implementation of EE requires $O(k^2)$ memory with k being the number of mentions extracted, while other HOI approaches requires $O(k)$. Under this limited setting, the poor performance (especially the recall of metrics) is expected for long documents whose number of mentions in gold labels exceeds 300. EE is a limited approach for long documents in terms of computational limitation.

Also, the evaluation on AFT shows that the best performing model on split 2 still maintains its performance with slight decrease of 1.07% (76.88% to 75.81%), which still surpasses the OntoNotes model. This shows the generalization ability of our model trained on GFT to fictional texts.

5 Error Analysis

For both OntoNotes model and our model, the predicted results of 9 stories, randomly selected from the test set, have been examined based on a number of error types. The error categories were added or modified by the annotators throughout the analysis, and the finalized error types are found in Table 8. The distribution of error types for OntoNotes and our model are shown in Figure 1 and Figure 2, respectively.

5.1 OntoNotes model

(simplified).pdf (simplified).pdf

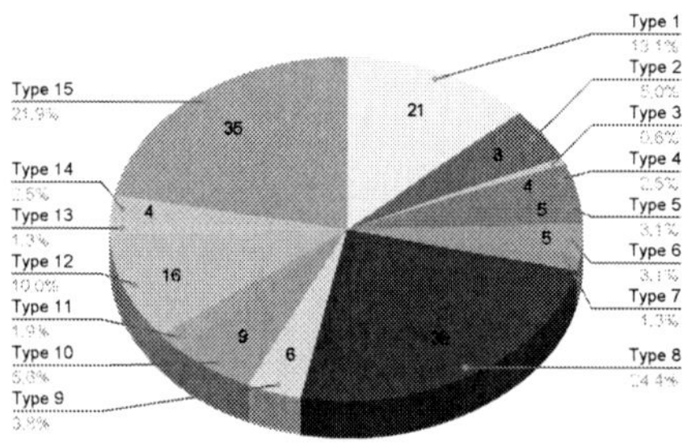

Figure 1: The distribution of error types for OntoNotes model. See Table 8 for details of the error types.

For OntoNotes model, 160 errors are observed and 46.3% of errors are found in Type 8 (Lexical Variations) and Type 15 (Miscellaneous) combined. Large proportion of Type 8 errors indicate that the ELIT system has a limited performance in capturing various metaphoric expressions or lexical variations as single entities, which frequently appear in literary texts. Moreover, Miscellaneous type errors mostly include cases in which ELIT captures an entity correctly but its referents only partially, while negligence of abstract concepts (e.g., *the power of three giants* and *their power*) or temporal expressions (e.g., *yesterday*) are also found.

Errors specific to literary texts are shown by Type 9 (Foretelling, Wishes, 3.8%), Type 5 (Plot-Twists, 3.1%), Type 6 (Changes in Appearance, 3.1%), and Type 4 (Mistakes, 2.5%), which consist of 12.5% of errors combined. The proportion is not dominant; however, the errors show that the current coreference resolution model (trained on OntoNotes) has limitations on linking referents such as follows: an imaginative concept to its realization, asymmetric information, and a character to its new identity after change.

5.2 Our model

(simplified).pdf (simplified).pdf

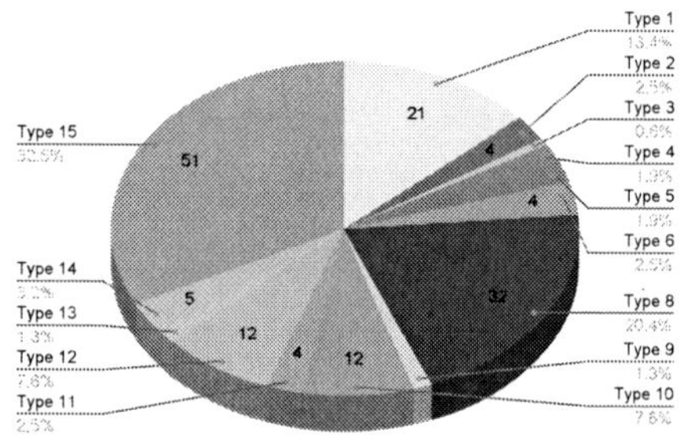

Figure 2: The distribution of error types for our model. See Table 8 for details of the error types.

For our model, the number of errors is 106, approximately 33.8% reduced compared to the result of OntoNotes model. The proportion of Type 15 (Miscellaneous, 32.5%), Type 8 (Lexical Variations, 20.4%), Type 1 (General Objects, 13.4%), Type 12 (Different entities, 7.6%), and Type 10 (Long Modifiers, 7.6%) combined are still dominant (81.5%), while the increased ratio of Type 15 is noticeable. The increase in the Type 15 errors and the reduced ratio of most of the other categories indicate the following: the model trained on our dataset better distinguishes separate entities and better predicts entities with respect to literary-specific issues, and now, more errors are of 'missing referents', rather than 'missing entities'.

Comparing our model to OntoNotes model, the performance improves with respect to Type 2 (Long Distance, 5.0% to 4.0%). The average distance of

Error Types	Description
1. General Objects	A general object that does not appear frequently in a text and thus not captured as an entity.
2. Long Distance	A referent that is far apart (more than 700 tokens) from its preceding referent is not linked to its preceding referent.
3. Lies	Two or more referents involved in a character's lying (deception) are not correctly linked.
4. Mistakes	When a character mistakes an object or a person for something or someone else (but the referents need to be categorized under a single entity based on OWV), referents involed in such case are not correctly predicted.
5. Plot-Twists	Two or more referents that are involved in a plot-twist are not correctly linked.
6. Changes in Appearance	Referents are not correctly linked when they refer to a single entity which has undergone a change in its appearance (e.g., metamorphosis, physical growth)
7. Changes in Status	When a character goes through a change in status (e.g., demotion, promotion), terms of address used and after the change are not correctly linked.
8. Lexical Variations	Two or more terms of address referring to a single entity (e.g., anaphora, metaphorical expressions) are not correctly linked.
9. Foretelling, Wishes	A referent which seem separate from its entity due to a character's lying, but in fact is linked to its entity is not captured by the model.
10. Long Modifiers	A referent is not correctly linked to its entity when the referent is an NP with a long post-modifier (e.g., *a great neck-kerchief of silk embroidered with gold*).
11. NP+VP+Rel Clause	A referent having the structure of (NP+VP+relative clause modifying NP) is not marked as an entity (e.g., *a sword was hanging on the wall which was made of pure silver*).
12. Different Entities	A model groups separate entities and their referents under a single group.
13. Verbs & Nominalizations	A verb and its nominalizations (e.g., *flew-flight*) are not linked.
14. Nouns w/o Determiners	An NP used without a determiner is not linked with other referents (e.g., *table-the table*).
15. Miscellaneous	Errors which do not fall into the types above are categorized as 15. Miscellaneous.

Table 8: Error types used during the error analysis and the description of each error type.

the correct group becomes 43.34 tokens from 41.65 tokens and that of the error group becomes 88.96 tokens from 94.62 tokens. This implies that the model has improved towards capturing the mentions of the same entity in long distance after training with our dataset.

Moreover, a couple of errors from literary-specific categories, (Type 4 (Mistakes), Type 5 (Plot-Twists), Type 6 (Changes in Appearance), and Type 9 (Foretelling, Wishes) are now predicted correctly, which shows that training with our dataset has an effect of remedying issues caused during the coreference resolution of literary styles or concepts. As an example of Type 4, in the story *Frederick and Catherine*, a group of robbers under a tree mistakes *Catherine* for *the devil*, when she drops an object from up the tree. While the two referents, *Catherine* and *the devil* are grouped under separate entities in OntoNotes model, they are correctly captured under the *Catherine* cluster in our model. Moreover, a Type 5 error is exemplified by the story *The Girl without Hands*. In the text, *an old man* comes across *a stranger* on the street, who turns out to be *the devil* in the latter part of the story. The two referents, *a stranger* and *the devil*, which used to be in separate entity clusters are grouped under a single cluster in our model. Finally, a Type 6 error is shown by the story, *The Sea-Hare*: In the story, *a fox* transforms into a human *merchant*, and the two categories are correctly linked in our model.

The low proportion of errors specific to literary (fictional) texts may also be due to characteristics of texts randomly selected from the test set. Hence, large data sets of literary texts are in need to train the pre-exsiting coreference resolution systems and boost their performance with respect to literary-specific features.

6 Conclusion

In this work, we present *FantasyCoref*, a new English annotated dataset of 367,891 tokens from Grimms' Fairy Tales and additional fantasy literature. *FantasyCoref* is larger in size compared to the existing coreference corpora in literature, and takes into consideration a number of issues specific to this genre. These issues are organized as guidelines having four categories of the following: 1) Asymmetry of Knowledge, 2) Changes in Entities, 3) Foretelling or Wishes, and 4) Lexical Variations. The state-of-the-art coreference system trained on our annotated corpus results in a significant improvement on fictional texts and a decrease in genre-specific errors. However, the best performance with 76.88% still has room for improvement compared to the those shown in the OntoNotes dataset. Hence, we believe that *FantasyCoref* is a highly valuable resource that can be utilized to develop the current coreference resolution models and, by extension, language comprehension tasks.

Acknowledgments

This work was supported by the Ministry of Education of the Republic of Korea and the National Research Foundation of Korea (NRF-2020S1A5B1104865).

References

Amit Bagga and Breck Baldwin. 1998. Algorithms for scoring coreference chains. In *In The First International Conference on Language Resources and Evaluation Workshop on Linguistics Coreference*, pages 563–566.

David Bamman, Olivia Lewke, and Anya Mansoor. 2020. An annotated dataset of coreference in English literature. In *Proceedings of the 12th Language Resources and Evaluation Conference*, pages 44–54, Marseille, France. European Language Resources Association.

David Bamman, Sejal Popat, and Sheng Shen. 2019. An annotated dataset of literary entities. In *Proceedings of the 2019 Conference of the North American Chapter of the Association for Computational Linguistics: Human Language Technologies, Volume 1 (Long and Short Papers)*, pages 2138–2144, Minneapolis, Minnesota. Association for Computational Linguistics.

Jacob Cohen. 1960. A coefficient of agreement for nominal scales. *Educational and Psychological Measurement*, 20(1):37–46.

Andreas Cranenburgh, van. 2019. A dutch coreference resolution system with an evaluation on literary fiction. *Computational Linguistics in the Netherlands Journal*, 9.

Tian Ye He. 2007. Coreference resolution on entities and events for hospital discharge summaries. *Thesis (M. Eng.)–Massachusetts Institute of Technology, Dept. of Electrical Engineering and Computer Science.*

Felix Hill, Antoine Bordes, Sumit Chopra, and Jason Weston. 2016. The goldilocks principle: Reading children's books with explicit memory representations. In *4th International Conference on Learning Representations, ICLR 2016, San Juan, Puerto Rico, May 2-4, 2016, Conference Track Proceedings.*

Eduard H. Hovy, Mitchell P. Marcus, Martha Palmer, Lance A. Ramshaw, and Ralph M. Weischedel. 2006. Ontonotes: The 90% solution. In *Human Language Technology Conference of the North American Chapter of the Association of Computational Linguistics, Proceedings, June 4-9, 2006, New York, New York, USA*. The Association for Computational Linguistics.

Mandar Joshi, Danqi Chen, Yinhan Liu, Daniel S. Weld, Luke Zettlemoyer, and Omer Levy. 2020. Spanbert: Improving pre-training by representing and predicting spans. *Transactions of the Association for Computational Linguistics*, 8:64–77.

Mandar Joshi, Omer Levy, Luke Zettlemoyer, and Daniel S Weld. 2019. Bert for coreference resolution: Baselines and analysis. In *Proceedings of the 2019 Conference on Empirical Methods in Natural Language Processing and the 9th International Joint Conference on Natural Language Processing (EMNLP-IJCNLP)*, pages 5803–5808.

Ben Kantor and Amir Globerson. 2019. Coreference resolution with entity equalization. In *Proceedings of the 57th Annual Meeting of the Association for Computational Linguistics*, pages 673–677, Florence, Italy. Association for Computational Linguistics.

Kenton Lee, Luheng He, and Luke Zettlemoyer. 2018. Higher-order coreference resolution with coarse-to-fine inference. In *Proceedings of the 2018 Conference of the North American Chapter of the Association for Computational Linguistics: Human Language Technologies, Volume 2 (Short Papers)*, pages 687–692, New Orleans, Louisiana. Association for Computational Linguistics.

Xuansong Li, Martha Palmer, Nianwen Xue, Lance Ramshaw, Mohamed Maamouri, Ann Bies, Kathryn Conger, Stephen Grimes, and Stephanie Strassel. 2016. Large multi-lingual, multi-level and multi-genre annotation corpus. In *Proceedings of the Tenth International Conference on Language Resources and Evaluation (LREC'16)*, pages 906–913, Portorož, Slovenia. European Language Resources Association (ELRA).

Xiaoqiang Luo. 2005. On coreference resolution performance metrics. In *Proceedings of Human Language Technology Conference and Conference on Empirical Methods in Natural Language Processing*, pages 25–32, Vancouver, British Columbia, Canada. Association for Computational Linguistics.

Sameer Pradhan, Alessandro Moschitti, Nianwen Xue, Olga Uryupina, and Yuchen Zhang. 2012. CoNLL-2012 shared task: Modeling multilingual unrestricted coreference in OntoNotes. In *Joint Conference on EMNLP and CoNLL - Shared Task*, pages 1–40, Jeju Island, Korea. Association for Computational Linguistics.

Sameer Pradhan, Lance Ramshaw, Mitchell Marcus, Martha Palmer, Ralph Weischedel, and Nianwen Xue. 2011. CoNLL-2011 shared task: Modeling unrestricted coreference in OntoNotes. In *Proceedings of the Fifteenth Conference on Computational Natural Language Learning: Shared Task*, pages 1–27, Portland, Oregon, USA. Association for Computational Linguistics.

Nils Reiter. 2018. CorefAnnotator - A New Annotation Tool for Entity References. In *Abstracts of EADH: Data in the Digital Humanities*.

Ina Roesiger, Sarah Schulz, and Nils Reiter. 2018. Towards coreference for literary text: Analyzing domain-specific phenomena. In *Proceedings of the Second Joint SIGHUM Workshop on Computational Linguistics for Cultural Heritage, Social Sciences, Humanities and Literature*, pages 129–138, Santa Fe, New Mexico. Association for Computational Linguistics.

Marc Vilain, John Burger, John Aberdeen, Dennis Connolly, and Lynette Hirschman. 1995. A model-theoretic coreference scoring scheme. In *Proceedings of the 6th Conference on Message Understanding*, MUC6 '95, page 45–52, USA. Association for Computational Linguistics.

Wei Wu, Fei Wang, Arianna Yuan, Fei Wu, and Jiwei Li. 2020. CorefQA: Coreference resolution as query-based span prediction. In *Proceedings of the 58th Annual Meeting of the Association for Computational Linguistics*, pages 6953–6963, Online. Association for Computational Linguistics.

Liyan Xu and Jinho D. Choi. 2020. Revealing the myth of higher-order inference in coreference resolution. In *Proceedings of the 2020 Conference on Empirical Methods in Natural Language Processing (EMNLP)*, pages 8527–8533, Online. Association for Computational Linguistics.

Michael Yoder, Sopan Khosla, Qinlan Shen, Aakanksha Naik, Huiming Jin, Hariharan Muralidharan, and Carolyn Rosé. 2021. FanfictionNLP: A text processing pipeline for fanfiction. In *Proceedings of the Third Workshop on Narrative Understanding*, pages 13–23, Virtual. Association for Computational Linguistics.

Ethan Zhou and Jinho D. Choi. 2018. They exist! introducing plural mentions to coreference resolution and entity linking. In *Proceedings of the 27th International Conference on Computational Linguistics*, pages 24–34, Santa Fe, New Mexico, USA. Association for Computational Linguistics.

A Appendix

We provide several paragraphs from *Grimms' Fairy Tales* which serve as an example for each annotation guideline.

A.1 Asymmetry of Knowledge

(1) (*Deception*) "If thou wilt invite [us]$_x$ to the wedding, not be ashamed of [us]$_x$, and wilt call [us]$_x$ thine aunts, (...) "I have [three aunts]$_x$," said the girl, "(...) allow me to invite [them]$_x$ to the wedding, and let [them]$_x$ sit with us at table."

In *The Three Spinners*, the girl lies that 'the three spinners' are her aunts. Nevertheless the spinners are not the girl's aunts in fact, the reader knows that the girl is referring to the same people. We connect 'the spinners' and 'the girl's aunts'.

(2) (*Mistaking*) He was dreadfully frightened, and ran to the back-door, but [the dog, who lay there]$_x$ sprang up and bit his leg; and as he ran across the yard by the straw-heap, [the donkey]$_y$ gave him a smart kick with its hind foot. (...) Then the robber ran back as fast as he could to his captain, and said, "Ah, (...) and by the door stands [a man with a knife, who stabbed me in the leg]$_x$; and in the yard there lies [a black monster, who beat me with a wooden club]$_y$ (...)"

In *The Bremen Town-Musicians* the robber mistakes animals for different things though the animals were not intended to deceive him. In (3), 'dog' is mistaken as 'a man with a knife' and 'the donkey' is mistaken as 'a black monster'. As the reader knows that the robber refers to the same thing, we annotate them as co-referents.

(3) (*Secret*) Then he took him about everywhere, up and down, and let him see all the riches, and the magnificent apartments, only there was one room which he did not open, that in which hung [the dangerous picture]$_x$. (...) "Ah, no," replied the young King, "if I do not go in, it will be my certain destruction.I should have no rest day or night until I had seen [it]$_x$ with my own eyes.

In *Faithful John*, Faithful John keep in secret to the young King that the dangerous picture is in the chamber. The young King says he will not move until he sees 'it'. Even though the young King does not know whether 'it' is the dangerous picture, the reader knows that, therefore we treated them as the same entity.

(4) (*Twist*) [He]$_x$ said to her kindly, "Do not be afraid, [I]$_x$ and [the fiddler who has been living with you in that wretched hovel]$_x$ are one. For love of you [I]$_x$ disguised [myself]$_x$ so; and [I]$_x$ also was the hussar who rode through your crockery. (...)"

In *King Thrushbeard*, it turns out that 'king Thrushbeard', 'the fiddler' and 'the hussar' were the same person at the end of the story. The reader may not notice it in the middle of the plot since it is the twist, however, we annotate all as the same referents with the knowledge after reading through all the text.

A.2 Changes in Entities

(5) (*Metamorphosis*) [The lion]$_x$, however, was an enchanted prince (...) a ray about the breadth of a hair fell on [the King's son]$_x$, and when this ray touched [him]$_x$, [he]$_x$ was transformed in an instant, and when she came in and looked for [him]$_x$, she did not see [him]$_x$, but [a white dove]$_x$ was sitting there.

In *The Singing, Springing Lark*, 'the lion' changes into 'a white dove' by being touched by 'a ray'. Since the identity of 'the lion' has not changed by its appearance, we annotate 'the lion' and 'a white dove' under the same entity.

(6) (*Change in Status*) There was once on a time [a girl who was young and beautiful]$_x$, (...). At last [she]$_x$ hired [herself]$_x$ to a farmer as a cow-herd, and buried [her]$_x$ dresses and jewels beneath a stone.(...) [she]$_x$ said,"Little calf, little calf, kneel by [my]$_x$ side, And do not forget [thy shepherd-maid]$_x$, As the prince forgot [his betrothed bride, Who waited for him 'neath the lime-tree's shade]$_x$."

In *The True Sweethearts*, a girl become a shepherd-maid and prince's bride during the story. Though a girl is not a shepherd-maid nor a bride in the beginning of the story, we group 'a girl', 'a shepherd-maid' and 'a bride' together.

(7) (*Growth*) (...) from [the two pieces]$_x$ that were buried in the ground [two golden lilies]$_x$ sprang up, (...)

In *The Gold-Children*, 'the two pieces (of a golden fish)' is buried, then grows into 'two golden lilies'. Although the appearance has changed throughout the growth, no further mention of 'the two pieces' appear after their growth. Hence, we consider 'the two pieces' and 'two golden lilies' to be the referents.

A.3 Foretelling and Wishes

(8) (*Prophecy*) "you must not drink [the wine which will be brought to you at night]$_x$, and must pretend to be sound asleep." (...) the eldest came and brought him [a cup of wine]$_x$ (...)

In *The Shoes that were Danced to Pieces*, 'an old woman' foretells and warns 'a poor soldier' that he must not drink 'the wine' that will be served that night, and 'a cup of wine' is indeed offered to him as the warning said. We link the first appearance of an entity in a prophecy, curse, or dream (in this example, 'the wine which will be brought to you at night') to its realization in the real-world (in this example, 'a cup of wine').

(9) (*Wish*) "Will you wish for [a new house]$_x$ instead of this old one?" "Oh, yes," said the man; "if I can have [that]$_x$, too, I should like it very much." And the Lord fulfilled his wish, and changed their old house into [a new one]$_x$, (...) on the opposite side of the way, [a new clean-looking house with red tiles and bright windows where the old hut used to be]$_x$.

In *The Poor Man and the Rich Man*, the man wishes for 'a house' and this wish is fulfilled as a form of 'a new clean-looking house with red tiles and bright windows'. When an entity that is wished or requested for in a story is realized into a real-world entity, we link the two as referents.

(10) (*Favor*) (...)"Here, put on this dress and go out into the wood, and fetch me [a little basketful of strawberries],—I have a fancy for some." (...) she answered, "I am to look for [a basketful of strawberries], and am not to go home until I can take them with me."

In *The Three Little Men in the Wood*, the mother makes the girl fetch her some strawberries and later, the girl says about strawberries. In this case, since 'a basketful of strawberries' are general, we do not annotate them as the same entity. If the mother asked the girl to find some 'special strawberries', strawberries should be annotated.

A.4 Lexical Variations

(11) (*Variations in terms of Address*) When Fir-twister was busy cooking, [a little shrivelled-up old mannikin]$_x$ came to him (...) "Be off, [sly hypocrite]$_x$," (...) But how astonished Fir-twister was when [the little insignificant dwarf]$_x$ sprang up at him, (...) "(...) they may just try their chance with [the little scrubbing-brush]$_x$;" (...) Then [the malicious dwarf]$_x$ wanted to spring on him (...)

In *Strong Hans*, 'a little shrivelled-up old manikins' is referred to as various expressions according to how other characters perceive him in the story or how the narrator depicts his appearance or personality. Regardless of the variation, when a reader can perceive that several anaphoric terms of address point to a single character, these terms are grouped under the same entity.

(12) (*Metaphoric Expression*) Then at last [the children]$_x$ became so impatient, (...) and ran away. But when church was over, the nix saw that [the birds]$_x$ were flown, and followed [them]$_x$ with great strides.

In *The Water-Nix*, 'the birds' is used as an metaphoric expression referring to 'the children' who have run away. We link metaphoric expressions to its referent when the connection between them can be perceived by the reader.

DramaCoref: A Hybrid Coreference Resolution System for German Theater Plays

Janis Pagel
Institute for Natural Language Processing
University of Stuttgart
pageljs@ims.uni-stuttgart.de

Nils Reiter
Department of Digital Humanities
University of Cologne
nils.reiter@uni-koeln.de

Abstract

We present a system for resolving coreference on theater plays, *DramaCoref*. The system uses neural network techniques to provide a list of potential mentions. These mentions are assigned to common entities using generic and domain-specific rules. We find that DramaCoref works well on the theater plays when compared to corpora from other domains and profits from the inclusion of information specific to theater plays. On the best-performing setup, it achieves a CoNLL score of 32% when using automatically detected mentions and 55% when using gold mentions. Single rules achieve high precision scores; however, rules designed on other domains are often not applicable or yield unsatisfactory results. Error analysis shows that the mention detection is the main weakness of the system, providing directions for future improvements.

1 Introduction

We present experiments on resolving coreferences in theater plays/dramas. *Coreference resolution* (CR) aims to assign all mentions in a text to their respective discourse entities. Doing so offers many benefits for working with theater plays, yet CR on this type of text is rarely performed.

Next to prose and poetry, drama is considered one of the three main literary genres since Ancient Greece (Aristoteles, 1982). Dramas are scripts to be performed in theatre. Furthermore, drama is a highly structured text type: To a large extent, it consists of character speech with clear indication of the speaker, as well as some stage directions and a segmentation into acts/scenes. Usually, dramas also contain a so called *dramatis personæ*, which is a list of cast members which will appear during the course of the play. This list typically contains further information about the characters, like family relations, which in turn can be exploited to better resolve certain coreferent mentions.

ACT I, Scene I. *The Prince's Cabinet*
The Prince, seated at a desk, which is covered with papers.
PRINCE. Complaints; nothing but complaints! [...] To be sure, if we could relieve every one, we might indeed be envied. Emilia? *opening a petition, and looking at the signature.* An Emilia? Yes—but an Emilia Bruneschi—not Galotti. Not Emilia Galotti. What does she want, this Emilia Bruneschi? *Reads* She asks much—too much. But her name is Emilia. It is granted *signs the paper, and rings.*

Figure 1: Opening scene of Gotthold Ephraim Lessing's *Emilia Galotti*. Translation from German by the authors.

Characters are a constitutive ingredient for theater plays, and scholarly analysis often revolves around characters, their depiction, and their relations. While dramas make it straightforward to detect character speech, references to characters within the speech of other characters can really only be detected using CR.[1] These character references provide insight into how characters are introduced and seen by other characters, sometimes well before appearing on stage themselves. This can already be seen in Figure 1, which is the opening scene of a play. The character Emilia Galotti only enters the stage in the second act, but from the very beginning, other characters talk about her, thus shaping her reception by readers and audience.

In this paper, we present a system to automatically resolve these coreferences. It makes use of both neural network and rule-based components. Both have been adapted to the dramatic text type, either through fine-tuning or the addition of specific rules.

2 Related work

CR has received a lot of attention, mostly focused on the English language and evaluated on news texts (Lee et al., 2013; Björkelund and Kuhn, 2014; Clark and Manning, 2016; Martschat, 2017; Lee et al., 2017, 2018; Joshi et al.,

[1] Andresen and Vauth (2018) point out similar things for prose texts.

Proceedings of the 4th Workshop on Computational Models of Reference, Anaphora and Coreference (CRAC 2021), pages 36–46
Punta Cana, Dominican Republic, November 10–11, 2021.

2019). The two published CR systems for German are CorZu (Tuggener, 2016) and IMS HotCoref DE (Rösiger and Kuhn, 2016). CorZu is a rule-based system that iteratively eliminates possible mention pairs by checking a number of linguistic features. It achieves 64.79 MELA F-Score (Pradhan et al., 2012) on TüBa-D/Z, an annotated corpus of German news text (Naumann, 2007)[2]. IMS HotCoref DE is a machine learning system that is based on the multi-language IMS HotCoref system by Björkelund and Kuhn (2014). IMS HotCoref searches for possible antecedents based on latent search trees and uses global features to train a perceptron for classification. IMS HotCoref DE modifies IMS HotCoref by adding language-specific properties such as morphological information and making use of GermaNet (Hamp and Feldweg, 1997). Recently, Schröder et al. (2021) presented a system for neural end-to-end coreference resolution on German data, including literary data. Their system outperforms the previous state-of-the-art system IMS HotCoref DE by up to 30 percentage points.[3]

There are only few publications that focus on **CR for literary texts**. BookNLP (Bamman et al., 2014) is a full NLP pipeline optimised for (English) long texts. To resolve coreferential links, noun phrases are clustered, following Davis et al. (2003) (without evaluation). The resolution of anaphora is based on linguistically motivated features and a Bayesian classifier. It achieves an accuracy of 82%, evaluated on under 900 mention pairs from three literary novels. Krug et al. (2015) describe a CR system that only resolves references to literary characters. The system is an adaptation of Lee et al. (2011) and achieves a performance of about 56 B^3 F-Score (outperforming CorZu). Van Cranenburgh (2019) also build upon Lee et al. (2011) and present results for CR on Dutch novels. Like Krug et al. (2015), they limit their annotation of mentions to literary characters, but also include inanimate objects. Table 1 shows self-reported results from the two aforementioned works for CR on literary texts, contrasted with results from Lee et al. (2011), on which system both works are build upon.

To our knowledge, no system has been published for German data that is tailored to dramatic or dialogical texts. Only a few publications deal explicitly with domain adaptation for CR systems (Apostolova et al., 2012; Yang et al., 2012; Zhao and Ng, 2014). Do et al. (2015) describe a method for adapting the Berkeley CR system to narrative texts using linear programming.

In terms of **data sets**, there are only a few readily available. Bamman et al. (2019) released a corpus with annotated entity types (following the ACE standard) on English literary texts. Rösiger et al. (2018) describe challenges in the annotation of literary texts, including plays. In previous own work (Pagel and Reiter, 2020), we have presented a corpus of 31 German language plays annotated for coreference, which will be used as the main resource in this paper.

3 DramaCoref

We propose a hybrid system, using neural and rule-based components, for resolving coreference on theater plays, called *DramaCoref*. The system follows the classic distinction into mention detection and coreference resolution component. For mention detected, we apply a system that is based on a BERT-model, and fine-tune it to our task and domain. We generally see mention detected as similar to named entity recognition (NER), and follow best practices and settings for NER.

The coreference resolution component is based on Stanford's Multi-Pass Sieve Coreference Resolution System (Raghunathan et al., 2010; Lee et al., 2011, 2013). Rule-based systems have been shown to provide good results for CR on literary data (Krug et al., 2015; van Cranenburgh, 2019). For this type of data, rule-based systems also come with certain advantages, as (i) no training data is needed, which is usually sparse for the literary domain (cf. Krug et al., 2015), (ii) rule-based systems tend to generalize better on unseen domains (Lee et al., 2013, p. 886) and (iii) the rules can be easily crafted and changed to fit the needs of the specific domain (van Cranenburgh, 2019, p. 28).

We adopt all passes of Raghunathan et al. (2010) and Lee et al. (2011) to test how general purpose rules fair on dramas and add passes designed to yield high precision on this type of text. In particular, we add a pass that matches lemmas of heads of mentions, since the dramas are in German language and head words can be morphologically complex. Furthermore, we advance the pronoun related rule of Lee et al. (2011) and split it into first, second and third person rules. This allows us to specifically target these different cases and exploit the fact that

[2]https://uni-tuebingen.de/de/134290

[3]The paper got released during the final preparation of this paper.

Paper	Mentions	MUC	B^3	$CEAF_e$	CoNLL
Lee et al. (2011)	auto	0.61	0.69	0.45	0.58
	gold	0.65	0.71	0.48	0.61
Krug et al. (2015)	auto	0.86	0.56	NA	NA
	gold	NA	NA	NA	NA
van Cranenburgh (2019)	auto	0.71	0.62	0.67	0.67
	gold	0.78	0.72	0.78	0.76

Table 1: Comparison of results from different papers. All scores for the different evaluation measures are F1 scores.

dramas mark speaker turns.

Like in Lee et al. (2011), single passes are tested for their precision on a held-out dataset and then ordered by precision; the pass with the highest precision is applied first. Passes which are applied later receive the clusters of previous passes as input, so clusters are build up successively.

Table 2 gives an overview of all passes deployed within DramaCoref. Pass 1 groups mentions into clusters that have identical surface strings. Pass 2 matches structurally predictable constructions, such as appositions and relative clauses (cf. Raghunathan et al., 2010). Pass 3 matches for identical heads of two mentions, while disallowing mentions that are embedded within each other or that do not contain stop words or modifiers present in the cluster of the other mentions. Passes 4 and 5 are variations on this and drop the aforementioned constraints, respectively. Pass 6 drops the constraints of passes 4 and 5, but requires two mentions to share the same named entity category. Pass 7 and 9 resolve pronouns. Pass 10 matches mentions that are identical after dropping any words following the head words. Pass 11 matches mentions with proper nouns as head words. Pass 12 handles information from lexical resources and matches mentions which heads are in a synonymy or hyponymy relationship. For a detailed description of the functionality of passes 1–12, see Raghunathan et al. (2010) and Lee et al. (2011). Pass 2 from Raghunathan et al. (2010) and pass 12 and 14 (here pass 9) from Lee et al. (2011) have been subdivided into passes 2a-c, 9a-b and 12a-b to enable a more detailed evaluation, but still serve the same purpose as in the original papers. While pass 7 from Raghunathan et al. (2010) originally resolved general pronouns, it here only resolves third person pronouns. Pass 11 from Raghunathan et al. (2010) has been extended by a new variation 11a. All changes to passes from Lee et al. (2011) and Raghunathan et al. (2010) as well as passes newly introduced to the system are listed below:

Pass 11a Like pass 11, but adds the constraint that modifiers of either candidates cannot contain a first person pronoun if the speakers differ or a second person pronoun if the next or previous speaker differs.

Pass 12a and 12b Like pass 12 in Lee et al. (2011), but instead of WordNet (Fellbaum, 1998), GermaNet (Hamp and Feldweg, 1997) is used.

Pass 14 This pass works the same as pass 1, except it does not operate on tokens but lemmas only. This change targets the morphological complexity of German, so that inflected word forms are not counted as a mismatch.

Post-processing In a post-processing step, clusters are merged when they contain at least one mention that is referring to the same cast member of the play. In the cases of first-person pronouns, the speaker can be identified as the referred cast member. In the cases of proper names, DramaCoref gets a list of all cast members from the *dramatis personæ* as input and tries to assign the correct cast member via string comparison between all mentions in the dramatis personæ and all mentions in the cluster.

In a very last step, all singletons, i.e. clusters that only contain one single mention, are removed, since all the datasets used in the experiments do not contain singletons.

4 Experiments

4.1 Data

The experiments are performed on the GerDraCor-Coref data (Pagel and Reiter, 2020). GerDraCor-Coref is a corpus of coreference annotations on dramas in German language, including 31 texts

Pass ID	Short Name	Source
1	ExactMatch	Raghunathan et al. (2010)
2a	Acronyms	Raghunathan et al. (2010)
2b	Appositions	Raghunathan et al. (2010)
2c	RelPron	Raghunathan et al. (2010)
3	StrictHeadMatch	Raghunathan et al. (2010)
4	StrictHeadMatchVar1	Raghunathan et al. (2010)
5	StrictHeadMatchVar2	Raghunathan et al. (2010)
6	HeadEntail	Raghunathan et al. (2010)
7	Pron3rdPers	Raghunathan et al. (2010)
9a	SpeakerPron1stPers	Lee et al. (2011), modified
9b	SpeakerPron2ndPers	Lee et al. (2011), modified
10	RelaxedStringMatch	Lee et al. (2011)
11	ProperHeadWordMatch	Lee et al. (2011)
11a	PoperHeadWordMatchVar1	New
12a	LexicalSynonym	Lee et al. (2011), modified
12b	LexialHyponym	Lee et al. (2011), modified
14	ExactLemmaMatch	New

Table 2: All passes of DramaCoref.

from 1732 to 1921. All texts come from GerDraCor (Fischer et al., 2019), a corpus of German dramas, which is encoded in TEI/XML to mark act and scene segmentations and speaker changes, among others. In total, the dataset is comprised of 298,352 tokens, 61,126 mentions and 5,473 entities. The most frequent part-of-speech for mentions are pronouns with 40% of the overall number of mentions, followed by noun phrases and named entities.

Pagel and Reiter (2020) point out several observations about the data and regarding the use of coreference in the texts: Since the texts are considerably longer than in common domains, such as newspaper texts, coreference chains can become quite long as well. Especially chains involving main characters of the plays entail many mentions and span the entirety of the text. On average, dramas contain more mentions, but less entities when compared to news and interview corpora. Additionally, the number of pronouns in coreference chains is much higher compared to other domains (40% for GerDraCor-Coref, compared to 20% in TüBa-D/Z).

For the experiments, we use all mentions and coreference clusters from GerDraCor-Coref except for clusters containing non-nominal antecedents (cf. Kolhatkar et al., 2018).

4.2 Neural mention detection

We extract all possible mentions using a transformer-based approach via fine-tuning a pre-trained German BERT model (Devlin et al., 2019) provided by HuggingFace[4]. While the pre-trained BERT model is not specifically tuned to work on Named Entity Recognition (NER) or similar tasks, it nevertheless performs well on German benchmark NER evaluation datasets, like CoNLL 2003 (0.80 F1) or GermEval14 (0.84 F1)[5].

We also compare the performance to HuggingFace's DistilBERT model[6] (Sanh et al., 2019), a smaller version of BERT with comparable performance, and a BERT model fine-tuned on German literary texts and NER, also hosted by HuggingFace[7].

While mention detection is not identical with NER, we assume that the tasks are similar enough that a model for mention detection will benefit from knowledge about named entities.

Experimental setup The pre-trained BERT models all have embedding and hidden state dimension size of 768. Dropout was set to 0.1 and 12 attention

[4] `https://huggingface.co`

[5] `https://huggingface.co/bert-base-german-cased`

[6] `https://huggingface.co/distilbert-base-german-cased`

[7] `https://huggingface.co/severinsimmler/literary-german-bert`

heads were used while training. In all cases, we run fine-tuning over 4 epochs with an early stopping criterion of 3 and use a train-test split of 80%-20%. AdamW was used as optimizer. Learning rate was set to 4e−5 and the batch size to 8. The maximum length a sequence could have was set to 128.

The BERT-based models are compared to a baseline that uses the Berkeley Parser (Petrov et al., 2006). From the parser's output, we treat all predicted noun phrases as mentions[8].

Results The results of our neural mention detection experiments are shown in Table 3. We find that our setup outperforms the baseline based on parsing in terms of accuracy and precision, however, the baseline yields slightly better results in the macro F1 score. Using a BERT-based model fine-tuned on German literary text is not able to outperform the generic German BERT model, but rather lowers the performance quite notably. We do not find a difference in the performance of the base BERT model and DistilBERT.

Considering the higher score in accuracy with an almost identical F1 score, we opt to use the output of DistilBERT over the parser output as input for the coreference resolution component.

4.3 Sieve-based coreference resolution

We use the best performing model of the experiment in Section 4.2 as input for *DramaCoref*, which is DistilBERT. This component works as described in Section 3. All evaluation scores are measured using the coreference scorer from Pradhan et al. (2014). For the development set, on which the ordering of the passes will be determined, we randomly assign 20% of the documents from GerDraCor-Coref, while the rest is used for testing.

Baselines Before discussing the results of our resolution component, we show different baselines on the GerDraCor-Coref data in order to get a better understanding of the general performance of DramaCoref, since there are no other results to compare with on this dataset.

We showcase three different baselines[9]: (B1) N mentions in N clusters, meaning that every mention is assigned to its own cluster, so that we end up with as many clusters as mentions, each containing exactly one mention, (B2) N mentions in 1 cluster, meaning all mentions are grouped together in a single cluster and (B3) Closest agreeing candidate, which assigns each mention to the closest previous mention it agrees with syntactically and semantically, i.e. in number, gender and NE class.

We can see from Table 4 that B2, which groups all mentions in a single cluster, performs best, closely followed by B3. Looking at the structure of coreference clusters in the data, this makes sense, since the clusters with the most mentions are clusters for dramatic characters, making up a large amount of all mentions, and resemble the setup in the second baseline very closely. Still, performance scores are rather low.

Results Table 6 shows the main results of our coreference resolution component. We show both results on predicted and gold mentions and for different setups. For *act* and *scene*, DramaCoref is applied on whole acts or scenes contained within these acts, respectively. For all following setups, the *scene* setup has been used as a basis. For the setup of *castmembers-only*, we remove all mentions that are not listed in the dramatis personæ, so only literary characters are considered as mentions and resolved. This resembles more closely the setups by Krug et al. (2015) and van Cranenburgh (2019). The setup *dramatispersonae* applies the post-processing step described before, i.e. it merges clusters where it can find common strings found in the dramatis personæ.

All setups perform relatively equal, with *dramatispersonae* boosting the results slightly compared to *act*. The best results on automatic mentions is achieved by the *scene* setup, but for gold mentions, *dramatispersonae* is best. Applying DramaCoref only on cast members yields worst results, mainly because of the $CEAF_e$ score dropping. This shows a need to find better ways of resolving clusters of literary characters, as approximately 61% of all mentions in GerDraCor-Coref refer to literary characters.

We also show the results of DramaCoref on texts from other domains, namely TüBa-D/Z (Naumann, 2007) as newspaper domain, DIRNDL (Björkelund et al., 2014) as radio news domain and CRETA (Rösiger et al., 2018) as a corpus on other literary texts which are not dramas, in Table 7. For the other corpora, the automatic mentions were provided with them, while for GerDraCor-Coref, we again

[8]The parser uses the PennTree format (Marcus et al., 1993), for which in the used implementation, pronouns are not marked as noun phrases and noun phrases inside prepositional phrases are completely neglected. We therefore additionally add these to our set of output mentions.

[9]B1 and B2 are identical to baselines also applied in Krug et al. (2015)

Model	MacroPrec	MacroRec	MacroF1	Acc
Parsing Baseline	0.5	**0.57**	**0.53**	0.7
DistilBERT	**0.54**	0.51	0.52	**0.84**
Base BERT	**0.54**	0.51	0.52	**0.84**
Literary BERT	0.24	0.33	0.28	0.73

Table 3: Results of the mention detection experiments.

	auto			gold		
Baseline	Precision	Recall	F1	Precision	Recall	F1
B1: N mentions in N clusters	0.23	0.13	NA	0.35	0.21	NA
B2: N mentions in 1 cluster	**0.29**	**0.33**	**0.22**	**0.45**	**0.67**	**0.38**
B3: Closest agreeing candidate	0.24	0.23	**0.22**	0.39	0.41	0.37

Table 4: CoNLL scores for running the different baselines on GerDraCor-Coref.

use the mentions coming from the BERT model in Section 4.2.

Looking at the CoNLL scores, DramaCoref works very well on CRETA and DIRNDL when using automatically detected mentions. The results on GerDraCor-Coref are slightly higher than on TüBa-D/Z. For the gold mentions, the CoNLL scores for TüBa-D/Z are highest and lowest for GerDraCor-Coref. On the one hand, this shows that DramaCoref is working in general, as it is able to predict coreference on texts of a different type. On the other hand, it shows that dramas might have properties that require more domain-specific rules and are not covered by systems build for newspaper texts. What can furthermore be seen is that with gold mentions, DramaCoref is able to predict much better than with the automatically detected mentions, showing the need for a more sophisticated mention detection for dramas.

System	MUC	B^3	$CEAF_e$	CoNLL
HotCoref	**56.55**	14.98	14.84	**28.79**
DramaCoref	42.54	**19.87**	**18.97**	27.12

Table 5: Results for comparing DramaCoref and IMS HotCoref DE.

We also compare the results of DramaCoref to IMS HotCoref DE on the plays. To allow for a comparison, we split the data in training and test set of 70% and 30%, respectively. IMS HotCoref DE is then trained on the training set, while for DramaCoref, the ordering of rules is determined on this set. Both systems are tested on the same test set. The results can be seen in Table 5. We can see that DramaCoref achieves comparable results to IMS HotCoref DE, outperforming it in the B^3 and $CEAF_e$ scores. However, IMS HotCoref DE performs better for the MUC score, resulting in a slightly higher CoNLL score.

5 Error analysis

By having a closer look at the performance of the single passes in Figure 2, we can see that, as expected, passes 9a and 9b, which handle first and second person pronouns, perform very well. Also pass 1 for exact string matches is relatively reliable, the remaining passes perform relatively on par. Only passes 2a-c have almost no hits, as they handle constructions normally not present in dramas. We also include the three baselines B1-3 for comparison, which manage to outperform several passes. Pass 9a performing well is not surprising, as first person pronouns can often be assigned very reliably to the cluster of the current speaker. Assigning second person pronouns with pass 9b works surprisingly well, showing that a simple heuristic of assuming that the current character addresses the previous or following speaker works in many cases. Pass 1, which performed highest for Raghunathan et al. (2010), is also strong for GerDraCor-Coref, but does not achieve a precision of 90+% as in Raghunathan et al. (2010). This might be due to the length of the texts, where mentions with identical surface forms can appear many times in different contexts. Using lemmas instead of tokens for pass 14 does not outperform pass 1.

	Mentions	MUC	B^3	$CEAF_m$	$CEAF_e$	CoNLL
act	auto	0.45	0.23	0.32	0.19	0.29
	gold	0.79	0.42	0.43	0.41	0.54
castmembers-only	auto	0.44	0.26	0.35	0.15	0.28
dramatispersonae	auto	0.46	0.23	0.33	0.19	0.29
	gold	0.79	0.44	0.45	0.42	0.55
scene	auto	0.43	0.27	0.37	0.24	0.32
	gold	0.72	0.47	0.49	0.42	0.54

Table 6: Results of DramaCoref on GerDraCor-Coref with different setups. All scores are F1 scores.

Mentions	Corpus	Mention Fscore	MUC	B^3	$CEAF_m$	$CEAF_e$	CoNLL
auto	CRETA	0.70	0.51	0.30	0.34	0.26	0.36
	DIRNDL	0.43	0.36	0.30	0.38	0.37	0.38
	TüBa-D/Z	0.46	0.26	0.25	0.33	0.31	0.28
	GerDraCor-Coref	0.60	0.45	0.23	0.32	0.19	0.29
gold	CRETA	0.96	0.72	0.46	0.46	0.47	0.55
	DIRNDL	0.70	0.61	0.58	0.63	0.61	0.61
	TüBa-D/Z	0.86	0.66	0.62	0.65	0.64	0.64
	GerDraCor-Coref	0.96	0.79	0.42	0.43	0.40	0.54

Table 7: Scores for running DramaCoref on different corpora. All scores are F1 scores.

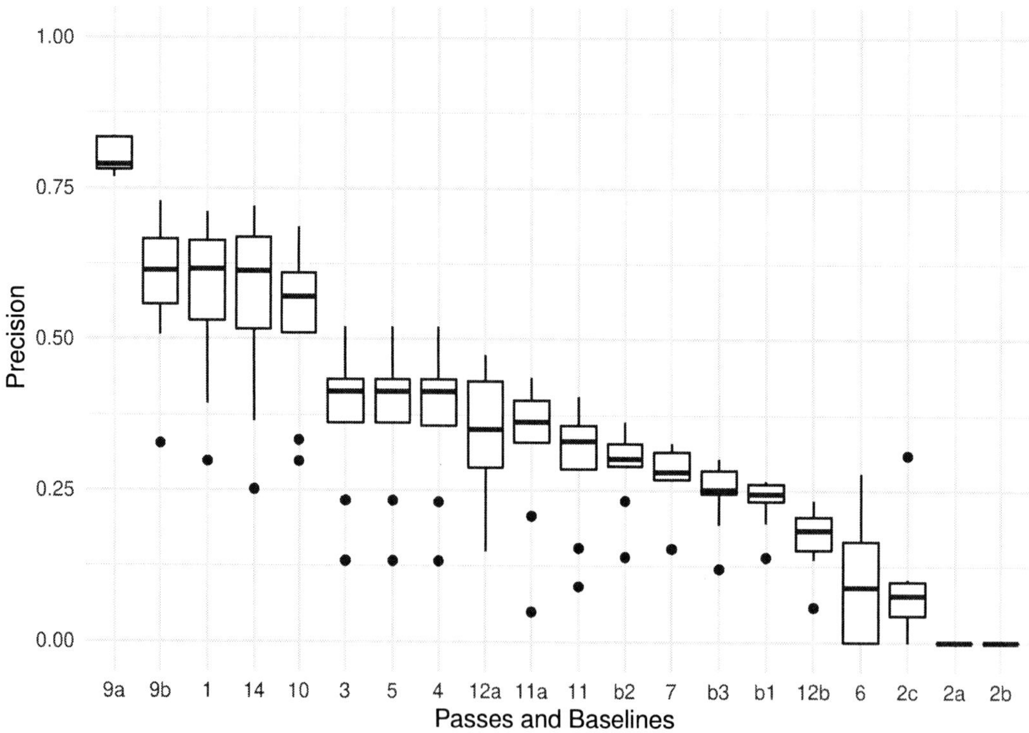

Figure 2: Performance of passes on the development set, ordered by precision. The precision is measured using the CoNLL score.

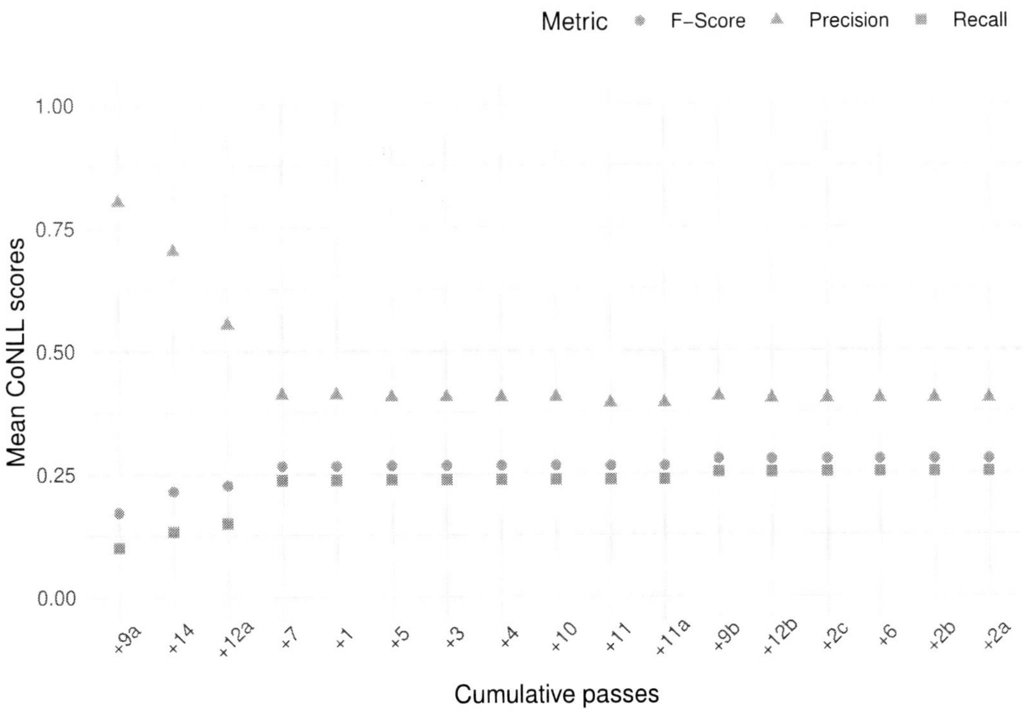

Figure 3: Passes ordered by their precision on the test set and applied cumulatively, showing mean precision, recall and F1 for the CoNLL score. Cumulatively means that from left to right, the given pass is added to all previously applied passes.

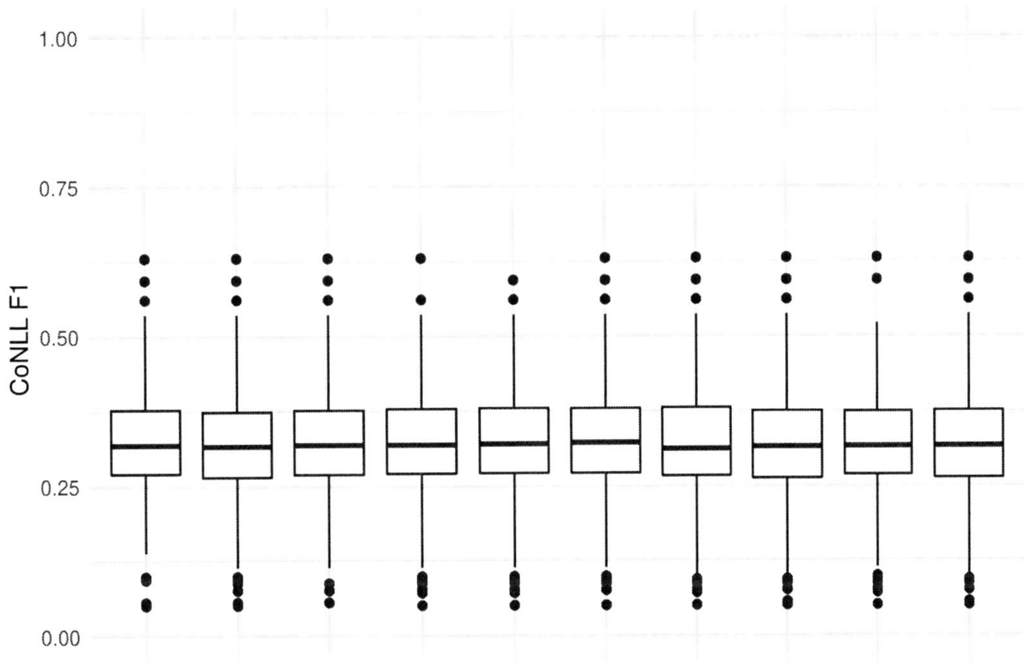

Figure 4: Results in a 10-fold cross validation setting.

Figure 3 shows all passes applied cumulatively. This means that the pass with the highest precision on the development set is evaluated on the test, then the pass with the highest and second-highest precision, and so on. This enables us to see how the evaluation scores change when more and more passes are added. Other than in Figure 2, the passes are evaluated on the test set instead of the development set, in order to get more meaningful numbers on a larger dataset. Thus, the ordering of the passes is different to Figure 2. Figure 3 emphasizes that, while the overall precision naturally falls when more passes with lower individual precision are added, the recall does not rise significantly. This calls for passes that are able to increase recall while not dropping precision too much. While the used passes did exactly that in the experiments of Raghunathan et al. (2010) and Lee et al. (2011), and also for van Cranenburgh (2019) on Dutch novels, this seemingly does not apply to the dramas in GerDraCor-Coref.

In general, passes from Lee et al. (2011), which are meant for general purpose domains, do not perform well enough on dramas, while passes specifically engineered for this domains, do not perform well enough in order to achieve results comparable to other domains like newspaper texts.

Lastly, we make sure that the results are not caused by splitting the data into a certain train-test split by applying 10-fold cross validation. The results are shown in Figure 4. As can be seen, the results are relatively constant across folds, meaning that the plays form a homogeneous whole.

6 Conclusion and future work

We present a system, DramaCoref, for coreference resolution on German theater plays. DramaCoref is hybrid in the sense that it uses a transformer architecture to retrieve potential mentions and in a second step clusters the retrieved mentions using ordered sieves. It performs comparable to other attempts of CR on literary data, however, theater plays appear to be a more difficult type of data for CR than texts of other types, e.g. newspaper texts. While some passes that work well on newspaper texts do not apply or underperform on the theater plays, specific passes and newly added passes perform reasonably well. Our goal for future research is the exploration of new passes, utilizing information coming from the plays like speaker turns and informations from the dramatis personæ like family relations, and improving the mention detection component. Developing an end-to-end neural network based system might also be worthwhile, as it makes the need for two distinct components obsolete; however, at this point, the available training data does not seem to be sufficient for such an approach.

Acknowledgements

The work described has been conducted in the QuaDramA project, funded by the Volkswagen foundation and in the Q:TRACK project, funded by the German Research Foundation (DFG) in the context of SPP 2207 *Computational Literary Studies*. We thank both for making this possible.

References

Melanie Andresen and Michael Vauth. 2018. Added value of coreference annotation for character analysis in narratives. In *Proceedings of the Workshop on Annotation in Digital Humanities (annDH)*, pages 1–6.

Emilia Apostolova, Noriko Tomuro, Pattanasak Mongkolwat, and Dina Demner-Fushman. 2012. Domain adaptation of coreference resolution for radiology reports. In *Proceedings of the 2012 Workshop on Biomedical Natural Language Processing (BioNLP)*, pages 118–121.

Aristoteles. 1982. *Poetik*. Reclam, Stuttgart, Germany.

David Bamman, Sejal Popat, and Sheng Shen. 2019. An annotated dataset of literary entities. In *Proceedings of the 2019 Conference of the North American Chapter of the Association for Computational Linguistics: Human Language Technologies (NAACL-HLT)*, pages 2138–2144.

David Bamman, Ted Underwood, and Noah A. Smith. 2014. A bayesian mixed effects model of literary character. In *Proceedings of the 52nd Annual Meeting of the Association for Computational Linguistics (ACL)*, pages 370–379.

Anders Björkelund, Kerstin Eckart, Arndt Riester, Nadja Schauffler, and Katrin Schweitzer. 2014. The extended DIRNDL corpus as a resource for automatic coreference and bridging resolution. In *Proceedings of the 9th International Conference on Language Resources and Evaluation (LREC)*, pages 3222–3228.

Anders Björkelund and Jonas Kuhn. 2014. Learning structured perceptrons for coreference resolution with latent antecedents and non-local features. In *Proceedings of the 52nd Annual Meeting of the Association for Computational Linguistics (ACL)*, pages 47–57.

Kevin Clark and Christopher D. Manning. 2016. Improving coreference resolution by learning entity-level distributed representations. In *Proceedings of the 54th Annual Meeting of the Association for Computational Linguistics (ACL)*, pages 643–653.

Andreas van Cranenburgh. 2019. A Dutch coreference resolution system with an evaluation on literary fiction. *Computational Linguistics in the Netherlands Journal*, 9:27–54.

Peter T. Davis, David K. Elson, and Judith L. Klavans. 2003. Methods for precise named entity matching in digital collections. In *Proceedings of the 3rd ACM/IEEE-CS Joint Conference on Digital Libraries (JCDL)*, pages 125–127.

Jacob Devlin, Ming-Wei Chang, Kenton Lee, and Kristina Toutanova. 2019. BERT: Pre-training of deep bidirectional transformers for language understanding. In *Proceedings of the 2019 Conference of the North American Chapter of the Association for Computational Linguistics: Human Language Technologies (NAACL-HLT)*, pages 4171–4186.

Quynh Ngoc Thi Do, Steven Bethard, and Marie-Francine Moens. 2015. Adapting coreference resolution for narrative processing. In *Proceedings of the 2015 Conference on Empirical Methods in Natural Language Processing (EMNLP)*, pages 2262–2267.

Christiane Fellbaum, editor. 1998. *WordNet: An Electronic Lexical Database*. MIT, Cambridge, MA.

Frank Fischer, Ingo Börner, Mathias Göbel, Angelika Hechtl, Christopher Kittel, Carsten Milling, and Peer Trilcke. 2019. Programmable corpora: Introducing DraCor, an infrastructure for the research on European drama. In *Proceedings of DH2019: "Complexities"*.

Birgit Hamp and Helmut Feldweg. 1997. GermaNet - a lexical-semantic net for German. In *Proceedings of the ACL workshop Automatic Information Extraction and Building of Lexical Semantic Resources for NLP Applications*, pages 9–15.

Mandar Joshi, Omer Levy, Luke Zettlemoyer, and Daniel Weld. 2019. BERT for coreference resolution: Baselines and analysis. In *Proceedings of the 2019 Conference on Empirical Methods in Natural Language Processing and the 9th International Joint Conference on Natural Language Processing (EMNLP-IJCNLP)*, pages 5803–5808.

Varada Kolhatkar, Adam Roussel, Stefanie Dipper, and Heike Zinsmeister. 2018. Anaphora with non-nominal antecedents in computational linguistics: A survey. *Computational Linguistics*, 44(3):547–612.

Markus Krug, Frank Puppe, Fotis Jannidis, Luisa Macharowsky, Isabella Reger, and Lukas Weimer. 2015. Rule-based coreference resolution in German historic novels. In *Proceedings of the Fourth Workshop on Computational Linguistics for Literature*, pages 98–104.

Heeyoung Lee, Angel Chang, Yves Peirsman, Nathanael Chambers, Mihai Surdeanu, and Dan Jurafsky. 2013. Deterministic coreference resolution based on entity-centric, precision-ranked rules. *Computational Linguistics*, 39(4):885–916.

Heeyoung Lee, Yves Peirsman, Angel Chang, Nathanael Chambers, Mihai Surdeanu, and Dan Jurafsky. 2011. Stanford's multi-pass sieve coreference resolution system at the CoNLL-2011 shared task. In *Proceedings of the Fifteenth Conference on Computational Natural Language Learning: Shared Task (CoNLL)*, pages 28–34.

Kenton Lee, Luheng He, Mike Lewis, and Luke Zettlemoyer. 2017. End-to-end neural coreference resolution. In *Proceedings of the 2017 Conference on Empirical Methods in Natural Language Processing (EMNLP)*, pages 188–197.

Kenton Lee, Luheng He, and Luke Zettlemoyer. 2018. Higher-order coreference resolution with coarse-to-fine inference. In *Proceedings of the Conference of the North American Chapter of the Association for Computational Linguistics: Human Language Technologies (NAACL-HLT)*, pages 687–692.

Mitchell P. Marcus, Beatrice Santorini, and Mary Ann Marcinkiewicz. 1993. Building a large annotated corpus of English: The Penn Treebank. *Computational Linguistics*, 19(2):313–330.

Sebastian Martschat. 2017. *Structured Representations for Coreference Resolution*. Ph.D. thesis, Heidelberg University.

Karin Naumann. 2007. *Manual for the Annotation of in-document Referential Relations*. Abt. Computerlinguistik Universität Tübingen.

Janis Pagel and Nils Reiter. 2020. GerDraCor-Coref: A coreference corpus for dramatic texts in German. In *Proceedings of the Language Resources and Evaluation Conference (LREC)*, pages 55–64.

Slav Petrov, Leon Barrett, Romain Thibaux, and Dan Klein. 2006. Learning accurate, compact, and interpretable tree annotation. In *Proceedings of the 21st International Conference on Computational Linguistics and the 44th Annual Meeting of the Association for Computational Linguistics*, pages 433–440, Stroudsburg, PA, USA. Association for Computational Linguistics.

Sameer Pradhan, Xiaoqiang Luo, Marta Recasens, Eduard Hovy, Vincent Ng, and Michael Strube. 2014. Scoring coreference partitions of predicted mentions: A reference implementation. In *Proceedings of the 52nd Annual Meeting of the Association for Computational Linguistics (ACL)*, pages 30–35.

Sameer Pradhan, Alessandro Moschitti, Nianwen Xue, Olga Uryupina, and Yuchen Zhang. 2012. CoNLL-2012 shared task: Modeling multilingual unrestricted coreference in OntoNotes. In *Joint Conference on EMNLP and CoNLL - Shared Task*, CoNLL 2012, pages 1–40, Stroudsburg, PA, USA. Association for Computational Linguistics.

Karthik Raghunathan, Heeyoung Lee, Sudarshan Rangarajan, Nathanael Chambers, Mihai Surdeanu, Dan Jurafsky, and Christopher Manning. 2010. A multi-pass sieve for coreference resolution. In *Proceedings of the 2010 Conference on Empirical Methods in Natural Language Processing (EMNLP)*, pages 492–501.

Ina Rösiger and Jonas Kuhn. 2016. IMS HotCoref DE: A data-driven co-reference resolver for German. In *Proceedings of the 10th International Conference on Language Resources and Evaluation (LREC)*, pages 155–160.

Ina Rösiger, Sarah Schulz, and Nils Reiter. 2018. Towards coreference for literary text: Analyzing domain-specific phenomena. In *Proceedings of the Second Joint SIGHUM Workshop on Computational Lingusitics for Cultural Heritage, Social Sciences, Humanities and Literature*, pages 129–138.

Victor Sanh, Lysandre Debut, Julien Chaumond, and Thomas Wolf. 2019. DistilBERT, a distilled version of BERT: smaller, faster, cheaper and lighter. *CoRR*, abs/1910.01108.

Fynn Schröder, Hans Ole Hatzel, and Chris Biemann. 2021. Neural end-to-end coreference resolution for German in different domains. In *Proceedings of the 17th Conference on Natural Language Processing (KONVENS)*.

Don Tuggener. 2016. *Incremental Coreference Resolution for German*. Ph.D. thesis, University of Zürich.

Jian Bo Yang, Qi Mao, Qiao Liang Xiang, Ivor W. Tsang, Kian Ming A. Chai, and Hai Leong Chieu. 2012. Domain adaptation for coreference resolution: An adaptive ensemble approach. In *Proceedings of the 2012 Joint Conference on Empirical Methods in Natural Language Processing and Comutational Natural Language Learning (EMNLP-CoNLL)*, pages 744–753.

Shanheng Zhao and Hwee Tou Ng. 2014. Domain adaptation with active learning for coreference resolution. In *Proceedings of the 5th International Workshop on Health Mining and Information Analysis (Louhi)*, pages 21–29.

A Overview table with detailed results

Table 8 shows detailed results for applying DramaCoref on different corpora, for several evaluation metrics broken down by precision, recall and F1-score.

Mentions	Corpus	Mention Fscore	MUC			B^3			$CEAF_m$			$CEAF_e$			CoNLL		
			Prec.	Rec.	F1	Prec.	Rec.	F1	Prec.	Rec.	F1	Prec.	Rec.	F1	Prec.	Rec.	F1
auto	CRETA	0.70	0.51	0.51	0.51	0.39	0.25	0.30	0.33	0.36	0.34	0.21	0.35	0.26	0.37	0.37	0.36
	DIRNDL	0.43	0.19	0.21	0.36	0.22	0.24	0.30	0.28	0.30	0.38	0.27	0.28	0.37	0.23	0.24	0.38
	TüBa-D/Z	0.46	0.18	0.25	0.26	0.21	0.28	0.25	0.26	0.38	0.33	0.23	0.38	0.31	0.21	0.30	0.28
	GerDraCor-Coref	0.60	0.58	0.38	0.45	0.49	0.16	0.23	0.38	0.28	0.32	0.15	0.26	0.19	0.41	0.26	0.29
gold	CRETA	0.96	0.76	0.69	0.72	0.59	0.38	0.46	0.48	0.45	0.46	0.45	0.49	0.47	0.60	0.52	0.55
	DIRNDL	0.70	0.57	0.31	0.61	0.60	0.30	0.58	0.59	0.34	0.63	0.55	0.35	0.61	0.57	0.32	0.61
	TüBa-D/Z	0.86	0.71	0.51	0.66	0.73	0.47	0.62	0.68	0.51	0.65	0.63	0.54	0.64	0.69	0.51	0.64
	GerDraCor-Coref	0.96	0.83	0.74	0.79	0.66	0.31	0.42	0.44	0.41	0.43	0.37	0.46	0.40	0.62	0.51	0.54

Table 8: Overview of all results of the baselines and DramaCoref on the different corpora.

A Hybrid Rule-Based and Neural Coreference Resolution System with an Evaluation on Dutch Literature

Andreas van Cranenburgh, Esther Ploeger, Frank van den Berg, Remi Thüss
University of Groningen
Department of Information Science
a.w.van.cranenburgh@rug.nl

Abstract

We introduce a modular, hybrid coreference resolution system that extends a rule-based baseline with three neural classifiers for the subtasks mention detection, mention attributes (gender, animacy, number), and pronoun resolution. The classifiers substantially increase coreference performance in our experiments with Dutch literature across all metrics on the development set: mention detection, LEA, CoNLL, and especially pronoun accuracy. However, on the test set, the best results are obtained with rule-based pronoun resolution. This inconsistent result highlights that the rule-based system is still a strong baseline, and more work is needed to improve pronoun resolution robustly for this dataset. While end-to-end neural systems require no feature engineering and achieve excellent performance in standard benchmarks with large training sets, our simple hybrid system scales well to long document coreference (>10k words) and attains superior results in our experiments on literature.

1 Introduction

This paper reports on a hybrid rule-based and neural coreference resolution system[1] evaluated on Dutch literary texts. We use neural classifiers for the following three subtasks:

1. Mention span identification;
2. Mention attributes: gender, animacy, number;
3. Pronoun resolution.

These subtasks have been selected based on the expected return on investment given the particular weaknesses of the rule-based model (Lee et al., 2017a) and specific challenges of literary coreference (Rösiger et al., 2018). To keep the approach as simple as possible, we implement these classifiers as independent modules operating in a pipeline.

[1] Code and models are available at https://github.com/andreasvc/dutchcoref

The classifiers can be trained on a laptop without GPU in ten minutes, and are therefore substantially less resource-intensive than state-of-the-art neural models; e.g., SpanBERT (Joshi et al., 2020) requires pre-training a BERT model with span representations on specialized hardware (TPU); moreover, end-to-end neural coreference resolution systems are generally memory and CPU intensive, especially when longer contexts are taken into account (Toshniwal et al., 2020).

The output of coreference resolution is a set of mention spans, partitioned into clusters (example based on Rudinger et al., 2018):

(1) [De chirurg]$_1$ kon [de patiënt]$_2$ niet behandelen. [Hij]$_2$ was [[haar]$_1$ zoon]$_2$!
[The surgeon]$_1$ couldn't treat [the patient]$_2$. [He]$_2$ was [[her]$_1$ son]$_2$!

2 Related Work

Rule-based coreference resolution provides a reasonable baseline (Lee et al., 2011, 2013), and its advantages are that it can exploit global features of entities based on the whole document. In contrast to end-to-end systems, information from parse trees and named-entity recognition can be used, as well as other components from the Natural Language Processing (NLP) pipeline. Feature-based models also use the NLP pipeline, but use machine learning classifiers that make local decisions (mention-pair and mention-ranking architectures), or attempt to take global context into account, but this runs into computational challenges with long documents. End-to-end neural systems do not need the NLP pipeline and are able to optimize all steps of coreference resolution jointly, which has enabled large advances in standard benchmarks (Lee et al., 2017b, 2018; Wu et al., 2020). However, there are several challenges with end-to-end neural models: long documents with long coreference chains (Joshi et al., 2019; Toshniwal et al., 2020), domain and

Proceedings of the 4th Workshop on Computational Models of Reference, Anaphora and Coreference (CRAC 2021), pages 47–56
Punta Cana, Dominican Republic, November 10–11, 2021.

annotation differences across datasets (Zhu et al., 2021; Poot and van Cranenburgh, 2020), and needing a large number of training examples (Shalev-Shwartz and Shashua, 2016; Glasmachers, 2017). Moreover, gender bias is a general challenge in coreference resolution systems (Rudinger et al., 2018; Webster et al., 2018). Each of these areas is potentially easier to address with a well engineered rule-based or feature-based approach to coreference resolution, and we therefore choose to explore this direction.

Hybrid coreference resolution systems have been presented before; Lee et al. (2017a) present a system in which most steps of the rule-based system are implemented with random forest classifiers. They obtain improvements in accuracy and efficiency, but neural systems have since eclipsed these results. Their classifiers include mention detection and pronoun resolution, which we also pursue in this work.

In addition, previous work shows that neural representations and surface features have complementary strengths (Moosavi and Strube, 2017). This is another sense in which our system is hybrid: we use both manually selected features as well as contextualized word embeddings. Parts of the neural architecture and features are inspired by Clark and Manning (2016), but we use BERT (Devlin et al., 2019) for embedding features instead of static word embeddings, since BERT representations have shown to bring about significant improvements in natural language tasks that rely on the context.

There has been some work on improving detection of mention attributes (animacy, gender, number) using external datasets and machine learning. Bergsma and Lin (2006) extract attributes from a large corpus with dependency parses using heuristic patterns. Orasan and Evans (2007) focus on animacy and use Wordnet and SemCor combined with machine learning. These methods aim to learn general patterns for detecting attributes of noun phrases. In contrast, we will annotate attributes of the entities in our coreference corpus in context and train the classifier on those annotations. We hope to handle more difficult, ambiguous cases which require context with this approach.

Although most coreference resolution systems are trained and evaluated on domains contained in benchmark datasets, such as news texts and phone conversations in the case of OntoNotes, we train and evaluate our hybrid system on Dutch literature. The reason we are interested in the literary domain is that, while literary texts are increasingly subject to computational analysis in the field of digital humanities, there is still a lot of work required to adapt NLP models to the literary domain, of which coreference resolution is a particularly challenging instance. Importantly, the literary domain contains unique characteristics, such as long coreference chains and dialogue, which do not appear in typical benchmark data for coreference resolution (Rösiger et al., 2018; Bamman et al., 2020).

3 Data

We use RiddleCoref (van Cranenburgh, 2019), with the same train/dev/test splits as used in Poot and van Cranenburgh (2020). The corpus consists of 162k tokens of contemporary (2007–2012) bestselling novels in Dutch (translated and original), with a total of 33 documents (fragments of novels), and an average of 4897.4 tokens per document. The entity coreference annotations follow the dutchcoref annotation guidelines. The 38,466 mentions in the corpus have been manually corrected and exclude non-referring expressions.

We did an additional round of corrections on the whole corpus, mostly to fix mention boundaries to exclude relative clauses and remove non-referring expressions (idioms, verbal expressions, negated mentions). We also made small improvements to the mention detection of the rule-based system: bare nouns in conjunctions are extracted as mentions, and subordinate clauses are removed from mention spans, in accordance with the annotation guidelines.

Three mention attributes, namely animacy, gender, and number, have been manually annotated for each of the 11,684 entities in the training and development sets. The gender attribute has four possible values: f (female), m (male), fm (unknown or mixed gender), and n (neuter, non-human). Any gender except neuter implies a human (person) entity; the animacy attribute is therefore implied. Note that Dutch has noun classes with grammatically gendered and neuter words; however, our annotations concern the gender with which individuals are identified. For example, the noun phrase *het meisje* (the girl) is grammatically neuter, but annotated as female, since it would be referred to by female pronouns.

The number attribute has two possible values: sg (singular) and pl (plural; an entity consisting of multiple individuals/objects). We annotate the

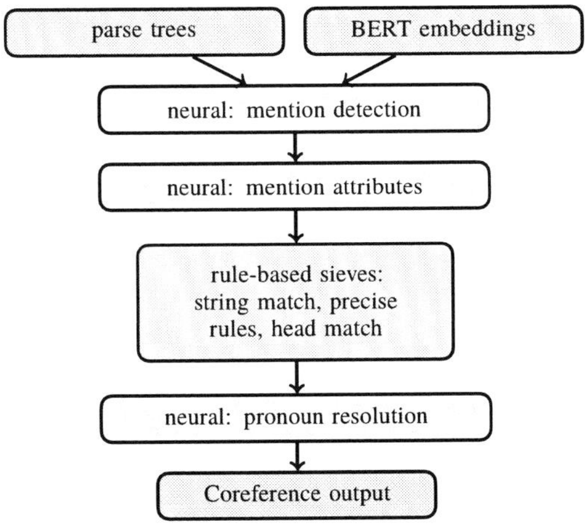

Figure 1: An overview of the hybrid system.

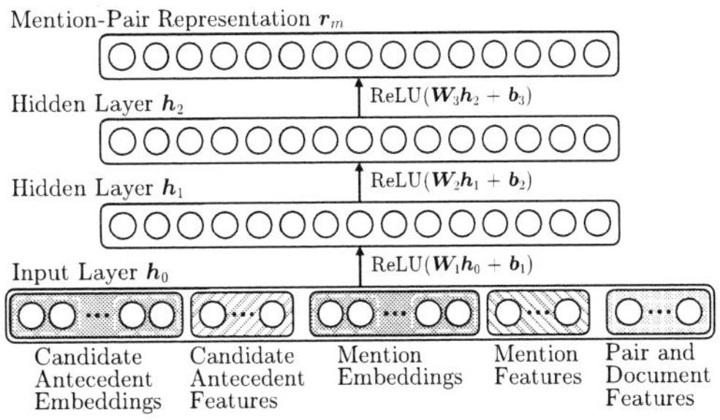

Figure 2: The mention-pair encoder for the pronoun resolution model; the other modules take a single mention as input; figure from Clark and Manning (2016)

semantic number (e.g., "the group" is plural since it is a collective noun that could be referred to by "they"), regardless of the syntactic number.

4 Method

The base system is a rule-based coreference resolution system (van Cranenburgh, 2019) which takes parse trees as input. We extend this system with neural classifiers for three subtasks; see Figure 1 for an overview of our hybrid system.

4.1 Rule-based system

The rule-based system starts by extracting mention candidates from parse trees based on rules. Mention attributes are heuristically assigned based on parse tree features and lexical resources. Mentions are then linked into entity clusters using several "sieves" for linking nominals, names, and finally pronouns. The pronoun resolution step is an implementation of the Hobbs (1978) system using heuristics of recency and syntactic prominence.

We use a feed-forward neural network classifier for the three subtasks (see Figure 2). The input consists of BERT token embeddings and several handpicked features. The network has two dense hidden layers with 500 and 150 neurons, respectively, both with ReLu activation and batch normalization. The output layer is a sigmoid function with the respective binary classification for the subtask and L_2 regularization of 0.05. We apply a dropout of 0.2 to the input layer and 0.5 to each hidden layer and fit the networks with a batch size of 32 and Adam with a learning rate of 0.0001. Each subtask is trained with early stopping until there are 5 successive epochs that do not show an improvement on the validation set.

BERT embeddings are produced using the monolingual, pre-trained BERTje model (de Vries et al., 2019). We use the BERT token embeddings from layer 9, since that layer was shown to perform best for the task of coreference resolution in Dutch (de Vries et al., 2020). For mentions consisting of multiple BERT tokens, we use the mean of the embeddings of all tokens as the mention representation. While neural systems (e.g., Lee et al., 2017b; Bamman et al., 2020) often use a recurrent layer (e.g., LSTM) to obtain contextualized representations of mentions, we follow Joshi et al. (2019) in using BERT embeddings directly. Unlike Joshi et al. (2019), we do not encode BERT embeddings for segments of multiple sentences, but encode each sentence independently.

4.2 Mention Span Classifier

To improve mention detection, we implement a mention span classifier that picks the best mention span from a list of candidates for a given head word (similar to Lee et al., 2017a), or classifies the spans as non-referring if none of them have a probability higher than a threshold (set at > 0.3 in our experiments based on experiments with development data).

Candidates are extracted based on the same syntactic rules as in van Cranenburgh (2019), but include alternative, shorter spans as candidates as well. Since mention spans that incorrectly include an adverb in the first position have been observed frequently in previous work (van Cranenburgh, 2019), we ensure that for each span (n, m), the span (n+1, m) is also considered. The system is trained on gold mention spans annotated in the corpus, as well as negative examples extracted from the parse trees. During evaluation and prediction, only spans extracted by rules are used as candidates. While it would be possible to train a classifier that works with arbitrary spans as candidates, the rest of the rule-based system depends on parse tree features, and we therefore stick with candidates extracted by parse tree queries.

The features presented to the neural network are as follows:

1. The BERT token embeddings of the first and last token of the span;
2. Whether the rule-based mention detection would extract the span as mention;
3. The grammatical function of the constituent matching the span (subject, object, predicative, apposition);
4. Whether the span contains another NP;
5. Whether the head word of the span is a named entity (PER/LOC/ORG/MISC);
6. The POS tag of the head word (noun, name, pronoun, or verb), the first word (adverb, adjective, punctuation) and the last word (punctuation);
7. The number of words in the mention, histogrammed as in Clark and Manning (2016).

Given the input of example (1), the candidates are (correct mention underlined): {De chirurg, chirurg}, {de patiënt, patiënt}, ..., {mijn zoon, zoon}

We also experimented with adding an anaphoricity classifier (e.g., Clark and Manning, 2016; Moosavi and Strube, 2017), but initial experiments did not improve the results, so we leave this for future work. Moreover, mentions could also be classified as singleton or coreferent; however, following Lee et al. (2017a), we have not pursued this, since it is better to leave this decision to later sieves, at which point more global information is available.

4.3 Mention Attributes Classifier

The rule-based system (van Cranenburgh, 2019) detects mention attributes heuristically using parse tree features and several lexicons and lexical resources:

1. Named-entity category and grammatical features;
2. a list of the most common Dutch first names for men and women;
3. gender and animacy attributes for nouns from the Dutch Wordnet equivalent Cornetto;
4. and heuristic number and gender frequencies derived from English web text (Bergsma and Lin, 2006).

To improve the detected attributes, we train a supervised classifier that predicts these attributes for a given mention in a sentence. We manually annotated the mention attributes for each entity in the corpus based on the whole coreference chain. During training, we train and predict these entity attributes for each mention. This means that some data points will be difficult, e.g., predicting the gender of the mention "the person" is not possible without further context. Similarly, *ze* is both a third person singular female pronoun as well as a third person plural pronoun; when not in subject position, gender and number are ambiguous. In early experiments, attributes were only predicted for names and nominals; however, predicting attributes for all mention types (i.e., including pronouns) substantially improved performance. Furthermore, annotating and predicting number, despite being relatively reliably marked syntactically, also boosts performance.

The task is set up as a multi-label classification task such that a mention is assigned probabilities for all possible labels; this multi-task setup means that attributes are trained and predicted jointly. For each attribute, we assign all labels with a probability > 0.5. Experimenting with different thresholds did not improve results. Given this setup, it is possible for the classifier to predict no attributes for a mention, which is interpreted as the attributes being unknown by the system; or a combination of features such as female and neuter, which is not part of the annotations, this is again interpreted as an uncertain feature by the rule-based system.

The features from which the neural network predicts mention attributes are as follows:

1. The averaged BERT token embeddings for the mention;
2. The heuristically detected attributes for gender, animacy, and number;
3. Whether the mention is a subject or object;
4. Whether the mention contains another NP.

Given the input of (1), the expected output is: De chirurg: fm, sg; de patiënt: fm, sg; Hij: m, sg; haar f, sg; haar zoon: m, sg. However, based on the context, the predicted gender of the first two mentions could be more specific.

	recall	prec.	F1
Rule-based	88.3	84.9	86.6
Classifier	**88.8**	**87.2**	**88.0**

Table 1: Mention span classifier results on dev set (N=6434 mentions).

4.4 Pronoun Resolution Classifier

We train a binary classifier on predicting whether a pair of mentions is coreferent; i.e., a mention-pair architecture (Soon et al., 2001). Pairs consist of a pronoun and antecedent candidate. The pronoun is a third person personal, possessive, indefinite, or demonstrative pronoun. The antecedent candidate is a mention within the preceding 22 mentions words relative to the pronoun (this distance is applied during both training and prediction). Mentions with a grammatical function of appositive or determiner are not considered as candidates, since these often lead to incorrect links. We also filter out mention pairs based on binding constraints (i-within-i and co-argument restrictions). Mention pairs are assigned a probability. For each pronoun, the candidate with the highest probability is selected as its antecedent, unless the highest probability is less than a threshold, in which case no antecedent is selected. Based on experiments with the development data, we set the threshold at 0.2.

The features given to the neural network are as follows:

1. The averaged BERT token embeddings for the pronoun, and for the candidate;
2. Candidate mention type (pronoun, noun, name);
3. Whether the grammatical function (subj, obj, etc.) of the pair is the same;
4. Attribute compatibility (gender, animacy, number);
5. Person (1, 2, 3) of candidate, if it is a pronoun;
6. Whether pronoun or candidate occurs in quoted speech;
7. Distance in sentences and words between pronoun and candidate; number of words in candidate. The distances and lengths are histogrammed as in Clark and Manning (2016).

Given the input of (1), the candidates are (correct antecedent underlined): Hij: {de patiënt, De chirurg}; haar: {Hij, de patiënt, De chirurg}.

Unfortunately, several simple features reported to be useful in previous work (e.g., string match, pronoun type, position in sentence) actually decreased development scores in our experiments, which is why we end up with this relatively small list of features. We also considered frequency features: how frequent is the candidate entity in the preceding context or whole document. We have not pursued this since it complicates the implementation as it makes predictions dependent on previous predictions. Another feature which is left for future work is incorporating external knowledge on selectional preferences, as used successfully by Zhang et al. (2019).

	RB	NEU	support
nonhuman	83.3	**94.5**	3073
human	85.0	**95.0**	3361
female	59.1	**73.4**	1347
male	85.8	**89.9**	3002
neuter	80.1	**94.5**	3073
singular	96.7	**98.6**	5224
plural	90.8	**93.6**	1210
macro avg	83.0	**91.3**	20290

Table 2: F1-scores for mention attributes on development set with rule-based baseline using word lists (RB) and the neural classifier (NEU).

5 Results

We first report the results for each module on the development set, and then report the results for the system in various configurations on the development and test sets.

The results for the mention span classifier are shown in Table 1. We obtain a decent improvement over the rule-based method: a difference of 1.4% F1 points for mentions, mainly due to higher precision. The mention recall is limited by the rules for mention candidate extraction and parse tree errors.

The results for the mention attributes classifier are shown in Table 2. We obtain a solid improvement over the baseline, with a macro averaged F1 improvement of 8.3% points and consistent improvement for each label. Female mentions show the largest improvement, but also remain the most difficult to detect. There is a striking contrast with male and neuter mentions, which show higher scores. Animacy detection is also improved substantially, and number to a lesser extent, since the baseline is already high for this attribute.

For coreference evaluation, we use the averaged CoNLL score (Pradhan et al., 2011) and the LEA coreference metric (Moosavi and Strube, 2016; Moosavi et al., 2019). In addition we report mention scores and pronoun accuracy. Pronoun accuracy includes demonstrative and indefinite pronouns in addition to third person personal and possessive pronouns.

See Table 3 for the main coreference results, presented incrementally. The original rule-based model is listed as "dutchcoref", with the modules proposed in this paper listed as span (mention span classifier), attr (mention attributes classifier), and pron (pronoun resolution), respectively. The line "dutchcoref+span" means that the mention span classifier is used, but the rest of the system remains rule-based. For transparency, we report results both on the development and test sets; the parameters and models were tuned only on the development set. Since the annotations and the rule-based system were improved, we report results from Poot and van Cranenburgh (2020) for comparison. Each neural module improves performance scores on the development set, across all metrics. Unfortunately, on the test set the results are less consistent. On several metrics, the rule-based "dutchcoref" performs best, while the pronoun resolution classifier does not improve the pronoun accuracy with respect to the previous line "dutchcoref+span,attr" with results for the rule-based model with neural mention detection and mention attributes, but rule-based pronoun resolution; however, the mention span and attributes modules perform well.

In order to isolate the effect of mention detection (which is known to introduce pipeline errors), we also perform an evaluation on the test set with gold mentions, see Table 4. Here we find that the mention attribute classifier improves the performance across the board. Again the pronoun resolution module does not improve the results compared to the result for 'dutchcoref+attr'. (it does improve the results compared with the purely rule-based system).

All our evaluations include singletons; evaluating without singletons does not change the ranking of the systems on each metric. We conclude that the mention attribute classifier robustly improves the performance, but that the pronoun resolution classifier yields inconsistent results. Finally, while the result is puzzling, a similar result was reported by Poot and van Cranenburgh (2020), where the rule-based system performed better on the test set than on the development set, while the end-to-end neural system showed the opposite effect (better on development set than on test set).

6 Analysis

6.1 Analysis of Differences

It could be that the development and test set differ in difficulty. We consider several basic statistics to compare the two sets. We first consider differences in the out-of-vocabulary (OOV) rate and word frequencies with the Jensen-Shannon distance. We find that the development set actually has a lower OOV rate than the test set, with respect to the training set (16.3% and 13.3%, respectively). The Jensen-Shannon distance shows the same pattern (0.307 vs 0.290, respectively). Moreover, the average sentence length is similar between the development and test sets (18.39 and 18.26, respectively), but higher than the train set (15.51). The development set does have a lower number of mentions (6548 vs 6869) and entities (2643 vs 3008). Finally, the development set has a higher percentage of names (14.9 vs 9.1).

Genre is another potential explanation for the difference. There are four different genres in the RiddleCoref dataset: (Literary) Fiction, Suspense, Romance, and Other. The development set contains 4 Fiction and 1 Other novel, while the test set contains 3 Fiction, 1 Romance, and 1 Suspense novel. We now take a closer look at the difficulty of these genres using an out-of-domain training set. We evaluate the pronoun resolution module on each genre in RiddleCoref; the results are in Table 5. We evaluate on two novels for each genre. The two documents of the Other genre are three chapters from Harry Potter and The Hunger Games, and are therefore considerably longer than the other documents. Since these documents from varying genres all originate from the RiddleCoref training set, we train the pronoun resolution model on a different corpus: SoNar-1 (Schuurman et al., 2010). This model achieved a CoNLL score of 70.76 on the RiddleCoref test set, which is comparable to that of the model trained on RiddleCoref. This is in line with our expectations: on the one hand, SoNaR-1 is much larger with 1 million tokens, providing more training data, but on the other hand, there is a difference in domain. Moreover, as noted by van Cranenburgh (2019) and Poot and van Cranenburgh (2020), there are differences in the annotation

System	set	Mentions			LEA			CoNLL	Pron
		R	P	F1	R	P	F1		Acc
Poot and van Cranenburgh (2020):									
e2e-Dutch	dev	83.12	87.65	85.33	48.37	50.99	49.65	64.81	
dutchcoref	dev	86.85	85.84	86.34	49.18	58.03	53.24	65.91	
This work:									
dutchcoref	dev	88.34	84.87	86.57	50.60	58.06	54.07	66.55	52.16
dutchcoref+span	dev	**88.76**	**87.23**	**87.99**	50.54	59.33	54.58	67.32	53.37
dutchcoref+span,attr	dev	**88.76**	**87.23**	**87.99**	52.27	60.98	56.29	68.80	61.30
dutchcoref+span,attr,pron	dev	**88.76**	**87.23**	**87.99**	**53.68**	**61.27**	**57.23**	**69.37**	**65.38**
Poot and van Cranenburgh (2020):									
e2e-Dutch	test	81.95	89.00	85.33	44.82	50.48	47.48	63.55	
dutchcoref	test	87.65	90.80	89.20	50.83	64.78	56.97	69.86	
This work:									
dutchcoref	test	89.41	90.35	89.88	52.90	**64.93**	**58.30**	70.90	62.82
dutchcoref+span	test	**89.71**	**90.47**	**90.09**	52.02	63.10	57.03	70.07	64.96
dutchcoref+span,attr	test	**89.71**	**90.47**	**90.09**	53.46	63.39	58.00	**71.00**	**68.73**
dutchcoref+span,attr,pron	test	**89.71**	**90.47**	**90.09**	**54.29**	61.34	57.60	70.90	67.81

Table 3: Coreference results on the RiddleCoref dataset (predicted mentions, including singletons).

System	set	Mentions			LEA			CoNLL	Pron
		R	P	F1	R	P	F1		Acc
dutchcoref	test	100	100	100	59.55	69.70	64.22	77.75	69.59
dutchcoref+attr	test	100	100	100	61.16	**70.69**	**65.58**	**78.88**	**74.07**
dutchcoref+attr,pron	test	100	100	100	**61.87**	67.08	64.37	78.44	71.44

Table 4: Coreference results on the RiddleCoref dataset (gold mentions, including singletons).

	Fiction	Romance	Suspense	Other
tokens	9664	4046	4533	34,354
avg sent len	15.5	14.9	17.5	16.1
ment. / ent.	3.0	2.6	2.2	3.5
ent. / tok.	0.08	0.10	0.11	0.07
% pronoun	35.1	42.6	37.9	42.0
% nominals	54.8	45.1	50.2	41.2
% names	10.2	12.2	11.9	16.8
CoNLL score	67.76	71.30	72.45	70.22

Table 5: Evaluation of the pronoun resolution module trained on SoNaR-1, evaluated on different genres with two documents per genre.

scheme of RiddleCoref and SoNaR-1; however, for pronoun resolution, these differences do not prevent the model from achieving a decent score. Comparing the results for the different genres in Table 5 reveals that the genre Fiction resulted in the lowest scores and Suspense resulted in the best scores, the difference being 4.69 percentage points in the CoNLL score. It is quite noticeable that the genres with more tokens in this experiment performed worse. This is in line with the performance of the end-to-end neural model from Poot and van Cranenburgh (2020) where a similar effect was noticed. Furthermore there does not seem to be a clear correlation between the percentage of pronouns and the CoNLL score in this experiment. As some of the most common link errors involve pronouns, genres with more pronouns were expected to result in lower scores. This, however, does not seem to be the case in this sample, as the second best performing genre contained the highest percentage of pronouns and the worst performing genre contained the lowest percentage of pronouns. Lastly, the length of a sentence does not seem to have a substantial effect on the scores. A longer sentence could possibly be more complex with more mentions and therefore create more room for mistakes for the model, how-

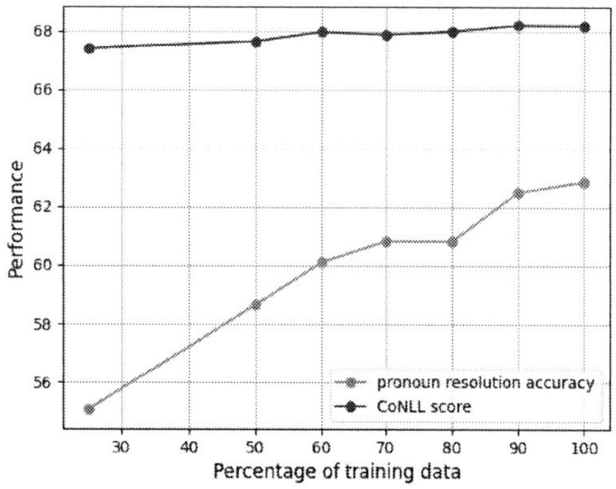

Figure 3: A training curve showing the effect of varying the amount of training data.

ever this does not seem to be the case here. The genre with the highest number of tokens per sentence actually performed the best.

Figure 3 shows training curves for the pronoun resolution model (i.e., these results do not include the mention span and attribute modules), with predicted mentions. From the curve we see the benefit of more training data for pronoun resolution accuracy (and to a lesser extent for the overall CoNLL score). Since the training curve keeps rising without reaching a plateau, we expect that adding more training data will improve pronoun resolution more. Still, since the curve gradually becomes less steep with supplying more data, we expect that there will be diminishing returns as more annotated training data is added.

6.2 Probing for gender bias

The results for the mention attribute classifier show that recognizing female mentions is most difficult. We suspect that the difficulty may lie in mentions that can be both male or female, in which the system may assume male as the most likely label. As a simple probe for gender bias, we experiment with the running example (1) which is a *Winogender* sentence (Rudinger et al., 2018).

Interestingly, the rule-based system correctly identifies *De chirurg* (the surgeon) as male or female (based on the Cornetto lexical resource), while the neural mention attribute classifier predicts it as male. How did this gender bias get introduced? The training data contains only one instance of *chirurg*, which is correctly annotated as male or female, since the context does not identify the surgeon's gender. Another potential source of gender bias is the BERT embeddings. If we present BERT with the following sentence:

(2) De chirurg kon [MASK] patiënt niet behandelen.
The surgeon couldn't treat [MASK] patient.

We find that BERT considers *de, zijn* (the, his) as overwhelmingly most probable, with *een, deze, die* (a, this, that) as distant runner ups, but no female possessive pronoun in the top 5. We therefore conclude that the pre-trained BERTje model has introduced a source of gender bias, which is in line with previous results for Dutch (Chávez Mulsa and Spanakis, 2020). Unless an effective bias mitigation technique is applied, this presents a dilemma: the goal is either to maximize overall accuracy, in which case for example the gender most commonly associated with an occupation is assumed, or gender bias is removed using constraints that lower overall performance.

Moreover, while the mention attribute classifier mistakenly classifies *De chirurg* (the surgeon) as male, the neural pronoun resolution module ignores this misclassification, and correctly links *haar*. This demonstrates the advantage of the neural classifiers which exploit mention attributes as features, but do not treat them as hard constraints, as the rule-based pronoun resolution sieve does.

7 Discussion and Conclusion

We have presented a hybrid coreference resolution system that extends a rule-based baseline with three simple neural classifiers. The classifiers substantially increase the coreference performance in our experiments on Dutch literature, except for pronoun resolution on the test set. The strongest improvements is on pronoun accuracy, which is especially important in longform narrative text.

There are several areas in which the system can be improved. In our approach we erred on the side of simplicity, but in the case of pronoun resolution the approach was too simple, leading to an improvement on the development set but not on the test set. The simplicity can be relaxed in several ways. The modules are trained with gold standard input, but using predictions of previous modules may give better results. If possible, the modules should be trained jointly. Adding more and more varied training data, such as from SoNaR-1 can be expected to yield better results. BERT performs better when finetuned and when encoding segments of 128 tokens, as reported by Joshi et al. (2019). Finally, other modules could be added. Anaphoricity classifiers are used in most state-of-the-art systems. In literature, dialogue is particularly important; annotating and predicting speakers of direct speech will help in resolving first and second person pronouns.

Future work should investigate in more detail the trade-offs between rule-based systems using an NLP pipeline and modern end-to-end neural models, especially in the challenging case of long-document coreference in narrative text.

Acknowledgments

We are grateful to Tommaso Caselli and three anonymous reviewers for helpful comments.

References

David Bamman, Olivia Lewke, and Anya Mansoor. 2020. An annotated dataset of coreference in English literature. In *Proceedings of LREC*, pages 44–54.

Shane Bergsma and Dekang Lin. 2006. Bootstrapping path-based pronoun resolution. In *Proceedings of COLING-ACL*, pages 33–40.

Rodrigo Alejandro Chávez Mulsa and Gerasimos Spanakis. 2020. Evaluating bias in Dutch word embeddings. In *Proceedings of GeBNLP*, pages 56–71.

Kevin Clark and Christopher D. Manning. 2016. Improving coreference resolution by learning entity-level distributed representations. In *Proceedings of ACL*, pages 643–653.

Wietse de Vries, Andreas van Cranenburgh, Arianna Bisazza, Tommaso Caselli, Gertjan van Noord, and Malvina Nissim. 2019. BERTje: A Dutch BERT model. arXiv:1912.09582.

Wietse de Vries, Andreas van Cranenburgh, and Malvina Nissim. 2020. What's so special about BERT's layers? A closer look at the NLP pipeline in monolingual and multilingual models. In *Findings of EMNLP*, pages 4339–4350.

Jacob Devlin, Ming-Wei Chang, Kenton Lee, and Kristina Toutanova. 2019. BERT: Pre-training of deep bidirectional transformers for language understanding. In *Proceedings of NAACL*, pages 4171–4186.

Tobias Glasmachers. 2017. Limits of end-to-end learning. In *Asian Conference on Machine Learning*, pages 17–32. PMLR.

Jerry R Hobbs. 1978. Resolving pronoun references. *Lingua*, 44(4):311–338.

Mandar Joshi, Danqi Chen, Yinhan Liu, Daniel S. Weld, Luke Zettlemoyer, and Omer Levy. 2020. SpanBERT: Improving pre-training by representing and predicting spans. *Transactions of the Association for Computational Linguistics*, 8:64–77.

Mandar Joshi, Omer Levy, Luke Zettlemoyer, and Daniel Weld. 2019. BERT for coreference resolution: Baselines and analysis. In *Proceedings of EMNLP-IJCNLP*, pages 5807–5812.

Heeyoung Lee, Angel Chang, Yves Peirsman, Nathanael Chambers, Mihai Surdeanu, and Dan Jurafsky. 2013. Deterministic coreference resolution based on entity-centric, precision-ranked rules. *Computational Linguistics*, 39(4):885–916.

Heeyoung Lee, Yves Peirsman, Angel Chang, Nathanael Chambers, Mihai Surdeanu, and Dan Jurafsky. 2011. Stanford's multi-pass sieve coreference resolution system at the CoNLL-2011 shared task. In *Proceedings of CoNLL*, pages 28–34.

Heeyoung Lee, Mihai Surdeanu, and Dan Jurafsky. 2017a. A scaffolding approach to coreference resolution integrating statistical and rule-based models. *Natural Language Engineering*, 23(5):733–762.

Kenton Lee, Luheng He, Mike Lewis, and Luke Zettlemoyer. 2017b. End-to-end neural coreference resolution. In *Proceedings of EMNLP*, pages 188–197.

Kenton Lee, Luheng He, and Luke Zettlemoyer. 2018. Higher-order coreference resolution with coarse-to-fine inference. In *Proceedings of NAACL*, pages 687–692.

Nafise Sadat Moosavi, Leo Born, Massimo Poesio, and Michael Strube. 2019. Using automatically extracted minimum spans to disentangle coreference evaluation from boundary detection. In *Proceedings of ACL*, pages 4168–4178.

Nafise Sadat Moosavi and Michael Strube. 2016. Which coreference evaluation metric do you trust? A proposal for a link-based entity aware metric. In *Proceedings of ACL*, pages 632–642.

Nafise Sadat Moosavi and Michael Strube. 2017. Use generalized representations, but do not forget surface features. In *Proceedings of CORBON*, pages 1–7.

Constantin Orasan and Richard J Evans. 2007. NP animacy identification for anaphora resolution. *Journal of Artificial Intelligence Research*, 29:79–103.

Corbèn Poot and Andreas van Cranenburgh. 2020. A benchmark of rule-based and neural coreference resolution in Dutch novels and news. In *Proceedings of CRAC*, pages 79–90.

Sameer Pradhan, Lance Ramshaw, Mitchell Marcus, Martha Palmer, Ralph Weischedel, and Nianwen Xue. 2011. CoNLL-2011 shared task: Modeling unrestricted coreference in OntoNotes. In *Proceedings of CoNLL*, pages 1–27.

Ina Rösiger, Sarah Schulz, and Nils Reiter. 2018. Towards coreference for literary text: Analyzing domain-specific phenomena. In *Proceedings of LaTeCH-CLfL*, pages 129–138.

Rachel Rudinger, Jason Naradowsky, Brian Leonard, and Benjamin Van Durme. 2018. Gender bias in coreference resolution. In *Proceedings of ACL*, pages 8–14.

Ineke Schuurman, Véronique Hoste, and Paola Monachesi. 2010. Interacting semantic layers of annotation in SoNaR, a reference corpus of contemporary written Dutch. In *Proceedings of LREC*, pages 2471–2477.

Shai Shalev-Shwartz and Amnon Shashua. 2016. On the sample complexity of end-to-end training vs. semantic abstraction training. arXiv preprint arXiv:1604.06915.

Wee Meng Soon, Hwee Tou Ng, and Daniel Chung Yong Lim. 2001. A machine learning approach to coreference resolution of noun phrases. *Computational Linguistics*, 27(4):521–544.

Shubham Toshniwal, Sam Wiseman, Allyson Ettinger, Karen Livescu, and Kevin Gimpel. 2020. Learning to Ignore: Long Document Coreference with Bounded Memory Neural Networks. In *Proceedings of EMNLP*, pages 8519–8526.

Andreas van Cranenburgh. 2019. A Dutch coreference resolution system with an evaluation on literary fiction. *Computational Linguistics in the Netherlands Journal*, 9:27–54.

Kellie Webster, Marta Recasens, Vera Axelrod, and Jason Baldridge. 2018. Mind the GAP: A balanced corpus of gendered ambiguous pronouns. *Transactions of the Association for Computational Linguistics*, 6:605–617.

Wei Wu, Fei Wang, Arianna Yuan, Fei Wu, and Jiwei Li. 2020. CorefQA: Coreference resolution as query-based span prediction. In *Proceedings of ACL*, pages 6953–6963.

Hongming Zhang, Yan Song, and Yangqiu Song. 2019. Incorporating context and external knowledge for pronoun coreference resolution. In *Proceedings of NAACL*, pages 872–881.

Yilun Zhu, Sameer Pradhan, and Amir Zeldes. 2021. OntoGUM: Evaluating contextualized SOTA coreference resolution on 12 more genres. In *Proceedings of ACL*, pages 461–467.

Lazy Low-Resource Coreference Resolution: a Study on Leveraging Black-Box Translation Tools

Semere Kiros Bitew, Johannes Deleu, Chris Develder and Thomas Demeester

IDLab, Ghent University - imec
{semerekiros.bitew, firstname.lastname}@ugent.be

Abstract

Large annotated corpora for coreference resolution are available for few languages. For machine translation, however, strong black-box systems exist for many languages. We empirically explore the appealing idea of leveraging such translation tools for bootstrapping coreference resolution in languages with limited resources. Two scenarios are analyzed, in which a large coreference corpus in a high-resource language is used for coreference predictions in a smaller language, i.e., by machine translating either the training corpus, or the test data. In our empirical evaluation of coreference resolution using the two scenarios on several medium-resource languages, we find no improvement over monolingual baseline models. Our analysis of the various sources of error inherent to the studied scenarios, reveals that in fact the quality of contemporary machine translation tools is the main limiting factor.

1 Introduction

End-to-end coreference resolution is the task of identifying and clustering all spans of text that refer to the same entity in a document. It serves as an important step for several downstream NLP tasks that involve natural language understanding, including question answering (Morton, 1999), information retrieval, and text summarization (Azzam et al., 1999; Baldwin and Morton, 1998). Recent advances in deep learning have resulted in state-of-the-art performance on coreference resolution (Lee et al., 2017; Fei et al., 2019; Kantor and Globerson, 2019; Joshi et al., 2020; Wu et al., 2020). The performance of these models, however, highly depends on the existence of large annotated datasets. Still, for many languages that lack large annotated coreference corpora, machine translation (MT) tools of an ever increasing quality are available. The idea studied in this work, is whether existing black-box translation tools can be readily leveraged for transferring the task of coreference resolution from one language to another.

We tackle the setting in which a large labeled corpus exists in a resource-rich language (i.e., the 'source' language) whereas only a smaller corpus exists in a smaller-resource language (called the 'target' language). Specifically, we consider two scenarios in which black-box MT tools can be integrated into a cross-lingual end-to-end coreference resolution system. The first scenario, `Translate-train`, uses an MT tool to translate the large source corpus into the target language, after which a coreference model is trained in the target language. In the second scenario, `Translate-test`, test examples in the target language are first machine translated to the source language, after which a pre-trained coreference model is used to predict the labels. The second scenario has the disadvantage that an MT tool is required at inference time.

Similar transfer learning setups for basic sequence tagging tasks gave encouraging results (as discussed in Section 4), but we find this is no longer the case for the task of coreference resolution.

We analyze the different sources of error related to integrating the MT tool in the pipeline. As it turns out, translation errors have the strongest impact on the effectiveness of the proposed methods, followed by prediction errors and alignment issues.

2 Approach

2.1 Translate-train

The goal of the `Translate-train` approach (visualized in Fig. 1a) is to create a dataset in the target language, on which a model can be trained. We follow the approach used by Jain et al. (2019) for NER, but we now apply it for coreference resolution.

We assume access to labeled training data in the source language, a MT tool, an alignment tool, and a test set in the target language. First, we use the MT tool to translate the entire training set from the

Proceedings of the 4th Workshop on Computational Models of Reference, Anaphora and Coreference (CRAC 2021), pages 57–62
Punta Cana, Dominican Republic, November 10–11, 2021.

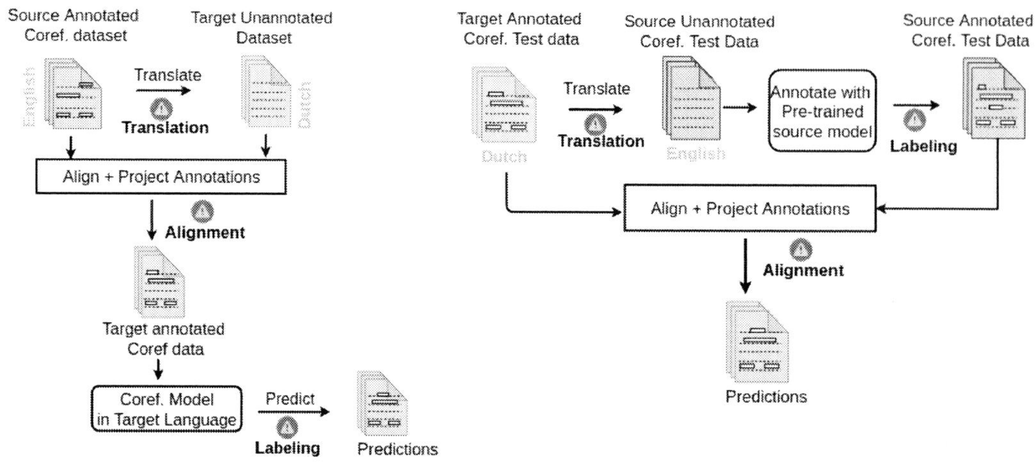

(a) Translate-train procedure

(b) Translate-test procedure

Figure 1: Annotation projection approaches, with indication of the main sources of error through the icon.

source to the target language. This results in an unannotated dataset in the target language. Second, we identify and label all mentions of entities in the translated target document by aligning the source and target documents using the alignment tool. Finally, a competitive monolingual method is used to train a coreference model directly in the target language, which is then evaluated on the test data.

2.2 Translate-test

The Translate-test approach (see Fig. 1b) follows Shah et al. (2010), and assumes access to a large training corpus in the source language, an off-the-shelf MT system, an alignment tool, and a test set in the target language. First, the test set is translated into the source language. A competitive model trained on the source language training corpus is used to annotate the translated test set (i.e., identify and cluster mentions into groups). With the alignment tool, the translated documents in the source language are aligned with the original ones in the target language, after which the predicted labels are projected onto them for evaluation.

3 Experimental Evaluation

Data — Our evaluation set was created for the SemEval-2010 (Recasens et al., 2010) shared task, and contains coreference annotations for six languages (see Table 1 for dataset statistics). We use Dutch, Spanish, Italian, and Catalan as our target languages, and the corresponding SemEval-2010 datasets are used to train and test the respective monolingual coreference models. As our large and high-quality source dataset, we use the English OntoNotes 5.0 coreference dataset from the CoNLL 2012 shared task (Pradhan et al., 2012).

Coreference Models — For the Translate-train scenario, we use the end-to-end neural coreference resolution method from Lee et al. (2017) to train and evaluate on the target languages. This model considers all spans of text as potential mentions and finds the most probable antecedents for each span. For each span, a span ranking model is used to decide which of the previous spans are good antecedents, whereby a trained pruner eliminates less likely mentions. During training, the marginal log-likelihood of all correct antecedents in the gold clusters is optimized. In our Translate-test experiments, we use SpanBert (Joshi et al., 2020), an English end-to-end coreference resolver, trained on the OntoNotes corpus.

Translation Tool — In both scenarios, we use Google Translate[1] as our publicly available MT tool of choice.

Alignment — For the alignment step, we compare Fast-Align from Dyer et al. (2013), a simple unsupervised statistical word alignment model, with the Heuristics method from the work of Jain et al. (2019).

Baselines — We compare our translate-train and translate-test approaches with a model trained on annotated data in the target language (i.e., End2end Coref). We also consider two alternative baseline systems for which end-to-end coref-

[1]The translation of documents using Google Translate was done on 02-12-2020.

	Training			Development			Test		
	#docs	#sents	#tokens	#docs	#sents	#tokens	#docs	#sents	#tokens
Catalan	829	8,709	253,513	142	1,445	42,072	167	1,698	49,260
Dutch	145	2,544	46,894	23	496	9,165	72	2,410	48,007
English	229	3,648	79,060	39	741	17,044	85	1,141	24,206
Italian	80	2,951	81,400	17	551	16,904	46	1,494	41,586
Spanish	875	9,022	284,179	140	1,419	44,460	168	1,705	51,040

Table 1: SemEval-2010 Dataset Statistics

Method	Alignment tool	Dutch	Spanish	Catalan	Italian
Translate-train	Fast-Align	0.280	0.410	0.410	0.340
Translate-train	Heuristics	0.260	0.390	0.370	0.307
Translate-test	Fast-Align	0.365	0.461	0.480	0.362
Translate-test	Heuristics	0.358	0.438	0.453	0.347
End2end Coref	-	**0.380**	**0.516**	**0.533**	0.430
Sucre or Tan-1*	-	0.191	0.490	0.482*	**0.607**

Table 2: Monolingual and Cross-Lingual results in terms of Average Coreference F1

erence results were reported on the SemEval 2010 shared task data: Sucre and Tan-1. The Sucre system (Kobdani and Schütze, 2010) uses engineered features for words, mentions and mention pairs and uses classical machine learning classifiers to cluster mentions. It reports the best results for Spanish, Italian and Dutch. The Tan-1 system (Attardi et al., 2010) uses dependency parse trees to detect mentions and trains a binary classifier to decide the pairwise relationship between the extracted mentions and reports the best result for Catalan. Works such as van Cranenburgh (2019) and Rahman and Ng (2012) are not used as baselines because they make use of external resources (mention detectors, NER, Alpino parse trees[2], etc.).

Metrics — For evaluation, we report the average F1 of the MUC, B3, and CEAF4 coreference resolution metrics, as proposed in Denis and Baldridge (2007).

3.1 Results

Our end-to-end monolingual baseline outperforms the Sucre and Tan-1 systems on Catalan, Spanish and Dutch, as shown in Table 2. For Italian, our baseline shows inferior performance, possibly due to the small number of training examples (i.e., only 80 documents). Interestingly, our cross-lingual models remain unable to surpass the effectiveness of their monolingual counterparts, although the former leverage a much larger coreference corpus than the latter. The Translate-test is consistently better than Translate-train, which we hypothesize is due to the superior quality of the English SpanBert model,especially in comparison with the End2end Coref models trained on the translated (i.e., noisy) source corpus. The Fast-Align alignment strategy consistently outperforms the Heuristics based alignment method in both the Translate-train and Translate-test approaches. Jain et al. (2019) showed that the Heuristics improved on their Fast-align and indicated the reason to be that named entities are low-frequency words. To improve its performance, we trained Fast-Align on the additional parallel corpus Europarl (Koehn, 2005).

[2]http://www.let.rug.nl/vannoord/alp/Alpino/

3.2 Error Analysis

In this section we discuss the contributing factors to the low performance of the Translate-test setup (being the better of both scenarios). From 10 randomly sampled test documents, which contain a total of 424 mentions and 127 cluster chains, we quantify three particular sources of error (see Fig. 1b):

Translation Error — To measure the impact of the imperfect translation step, we annotate the Dutch-to-English translated documents with coreference labels (i.e., perfect annotation on the noisy translations). We also manually align the noisy English documents with the original Dutch documents (i.e., to simulate perfect alignment).

Automatic Labeling Error — To see the impact of the prediction model, we use SpanBert to annotate the manually translated documents (i.e., assuming perfect translation), again followed by a manual

	Source text	Google Translate	Correct translation
1.	Het gesprek ging onder meer over *[Punt]*.	The conversation was about *[Dot]*.	The conversation, amongst others, was about *[Punt]*
2.	*[Mark Grammens]* ...	*[Mark Grams man]* ...	*[Mark Grammens]* ...
3.	... en *[zijn]* stelling is bekend	... and *[its]* position is well known	... [his] position is well known
4.	*[Die]* nam daar genoegen mee.	*[Which]* was content with that.	*[He]* was content with that

Table 3: Literal translation error (1 & 2) and pronoun mistranslation (3 & 4) examples

Model	F1
Translate-test	0.415
only *translation* error	0.490
only *labeling* error	0.613
only *alignment* error	0.896

Table 4: Error breakdown for a random sample of 10 Dutch SemEval-2010 documents.

alignment step (i.e., to avoid alignment errors).

Alignment Error — To quantify the noise induced by the alignment step, we manually translate the documents to English and manually assign the coreference labels, after which Fast-Align is applied for alignment with the original Dutch documents for evaluation.

Our analysis on the error breakdown is shown in Table 4. The largest source of error for the translate-test model appears to be the MT step followed by the labeling error, whereas the impact of the alignment error is rather small. We looked into the translation errors, and observed that the coreference results are most degraded due to incorrectly translated pronouns, and literal translations of (parts of) named entities.

The labeling error leads to a hypothetical F1 (i.e., in the absence of other errors) of 0.613 on the selected documents. This is considerably below the reported SpanBert performance of 0.796 on the Ontonotes test set (Joshi et al., 2020). We hypothesize this is partly due to the shift in domain between the English Ontonotes data and the SemEval data in Dutch, as well as some differences in coreference annotation guidelines between both datastets. For example, coreference relations with verbs are annotated in Ontonotes but not in SemEval.

4 Related Work

The key concept used in the presented transfer learning scenarios, is *annotation projection*, as originally proposed by Yarowsky et al. (2001) for part-of-speech tagging. It relies on the transfer of annotations from the source language to the target language. Most annotation projection methods depend on parallel corpora in which the source data is labeled using a trained model before projecting the labels onto the data in the target language (Hwa et al., 2005; Postolache et al., 2006; Zeman and Resnik, 2008; Ehrmann et al., 2011; de Souza and Orăsan, 2011; Fu et al., 2014; Ni et al., 2017; Grishina, 2019).

Alternatively, other works relied on the use of bilingual dictionaries for annotation projection (Mayhew et al., 2017; Xie et al., 2018). The Translate-train idea of creating a noisy translated corpus with projected annotations has been proposed as well (Tiedemann et al., 2014; Jain et al., 2019), for the task of dependency parsing and NER, respectively. Shah et al. (2010) used MT in the other direction (Translate-test) for the task of NER.

A common problem in both annotation projection scenarios is the alignment of text spans between languages, for which unsupervised statistical alignment models can be used (Shah et al., 2010; Ni et al., 2017), such as the IBM models 1-6 (Brown et al., 1993; Och and Ney, 2000). A few recent works (Mayhew et al., 2017; Xie et al., 2018) perform translation on a word or span level to avoid the alignment problem. Others explored alignment heuristics such as matching words based on their surface forms and translations (Ehrmann et al., 2011; Jain et al., 2019), or using external information such as Wikipedia links (Nothman et al., 2013; Al-Rfou et al., 2015).

The prior works applied annotation projection to the tasks of NER, POS, or dependency parsing, and proved relatively successful (i.e., close to monolingual models in the target language). Postolache et al. (2006); de Souza and Orăsan (2011) are notable prior works that applied the idea of annotation projection to the task of coreference resolution. Unlike our work, they depend on the existence of a parallel corpora and are focused on a single language pair to test their ideas. Moreover, they have a pipeline that extracts mentions using external annotation tools or manually before clustering them into coreference chains. We, on the other hand, do both the mention identification and clustering in an end-to-end fashion by considering all the possible text spans on a document.

For the task of end-to-end coreference resolution, we explore the use machine translation for annotation projection, especially for medium-resource languages for which strong MT systems exist. We investigate if MT systems can be used for transferring coreference knowledge (model, dataset) without having to rely on parallel corpora.

5 Conclusion and Future work

While the idea of leveraging MT to improve NLP task performance for low resource languages is not new, this idea to the best of our knowledge has not been pursued for coreference resolution. We contribute by comparing two conceptually different methods; the `Translate-train` and `Translate-test` approaches. We further present a rigorous quantitative error analysis. From our work, we conclude that (i) for coreference resolution the MT approaches are not very successful. (ii) our error analysis suggests this is mainly due by translation errors followed by labeling and alignment errors.

We believe MT models can be still leveraged in cross-lingual transfer learning for coreference resolution, but we speculate that access to the internals of the models, such as attention weights, will be needed. Moreover, future work will need to investigate hybrid strategies, combining transfer learning from other languages with the available data in the target language, to override issues due to MT uncertainty or differences in annotation guidelines.

References

Rami Al-Rfou, Vivek Kulkarni, Bryan Perozzi, and Steven Skiena. 2015. Polyglot-ner: Massive multilingual named entity recognition. In *Proceedings of the 2015 SIAM International Conference on Data Mining*, pages 586–594. SIAM.

Giuseppe Attardi, Maria Simi, and Stefano Dei Rossi. 2010. Tanl-1: coreference resolution by parse analysis and similarity clustering. In *Proceedings of the 5th International Workshop on Semantic Evaluation*, pages 108–111.

Saliha Azzam, Kevin Humphreys, and Robert Gaizauskas. 1999. Using coreference chains for text summarization. In *Coreference and Its Applications*.

Breck Baldwin and Thomas S Morton. 1998. Dynamic coreference-based summarization. In *Proceedings of the Third Conference on Empirical Methods for Natural Language Processing*, pages 1–6.

Peter F Brown, Stephen A Della Pietra, Vincent J Della Pietra, and Robert L Mercer. 1993. The mathematics of statistical machine translation: Parameter estimation. *Computational linguistics*, 19(2):263–311.

José Guilherme Camargo de Souza and Constantin Orăsan. 2011. Can projected chains in parallel corpora help coreference resolution? In *Discourse Anaphora and Anaphor Resolution Colloquium*, pages 59–69. Springer.

Pascal Denis and Jason Baldridge. 2007. Joint determination of anaphoricity and coreference resolution using integer programming. In *Human Language Technologies 2007: The Conference of the North American Chapter of the Association for Computational Linguistics; Proceedings of the Main Conference*, pages 236–243.

Chris Dyer, Victor Chahuneau, and Noah A Smith. 2013. A simple, fast, and effective reparameterization of ibm model 2. In *Proceedings of the 2013 Conference of the North American Chapter of the Association for Computational Linguistics: Human Language Technologies*, pages 644–648.

Maud Ehrmann, Marco Turchi, and Ralf Steinberger. 2011. Building a multilingual named entity-annotated corpus using annotation projection. In *Proceedings of the International Conference Recent Advances in Natural Language Processing 2011*, pages 118–124.

Hongliang Fei, Xu Li, Dingcheng Li, and Ping Li. 2019. End-to-end deep reinforcement learning based coreference resolution. In *Proceedings of the 57th Annual Meeting of the Association for Computational Linguistics*, pages 660–665.

Ruiji Fu, Bing Qin, and Ting Liu. 2014. Generating chinese named entity data from parallel corpora. *Frontiers of Computer Science*, 8(4):629–641.

Yulia Grishina. 2019. *Assessing the applicability of annotation projection methods for coreference relations*. Ph.D. thesis, Universität Potsdam.

Rebecca Hwa, Philip Resnik, Amy Weinberg, Clara Cabezas, and Okan Kolak. 2005. Bootstrapping parsers via syntactic projection across parallel texts. *Natural language engineering*, 11(3):311–326.

Alankar Jain, Bhargavi Paranjape, and Zachary C Lipton. 2019. Entity projection via machine-translation for cross-lingual ner. *arXiv preprint arXiv:1909.05356*.

Mandar Joshi, Danqi Chen, Yinhan Liu, Daniel S Weld, Luke Zettlemoyer, and Omer Levy. 2020. Spanbert: Improving pre-training by representing and predicting spans. *Transactions of the Association for Computational Linguistics*, 8:64–77.

Ben Kantor and Amir Globerson. 2019. Coreference resolution with entity equalization. In *Proceedings of the 57th Annual Meeting of the Association for Computational Linguistics*, pages 673–677.

Hamidreza Kobdani and Hinrich Schütze. 2010. Sucre: A modular system for coreference resolution. In *Proceedings of the 5th International Workshop on Semantic Evaluation*, pages 92–95. Association for Computational Linguistics.

Philipp Koehn. 2005. Europarl: A parallel corpus for statistical machine translation. In *MT summit*, volume 5, pages 79–86. Citeseer.

Kenton Lee, Luheng He, Mike Lewis, and Luke Zettlemoyer. 2017. End-to-end neural coreference resolution. *arXiv preprint arXiv:1707.07045*.

Stephen Mayhew, Chen-Tse Tsai, and Dan Roth. 2017. Cheap translation for cross-lingual named entity recognition. In *Proceedings of the 2017 conference on empirical methods in natural language processing*, pages 2536–2545.

Thomas S Morton. 1999. Using coreference for question answering. In *Coreference and Its Applications*.

Jian Ni, Georgiana Dinu, and Radu Florian. 2017. Weakly supervised cross-lingual named entity recognition via effective annotation and representation projection. *arXiv preprint arXiv:1707.02483*.

Joel Nothman, Nicky Ringland, Will Radford, Tara Murphy, and James R Curran. 2013. Learning multilingual named entity recognition from wikipedia. *Artificial Intelligence*, 194:151–175.

Franz Josef Och and Hermann Ney. 2000. Improved statistical alignment models. In *Proceedings of the 38th annual meeting of the association for computational linguistics*, pages 440–447.

Oana Postolache, Dan Cristea, and Constantin Orasan. 2006. Transferring coreference chains through word alignment. In *LREC*, pages 889–892.

Sameer Pradhan, Alessandro Moschitti, Nianwen Xue, Olga Uryupina, and Yuchen Zhang. 2012. Conll-2012 shared task: Modeling multilingual unrestricted coreference in ontonotes. In *Joint Conference on EMNLP and CoNLL-Shared Task*, pages 1–40.

Altaf Rahman and Vincent Ng. 2012. Translation-based projection for multilingual coreference resolution. In *Proceedings of the 2012 Conference of the North American Chapter of the Association for Computational Linguistics: Human Language Technologies*, pages 720–730.

Marta Recasens, Lluís Màrquez, Emili Sapena, M Antònia Martí, Mariona Taulé, Véronique Hoste, Massimo Poesio, and Yannick Versley. 2010. Semeval-2010 task 1: Coreference resolution in multiple languages. In *Proceedings of the 5th International Workshop on Semantic Evaluation*, pages 1–8.

Rushin Shah, Bo Lin, Anatole Gershman, and Robert Frederking. 2010. Synergy: a named entity recognition system for resource-scarce languages such as swahili using online machine translation. In *Proceedings of the Second Workshop on African Language Technology (AfLaT 2010)*, pages 21–26.

Jörg Tiedemann, Željko Agić, and Joakim Nivre. 2014. Treebank translation for cross-lingual parser induction. In *Eighteenth Conference on Computational Natural Language Learning (CoNLL 2014)*.

Andreas van Cranenburgh. 2019. A dutch coreference resolution system with an evaluation on literary fiction. *Computational Linguistics in the Netherlands Journal*, 9:27–54.

Wei Wu, Fei Wang, Arianna Yuan, Fei Wu, and Jiwei Li. 2020. Corefqa: Coreference resolution as query-based span prediction. In *Proceedings of the 58th Annual Meeting of the Association for Computational Linguistics*, pages 6953–6963.

Jiateng Xie, Zhilin Yang, Graham Neubig, Noah A Smith, and Jaime Carbonell. 2018. Neural cross-lingual named entity recognition with minimal resources. *arXiv preprint arXiv:1808.09861*.

David Yarowsky, Grace Ngai, and Richard Wicentowski. 2001. Inducing multilingual text analysis tools via robust projection across aligned corpora. Technical report, JOHNS HOPKINS UNIV BALTIMORE MD DEPT OF COMPUTER SCIENCE.

Daniel Zeman and Philip Resnik. 2008. Cross-language parser adaptation between related languages. In *Proceedings of the IJCNLP-08 Workshop on NLP for Less Privileged Languages*.

Resources and Evaluations for Danish Entity Resolution

Maria Barrett† **Hieu Trong Lam**† **Martin Wu**†
Ophélie Lacroix◇ **Barbara Plank**† **Anders Søgaard** ○

† Computer Science Department, IT University of Copenhagen, Denmark
[mbarrett,trol,mawu,bapl]@itu.dk
◇ Alexandra Institute, Denmark, ophelie.lacroix@alexandra.dk
○ Department of Computer Science, University of Copenhagen, Denmark
soegaard@di.ku.dk

Abstract

Automatic coreference resolution is understudied in Danish even though most of the Danish Dependency Treebank (Buch-Kromann, 2003) is annotated with coreference relations. This paper describes a conversion of its partial, yet well-documented, coreference relations into coreference clusters and the training and evaluation of coreference models on this data. To the best of our knowledge, these are the first publicly available neural coreference models for Danish. We also present a new entity linking annotation on the dataset using WikiData identifiers, a named entity disambiguation (NED) dataset, and a larger automatically created NED dataset enabling wikily supervised NED models. The entity linking annotation is benchmarked using a state-of-the-art neural entity disambiguation model.

1 Introduction

The Danish Dependency Treebank (DDT) (Buch-Kromann, 2003) is a beneficial resource for Danish NLP that contains several annotation layers. Most of the layers were annotated as part of the Copenhagen Dependency Treebank project, but a conversion of the dependency syntax annotation into Universal dependencies (Johannsen et al., 2015; Nivre et al., 2020) and the addition of named entities annotation layers (Hvingelby et al., 2020; Plank, 2019; Plank et al., 2020) are newer additions. The partial coreference annotation has received no attention for NLP purposes despite being very well documented. This paper describes converting the coreference relations into coreference clusters and a new entity linking annotation with unique Wikidata item identification codes (QIDs) (Vrandečić, 2012) on the same data.

Entity linking is the task of detecting mentions and matching the mentions to a knowledge base. The two annotation layers—coreference and entity linking—complement each other as two types of entity resolution. In practice, entity linking can be reduced to a binary classification task, called named entity disambiguation (NED), thereby simplifying the task and omitting mention detection.

The coreference-annotated data is benchmarked using a strong neural model. The entity linking annotation is turned into a NED dataset and benchmarked using a state-of-the-art NED model. We automatically create a larger NED train set from Wikipedia articles for train set augmentation, and we observe an improvement for the wikily supervised models. All data and models are publicly available.[1]

2 Related work

Danish anaphors have received some attention: Navarretta (2000) shows that Danish deictics are used in more contexts than the English ones and Houser et al. (2006) specifically discuss the use of verb phrase pronominalization in Danish. Danish has gendered possessive pronouns, but non-gendered reflexive pronouns. This has made it useful as an unambiguous testbed for gender bias in natural language inference models, machine translation models, and language models (González et al., 2020). But automatic coreference resolution for Danish has received no attention, and there was no established evaluation set for this task.

Linked resources such as Wikipedia enable multi-lingual entity linking/NED models and datasets, and Danish is often among the evaluation languages (Pan et al., 2017; McNamee et al., 2011). DBpedia Spotlight[2] is the most recent entity linking system that also supports Danish. But due to this being a different task from NED, we can not compare our model to DBpedia Spotlight.

[1] https://github.com/alexandrainst/danlp

[2] https://www.dbpedia-spotlight.org/

Proceedings of the 4th Workshop on Computational Models of Reference, Anaphora and Coreference (CRAC 2021), pages 63–69
Punta Cana, Dominican Republic, November 10–11, 2021.

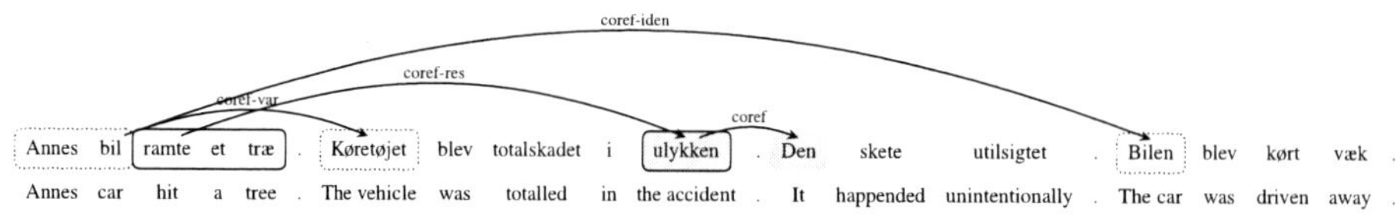

Figure 1: A constructed example of a coreference-annotated paragraph with binary relations as graphs and three clusters marked with background colour or borders around the word spans. The English word-by-word translation is below. Translation: "Anne's car crashed into a tree. The vehicle was damaged beyond repair in the accident. It happened unintentionally. The car was towed."

	N	LA	UA	REL
COREF	238	61	64	89
COREF-VAR	146	59	72	73
REF	70	90	91	94
COREF-IDEN	62	73	81	77
COREF-RES	36	62	67	75
COREF-EVOL	1	0	100	0

Table 1: Labelled agreement (LA), Unlabelled agreement (UA), only relation name (REL) and support (N) for the doubly annotated subset. Numbers are taken directly from the DDT documentation.[3]

3 Dataset

The coreference-annotated part spans 2/3 of the DDT and is documented in Korzen and Buch-Kromann (2011). This subset encompasses 341 documents/3,403 sentences/64,076 tokens. The source is the PAROLE Corpus (Bilgram and Keson, 1998). The domain is mostly newswire (299 documents) but also a small fraction of magazine text (41 documents) and news broadcast (1 document). We refer to this dataset as DACOREF.

4 Coreference

Annotation and conversion The DDT documentation[3] is extensive and this section's details concerning the annotation come from this resource. We refer to the DDT documentation for more details.

Key observations about the annotation scheme: Like the Ontonotes (Weischedel et al., 2013) coreference annotation, singletons are not annotated. The annotation does not label attributive noun phrases connected through copula verbs such as "to be" ("at være"). Verb phrases can only be linked if they are coreferent with a noun phrase.

The dataset is annotated with binary relations between core nodes. We consider nine different coreference labels that we merge heuristically into clusters. We omit the associative anaphors. Coreference clusters are sets of text spans that all refer to the same entity and labels are omitted. Each cluster is uniquely numbered.

We merge the following relations if they span the same target words: COREF (coreferential personal pronoun), COREF-ELL (elliptic anaphor demonstrative pronoun), COREF-EVOL (evolving anaphor), COREF-IDEN (coreferential noun phrase with complete lexical identity), COREF-IDEN.SB (coreferential noun phrase with lexical identity in the noun but lexical variety in some other (typically attributive) component), COREF-VAR (coreferential noun phrase with lexical variety in the noun), and REF (syntactically determined coreference, e.g., relative pronouns).

COREF-RES (resumptive anaphor clause or predicate) and COREF-RES.PRG (pragmatic resumptive anaphor) are also used for clustering but not merged with any other label, nor each other. Figure 1 shows a constructed example where COREF-VAR, COREF-IDEN and COREF are merged when on the same target word(s), but COREF-RES is not, thereby making `ulykken` part of two clusters.

Seven documents are doubly annotated, and they are assumed to form the basis of the reported annotation quality in the documentation, which we reprint in Table 1. COREF-ELL, COREF-IDEN.SB, and COREF-RES.PRG are subclasses of COREF, COREF-IDEN and COREF-RES, respectively. Separate scores were not reported for those but they are assumed to be included in the parent class score. DACOREF use the annotations of one annotator, "Lotte".

The coreference annotation only contains a label on the core node. For DACOREF, we propagate the label to the relevant span. Due to several instances of the label not being on the core node, this is done manually by one annotator. The spans encompass the relevant noun phrases. When linking

[3] `https://github.com/mbkromann/copenhagen-dependency-treebank/blob/master/manual/cdt-manual.pdf`

verb phrases, the span covers the entire verb phrase. This is different from Ontonotes (Weischedel et al., 2013), where the span only covers the head verb.

Even though the DDT has been split into train, development and test sets as part of the Universal Dependencies (UD) conversion (Johannsen et al., 2015), a new split is created for document-level coreference resolution since the UD dataset scrambled the sentences across documents. The train split contains 290 documents, the development set 23, and the test set 28 documents.

Coreference models We provide benchmark scores for two strong neural models using three different transformer representations. Lee et al. (2017) (LEE2017) presented the first neural end-to-end coreference model in which the spans are learned in the same training pass as the pairwise clustering. The pairwise clustering may produce globally inconsistent clusters, and Lee et al. (2018) (LEE2018) presented a higher-order upgrade that did not only consider pairs of spans but a matrix of all spans to counter global inconsistencies. Joshi et al. (2019) showed that the model from Lee et al. (2018) performed even better on English data when using transformer-based models instead of the word embeddings of the original implementations. We follow their approach and try representations from three different pre-trained models: Danish BERT (DABERT)[4] and two multilingual, cased models: multilingual BERT (MBERT) (Devlin et al., 2019) and the base model of XLM-Roberta (XLM-R) (Conneau et al., 2020). Instead of the TensorFlow implementations released by Joshi et al. (2019), we use the PyTorch-based implementation from AllenNLP 1.3.0.[5] with PyTorch version 1.7.1. A description of the tuning process is in Appendix A. After model selection, we retrain the models for a maximum of 1200 epochs with early stopping and a patience of 10.

Coreference results The coreference benchmark results are presented in Table 2. Models based on the two multi-lingual, cased transformer models perform a lot better than the uncased DABERT. The best model is LEE2018 trained with XLM-R.

5 Entity linking

Entity linking annotation The resource was annotated with QIDs in the spring of 2020 with the

[4]https://github.com/botxo/nordic_bert

[5]https://github.com/allenai/allennlp

	MODEL	F1	P	R	MR
DABERT	LEE2017	0.477	0.587	0.402	0.729
	LEE2018	0.313	0.655	0.207	0.683
MBERT	LEE2017	0.630	0.679	0.587	0.870
	LEE2018	0.532	0.625	0.463	0.854
XLM-R	LEE2017	0.623	0.668	0.585	0.822
	LEE2018	**0.640**	**0.699**	**0.592**	**0.880**

Table 2: Coreference results: M(ention) R(ecall), average P(recision), R(ecall) and F1 across MUC, B^3, and CEAFe. The best result per column is boldfaced.

WikiData entries available at that time in a semi-manual process: First, all tokens in named entities were used to search the MediaWiki API. Given the entire list of WikiData matches for each token, one annotator decided which QID match was correct for each. We did not search for entire mentions since mentions were not always equal to the WikiData label and thus returned too many wrong QID suggestions leaving this method inefficient. In the case of multi-word entity names, we searched for possible QID matches for each token and manually selected the correct one. One annotator decided in each case whether "Margrethe" referred to the Danish queen, a foundation in her name or another person/ship etc. This was checked by another annotator, who also manually added the QID to the correct span in the text. Both were native speakers of Danish. The average accuracy of the set of QIDs per document of annotator 1 compared to annotator 2 is 0.98 (std. 0.05). Furthermore, the second annotation process also included adding a generic QID for words that matched one of 47 categories (Ship Q11446, Award Q618779, Automobile model Q3231690, Hospital Q16917 etc.) for which no specific Wikidata entry existed. The list of all generic QIDs can be seen in Appendix B. In total, 7,173 tokens were annotated with a QID. 2,193 unique QIDs were used.

Construction of the DANED dataset Entity disambiguation is a binary classification variant of entity linking. Given a sentence, the entity name as printed in the sentence, and a QID; the model classifies whether this QID is the mentioned entity in the sentence. The task requires creating a new classification dataset also containing negative examples. Only sentences from DACOREF that have at least one QID annotation are part of the datasets.

We create the negative examples in the following manner: For each token annotated with a QID in the train, development, and test set, we search

SENTENCE	ENTITY	QID	KG CONTEXT	LABEL
The same sentence could be heard when Elvis had left the scene after a Las Vegas show.	Elvis	Q303	birth name Elvis Aaron Presley given name Elvis given name Aaron country of citizenship USA place of birth Tupelo place of death Graceland spouse Priscilla Presley child Lisa Marie Presley place of burial Graceland Commons category Elvis Presley LCAuth n78079487 VIAF 23404836 GND identificator 118596357 ISNI 0000 0001 2124 1960 ISNI 0000 0003 6863 8871 occupation film actor occupation rock singer occupation screen writer occupation guitarist occupation soldier occupation pianist occupation actor	1
The same sentence could be heard when Elvis had left the scene after a Las Vegas show.	Elvis	Q5368160	Commons category Firefighting helicopters in Australia image N179AC-Elvis-739.jpg instance of aircraft Freebase-ID /m/0271gwk	0

Table 3: Example of the representation of two samples for the NED model. All input to the model is in Danish; only this example is shown in English.

WikiData using SPARQL for other matches than the correct QID but with the same label name. If possible, up to two negative examples per QID are included. The same sentence occurs several times in each split due to negative examples and possibly multiple QIDs in the same sentence, but the same sentence does not occur across splits.

We used the MediaWiki API to obtain all WikiData knowledge graph (KG) contexts in Danish for both the positive and negative examples. Due to model constraints, we cut off the properties after 512 characters. An example of the representation of an instance is presented in Table 3.

The train-development-test split is determined by the DACOREF splits and ended in a 78-9-13% distribution. Class balance and split size after the construction of negative samples and dataset size are shown in Figure 2. This dataset is referred to as DANED.

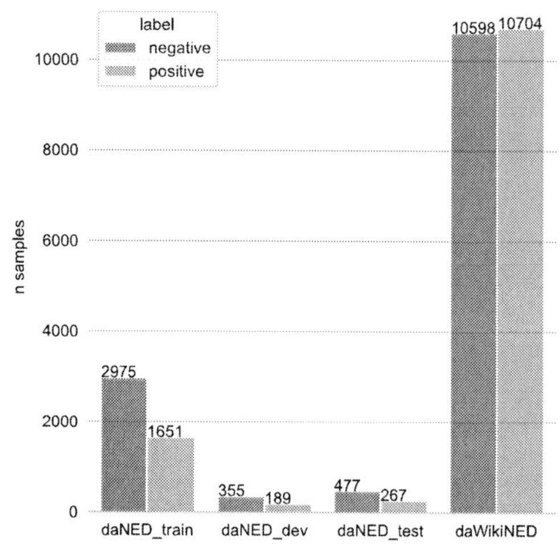

Figure 2: Distribution of class labels and data set sizes in the datasets for evaluating and training NED models.

Train set augmentation We automatically construct a large Danish NED dataset from Wikipedia, DAWIKINED. We use a list of 391,102 Danish articles names from the latest Wiki dump[6]. Initially, we further gather 82,150 person names that have Danish articles from the SPARQL endpoint. We fetch the Wikipedia text using the SPARQL API for each of the article names and split it into sentences using the NLTK library. We then pick the longest sentence that also contains the article title[7]. If possible, we fetch the corresponding QID, the corresponding KG context and the description for this entity and add it to the dataset. We fetch up to two negative examples per QID. Final DAWIKINED dataset size is in Figure 2.

NED model The model by Mulang' et al. (2020) takes the best model from Yang et al. (2019) called dynamic context augmentation with supervised learning (DCA-SL) but fine-tunes transformer model representation during training. The model leverages KG contexts from a knowledge base during training and evaluation. Mulang' et al. (2020) reported state-of-the-art performance on the AIDA-CONLL dataset (Hoffart et al., 2011). During training, we fine-tune either DABERT and XLM-R representations. In the code, we modify

	TRAIN SET	P	R	F1
XLM-R	DANED	0.76	0.90	0.82
	DAWIKINED	0.64	0.62	0.63
	BOTH	**0.84**	0.85	0.85
DABERT	DANED	0.8	**0.91**	0.85
	DAWIKINED	0.82	0.54	0.65
	BOTH	**0.84**	0.88	**0.86**

Table 4: NED results on the DANED test set. The best result per column is boldfaced.

[6]https://dumps.wikimedia.org/dawiki/

[7]We use fuzzy string matching with a similarity threshold of 85 to match the article name in the sentence because some of the article names are slightly different when appearing in the text, especially personal names.

that the KG context was not scrambled and reduced to the vocabulary using the `set()` function but keep the rest as-is. The tuning process is described in Appendix C.

NED results Table 4 presents the results of the NED evaluation. DABERT is slightly better than XML-R. We observe that the augmented training with DAWIKINED seems to help both models. The best model builds on DABERT and trains on the DANED train set and DAWIKINED (BOTH).

6 Conclusion

We have presented a semi-manual conversion of coreference relations into coreference clusters and a novel entity linking annotation for Danish. The latter annotation is transformed into a named entity disambiguation dataset, and we further described the automatic construction of a Danish Wikipedia named entity disambiguation dataset. We have reported the first benchmarks for Danish coreference resolution and an evaluation of our named entity disambiguation dataset with train set augmentation.

Acknowledgements

Maria Barrett is supported by a research grant (34437) from VILLUM FONDEN. Barbara Plank is in part supported by the Independent Research Fund Denmark (DFF) grant 9131-00019B. The Alexandra Institute is supported by the performance contract *"Digital sikkerhed, tillid og dataetik"* funded by the Danish Ministry of Higher Education and Science.

7 Bibliographical References

References

Thomas Bilgram and Britt Keson. 1998. The construction of a tagged Danish corpus. In *Proceedings of the 11th Nordic Conference of Computational Linguistics (NODALIDA 1998)*, pages 129–139, Copenhagen, Denmark. Center for Sprogteknologi, University of Copenhagen.

Matthias Buch-Kromann. 2003. The Danish Dependency Treebank and the DTAG treebank tool. In *2nd Workshop on Treebanks and Linguistic Theories (TLT)*, pages 217–220, Växjö, Sweden. Växjö University Press.

Alexis Conneau, Kartikay Khandelwal, Naman Goyal, Vishrav Chaudhary, Guillaume Wenzek, Francisco Guzmán, Edouard Grave, Myle Ott, Luke Zettlemoyer, and Veselin Stoyanov. 2020. Unsupervised cross-lingual representation learning at scale. In *Proceedings of the 58th Annual Meeting of the Association for Computational Linguistics*, pages 8440–8451, Online. Association for Computational Linguistics.

Jacob Devlin, Ming-Wei Chang, Kenton Lee, and Kristina Toutanova. 2019. BERT: Pre-training of deep bidirectional transformers for language understanding. In *Proceedings of the 2019 Conference of the North American Chapter of the Association for Computational Linguistics: Human Language Technologies, Volume 1 (Long and Short Papers)*, pages 4171–4186, Minneapolis, Minnesota. Association for Computational Linguistics.

Ana Valeria González, Maria Barrett, Rasmus Hvingelby, Kellie Webster, and Anders Søgaard. 2020. Type B reflexivization as an unambiguous testbed for multilingual multi-task gender bias. In *Proceedings of the 2020 Conference on Empirical Methods in Natural Language Processing (EMNLP)*, pages 2637–2648, Online. Association for Computational Linguistics.

Johannes Hoffart, Mohamed Amir Yosef, Ilaria Bordino, Hagen Fürstenau, Manfred Pinkal, Marc Spaniol, Bilyana Taneva, Stefan Thater, and Gerhard Weikum. 2011. Robust disambiguation of named entities in text. In *Proceedings of the 2011 Conference on Empirical Methods in Natural Language Processing*, pages 782–792, Edinburgh, Scotland, UK. Association for Computational Linguistics.

Michael J Houser, Line Mikkelsen, Maziar Toosarvandani, Erin Brainbridge, and Brian Agbayani. 2006. Verb phrase pronominalization in Danish: Deep or surface anaphora? In *Proceedings of the thirty-fourth Western Conference On Linguistics (WECOL)*, volume 17, Fresno, CA, US. California State University.

Rasmus Hvingelby, Amalie Brogaard Pauli, Maria Barrett, Christina Rosted, Lasse Malm Lidegaard, and Anders Søgaard. 2020. DaNE: A named entity resource for Danish. In *Proceedings of the 12th Language Resources and Evaluation Conference*, pages 4597–4604, Marseille, France. European Language Resources Association.

Anders Johannsen, Héctor Martínez Alonso, and Barbara Plank. 2015. Universal dependencies for Danish. In *International Workshop on Treebanks and Linguistic Theories (TLT14)*, pages 157–167, Warsaw, Poland. Institute of Computer Science, Polish Academy of Sciences.

Mandar Joshi, Omer Levy, Luke Zettlemoyer, and Daniel Weld. 2019. BERT for coreference resolution: Baselines and analysis. In *Proceedings of the 2019 Conference on Empirical Methods in Natural Language Processing and the 9th International Joint Conference on Natural Language Processing (EMNLP-IJCNLP)*, pages 5803–5808, Hong Kong, China. Association for Computational Linguistics.

Iørn Korzen and Matthias Buch-Kromann. 2011. Anaphoric relations in the Copenhagen Dependency Treebanks. In *Proceedings of DGfS Workshop – Göttingen, Germany*, pages 83–98, Bochum, Germany. Ruhr-Universität Bochum, Sprachwissenschaftliches Institut.

Kenton Lee, Luheng He, Mike Lewis, and Luke Zettlemoyer. 2017. End-to-end neural coreference resolution. In *Proceedings of the 2017 Conference on Empirical Methods in Natural Language Processing*, pages 188–197, Copenhagen, Denmark. Association for Computational Linguistics.

Kenton Lee, Luheng He, and Luke Zettlemoyer. 2018. Higher-order coreference resolution with coarse-to-fine inference. In *Proceedings of the 2018 Conference of the North American Chapter of the Association for Computational Linguistics: Human Language Technologies, Volume 2 (Short Papers)*, pages 687–692, New Orleans, Louisiana. Association for Computational Linguistics.

Paul McNamee, James Mayfield, Dawn Lawrie, Douglas W. Oard, and David Doermann. 2011. Cross-language entity linking. In *Proceedings of 5th International Joint Conference on Natural Language Processing*, pages 255–263, Chiang Mai, Thailand. Asian Federation of Natural Language Processing.

Isaiah Onando Mulang', Kuldeep Singh, Chaitali Prabhu, Abhishek Nadgeri, Johannes Hoffart, and Jens Lehmann. 2020. Evaluating the impact of knowledge graph context on entity disambiguation models. In *Proceedings of the 29th ACM International Conference on Information & Knowledge Management*, pages 2157–2160, Virtual event, Ireland. Association for Computing Machinery, NY, US.

Costanza Navarretta. 2000. Abstract anaphora resolution in Danish. In *1st SIGdial Workshop on Discourse and Dialogue*, pages 56–65, Hong Kong, China. Association for Computational Linguistics.

Joakim Nivre, Marie-Catherine de Marneffe, Filip Ginter, Jan Hajič, Christopher D. Manning, Sampo Pyysalo, Sebastian Schuster, Francis Tyers, and Daniel Zeman. 2020. Universal Dependencies v2: An evergrowing multilingual treebank collection. In *Proceedings of the 12th Language Resources and Evaluation Conference*, pages 4034–4043, Marseille, France. European Language Resources Association.

Xiaoman Pan, Boliang Zhang, Jonathan May, Joel Nothman, Kevin Knight, and Heng Ji. 2017. Cross-lingual name tagging and linking for 282 languages. In *Proceedings of the 55th Annual Meeting of the Association for Computational Linguistics (Volume 1: Long Papers)*, pages 1946–1958, Vancouver, Canada. Association for Computational Linguistics.

Barbara Plank. 2019. Neural cross-lingual transfer and limited annotated data for named entity recognition in Danish. In *Proceedings of the 22nd Nordic Conference on Computational Linguistics*, pages 370–375, Turku, Finland. Linköping University Electronic Press.

Barbara Plank, Kristian Nørgaard Jensen, and Rob van der Goot. 2020. DaN+: Danish nested named entities and lexical normalization. In *Proceedings of the 28th International Conference on Computational Linguistics*, pages 6649–6662, Barcelona, Spain (Online). International Committee on Computational Linguistics.

Denny Vrandečić. 2012. Wikidata: A new platform for collaborative data collection. In *Proceedings of the 21st international conference on world wide web*, pages 1063–1064, New York, NY, USA. Association for Computing Machinery.

Ralph Weischedel, Martha Palmer, Mitchell Marcus, Eduard Hovy, Sameer Pradhan, Lance Ramshaw, Nianwen Xue, Ann Taylor, Jeff Kaufman, Michelle Franchini, Mohammed El-Bachouti, Robert Belvin, and Ann Houston. 2013. OntoNotes release 5.0.

Fan Yang, Xiaochang Peng, Gargi Ghosh, Reshef Shilon, Hao Ma, Eider Moore, and Goran Predovic. 2019. Exploring deep multimodal fusion of text and photo for hate speech classification. In *Proceedings of the Third Workshop on Abusive Language Online*, pages 11–18, Florence, Italy. Association for Computational Linguistics.

A Tuning of coreference models

We tune the task learning rate (LR) and the transformer LR. Models are tuned individually using full grid search with early stopping for 50 epochs and a patience of 10 epochs. Tuned models are trained on the DACOREF train set, and the best settings are selected based on the DACOREF development set. Tuning the values with one step on the logarithmic scale hurt the model, so we tuned on smaller steps as outlined in Table 5.

The remaining parameters were kept fixed according to the original parameters. The development set was used both for early stopping and to select the best model. The criterion for model selection was the average F1 score over MUC, CEAF, and B3 F1 scores.

MODEL	TASK LR	TRANSFORMER LR
LEE2017	$\{9e{-}02, 1e{-}03, 2e{-}03\}$	$\{1e{-}05, 2e{-}05, 3e{-}05\}$
LEE2018	$\{2e{-}04, 3e{-}04, 4e{-}04\}$	$\{1e{-}05, 2e{-}05, 3e{-}05\}$

Table 5: Grid search parameters for tuning coreference models

B Generic QID's in entity linking annotation

Family name Q101352
Unisex nickname Q49614
Female given name Q11879590
Male given name Q12308941
Unisex name Q3409032
Artist name Q483501
Magazine Q41298
Hotel Q27686
Work of art Q838948
Governmental administrative unit in Denmark Q21268738
Municipal Police Q1758690
Road Q34442
Cohousing Q1107167
Postal address Q319608
Museum Q33506
Security (tradeable financial asset) Q169489
Geographic location Q2221906
Radio program Q1555508
Tv program Q15416
Product/goods Q2424752
Department within organisation Q2366457
Organization Q43229
Sports venue Q1076486
Dish Q746549 (only one instance)
Event Q1656682
Fleet Q189524
University Q3918
Disease Q12136
Coast Q93352
Ship Q11446
Award Q618779
Automobile model Q3231690
Project (also Inquiry) Q170584
Hospital Q16917
Amusement ride Q1144661
Sports team Q12973014
Building Q41176
Bill (proposed law) Q686822
Restaurant Q11707
People/ethnic group Q2472587
Educational institution Q2385804
Shop Q213441
Publication Q732577
Legislation Q49371
Night club Q622425
Newspaper Q11032
Prison Q40357
Army Q37726.

C Tuning of NED models

For training, we use the default settings from Mulang' et al. (2020) apart from the following values: train batch size, number of training epochs, LR, and warm-up ratio. Values are trained on the DANED train set, and the best models are selected based on the development set F1 score.

We tuned models using both pre-trained representations individually without any train set augmentation. The optimal hyperparameters are subsequently used for all models with this transformer architecture. During tuning, the models are trained with the following hyperparameters apart from the default settings: batch size of 8, for 1 epoch, the learning rate set to 4e-5, and the warm-up ratio set to 0.06. For hyperparameter tuning, we change one of the hyper-parameters from the default hyperparameter setting. Below are the tried values. The best value, which accidentally is the same for both transformer representations, is marked with bold:

- train batch size: **8**, 16
- num train epochs: 4, **8**
- learning rate: **4e-05**, 4e-06
- warmup ratio: **0.07**, 0.08, 0.1

CoreLM: Coreference-aware Language Model Fine-Tuning

Nikolaos Stylianou and **Ioannis Vlahavas**
Aristotle University of Thessaloniki
School of Informatics
Thessaloniki, Greece
{nstylia,vlahavas}@csd.auth.gr

Abstract

Language Models are the underpin of all modern Natural Language Processing (NLP) tasks. The introduction of the Transformers architecture has contributed significantly into making Language Modeling very effective across many NLP task, leading to significant advancements in the field. However, Transformers come with a big computational cost, which grows quadratically with respect to the input length. This presents a challenge as to understand long texts requires a lot of context. In this paper, we propose a Fine-Tuning framework, named CoreLM, that extends the architecture of current Pretrained Language Models so that they incorporate explicit entity information. By introducing entity representations, we make available information outside the contextual space of the model, which results in a better Language Model for a fraction of the computational cost. We implement our approach using GPT2 and compare the fine-tuned model to the original. Our proposed model achieves a lower Perplexity in GUMBY and LAMBDADA datasets when compared to GPT2 and a fine-tuned version of GPT2 without any changes. We also compare the models' performance in terms of Accuracy in LAMBADA and Children's Book Test, with and without the use of model-created coreference annotations.

1 Introduction

Language Models (LMs) have seen significant improvements in performance due to the Transformers architecture (Vaswani et al., 2017). The resulting Pretrained Language Models (PLMs) such as BERT (Devlin et al., 2019), GPT2 (Radford et al., 2019) and XLNet (Yang et al., 2019) have contributed to significant advancements in many Natural Language Processing (NLP) tasks. PLMs, regardless of their training objective and methodology, aim to learn contextualized text representations. As such, the available context during training has a key role in the models performance.

The quadratic computation complexity in the attention mechanism of the Transformer architecture, in terms of input sequence length, has been a limiting factor to the amount of contextual information the models can have at each step. To make this architecture more efficient, a plethora of approaches have been introduced (Kitaev et al., 2020; Beltagy et al., 2020; Child et al., 2019, *inter alia*), aiming to lower the computational complexity without sacrificing performance. Tay et al. (2020) summarizes these approaches and categorizes them based on type of attention mechanism in their survey. Yet, even with linear complexity, physical resources will always limit the amount of contextual information that can be handled simultaneously.

In terms of language, entities represent a natural way to tie words together through large pieces of discource. In NLP, Coreference Resolution is the task that aims to identify and group these entity mentions together, when they refer to the same real world entity (Stylianou and Vlahavas, 2021). Therefore, Coreference Resolution presents a natural way to link the context that we are currently handling with distant information, far outside the capabilities model architectures and current hardware resources. However, while this information is present in the text, it is usually not annotated and when annotated are very sparse and in small quantities making it extremely difficult to train large LMs (Kunz and Hardmeier, 2019).

In this paper we present a framework to effectively use coreference annotations to further fine-tune large PLMs, increasing their performance far more than just by fine-tuning on the same data. By using large PLMs we take advantage of existing resources that are expensive to reproduce and come with a big environmental cost (Strubell et al., 2019). What is more, fine-tuning takes advantage of the massive amount of data that essentially initialize the model, making it possible to introduce

Proceedings of the 4th Workshop on Computational Models of Reference, Anaphora and Coreference (CRAC 2021), pages 70–81
Punta Cana, Dominican Republic, November 10–11, 2021.

new capabilities to models with small amounts of annotated data.

In our approach, we use GPT2 as our base model and extend its architecture with the addition of a new Entity-Gating layer that handles entity annotations along with a gating mechanism that handles information flow between the base model and the Entity-Gating layer. As such, our approach uses entity representations when they are available through both training and inference, without imposing any constraints to the model's functionality.

For our experiments, we compare the performance of GPT2, post and pre fine-tuning, with and without our changes in a series of relative tasks. Furthermore, since most coreference annotated datasets are either very small or hard to acquire, we use GUMBY (Gessler et al., 2020) as our fine-tuning dataset which is a model annotated corpus. In addition, by using noisy annotations we aim to show the resilience of our approach to noise and the universality of our framework. Our results highlight the effects of our framework in language modeling, modeling long-range dependencies, and in specific word types where our fine-tuned model achieves better performance than GPT2.

2 Background

This section provides a concise overview of the Transformers architecture (Vaswani et al., 2017), which is the foundation of our approach, followed by a brief explanation of autoregressive language modeling used by our base model, GPT2.

2.1 Transformers

The Transformers architecture is based on stacked Transformer blocks, which take as input a $k \times d$ input vector and return a same size vector after applying a sequence of operations, where k and d denote the context window size and hidden size respectively. Each block is consisted of a multi-head masked self attention layer and a two layer position-wise feed-forward network, each rapped with a layer normalization (`LayerNorm`) layer (Ba et al., 2016) and a residual connection (He et al., 2016). Formally, given an input X the encoder and decoder architecture is described as:

`Encoder:`

$$\begin{aligned} Y &= \texttt{LayerNorm}(\texttt{Self-Attention}(X)) + X \\ Z &= \texttt{LayerNorm}(\texttt{PositionFFN}(Y)) + Y \end{aligned} \tag{1}$$

`Decoder:`

$$\begin{aligned} T &= \texttt{LayerNorm}(\texttt{Self-Attention}(T)) + T \\ P &= \texttt{LayerNorm}(\texttt{Self-Attention}(T,Z)) + T \\ H &= \texttt{LayerNorm}(\texttt{PositionFFN}(P)) + P \end{aligned} \tag{2}$$

However, the decoder can also be used independently by eliminating the second Self-Attention layer.

Self-Attention: The self-attention mechanism takes as input a vector X and projects it into Q, K, V representations for the Query, Key, Value attention scheme. Using the projected vector, this mechanism is formalized as:

$$\texttt{Self-Attention} = \texttt{softmax}(\frac{QK}{\sqrt{d}})V \tag{3}$$

where d is the size of the Q, K, V vectors. Usually the self-attention is multi-headed, in which multiple attentions are calculated in parallel, with the outputs of the multi-headed attentions being concatenated.

PositionFFN: Given an input vector X, this layer applies two position-wise linear transformations with a ReLU activation in between. The PositionFFN layer is formalized as:

$$\texttt{PositionFFN} = max(0, XW_1 + b_1)W_2 + b_2 \tag{4}$$

with W_1, b_1 and W_2, b_2 being the trainable weight and bias parameters of each layer respectively.

2.2 Autoregressive Language Modeling

Autoregressive language models estimate the distribution over a sequence of word tokens by factorizing their joint probabilities as the product of conditional probabilities (Bengio et al., 2003). For a context vector of tokens $U = (u_1, \ldots, u_k)$, this is formally described as:

$$p(U) = \prod_{i=1}^{k} p(u_k | u_1, \ldots, u_{k-1}) \tag{5}$$

where, k is the context window size.

GPT2 is an autoregressive LM, based on the previously described Transformer's decoder architecture. In comparison to the previously described architecture, it uses masked multi-headed attention to prevent leftward information flow in the decoder. For further information about the model's architecture we refer readers to Radford et al. (2019).

3 Coreference-aware Language Modeling

Language models are limited to the amount of information they can process based on the available context window k (eq. (5)). However, increasing k will lead to an exponential increase in computation complexity. As such, we implicitly increase the available information, without increase the context window, using coreference annotations.

We do this by introducing entity-representations (§3.2), in the form of vectors, that are utilized by the model to infuse the respective entity information to all the tokens in the sequence that are part of entities. The entity-representations are created from the whole discourse available, hence holding contextual information that are very distant to the context window. As such, we make no alterations to the language modeling objective. These vector representations are introduced to the model via an Entity-Gating layer (§3.3) that is added to model architecture.

3.1 Architecture

Our base model, GPT2, is comprised of N stacked Transformer decoder blocks, where each is consisted of a multi-headed attention layer and a position-wise feedforward layer with residual connections and layer normalizations. We extend its architecture by adding an Entity-Gating layer after the Transformer decoders (eqs. (6) to (9)).

$$h_0 = UW_e + W_p \tag{6}$$

$$h_l = \texttt{transformer\_decoder}(h_{l-1}) \forall_i \in [1,n] \tag{7}$$

$$h_e = \texttt{entity\_gating}(h_n, E) \tag{8}$$

$$p(U) = \texttt{softmax}(h_e W_e^T) \tag{9}$$

Here, n is the number of layers, W_e is the token embedding matrix, W_p is the position embedding matrix and E is the context vector of entity representations. Figure 1 illustrates a high level view of the model of our proposed architecture.

3.2 Entity representations

Each entity is represented by a learned vector $E_i \in \mathbb{R}^{1 \times d_{embd}}$, where d_{embd} is the embedding dimension of the model (W_e). These entity vectors are stored

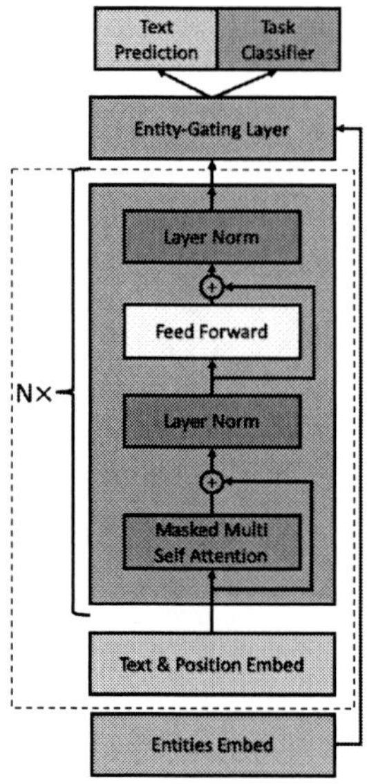

Figure 1: CoreLM Architecture as an extention of GPT2 model (area within dashed border).

in a persistent set of entities $\mathcal{E}$ so that they can be utilized through out the whole discourse scope. We use E_0 as a static entity representation for tokens that are not part of an entity.

The entity representations are initialized as a vector of ones. This design choice is based on the architecture of the Entity-Gating layer (§3.3) and the learning process. Specifically, as each token is accompanied with an entity representation. Initializing the entity representations this way introduces less noise during the first occurrence of an entity mention. It also provides a dynamic way of using the same architecture, even when no entity are available.

3.3 Entity-Gating

Our proposed Entity-Gating layer (Figure 2) follows the same design principles of the GPT2 Transformer decoder blocks, using a Multi-Headed Attention layer, Layer Normalization layers and residual connections. However, we replace the Masked Multi-Head Self Attention layer with an Entity-Attention layer and use a learnable gating mechanism to control flow of information. Formally, the Entity-Gating layer is described as:

$$EG_A = \texttt{LayerNorm}(\texttt{EntityAttention}(h_l)) + h_l \tag{10}$$

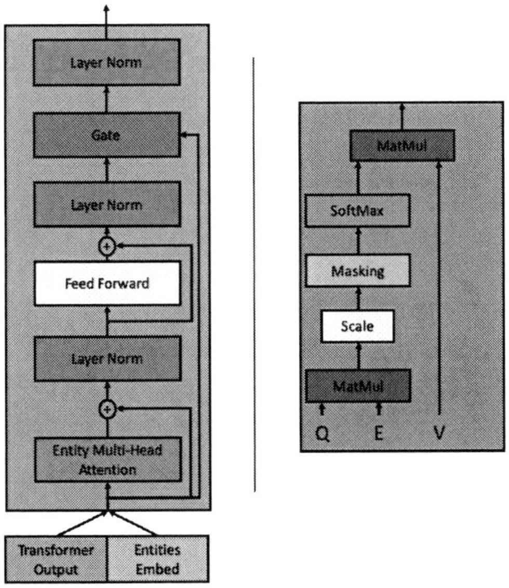

Figure 2: (left) Entity-Gating layer architecture. **(right)** Entity-Attention mechanism. In the illustration, we assume a single attention head for simplicity.

$$EG_B = \texttt{LayerNorm}(\texttt{PositionFFN}(EG_A)) + EG_A \tag{11}$$

$$h_e = \texttt{LayerNorm}(\texttt{Gate}(EG_B, h_l)) \tag{12}$$

The `LayerNorm` and `PositionFFN` are used as described in Section 2.1, from the original architecture.

Our `EntityAttention` layer uses the Query (Q), Entity (E), Value (V) scheme described in eq. (13) (Stylianou and Vlahavas, 2020). In comparison to their variation, we use a multi-headed approach so that we limit the effect of entity representation to the tokens closer to the entity mention. As such, the attention mechanism is defined as:

$$EntityAttention = \texttt{Softmax}(\frac{QE}{\sqrt{d_k}})V \tag{13}$$

where d_k is the dimension of the queries and entities in each head. Finally, the `Gate` layer combines the layer input h_l with EG_B using the following gating mechanism before applying a layer normalization to the output:

$$g_e = \delta(\sigma(Vh_l)) \tag{14}$$

$$z_e = (1 - g_e) \odot EG_B + g_e \odot h_l \tag{15}$$

in which σ is a sigmoid function, V is a parameter vector, $\odot$ is the Hadamard product and δ is a gate flow rate. We use a gate flow rate to ensure that the entity information is considered by our final model. By definition, $\delta \to 0$ results in no pass-through of information from the gate, $\delta \to 1$ results in completely dependent pass-through from the learned vector and $\delta \to 0.5$ enforces at least a fifty-fifty split of information.

4 Experiments

We Fine-Tune our entity-aware LM with the original training objective of maximizing the log-probability of U (eq. (5)). Language Models are evaluated in terms of Perplexity (PPL) which is the exponentiated average negative log probability per word prediction, as we are using a word-level base model. As such, PPL is a direct reflection of the model's loss. For Fine-Tuning we use GUMBY, a model annotated coreference corpus, containing 4960 documents.

The entity-aware fine-tuned LM is evaluated on GUMBY, using the created entity representations during Fine-Tuning and in a Zero-Shot setting, without any further training, on LAMBADA, WikiText2, WikiText103 in terms of PPL and on LAMBADA and CBT in terms of Accuracy. We also evaluate the effect of newly introduced entity annotations from a separate Coreference Resolution model on the Zero-Shot evaluated corpora, to investigate their effect in the model's performance. Detail information about the model parameters and experimental setup are provided in Appendix A. Appendix B enlists our methodology to annotate the LAMBADA and CBT corpora with coreference clusters, used in Zero-Shot evaluation only.

4.1 Fine-Tuning

In order to fine-tune the model, using the annotated entity information in the GUMBY corpus (Gessler et al., 2020), we re-formatted it by introducing a second input stream along the raw text, which assigns a unique entity identifier in the corresponding token in the text (Stylianou and Vlahavas, 2020).

We similarly use $\varnothing$ to identify tokens that are not part of an entity. However, in order to utilize the encapsulated entity information present, we create multiple instances of the source files each annotated with a single layer of entity annotations. This comes in comparison with their approach in which only the outer entities are considered. We

Table 1: Language Modeling performance evaluation on fine-tuning and zero-shot setting. The fine-tuned models are trained only on GUMBY and evaluated on LAMBADA, WikiText2 and WikiText103 test sets.

	GUMBY (PPL)	LAMBADA (PPL)	WikiText2 (PPL)	WikiText103 (PPL)
GPT2 Zero-Shot	66.19	26.49	**30.63**	35.81
GPT2 +Fine-Tuning	52.60	28.93	32.36	35.53
GPT2 +CoreLM +Fine-Tuning	**46.97**	**26.21**	31.80	**29.51**

treat all entities as encapsulated entities, so that the second instance of the source file is only annotated with the entities that were identified within the span of text of first entity layer (example in Appendix A - Table 3). As a result, our final data was consisted of 13070 documents, which is approximately triple the original size. As the original corpus does not provide with predefined split, we held out 10% of the data for evaluation while maintaining the balance between source types.

The fine-tuned model is compared against the base model (GPT2) and a fine-tuned version of the base model without any entity information, on the held out data of GUMBY. As shown in Table 1 our approach significantly improves the model's performance after fine-tuning compared to the original model.

4.2 Language Modeling

For the Language Modeling evaluation we use WikiText2, WikiText103 (Merity et al., 2016) and LAMBADA (Paperno et al., 2016) in a Zero-Shot evaluation setting. We compare the previously fine-tuned entity-aware LM with the base-model, with and without any Fine-Tuning on GUMBY. The results are showcased in Table 1.

We notice that fine-tuning GPT2 with GUMBY does not generalize well in other domains, leading in a significant drop in performance in both LAMBADA and WikiText2. In WikiText103, in which the unknown words are proper names, the fine-tuned version performs better. With CoreLM, our model avoids catastrophic forgetting and presents similar performance gains in all corpora, resulting in a slight improvement in LAMBADA and WikiText103 and a slight impairment in WikiText2 compared to the base model.

4.3 LAMBADA

The LAMBADA corpus is used to evaluate our approach, in a Zero-shot setting. LAMBADA is designed to test the model's ability to use long range dependencies in text. Long range dependency, in this context, is consider to be a context window of 50 tokens, which the architecture can handle due to the 1024 token window context. During evaluation, we use use model acquired coreference annotation to the corpus, using a pretrained model Coreference Resolution model (Appendix B). Hence, we also evaluate the effect of coreferent information.

Without Coreference: Comparing the model's performance to GPT2, our approach achieves increased Accuracy in correctly predicting the last word, with scores 46.67% for GPT2 and 48.11% for CoreLM (statistically significant with paired t-test $p << 0.01$ - Table 2). This increase in performance is slightly bigger if we compare it to the fine-tuned GPT2 model on GUMBY.

With Coreference: Coreference annotations offer a slight increase in performance, with 0.28% Accuracy increase compared to the CoreLM version without coreference annotations. While this increase is not a statistically significant contribution, it is an expected behavior given that the entity representations were initialized during the zero-shot evalutation (Appendix B). Furthermore, the context of each of LAMBADA entries is well inside the capabilities of the GPT2 model architecture and consequently the coreference annotations did not provide any information that were not already accessible by the model.

4.4 Children's Book Test

The Children's Book Test (CBT) (Hill et al., 2016) was designed to evaluate LMs in different word cat-

Table 2: Zero-Shot evaluation on LAMBADA and Children's Book Test (CBT) with and without coreference annotations.

	LAMBADA (Acc)	CBT-CN (Acc)	CBT-NE (Acc)	CBT-V (Acc)	CBT-P (Acc)
GPT2 Zero-Shot	46.67	**84.48**	64.52	92.24	91.00
GPT2 +Fine-Tuning	46.63	84.02	64.24	92.04	90.80
GPT2 +CoreLM +Fine-Tuning	48.11	84.16	64.48	**92.40**	90.88
GPT2 +CoreLM +Fine-Tuning +Coref	**48.39**	84.16	**64.56**	**92.40**	**91.97**

egories. In comparison to GPT2, we report scores in all categories, i.e. Common Nouns (CN), Named Entities (NE), Verbs (V) and Prepositions (P). CBT is designed as a cloze test, in which a hidden word should be predicted, given ten possible options. We formulate this task as a language modeling task, similar to Radford et al. (2019), in which we condition the sentence with each option and calculate its probability, choosing the one with the highest probability as the final prediction. Similarly to LAMBADA, we use a pretrained Coreference Resolution model to annotate the corpus with newly initialized entity mentions.

Table 2 shows the results in terms of Accuracy with and without the use of coreference annotations.

Without Coreference: Comparing the base model, with a fine-tuned version of the base model and CoreLM, it becomes obvious that the GUMBY does not generalize well with CBT. As a result, we note a drop in performance by just fine-tuning the model in all word categories. However, the CoreLM fine-tuned version results in better performance compared to the GPT2 fine-tuned model, with insignificant differences from the base model in almost all categories, with the exceptions of Verbs in which we notice a slightly better Accuracy.

With Coreference: Including coreference annotation to the CoreLM model results in small changes in performance in all categories. Specifically, there is no gain in performance when using entities in CN corpus variant. However, in the NE variant we achieve a 0.16% increase. This very small increase is because in the majority of the cases, the cloze test answers are similar to the surface forms of the entities as found in the context and as such the correlation is very easy for model to make without the need of extra information. For the V variant of the corpus, there is no change to the performance while using coreference annotations as expected, while for the P variant, there is a increase of 1.09% (statistically significant with t-test $p < 0.01$). This increase in prepositions is attributed to the accurate resolution of the nouns as mentions of entities that changed their representations.

The performance changes, while using coreference annotation are indicative of the impact of entity representations in CoreLM. As our base model is capable of contextualizing each entry in CBT due to it's context window, we expect these improvements to be bigger in corpora which the information outside the context window of the model is required.

5 Error Analysis

In our experiments, we showcased the effects of CoreLM on the base model, in different scenarios. In this section we investigate the cases in which the base model performed better than the CoreLM model and vice-versa. For that reason, we manually compared the predictions made between the two models, using the GUMBY Fine-Tuned GPT2 model as the deciding factor in our observations between the effects of CoreLM Fine-Tuning and simple Fine-Tuning. We limit our analysis on the

CBT corpus which provides a meaningful way to evaluate the changes due to its word category variants.

In our analysis, we noticed that fine-tuning on GUMBY lead to wrong choices by the model in all categories, which were not made by the GPT2. However, when CoreLM was used with coreference annotations, 83% of those cases were corrected. The vast majority of the corrected cases were in the Prepositions and Named Entities word categories, with only 19% of the corrected ones in Verbs and Common Noun word categories. A positive correlation between corrected cases and correct coreference annotations was noticed, as cases in which CoreLM persisted on the wrong option also had different coreferent annotations than the correct sentence.

In the cases where CoreLM performed better than both the fine-tuned and base model, we noticed the same correlation between coreference annotations that directly affected the available options. Unavailingly, a small number of cases in which, the nouns following a preposition or the Named Entities themselves were annotated in a wrong coreference cluster, lead to different probability distributions for the available options and eventually to making the wrong selection. Furthermore, comparing the predictions made by CoreLM with and without the use of coreference annotations, we notice that the majority of the errors persisted when the option was not directly annotated in a coreference cluster.

6 Discussion

Our approach takes advantage of PLMs and increases their performance by exploiting distant contextual information in the form of entity representations using coreference annotations. What is more, it can be used with and without the existence of such information, hence not hindering the flexibility of PLMs. Our experiements when Fine-Tuning GPT2 and the GPT2 with CoreLM on the same data, without using coreference information show that even when the fine-tuning data are not best suited for the downstream tasks, CoreLM maintains more of the original model's performance, making it a more resilient Fine-Tuning methodology. In addition, as CoreLM is very modular, it can be applied to the majority of LMs, including non-autoregressive approaches such as BERT.

In Language Modeling, our approach achieved significantly lower Perplexity in all corpora compared to the GPT2 Fine-Tuned version. What is more, GUMBY proved to be an ill-suited corpus to fine-tune for both LAMBADA and WikiText based on the post Fine-Tuning performance. Regardless, Fine-Tuning with CoreLM demonstrated significant gains, even compared to the pre Fine-Tuned model.

In both LAMBADA and CBT, we show increase in Accuracy compared to GPT2 pre and post Fine-Tuning. Most notably, the Named Entity and Prepositions word types showed the biggest increase in CBT, with Common Nouns suffering in comparison compared to the pre Fine-Tuned version and Verbs attaining a slightly better Accuracy. Our error analysis highlights the effect of coreference annotations to these changes in performance. In all cases, Fine-Tuned GPT2 achieved lower scores in all word categories compared to CoreLM Fine-Tuned, which indicated that GUMBY is not a suitable fine-tuning corpus for these tasks.

Using model-created coreference annotations during Zero-Shot evaluation did increase the performance slightly. While the performance increase is minor, the entity representations used were only initialized from the scope of each example as there was not long contextual information to take advantage off. What is more, coreference annotations increased the performance regardless of the information being within the context window in all the examples, indicating that further gains can be achieved by using coreference annotations extensively over large pieces of discourse.

Unavailingly, our approach is based on the ability of other models to accurately predict coreference clusters so that CoreLM can exploit the coreferent mentions. The errors in the predicted clusters introduce noise, to both entity representations and the final model. What is more, maintaining a persistent set of entity representations, is computationally expensive and can be very burdening when considering a large collection of documents. As a result, an entity management mechanism, similar to the one used in Toshniwal et al. (2020), would be required for CoreLM to scale efficiently to bigger document collections.

7 Related Work

Early entity-aware LMs were trained from scratch with entity information available through the training process. Specifically, Yang et al. (2017) and Ji et al. (2017) both introduced models that used reference information with attention-based mechanisms to incorporate them into the model. Yang et al.'s (2017) model made use of both intra-linguistic, coreferring mentions in text, and extra-linguistic, tables and lists, features through three different components, only creating learnable embeddings for intra-linguistic features. Ji et al.'s (2017) model was focused only on intra-linguistic mentions, i.e. corefererring mentions, and introduced additional control variables indicating if the next token is part of an entity as well as the number of remaining entity tokens. Recently, Kunz and Hardmeier (2019) extended Yang et al.'s (2017) approach by using learnable entity embeddings. These approaches also have the ability to autoregressively predict the entity of the following word and constrain the word generation to a specific entity.

EnGen combines EntityNLM (Ji et al., 2017) with S2SA (Sutskever et al., 2014), to train a generative language model that uses both previous sentence representations and entity representations in order to generate coherent text (Clark et al., 2018). In comparison to their approach, our approach handles entities and information flow differently. Stylianou and Vlahavas (2020) also introduced a Transformer-based approach towards incorporating learnable entity representations, using multi-head attentions inside all the Transformer blocks of the model. In comparison to past approaches, this approach was only focused on the effective use of entity information in a LM and did not predict the following entity information. However, all of these models required high quality annotated data to be trained from scratch which were limited and of specific genre (Kunz and Hardmeier, 2019; Stylianou and Vlahavas, 2020).

Other methods have focused on using only extra-linguistic information, ignoring pronouns and nominal mentions in text. ERNIE (Zhang et al., 2019) uses Knowledge Graphs (KG) to extract entities for identified named entities. However, ERNIE represents entity information using a pre-trained knowledge embedding model, trained on the used KG, and does not create dynamic entity representations. Liu et al. (2019) use Knowledge Bases to learn word type embeddings based on the learned type representations. Similar to past approaches (Ji et al., 2017; Kunz and Hardmeier, 2019) it can autoregressively constrain the prediction to a certain entity type. The type information is restricted using pre-defined vocabularies making the model less dynamic in its entity predictions. Both approaches have been found to be very effective for the tasks that were respectively designed, however they lack in expandability of their domain of application without requiring complete retraining.

8 Conclusions and Future Work

In this paper we presented CoreLM, a modular Fine-Tuning framework for PLMs to exploit model-created coreference annotations in order to create better mention representations and an overall better LM. In our experiments we showcased a performance increase when evaluating in a zero-shot setting, compared to the similarly fine-tuned model, even when the fine-tuning corpus did not generalize well to the end tasks. Our analysis shows that coreference annotations play a significant role in both Fine-Tuning and in downstream task performance, with correct annotations leading to better performance when used.

In addition, our work helps in adding a new frontier to Coreference Resolution through the effective use of coreference annotations in Language Modeling. In this paper we showcased the effects of coreference annotation even when the information is within the context window of the model. Using coreference annotations can further lead to the decrease of the required context window and boost approaches like Shortformer (Press et al., 2020), leading to better and more efficient LMs.

In the future we aim to create a more efficient approach to LM through the use of both intra-linguistic (Coreference) and extra-linguistic (KG) features. Undeniably, KGs provide a means for structured, high quality information that cannot be found in a single text. We believe that an information fusion from coreference annotation and graph nodes, along with short context window will not be computationally prohibitive and lead in better, information rich, LMs.

Acknowledgements

This research is co-financed by Greece and the European Union (European Social Fund - ESF) through the Operational Programme "Human Resources Development, Education and Lifelong Learning" in the context of the project "Strengthening Human Resources Research Potential via Doctorate Research" (MIS-5000432), implemented by the State Scholarships Foundation (IKY).

References

Jimmy Lei Ba, Jamie Ryan Kiros, and Geoffrey E Hinton. 2016. Layer normalization. *arXiv preprint arXiv:1607.06450*.

Iz Beltagy, Matthew E. Peters, and Arman Cohan. 2020. Longformer: The long-document transformer. *arXiv:2004.05150*.

Yoshua Bengio, Réjean Ducharme, Pascal Vincent, and Christian Janvin. 2003. A neural probabilistic language model. *The journal of machine learning research*, 3:1137–1155.

Rewon Child, Scott Gray, Alec Radford, and Ilya Sutskever. 2019. Generating long sequences with sparse transformers. *arXiv preprint arXiv:1904.10509*.

Elizabeth Clark, Yangfeng Ji, and Noah A. Smith. 2018. Neural text generation in stories using entity representations as context. In *Proceedings of the 2018 Conference of the North American Chapter of the Association for Computational Linguistics: Human Language Technologies, Volume 1 (Long Papers)*, pages 2250–2260, New Orleans, Louisiana. Association for Computational Linguistics.

Jacob Devlin, Ming-Wei Chang, Kenton Lee, and Kristina Toutanova. 2019. BERT: Pre-training of deep bidirectional transformers for language understanding. In *Proceedings of the 2019 Conference of the North American Chapter of the Association for Computational Linguistics: Human Language Technologies, Volume 1 (Long and Short Papers)*, pages 4171–4186, Minneapolis, Minnesota. Association for Computational Linguistics.

Luke Gessler, Siyao Peng, Yang Liu, Yilun Zhu, Shabnam Behzad, and Amir Zeldes. 2020. Gumby–a free, balanced, and rich english web corpus. In *Proceedings of The 12th Language Resources and Evaluation Conference*, pages 5267–5275.

Kaiming He, Xiangyu Zhang, Shaoqing Ren, and Jian Sun. 2016. Deep residual learning for image recognition. In *Proceedings of the IEEE conference on computer vision and pattern recognition*, pages 770–778.

Felix Hill, Antoine Bordes, Sumit Chopra, and Jason Weston. 2016. The goldilocks principle: Reading children's books with explicit memory representations. In *4th International Conference on Learning Representations, ICLR 2016, San Juan, Puerto Rico, May 2-4, 2016, Conference Track Proceedings*.

Yangfeng Ji, Chenhao Tan, Sebastian Martschat, Yejin Choi, and Noah A. Smith. 2017. Dynamic entity representations in neural language models. In *Proceedings of the 2017 Conference on Empirical Methods in Natural Language Processing*, pages 1830–1839, Copenhagen, Denmark. Association for Computational Linguistics.

Nikita Kitaev, Łukasz Kaiser, and Anselm Levskaya. 2020. Reformer: The efficient transformer. *arXiv preprint arXiv:2001.04451*.

Jenny Kunz and Christian Hardmeier. 2019. Entity decisions in neural language modelling: Approaches and problems. In *Proceedings of the Second Workshop on Computational Models of Reference, Anaphora and Coreference*, pages 15–19, Minneapolis, USA. Association for Computational Linguistics.

Angli Liu, Jingfei Du, and Veselin Stoyanov. 2019. Knowledge-augmented language model and its application to unsupervised named-entity recognition. In *Proceedings of the 2019 Conference of the North American Chapter of the Association for Computational Linguistics: Human Language Technologies, Volume 1 (Long and Short Papers)*, pages 1142–1150, Minneapolis, Minnesota. Association for Computational Linguistics.

Liyuan Liu, Haoming Jiang, Pengcheng He, Weizhu Chen, Xiaodong Liu, Jianfeng Gao, and Jiawei Han. 2020. On the variance of the adaptive learning rate and beyond. In *International Conference on Learning Representations*.

Stephen Merity, Caiming Xiong, James Bradbury, and Richard Socher. 2016. Pointer sentinel mixture models. *arXiv preprint arXiv:1609.07843*.

Denis Paperno, Germán Kruszewski, Angeliki Lazaridou, Ngoc Quan Pham, Raffaella Bernardi, Sandro Pezzelle, Marco Baroni, Gemma Boleda, and Raquel Fernández. 2016. The LAMBADA dataset: Word prediction requiring a broad discourse context. In *Proceedings of the 54th Annual Meeting of the Association for Computational Linguistics (Volume 1: Long Papers)*, pages 1525–1534, Berlin, Germany. Association for Computational Linguistics.

Ofir Press, Noah A Smith, and Mike Lewis. 2020. Shortformer: Better language modeling using shorter inputs. *arXiv preprint arXiv:2012.15832*.

Alec Radford, Jeffrey Wu, Rewon Child, David Luan, Dario Amodei, and Ilya Sutskever. 2019. Language models are unsupervised multitask learners. *OpenAI blog*, 1(8):9.

Samyam Rajbhandari, Jeff Rasley, Olatunji Ruwase, and Yuxiong He. 2020. Zero: Memory optimizations toward training trillion parameter models. In *Proceedings of the International Conference for High Performance Computing, Networking, Storage and Analysis*, SC '20. IEEE Press.

Jeff Rasley, Samyam Rajbhandari, Olatunji Ruwase, and Yuxiong He. 2020. Deepspeed: System optimizations enable training deep learning models with over 100 billion parameters. In *Proceedings of the 26th ACM SIGKDD International Conference on Knowledge Discovery & Data Mining*, KDD '20, page 3505–3506, New York, NY, USA. Association for Computing Machinery.

Rico Sennrich, Barry Haddow, and Alexandra Birch. 2016. Neural machine translation of rare words with subword units. In *Proceedings of the 54th Annual Meeting of the Association for Computational Linguistics (Volume 1: Long Papers)*, pages 1715–1725, Berlin, Germany. Association for Computational Linguistics.

Emma Strubell, Ananya Ganesh, and Andrew McCallum. 2019. Energy and policy considerations for deep learning in NLP. In *Proceedings of the 57th Annual Meeting of the Association for Computational Linguistics*, pages 3645–3650, Florence, Italy. Association for Computational Linguistics.

Nikolaos Stylianou and Ioannis Vlahavas. 2020. E.T.: Entity-transformers. coreference augmented neural language model for richer mention representations via entity-transformer blocks. In *Proceedings of the Third Workshop on Computational Models of Reference, Anaphora and Coreference*, pages 1–10, Barcelona, Spain (online). Association for Computational Linguistics.

Nikolaos Stylianou and Ioannis Vlahavas. 2021. A neural entity coreference resolution review. *Expert Systems with Applications*, 168:114466.

Ilya Sutskever, Oriol Vinyals, and Quoc V Le. 2014. Sequence to sequence learning with neural networks. In *Advances in neural information processing systems*, pages 3104–3112.

Yi Tay, Mostafa Dehghani, Dara Bahri, and Donald Metzler. 2020. Efficient transformers: A survey. *arXiv preprint arXiv:2009.06732*.

Shubham Toshniwal, Sam Wiseman, Allyson Ettinger, Karen Livescu, and Kevin Gimpel. 2020. Learning to Ignore: Long Document Coreference with Bounded Memory Neural Networks. In *Proceedings of the 2020 Conference on Empirical Methods in Natural Language Processing (EMNLP)*, pages 8519–8526, Online. Association for Computational Linguistics.

Ashish Vaswani, Noam Shazeer, Niki Parmar, Jakob Uszkoreit, Llion Jones, Aidan N Gomez, Ł ukasz Kaiser, and Illia Polosukhin. 2017. Attention is all you need. In *Advances in Neural Information Processing Systems*, volume 30. Curran Associates, Inc.

Zhilin Yang, Zihang Dai, Yiming Yang, Jaime Carbonell, Russ R Salakhutdinov, and Quoc V Le. 2019. Xlnet: Generalized autoregressive pretraining for language understanding. In *Advances in Neural Information Processing Systems*, volume 32. Curran Associates, Inc.

Zichao Yang, Phil Blunsom, Chris Dyer, and Wang Ling. 2017. Reference-aware language models. In *Proceedings of the 2017 Conference on Empirical Methods in Natural Language Processing*, pages 1850–1859, Copenhagen, Denmark. Association for Computational Linguistics.

Zhengyan Zhang, Xu Han, Zhiyuan Liu, Xin Jiang, Maosong Sun, and Qun Liu. 2019. ERNIE: Enhanced language representation with informative entities. In *Proceedings of the 57th Annual Meeting of the Association for Computational Linguistics*, pages 1441–1451, Florence, Italy. Association for Computational Linguistics.

Table 3: Data example from the GUMBY corpus, as formatted for the task. Other corpora are similarly formatted, with multiple rows of entity annotation when coreference information were needed.

$X_{1:12}$	The	prime	minister	of	Israel	,	Binyamin	Netanyahu	,	told	a	news
$E_{1:12}$	11	11	11	11	11	∅	11	11	∅	∅	13	13
$E_{1:12}$	∅	∅	∅	∅	7	∅	∅	∅	∅	∅	∅	∅

A Experimental Setup

In all our experiments we use the GPT2-small configuration with 124M parameters, with 12 layers and 12 attention heads each for our base model. We add one Entity-Gating layer after the base model's Transformer layers, which has a masked multi-headed entity attention layer with 12 heads and a 10% dropout between layers. The gate flow rate (δ) is set to 0.5. These hyperparameters were found to perform best from [6, 8, 10, 12, 16] number of heads and [0.2, 0.5, 0.7, 1] gate flow rate (δ) after manual tuning.

All datasets are tokenized using the pre-trained GPT2 tokenizer, which uses Byte Pair Encoding (BPE) (Sennrich et al., 2016). We also apply a simple de-tokenization based on author's responses in the official GitHub repository as the exact de-tokenizer used to achieve the published results has not been made available.[1] We use the OpenAI LAMBADA split for evaluation and remove the The Jungle Book by Rudyard Kipling from CBT as it was found to be part of the GPT2 original training set (Radford et al., 2019). As such, all scores are based on our own experiments and in some cases vary (both positively and negatively) from the reported scores.

Our model has 132M parameters, a 6% increase, after the addition of the Entity-Gating layer and the entity representations. It is fine-tuned on the GUMBY corpus for 10 epochs, with a batch size of 128. Rectified Adam (Liu et al., 2020) was used as the optimizer with 100 steps of warm up and a linearly decaying learning rate with a starting value of 1e-5. During Fine-Tuning, the entity representations are updated after every training step. We freeze all 12 GPT2 Transformer layers and apply gradients only to the input layers (W_e and W_p), output layers (the language modeling head) and the Entity-Gating layer. During Zero-Shot evaluation we do not use any entity information and as such we discard the persistent entity representations.

All experiments were run on a single Titan V 12GB graphics card, using half precision floating-point format, Zero Stage 2 optimization (Rajbhandari et al., 2020) and DeepSpeed (Rasley et al., 2020). In this setup, fine-tuning takes approximately 8 hours, with no noticeable differences in terms of inference speed compared to GPT2.

[1] https://github.com/openai/gpt-2/issues/131

B Coreference Annotations

The vast majority of the datasets do not come with coreference annotations, a process which is very expensive and time consuming if it was to be done by human annotators. The same issue rises from the use of free text from web sources. In order to fully exploit our proposed framework, we uses the pre-trained Coreference Resolution model by Toshniwal et al. (2020) to create noisy coreference annotations for LAMBADA and Children's Book Test (CBT) corpora.

Our approach does not have an entity-linking component with which the originally identified entities from the GUMBY corpus could be linked with newly identified entities in the other corpora. As such, the persistent entity representation used in the original GUMBY corpus were reset for each corpora. Hence, the resulting entity representation are not as descriptive as the GUMBY created ones as, there was little context involved and we only used the corpora for zero-shot evaluation, not allowing for iteratively creating richer entity representations.

LAMBADA: No major preprocessing was required for the LAMBADA dataset. We did treat each entry in the dataset as a new document so that coreference annotations did not point to entities on other unrelated entities. The resulted entity representation were created as an average of the hidden representation of all the entity mention in that entry (§3.2), excluding the last word and its entity annotation which were to be predicted.

Children's Book Test: For CBT, we first formulated the corpus to fit our Language Modeling approach (§4.4), conditioning each choice with one of 10 possible candidates and annotating the document as if the candidate was the answer in the cloze test. During evaluation, we predicted coreference clusters for the context conditioned with all possible candidate choices.

Data Augmentation Methods for Anaphoric Zero Pronouns

Abdulrahman Aloraini[1,2], **Massimo Poesio**[1]
[1]Queen Mary University of London, United Kingdom
[2]Qassim University, Saudi Arabia
{a.aloraini, m.poesio}@qmul.ac.uk

Abstract

In pro-drop language like Arabic, Chinese, Italian, Japanese, Spanish, and many others, unrealized (null) arguments in certain syntactic positions can refer to a previously introduced entity, and are thus called anaphoric zero pronouns. The existing resources for studying anaphoric zero pronoun interpretation are however still limited. In this paper, we use five data augmentation methods to generate and detect anaphoric zero pronouns automatically. We use the augmented data as additional training materials for two anaphoric zero pronoun systems for Arabic. Our experimental results show that data augmentation improves the performance of the two systems, surpassing the state-of-the-art results.

1 Introduction

In pronoun-dropping (pro-drop) languages such as Arabic (Eid, 1983), Chinese (Li and Thompson, 1979), Italian (Di Eugenio, 1990) and other romance languages (e.g., Portuguese, Spanish), Japanese (Kameyama, 1985), and others (Kim, 2000), certain arguments can be omitted in which a pronoun is used in English: such arguments are called zero-pronouns (ZP) in NLP. Anaphoric zero pronouns (AZP) are a special case of zero pronouns. AZPs refer to one or more noun entities previously mentioned in a text, as in the following example from the Arabic portion of OntoNotes (in Arabic OntoNotes 5.0, ZPs are denoted as * in Arabic text).

.. المفارقة الأخرى عن بوش هي عدم حماسته للمؤتمر الدولي، اذ انه من البداية، يريد * اجتماعا مختلفا ....

Ironically, Bush did not show any enthusiasm for the international conference, because since the beginning, (he) wanted to attend another conference ...

In the example, the AZP, indicated with '*', refers to a singular masculine person that has been mentioned previously, Bush (بوش). English is not a pro-drop language (White, 1985) so the null argument in Arabic has to be expressed using an overt pronoun (he).

AZP resolution involves two tasks: identification and resolution. AZP identification is the task of identifying the locations where the pronoun was omitted (the * in the example). AZP resolution is the task of finding the antecedent that an AZP refers to (Bush in the example). Contextual information is required for these two tasks, such as that provided by the verb which has the AZP as an argument (in the example the verb is "wanted/يريد".

The AZP problem has inspired much research because AZP interpretation benefits many natural language processing (NLP) tasks such as machine translation (Mitkov and Schmidt, 1998). Although AZPs are common (Chen and Ng, 2016), they are not always annotated in NLP corpora. There are two reasons for this. First, AZPs have no surface realization and the focus in coreference is usually on arguments realized on the surface (Lee et al., 2005). Second, pro-drop languages have several types of ZPs, not all of which anaphoric, which can make it challenging to identify AZPs. Therefore, the number of datasets with annotated AZPs is small (Konno et al., 2020). We investigate therefore automatic methods for augmenting these existing data, applying them to Arabic. Our contributions are as follows:

- We apply various data augmentation methods to detect potential AZPs in unannotated sentences, and to generate sentences containing AZPs.
- We propose a method to automatically find the true antecedent of AZPs.
- The augmented data improve AZP identification and resolution for Arabic, and surpass the

Proceedings of the 4th Workshop on Computational Models of Reference, Anaphora and Coreference (CRAC 2021), pages 82–93
Punta Cana, Dominican Republic, November 10–11, 2021.

current state-of-the-art results.

The rest of the paper is organized as follows. We discuss AZP and data augmentation related literature in Section 2. We explain our data-augmentation methods in Section 3. We discuss the evaluation settings and results in Section 4 and Section 5 respectively. We conclude in Section 6.

2 Related Work

2.1 Anaphoric Zero Pronouns

Arabic: There have been a few proposals devoted to AZP tasks and null arguments in general. Green et al. (2009) proposed a conditional-random-field (CRF) sequence classifier to detect Arabic noun phrases, and captured ZPs implicitly. Bakr et al. (2009) applied a statistical approach to detect empty categories. Gabbard (2010) proposed a pipeline made of maximum entropy classifiers which jointly make a CRF to retrieve Arabic empty categories. Aloraini and Poesio (2020b) proposed the first neural model for resolving Arabic AZP, but they did not consider the AZP identification step. Aloraini and Poesio (2020a) showed a multilingual approach to detect AZPs for Arabic and Chinese using BERT (Devlin et al., 2018).

Other languages: for Chinese, Converse (2006) studied AZP resolution and applied a rule-based approach that employed Hobbs algorithm (Hobbs, 1978) to resolve ZPs in the Chinese Treebank; however, did not attempt to automatically identify AZP. Yeh and Chen (2006) is another rule-based approach for Chinese which used a set of hand-engineered rules to identify and resolve AZPs. Zhao and Ng (2007) proposed the first machine learning approach to Chinese AZPs identification and resolution. They applied decision trees incorporated with a set of syntactic and positional features. Other proposals followed the machine learning approach targeting Chinese (Kong and Zhou, 2010; Chen and Ng, 2013, 2014, 2015, 2016; Yin et al., 2016, 2017; Liu et al., 2017; Chang et al., 2017; Yin et al., 2018; Kong et al., 2019). There has been also a great deal of research on identification and resolution of AZPs, particularly in Japanese (Yoshimoto, 1988; Kim and Ehara., 1995; Aone and Bennett, 1995; Seki et al., 2002; Isozaki and Hirao, 2003; Iida et al., 2006, 2007; Sasano et al., 2008, 2009; Sasano and Kurohashi, 2011; Yoshikawa et al., 2011; Hangyo et al., 2013; Iida et al., 2015; Yoshino et al., 2013; Yamashiro et al., 2018), but also in other languages, including Korean (Han, 2004; Byron et al., 2006), Spanish (Ferrández and Peral, 2000; Rello and Ilisei, 2009), Portuguese (Rello et al., 2012), Romanian (Mihăilă et al., 2011), Bulgarian (Grigorova, 2013), and Sanskrit (Gopal and Jha, 2017). Iida and Poesio (2011) proposed the first multilingual approach for AZP resolution.

These proposals applied their AZP systems to labeled dataset. Even though data augmentation improved many NLP tasks, as discussed in Section 2.2, none of the above proposals considered augmenting AZPs datasets automatically. As far as we know, (Konno et al., 2020) is the only proposal to use data augmentation for AZP resolution. Konno et al applied a data augmentation method called contextual data augmentation (CDA) to Japanese AZPs. CDA method is based on language models to generate different variants of a labeled input by masking certain tokens and then predict them. Our work is different in that we apply various methods to detect, generate, and resolve AZPs while they focus generating samples for AZP resolution. The generated AZP samples are of numerous types and they are automatically prepared for both AZP tasks.

2.2 Data Augmentation

Data augmentation is an active research topic and has been applied in different areas of research of NLP (Feng et al., 2021; Chen et al., 2021). However, there has been very limited proposals for AZP data augmentation. Zhang et al. (2015) augmented data by replacing a word with its synonyms to improve text classification. Sennrich et al. (2015) augmented data by translating a sequence from one language to another, and then translating the sequence back into the original language. The new data were used to enhance the performance of neural machine translation models. Wang et al. (2018) examined various methods for data augmentation and proposed to randomly replace words in source and target languages to improve neural machine translation. Şahin and Steedman (2019) removed dependency links and modified tree nodes to create an augmented dataset for Part-of-Speech tagging. Gulordava et al. (2018) replaced words with other words that share the same Part-of-Speech, morphological features, and dependency labels, to improve subject-verb agreement models. Feng et al. (2019) introduced a pipeline called SMERTI which combines various data augmentation methods, such as, entity replacement, similarity masking, and text in-filling. Grundkiewicz et al. (2019) used a spellchecker to augment training data which are then used to pre-train sequence-to-sequence models. Singh et al. (2019) introduced a cross-lingual data augmentation called XLDA, evaluated on 14 languages on a natural language inference (XNLI) benchmark and question-answering task. XLDA replaces segments of an inputs text with its translation in other languages. Kumar et al. (2019) proposed DiPS, a model that generates various paraphrased sentences used to train conversational agents and in text summarization tasks. Andreas (2019) proposed rule-based data augmentation, which replaces segments of inputs that share similar context to improve the training of n-gram and sequence-to-sequence language models. Guo et al. (2020) proposed a statistical approach called SeqMix to decide which token to use at each position of an input, and they also provided a framework that combines several data augmentation approaches for several NLP tasks. Chen et al. (2020) represented datasets as graphs and proposed methods to augment data based on graph theory for paraphrasing. Ding et al. (2020) trained a language model on the linearized version of the input to synthesize data for low-resource sequence-tagging. Feng et al. (2020) inserted character-level synthetic noise and word hypernyms to augment data for text generation. Louvan and Magnini (2020) used a set of augmentation methods that span words and modify sentences for slot filling and intent detection. (Ri et al., 2021) proposed a method to augment ZPs (not AZPs). They delete personal overt pronouns which results in extra sentences with no pronouns, and use them in Japanese-English translation. Other proposals investigated data augmentation for neural machine translation (Vaibhav et al., 2019; Gao et al., 2019; Nguyen et al., 2019), text classification (Kobayashi, 2018; Wei and Zou, 2019; Anaby-Tavor et al., 2020; Jindal et al., 2020), and question-answering (Kafle et al., 2017; Yang et al., 2019).

Data augmentation methods helped to improve various NLP tasks; however, very few proposals (Konno et al., 2020) considered the methods for AZP tasks which was focused on generating AZPs for resolution. This paper explores the direction of exploiting several data augmentation methods for AZP resolution and identification, and how they can benefit both tasks.

3 Methodology

We applied the following five methods to generate AZPs:

1. **OntoNotes Patterns (ONP):** AZPs may occur more frequently in the company of certain verbs. To find the most frequent collocations, we apply the t-test on the Part-of-Speech sequences of AZP sentences. We tried a window of one, two, and three and we found empirically a window of two to detect many correct AZP collocations.

2. **Removing Subject Mention (RSM):** AZPs are dropped subjects of verbs. When an (explicit) mention is the subject of a verb phrase, we remove the mention to obtain an AZP sentence.

3. **Masking Candidate Mentions (MCM),** also known as contextual data augmentation (CDA). We mask the true antecedents of AZPs and use a language model to find the semantically most similar words, which are then used to produce new sentences by replacing the original word.

4. **Back Translation (BT):** the AZP examples in OntoNotes are in Arabic. We translate them into English using the GoogleTrans API,[1] and then translate them back to Arabic.

5. **Changing Subject–verb Agreement (CSA):** the verb in an AZP construction and its true antecedent agree on number which can be in singular, dual, or plural form. We change their agreement number from one form to another. For example, if the AZP verb and its reference are in singular form, we change the verb and its reference to dual or plural form.

Table 1 shows the number of collected data of each method. AZPs interpretation involves two steps: AZP detection, and AZP resolution. The detection step finds if a sentence has AZPs while the resolution resolves AZPs to their true antecedent. The true antecedent might be present in the same AZP sentence or any previous sentences. In our experiments, we decided to collect AZP samples such that each sample has two sentences: the first has the true antecedent and the second has its AZP. While it is possible to automatically create AZP

[1]https://pypi.org/project/googletrans/

Method	Training
OntoNotes Patterns (ONP)	369
Removing Subject (RSM)	1,196
Masking Candidate (MCM)	736
Back Translation (BT)	501
Changing Subject-Verb Agr. (CSA)	104
Total	2,906

Table 1: The number of the augmented data of each method, and their total.

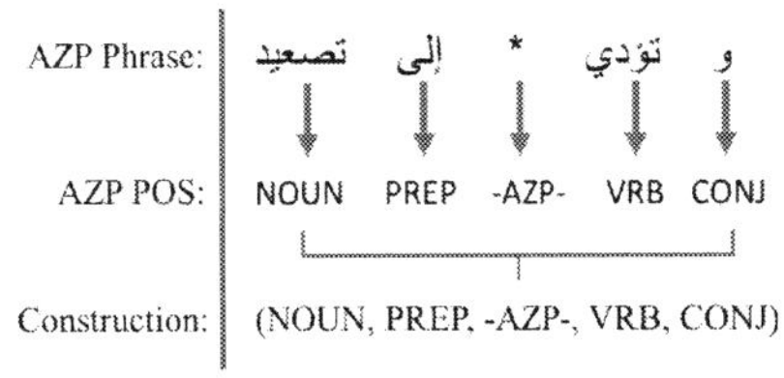

Figure 1: An example of one construction of an AZP from OntoNotes. For every AZP position, we extract the POS of two words before and two after, in order to create one construction.

samples of one sentence only (the AZP position and its true antecedent in the same sentence), but two-sentence samples provide more context and information about AZPs.

3.1 OntoNotes Patterns

AZP sentences may occur more frequently in certain constructions. To find these constructions, we apply a window of one, two, and three tokens on the Part-of-Speeches of AZP samples. We found a window of two (two words before an AZP and two words after as shown in Figure 1) to provide many correct collocations. We count the frequencies of the constructions and apply the t-test score as in (Manning and Schutze, 1999) to see how probable a construction is:

$$t = \frac{\bar{x} - \mu}{\sqrt{\frac{s^2}{N}}}$$

Where $\bar{x}$ is the sample mean of a Part-of-Speech, and s^2 is its sample variance, N is its sample size, and μ is its distribution mean. We choose the highest five t-test scores and apply them to large public text datasets i.e Wikipedia. We tag the sentences in Wikipedia summary sections with their Part-of-Speech using CAMeL tools (Obeid et al., 2020) and apply the OntoNotes constructions on each sentence except the first. When one sentence matches a pattern, it suggests that the sentence might be an AZP. The AZP true antecedent is usually in the first sentence of the summary section. We join the first sentence and the detected sentence together to represent one AZP sample, as shown in Figure 3. In Section 3.6, we discuss in details why we follow this approach and the challenges of finding the true antecedent of an AZP.

3.2 Removing Subject Mentions

Subject nouns or pronouns of a verb phrase might be optional. Removing these subjects transforms a sentence into a null-subject, as shown in the following example:

تقع لندن على نهر التامز

London is located on the Thames river.

In the example, removing 'London' from the Arabic sentence changes it into an AZP sentence and grammatically correct. However, when the subject is removed, readers might not know what the AZP refers unless they have access to more context i.e previous sentences. Therefore, in our experiments each AZP sample has two sentences. The first sentence contains the mention that the AZP refers to, and the second contains the AZP gap.

3.3 Masking Candidate Mentions

We use the multilingual BERT[2] to mask antecedents of AZPs and replace them with their most similar semantic token. We replace the antecedent token with [MASK][3], and predict its most similar semantic word. We replace the original mention with the predicted mention from BERT. However, even though the predicted token might be semantically similar to the original token, it might not agree in number or gender with the AZP verb. For example, the antecedent in the original sample can be *student* and BERT replaces it with *students*. Such samples can distort the training for machine learning algorithms because it associates the morphemes with wrong morphological features. We address this problem in Section 3.7.

3.4 Back Translation

It has been shown that translating a sentence from one language to another, and then translating it back to the original language to be beneficial to some NLP tasks (Xie et al., 2018; Vaibhav et al., 2019;

[2]https://github.com/google-research/bert

[3][MASK] is a special token in BERT which is used for prediction.

Zhang et al., 2019). Back Translation generates a paraphrased version of the original input adding noise, such as, semantic and syntactical changes. Therefore, we translate the Arabic samples to English, and translate them back to Arabic.

3.5 Changing Subject–verb Agreement

AZP verb and its antecedent usually agree on number, gender, and person. We change the verb and its antecedent number agreement from one form to another. For example, if the number of an AZP sample is singular, we change it to dual or plural. To find and generate verb inflections and mention number, we use CAMeL which consists of a set of NLP tools for Arabic.

The five methods we discussed are used create AZP samples, but they are applied differently. The first two (ONP and RSM) are used to detect AZPs on text while the other three (CSA, MCM, and BT) are used to generate AZP from existing AZP samples. Thus, we apply the two methods on the Wikipedia summary sections to initially collect AZPs, and then use the other three to generate extra samples. An illustration of all data augmentation methods and steps in Figure 2.

3.6 Finding the True Antecedent

An AZP refers to a preceding mention in a text. The mention can be in the same sentence as the AZP or in previous sentences. Finding the true mention in a sentence using patterns is not trivial because resolving AZPs involves reasoning, context, background knowledge of real world, and deep understanding of a language characteristic, such as, its morphology (Alnajadat, 2017). At the beginning of the experiment, we apply the two methods (ONP and RSM) on Arabic newspaper articles of Abu El-Khair corpus (El-Khair, 2017) to detect AZP locations. For resolving AZPs to their antecedents, we used AZP context features to find the true antecedent. The main features are the agreement morphemes between the AZP verb and its antecedent. The result was we managed to identify many AZP locations successfully; however, we encountered two problems when we tried finding their true antecedents. First, there were many mentions that share similar features as the true antecedent which led to many incorrect antecedent reference. Second, some locations of the true antecedents were very far from the AZP gap.

To alleviate the above-mentioned limitations of AZP resolution, we apply the two methods on Wikipedia articles. Every Wikipedia articles focuses on a single topic especially in the summary section. Summary sentences can contain AZPs and they usually refer to the Wikipedia title. Therefore, we apply the five methods on the summary sentences, and we consider the title to be the true antecedent of every AZP. The true antecedent always appears in the first sentence i.e the title of Wikipedia page or part of it. So for every AZP in the other sentences of the same page, they refer to the mention in the first sentence. So each AZP sample consists of the first sentence of the Wikipedia page and the sentence where it has the AZP. The reason why we apply the methods only on Wikipedia summary sections because their sentences usually focus on briefly describing the entity of the page. The sentences of other sections might have AZPs but they also include other mentions which can make it challenging to resolve the AZPs to their true antecedent. An illustration of creating one sample from Wikipedia is in Figure 3. After collecting the samples using ONP and RSM methods, we apply the other methods MCM, BT, CSA to generate extra samples.

3.7 Filtering Samples

After data creation and generation, we found some samples to be grammatically incorrect or not AZPs. For example, sometimes MCM method replaces the original antecedent of an AZP with a mention of a different number or gender. BT method can be problematic in some cases because it predicts the dropped subject which converts an AZP sample into a non-AZP sample. Another problem of BT method is that the AZP verb in the original sample is used to track the AZP location. If the AZP verb is translated back into another similar verb, the AZP location can not be retrieved back. To enhance the quality of the augmented data produced by the MCM method, we use Camel tools [4] which has a morphological analyser to find the gender and number of mentions. We use the analyser to see if the AZP verb and its antecedent agree on number and gender. For the grammatically incorrect cases, we remove samples that do not have complete agreements. For the added subject after the BackTranslation step, we remove the subjects in a similar way as we do in RSM method. If the verb of the original sample is absence after the BackTranslation, we remove the sample.

[4] https://github.com/CAMeL-Lab/camel_tools

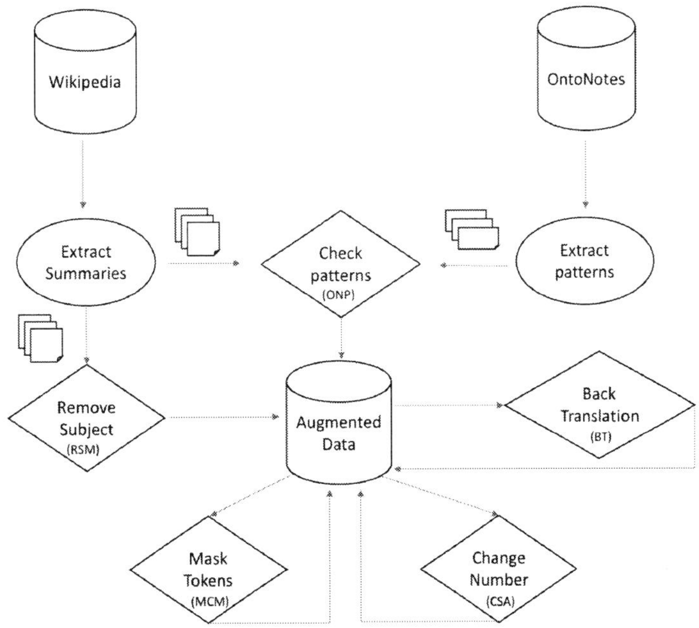

Figure 2: Overall picture of all data augmentation methods for Anaphoric Zero Pronouns. We extract patterns from OntoNotes and check them on Wikipedia summary sentences (ONP method). Removing Subject (RSM) is also applied to the summary sentences. after collecting AZP samples, We create extra data applying MCM, BT, and CSA methods.

4 Evaluation

4.1 Dataset

Most existing Arabic corpora do not have AZP annotated. As far as we know, OntoNotes 5.0 is the only source that has Arabic AZPs annotated. The distribution of documents, sentences, words, and AZPs in OntoNotes are in Table 2.

4.2 AZP systems

For AZP identification, we use the model by (Aloraini and Poesio, 2020a) which is a binary classifier that takes a candidate ZP location as input, and classifies whether it as an AZP or not. For AZP resolution, we use the model by (Aloraini and Poesio, 2020b) which combines BERT representations and additional task-related features of AZPS to learn their true antecedent. We adopt their systems and apply the same settings on Arabic AZPs. We then evaluate each method of our data augmentation for both systems to see its effect. We then try using all the collected data, and try various binary combinations as we will see in Section 5.

Category	Training	Dev	Test
Documents	359	44	44
Sentences	7,422	950	1,003
Words	264,589	30,942	30,935
AZPs	3,495	474	412

Table 2: Basic statistics about AZPs in Arabic OntoNotes. The total number of AZPs is 3495, 474, and 412 for training, development, and test respectively.

4.3 Data Preprocessing

Arabic is a morphologically rich language with a large set of morphological properties. Arabic text can suffer from sparsity (different forms for the same word) and ambiguity (same form for numerous words) if the text is not pre-processed. There are two reasons for these problems. First, certain letters can have different forms which are usually misspelled, such as the various forms of the letter “alif”. Second, same word can have a fully diacritized, partially diacritized or undiacritized forms. Retaining diacritics can complex word representation and model training (Habash and Sadat, 2006). Pre-processing Arabic text improves the overall performance. For example, Aloraini et al. (2020) fol-

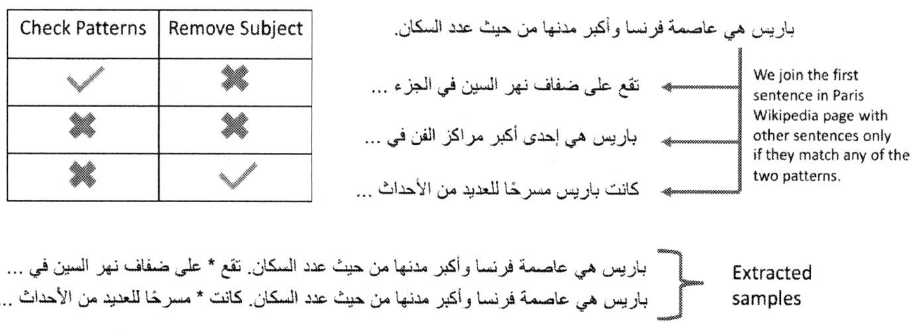

Figure 3: Illustration of finding AZPs using OntoNotes Patterns (ONP) and Remvoing Subject Mnetion (RSM) on Paris, from Arabic Wikipedia. Given a Wikipedia page, we join the first sentence with any other sentence in the summary only if they match any of the two data augmentation methods. The extracted samples are made of the first sentence and the matched sentences. The first sentence contains the true antecedent and the second the AZP.

Original text	لا بَأْسَ أَنْ تُقَال
pre-processed text	لا باس ان تقال

Table 3: An example of how we pre-process Arabic text. We normalize all 'alif' letters forms, and remove all diacritics.

lowed the pre-processing steps by Althobaiti et al. (2014) which led to a significant improvement in the performance of Arabic coreference resolution with an increase of 7% F1 score more than the baseline. Therefore, we follow their steps for pre-processing text which are:

- We normalize the various forms of the letter "alif" (إ,أ,آ) to the letter "ا".
- We remove all diacritic marks on words, such that each word has its undiacritized form.

We show an example of an original and pre-processed sentence from OntoNotes in Table 3.

5 Results

We use the systems from (Aloraini and Poesio, 2020a) and (Aloraini and Poesio, 2020b) as baselines for AZP identification and resolution respectively. To see the effect of the collected samples, we use their systems following the same settings. We evaluate the augmented data of each method with different settings, and see their performance on the precision, recall, and F1 scores.

AZP identification in Table 4, we train the baseline system with every data augmentation method and evaluate on the test portion. We see the results vary. RSM and BT improve the scores with an increase of +0.4 and +0.1 compared to the baseline F1 score. ONP and CSA hurt the scores with a decrease of -0.3 and -0.7 compared to the baseline F1 score. When we train the system with ALL the augmented data, it outperforms the baseline with an increase of +0.3, but still less than when we use RSM by itself. RSM method provides the best performance and outperforms the baseline and all other settings scores.

AZP resolution we evaluate each augmented-data method and the results are shown in Table 5. Almost every data augmentation method increases the overall performance when it is trained with CoNLL-2012 except for CSA method. ONP, RSM, MCM, and BT increase the F1 score with +0.5, +1.6, +0.8, and +1.0 F1 scores respectively while CSA decreases the score by -0.2, compared with the baseline's F1 score. The best settings when we train ALL the augmented data with CoNLL-2012 which results an increase of +1.8.

Combinations we also try combining two methods together to see if they can outperform when we use every method separately. We show the AZP identification results in Table 6 and Table 7 for AZP resolution. As shown in the tables, some combinations can improve the scores; however, no single combination outperforms the highest scores in Tables 4 and 5.

5.1 Discussion

The augmented data helps to improve the results for both AZP identification and resolution. The improvements in scores for AZP resolution are more than AZP identification. To understand the reasons,

Training settings	Test Evaluation			
	P	R	F1	diff
CoNLL-2012 [b]	**60.0**	78.9	68.2	-
+ ONP	59.4	79.3	67.9	-0.3
+ RSM	59.8	**80.4**	**68.6**	**+0.4**
+ MCM	59.6	79.8	68.2	0
+ BT	59.6	80.2	68.3	+0.1
+ CSA	59.3	78.5	67.5	-0.7
CoNLL-2012 + ALL	59.8	80.2	68.5	+0.3

Table 4: AZP identification training settings with each data augmentation technique, and their results on the test set. [b] is the baseline scores (Aloraini and Poesio, 2020a). *diff* is the difference between a method's F1 score and the baseline.

Training settings	Test Evaluation			
	P	R	F1	diff
CoNLL-2012 [b]	64.4	51.8	57.4	-
+ ONP	64.8	52.4	57.9	+0.5
+ RSM	65.6	53.7	59.0	+1.6
+ MCM	65.3	52.6	58.2	+0.8
+ BT	65.3	52.9	58.4	+1.0
+ CSA	64.4	51.6	57.2	-0.2
CoNLL-2012 + ALL	**65.8**	**53.9**	**59.2**	**+1.8**

Table 5: AZP resolution training settings with each data augmentation technique, and their results on the test set. [b] is the baseline scores (Aloraini and Poesio, 2020b). *diff* is the difference between a method's F1 score and the baseline.

Training settings	Test Evaluation			
	P	R	F1	diff
CoNLL-2012 [b]	**60.0**	78.9	68.2	-
+ ONP + RSM	59.6	79.7	68.2	0.0
+ ONP + MCM	59.5	79.7	68.1	-0.1
+ ONP + BT	59.8	79.8	68.3	+0.1
+ ONP + CSA	59.7	78.8	67.9	-0.3
+ RSM + MCM	59.8	79.0	68.1	-0.1
+ RSM + BT	59.8	79.8	68.4	+0.2
+ RSM + CSA	59.8	**80.2**	**68.5**	**+0.3**
+ MCM + BT	59.8	79.7	68.3	+0.1
+ MCM + CSA	59.7	79.7	68.2	0.0
+ BT + CSA	59.7	79.0	68.0	-0.2

Table 6: AZP identification training settings with different combinations of data augmentation methods, and their results on the test set.

Training settings	Test Evaluation			
	P	R	F1	diff
CoNLL-2012 [b]	64.4	51.8	57.4	-
+ ONP + RSM	65.3	53.7	58.9	+1.5
+ ONP + MCM	65.0	53.2	58.5	+1.1
+ ONP + BT	64.9	53.5	58.6	+1.1
+ ONP + CSA	64.6	52.7	58.0	+0.6
+ RSM + MCM	65.1	53.6	58.7	+1.4
+ RSM + BT	**65.4**	**53.8**	59.0	**+1.6**
+ MCM + BT	64.9	52.9	58.2	+0.8
+ MCM + CSA	65.1	53.4	58.6	+1.2
+ BT + CSA	64.6	52.4	57.8	+0.4

Table 7: AZP resolution training settings with different combinations of data augmentation methods, and their results on the test set.

we investigated the Arabic portion of CoNLL-2012 and the outputs of the two systems. In CoNLL-2012, we found that many AZP samples to be duplicates but they refer to different types of mentions. The augmented data has more variance of AZP verbs; however, many were not present in the test part which might have led the model to associate these newly seen AZP verbs to cases that are not AZPs in the test set. We also examined the identified and resolved AZPs, and we found several cases to be verbs or mentions that are not subset of the training or the augmented data. Even though the data augmentation methods we showed helped to alleviate this problem, we still need more annotated data and explore more data augmentation methods.

6 Conclusion

We tested five methods to detect and generate AZPs. We suggested a simple and effective way to resolve AZPs in the automatically generated samples. We evaluated the augmented data on the AZP identification and resolution tasks for Arabic. Training the models with the augmented data achieved new state-of-the-art results for both AZP tasks.

Acknowledgements

We would like to thank the anonymous reviewers for their insightful comments and suggestions which helped to improve an early version of the paper.

References

Bashir M. Alnajadat. 2017. Pro-drop in standard arabic. In *International Journal of English Linguistics 7.1*.

Abdulrahman Aloraini and Massimo Poesio. 2020a. Anaphoric zero pronoun identification: A multilingual approach. In *Proceedings of the Third Workshop on Computational Models of Reference, Anaphora and Coreference*, pages 22–32.

Abdulrahman Aloraini and Massimo Poesio. 2020b. Cross-lingual zero pronoun resolution. In *Proceedings of The 12th Language Resources and Evaluation Conference*, pages 90–98.

Abdulrahman Aloraini, Juntao Yu, and Massimo Poesio. 2020. Neural coreference resolution for arabic. *arXiv preprint arXiv:2011.00286*.

Maha Althobaiti, Udo Kruschwitz, and Massimo Poesio. 2014. Aranlp: A java-based library for the processing of arabic text.

Ateret Anaby-Tavor, Boaz Carmeli, Esther Goldbraich, Amir Kantor, George Kour, Segev Shlomov, Naama Tepper, and Naama Zwerdling. 2020. Do not have enough data? deep learning to the rescue! In *Proceedings of the AAAI Conference on Artificial Intelligence*, pages 7383–7390.

Jacob Andreas. 2019. Good-enough compositional data augmentation. *arXiv preprint arXiv:1904.09545*.

Chinatsu Aone and Scott William Bennett. 1995. Evaluating automated and manual acquisition of anaphora resolution strategies. In *ACL '95 Proceedings of the 33rd annual meeting on Association for Computational Linguistics*, pages 122–129.

Hitham M Abo Bakr, Khaled Shaalan, and Ibrahim Ziedan. 2009. A statistical method for detecting the arabic empty category. In *Proceedings of the Second International Conference on Arabic Language Resources and Tools, Cairo, Egypt*.

Donna K. Byron, Whitney Gegg-Harrison, and Sun-Hee Lee. 2006. Resolving zero anaphors and pronouns in korean. In *Traitement Automatique des Langues 46.1*, pages 91–114.

Tao Chang, Shaohe Lv, Xiaodong Wang, and Dong Wang. 2017. Zero pronoun identification in chinese language with deep neural networks. In *2017 2nd International Conference on Control, Automation and Artificial Intelligence (CAAI 2017)*. Atlantis Press.

Chen Chen and Vincent Ng. 2013. Chinese zero pronoun resolution: Some recent advances. In *Proceedings of the 2013 conference on empirical methods in natural language processing*, pages 1360–1365.

Chen Chen and Vincent Ng. 2014. Chinese zero pronoun resolution: An unsupervised probabilistic model rivaling supervised resolvers. In *Proceedings of the 2014 Conference on Empirical Methods in Natural Language Processing*.

Chen Chen and Vincent Ng. 2015. Chinese zero pronoun resolution: A joint unsupervised discourse-aware model rivaling state-of-the-art resolvers. In *Proceedings of the 53rd Annual Meeting of the Association for Computational Linguistics and the 7th International Joint Conference on Natural Language Processing (Volume 2: Short Papers)*, pages 320–326.

Chen Chen and Vincent Ng. 2016. Chinese zero pronoun resolution with deep neural network. In *Proceedings of the 54th Annual Meeting of the Association for Computational Linguistics (Volume 1: Long Papers)*, pages 778–788.

Hannah Chen, Yangfeng Ji, and David Evans. 2020. Finding friends and flipping frenemies: Automatic paraphrase dataset augmentation using graph theory. *arXiv preprint arXiv:2011.01856*.

Jiaao Chen, Derek Tam, Colin Raffel, Mohit Bansal, and Diyi Yang. 2021. An empirical survey of data augmentation for limited data learning in nlp. *arXiv preprint arXiv:2106.07499*.

Susan Converse. 2006. Pronominal anaphora resolution in chinese. In *PhD Thesis, University of Pennsylvania*.

Jacob Devlin, Ming-Wei Chang, Kenton Lee, and Kristina Toutanova. 2018. Bert: Pre-training of deep bidirectional transformers for language understanding. *arXiv preprint arXiv:1810.04805*.

B. Di Eugenio. 1990. Centering theory and the italian pronominal system. In *Proc. of the 13th COLING*, Helsinki, Finland.

Bosheng Ding, Linlin Liu, Lidong Bing, Canasai Kruengkrai, Thien Hai Nguyen, Shafiq Joty, Luo Si, and Chunyan Miao. 2020. Daga: Data augmentation with a generation approach for low-resource tagging tasks. *arXiv preprint arXiv:2011.01549*.

Mushira Eid. 1983. On the communicative function of subject pronouns in arabic. In *Journal of Linguistics 19.2*, pages 287–303.

Ibrahim Abu El-Khair. 2017. Abu el-khair corpus: A modern standard arabic corpus. *International Journal of Recent Trends in Engineering & Research (IJRTER) Volume*, 2.

Steven Y Feng, Varun Gangal, Dongyeop Kang, Teruko Mitamura, and Eduard Hovy. 2020. Genaug: Data augmentation for finetuning text generators. *arXiv preprint arXiv:2010.01794*.

Steven Y Feng, Varun Gangal, Jason Wei, Sarath Chandar, Soroush Vosoughi, Teruko Mitamura, and Eduard Hovy. 2021. A survey of data augmentation approaches for nlp. *arXiv preprint arXiv:2105.03075*.

Steven Y Feng, Aaron W Li, and Jesse Hoey. 2019. Keep calm and switch on! preserving sentiment and fluency in semantic text exchange. *arXiv preprint arXiv:1909.00088*.

Antonio Ferrández and Jesús Peral. 2000. A computational approach to zero-pronouns in spanish. In *Proceedings of the 38th Annual Meeting of the Association for Computational Linguistics*, pages 166–172.

Ryan Gabbard. 2010. Null element restoration. In *Ph.D Thesis, University of Pennsylvania.*

Fei Gao, Jinhua Zhu, Lijun Wu, Yingce Xia, Tao Qin, Xueqi Cheng, Wengang Zhou, and Tie-Yan Liu. 2019. Soft contextual data augmentation for neural machine translation. In *Proceedings of the 57th Annual Meeting of the Association for Computational Linguistics*, pages 5539–5544.

Madhav Gopal and Girish Nath Jha. 2017. Zero pronouns and their resolution in sanskrit texts. In *The International Symposium on Intelligent Systems Technologies and Application*, pages 255–267.

Spence Green, Conal Sathi, and Christopher Manning. 2009. Np subject detection in verb-initial arabic clauses. In *Proceedings of the Third Workshop on Computational Approaches to Arabic Script-based Languages (CAASL3). Vol. 112.*

Diana Grigorova. 2013. An algorithm for zero pronoun resolution in bulgarian. In *Proceedings of the 14th International Conference on Computer Systems and Technologies.*

Roman Grundkiewicz, Marcin Junczys-Dowmunt, and Kenneth Heafield. 2019. Neural grammatical error correction systems with unsupervised pre-training on synthetic data. In *Proceedings of the Fourteenth Workshop on Innovative Use of NLP for Building Educational Applications*, pages 252–263.

Kristina Gulordava, Piotr Bojanowski, Edouard Grave, Tal Linzen, and Marco Baroni. 2018. Colorless green recurrent networks dream hierarchically. *arXiv preprint arXiv:1803.11138.*

Demi Guo, Yoon Kim, and Alexander M Rush. 2020. Sequence-level mixed sample data augmentation. *arXiv preprint arXiv:2011.09039.*

Nizar Habash and Fatiha Sadat. 2006. Arabic preprocessing schemes for statistical machine translation. In *Proceedings of the Human Language Technology Conference of the NAACL, Companion Volume: Short Papers*, pages 49–52.

Na-Rae Han. 2004. A korean null pronouns: Classification and annotation. In *Proceedings of the 2004 ACL Workshop on Discourse Annotation. Association for Computational Linguistics, 2004.*, pages 33–40.

Masatsugu Hangyo, Daisuke Kawahara, and Sadao Kurohashi. 2013. Japanese zero reference resolution considering exophora and author/reader mentions. In *Proceedings of the 2013 Conference on Empirical Methods in Natural Language Processing*, pages 924–934.

Jerry Hobbs. 1978. Resolving pronoun references. In *Lingua*, pages 311–338.

Ryu Iida, Kentaro Inui, and Yuji Matsumoto. 2006. Exploiting syntactic patterns as clues in zero-anaphora resolution. In *Proceedings of the 21st International Conference on Computational Linguistics and 44th Annual Meeting of the Association for Computational Linguistic*, pages 625–632.

Ryu Iida, Kentaro Inui, and Yuji Matsumoto. 2007. Zero-anaphora resolution by learning rich syntactic pattern features. In *ACM Transactions on Asian Language Information Processing, 6(4).*

Ryu Iida and Massimo Poesio. 2011. A cross-lingual ilp solution to zero anaphora resolution. In *Proceedings of the 49th Annual Meeting of the Association for Computational Linguistics: Human Language Technologies-Volume 1*, pages 804–813.

Ryu Iida, Kentaro Torisawa, Chikara Hashimoto, Jong-Hoon Oh, and Julien Kloetzer. 2015. Intra-sentential zero anaphora resolution using subject sharing recognition. In *Proceedings of the 2015 Conference on Empirical Methods in Natural Language Processing*, pages 2179–2189.

Hideki Isozaki and Tsutomu Hirao. 2003. Japanese zero pronoun resolution based on ranking rules and machine learning. In *Proceedings of the 2003 Conference on Empirical Methods in Natural Language Processing,*, pages 184–191.

Amit Jindal, Arijit Ghosh Chowdhury, Aniket Didolkar, Di Jin, Ramit Sawhney, and Rajiv Shah. 2020. Augmenting nlp models using latent feature interpolations. In *Proceedings of the 28th International Conference on Computational Linguistics*, pages 6931–6936.

Kushal Kafle, Mohammed Yousefhussien, and Christopher Kanan. 2017. Data augmentation for visual question answering. In *Proceedings of the 10th International Conference on Natural Language Generation*, pages 198–202.

Megumi Kameyama. 1985. *Zero Anaphora: The case of Japanese*. Ph.D. thesis, Stanford University, Stanford, CA.

Yeun-Bae Kim and Terumasa Ehara. 1995. Zero-subject resolution method based on probabilistic inference with evaluation function. In *Proceedings of the 3rd Natural Language Processing Pacific- Rim Symposium*, pages 721—727.

YOUNG-JOO Kim. 2000. Subject/object drop in the acquisition of korean: A cross-linguistic comparison. In *Journal of East Asian Linguistics 9.4*, pages 325–351.

Sosuke Kobayashi. 2018. Contextual augmentation: Data augmentation by words with paradigmatic relations. *arXiv preprint arXiv:1805.06201.*

Fang Kong, Min Zhang, and Guodong Zhou. 2019. Chinese zero pronoun resolution: A chain-to-chain approach. *ACM Transactions on Asian and Low-Resource Language Information Processing (TALLIP)*, 19(1):1–21.

Fang Kong and Guodong Zhou. 2010. A tree kernel-based unified framework for chinese zero anaphora resolution. In *Proceedings of the 2010 Conference on Empirical Methods in Natural Language Processing. Association for Computational Linguistics*, pages 882–891.

Ryuto Konno, Yuichiroh Matsubayashi, Shun Kiyono, Hiroki Ouchi, Ryo Takahashi, and Kentaro Inui. 2020. An empirical study of contextual data augmentation for japanese zero anaphora resolution. *arXiv preprint arXiv:2011.00948*.

Ashutosh Kumar, Satwik Bhattamishra, Manik Bhandari, and Partha Talukdar. 2019. Submodular optimization-based diverse paraphrasing and its effectiveness in data augmentation. In *Proceedings of the 2019 Conference of the North American Chapter of the Association for Computational Linguistics: Human Language Technologies, Volume 1 (Long and Short Papers)*, pages 3609–3619.

Sun-Hee Lee, Donna K Byron, and Seok Bae Jang. 2005. Why is zero marking important in korean? In *International Conference on Natural Language Processing*, pages 588–599. Springer.

Charles N. Li and Sandra A. Thompson. 1979. Third person pronouns and zero anaphora in chinese discourse. In *Syntax and Semantics*, volume 12: Discourse and Syntax, pages 311–335. Academic Press.

Ting Liu, Yiming Cui, Qingyu Yin, Weinan Zhang, Shijin Wang, and Guoping Hu. 2017. Generating and exploiting large-scale pseudo training data for zero pronoun resolution. In *arXiv preprint arXiv:1606.01603*.

Samuel Louvan and Bernardo Magnini. 2020. Simple is better! lightweight data augmentation for low resource slot filling and intent classification. *arXiv preprint arXiv:2009.03695*.

Christopher Manning and Hinrich Schutze. 1999. *Foundations of statistical natural language processing*. MIT press.

Claudiu Mihăilă, Iustina Ilisei, , and Diana Inkpen. 2011. Zero pronominal anaphora resolution for the romanian language. In *Research Journal on Computer Science and Computer Engineering with Applications, POLIBITS, 42*.

Ruslan Mitkov and Paul Schmidt. 1998. On the complexity of pronominal anaphora resolution in machine translation. *STUDIES IN FUNCTIONAL AND STRUCTURAL LINGUISTICS*, pages 207–222.

Xuan-Phi Nguyen, Shafiq Joty, Wu Kui, and Ai Ti Aw. 2019. Data diversification: A simple strategy for neural machine translation. *arXiv preprint arXiv:1911.01986*.

Ossama Obeid, Nasser Zalmout, Salam Khalifa, Dima Taji, Mai Oudah, Bashar Alhafni, Go Inoue, Fadhl Eryani, Alexander Erdmann, and Nizar Habash. 2020. Camel tools: An open source python toolkit for arabic natural language processing. In *Proceedings of the 12th language resources and evaluation conference*, pages 7022–7032.

Luz Rello, Gabriela Ferraro, and Iria Gayo. 2012. A first approach to the automatic detection of zero subjects and impersonal constructions in portuguese. *Procesamiento del lenguaje natural*, 49:163–170.

Luz Rello and Iustina Ilisei. 2009. A rule-based approach to the identification of spanish zero pronouns. In *Proceedings of the Student Research Workshop*, pages 60–65.

Ryokan Ri, Toshiaki Nakazawa, and Yoshimasa Tsuruoka. 2021. Zero-pronoun data augmentation for japanese-to-english translation. *arXiv preprint arXiv:2107.00318*.

Gözde Gül Şahin and Mark Steedman. 2019. Data augmentation via dependency tree morphing for low-resource languages. *arXiv preprint arXiv:1903.09460*.

Ryohei Sasano, Daisuke Kawahara, and Sadao Kurohashi. 2008. A fully-lexicalized probabilistic model for japanese zero anaphora resolution. In *Proceedings of the 22nd International Conference on Computational Linguistics*, pages 769–776.

Ryohei Sasano, Daisuke Kawahara, and Sadao Kurohashi. 2009. The effect of corpus size on case frame acquisition for discourse analysis. In *Proceedings of Human Language Technologies: The 2009 Annual Conference of the North American Chapter of the Association for Computational Linguistics*, pages 521–529.

Ryohei Sasano and Sadao Kurohashi. 2011. discriminative approach to japanese zero anaphora resolution with large-scale lexicalized case frames. In *Proceedings of the 5th International Joint Conference on Natural Language Processing*, pages 758–766.

Kazuhiro Seki, Atsushi Fujii, and Tetsuya Ishikawa. 2002. A probabilistic method for analyzing japanese anaphora integrating zero pronoun detection and resolution. In *Proceedings of the 19th International Conference on Computational Linguistics - Volume 1*, pages 1–7.

Rico Sennrich, Barry Haddow, and Alexandra Birch. 2015. Improving neural machine translation models with monolingual data. *arXiv preprint arXiv:1511.06709*.

Jasdeep Singh, Bryan McCann, Nitish Shirish Keskar, Caiming Xiong, and Richard Socher. 2019. Xlda: Cross-lingual data augmentation for natural language inference and question answering. *arXiv preprint arXiv:1905.11471*.

Vaibhav Vaibhav, Sumeet Singh, Craig Stewart, and Graham Neubig. 2019. Improving robustness of machine translation with synthetic noise. *arXiv preprint arXiv:1902.09508*.

Xinyi Wang, Hieu Pham, Zihang Dai, and Graham Neubig. 2018. Switchout: an efficient data augmentation algorithm for neural machine translation. *arXiv preprint arXiv:1808.07512*.

Jason Wei and Kai Zou. 2019. Eda: Easy data augmentation techniques for boosting performance on text classification tasks. *arXiv preprint arXiv:1901.11196*.

Lydia White. 1985. The "pro-drop" parameter in adult second language acquisition. *Language learning*, 35(1):47–61.

Ziang Xie, Guillaume Genthial, Stanley Xie, Andrew Y Ng, and Dan Jurafsky. 2018. Noising and denoising natural language: Diverse backtranslation for grammar correction. In *Proceedings of the 2018 Conference of the North American Chapter of the Association for Computational Linguistics: Human Language Technologies, Volume 1 (Long Papers)*, pages 619–628.

Souta Yamashiro, Hitoshi Nishikawa, and Takenobu Tokunaga. 2018. Neural japanese zero anaphora resolution using smoothed large-scale case frames with word embedding. In *Proceedings of the 32nd Pacific Asia Conference on Language, Information and Computation*.

Wei Yang, Yuqing Xie, Luchen Tan, Kun Xiong, Ming Li, and Jimmy Lin. 2019. Data augmentation for bert fine-tuning in open-domain question answering. *arXiv preprint arXiv:1904.06652*.

Ching-Long Yeh and Yi-Chun Chen. 2006. Zero anaphora resolution in chinese with shallow parsing. In *Journal of Chinese Language and Computing 17 (1)*, pages 41–56.

Qingyu Yin, Yu Zhang, Weinan Zhang, and Ting Liu. 2016. A deep neural network for chinese zero pronoun resolution. In *arXiv preprint arXiv:1604.05800*.

Qingyu Yin, Yu Zhang, Weinan Zhang, and Ting Liu. 2017. Chinese zero pronoun resolution with deep memory network. In *Proceedings of the 2017 Conference on Empirical Methods in Natural Language Processing*, pages 1309–1318.

Qingyu Yin, Yu Zhang, Weinan Zhang, Ting Liu, and William Yang Wang. 2018. Zero pronoun resolution with attention-based neural network. In *Proceedings of the 27th International Conference on Computational Linguistics*, pages 13–23.

Katsumasa Yoshikawa, Masayuki Asahara, and Yuji Matsumoto. 2011. Jointly extracting japanese predicate-argument relation with markov logic. In *Proceedings of 5th International Joint Conference on Natural Language Processing*, pages 1125–1133.

Kei Yoshimoto. 1988. Identifying zero pronouns in japanese dialogue. In *Coling Budapest 1988 Volume 2: International Conference on Computational Linguistics*.

Koichiro Yoshino, Shinsuke Mori, and Tatsuya Kawahara. 2013. Predicate argument structure analysis using partially annotated corpora. In *Proceedings of the Sixth International Joint Conference on Natural Language Processing*, pages 957–961.

Xiang Zhang, Junbo Zhao, and Yann LeCun. 2015. Character-level convolutional networks for text classification. *Advances in neural information processing systems*, 28:649–657.

Yi Zhang, Tao Ge, Furu Wei, Ming Zhou, and Xu Sun. 2019. Sequence-to-sequence pre-training with data augmentation for sentence rewriting. *arXiv preprint arXiv:1909.06002*.

Shanheng Zhao and Hwee Tou Ng. 2007. Identification and resolution of chinese zero pronouns: A machine learning approach. In *Proceedings of the 2007 Joint Conference on Empirical Methods in Natural Language Processing and Computational Natural Language Learning*, pages 541–550.

Exploring Pre-Trained Transformers and Bilingual Transfer Learning for Arabic Coreference Resolution

Bonan Min
Raytheon BBN Technologies
10 Moulton Street, Cambridge, MA 02138
bonan.min@raytheon.com

Abstract

In this paper, we develop bilingual transfer learning approaches to improve Arabic coreference resolution by leveraging additional English annotation via bilingual or multilingual pre-trained transformers. We show that bilingual transfer learning improves the strong transformer-based neural coreference models by 2-4 F1. We also systemically investigate the effectiveness of several pre-trained transformer models that differ in training corpora, languages covered, and model capacity. Our best model achieves a new state-of-the-art performance of 64.55 F1 on the Arabic OntoNotes dataset. Our code is publicly available at https://github.com/bnmin/arabic_coref.

1 Introduction

Coreference resolution is the task of identifying all mentions which refers to the same discourse entity. It is a crucial step for many NLP tasks, and has been well-studied (Ng, 2010) for English. Recently, neural coreference resolution models based on pre-trained tranformers, e.g., BERT (Devlin et al., 2019) and SpanBERT (Joshi et al., 2020), have shown to be highly effective for English coreference resolution, achieving 80 F1 on the OntoNotes (Pradhan et al., 2012) dataset. However, coreference resolution in Arabic is still a challenging problem with previous systems (Björkelund and Kuhn, 2014; Chen and Ng, 2012; Fernandes et al., 2012; Zhekova et al., 2012; Stamborg et al., 2012; Xiong and Liu, 2012; Aloraini et al., 2020) performing significantly lower than the English systems.

A main problem is that Arabic coreference resolution datasets are much smaller than their English counterparts. For example, the widely useful benchmark dataset OntoNotes contains 7 times more documents in English than Arabic (Table 2).

Based on this observation, we develop bilingual transfer learning approaches to improve Arabic coreference resolution by leveraging additional English coreference annotation via bilingual or multilingual pre-trained transformers, e.g., multilingual BERT (Devlin et al., 2019). We summarize our contributions below:

- We develop several transformer-based models for Arabic coreference resolution. Our best model achieves a new state-of-the-art of 64.55 F1 in Arabic coreference resolution. Our source code are made publicly available.
- We develop two bilingual transfer learning approaches to improve Arabic coreference resolution. We show bilingual transfer learning, that combines English and Arabic coreference annotation via multilingual pre-trained transformers, leads to significant improvements in Arabic coreference resolution.
- We systemically investigate the effectiveness of several pre-trained transformer models that differ in training corpora, languages covered, and model capacity. We show that language-specific pre-training is a crucial success factor.

2 Related Work

Neural models for coreference resolution: State-of-the-art models for coreference resolution are based on neural networks (NN). E2E-COREF (Lee et al., 2018) is an NN model that performs span extraction and coreference classification in a single end-to-end model. BERT-based models (Joshi et al., 2019a, 2020) further improve E2E-COREF by replacing the Bi-LSTM text encoder with BERT (Devlin et al., 2019) or SPANBERT (Joshi et al., 2020). COREFQA (Wu et al., 2020) formulates coreference resolution as a QA task leveraging pre-trained transformers.

Arabic coreference resolution: Björkelund and Kuhn (2014) investigates structured perceptron models for Arabic coreference resolution. Chen

Proceedings of the 4th Workshop on Computational Models of Reference, Anaphora and Coreference (CRAC 2021), pages 94–99
Punta Cana, Dominican Republic, November 10–11, 2021.

and Ng (2012) uses a hybrid approach combining rule-based methods and learning-based methods. Fernandes et al. (2012) is a latent structure perceptron model along with entropy-guided feature induction. Zhekova et al. (2012) is a memory-based coreference resolution system. Stamborg et al. (2012) uses a mention classifier with features extracted from the dependency graphs of the sentences. Uryupina and Moschitti (2013) proposed an algorithm for multilingual mention detection by extracting mentions from parse trees via kernel-based SVM learning. Haponchyk and Moschitti (2017) improves structured prediction models for Arabic coreference resolution by using more expressive loss functions. Xiong and Liu (2012) is a projection-based model in which they first translate Arabic into English, run a coreference resolution system, and then map the coreference clusters back into Arabic. Aloraini and Poesio (2020) developed a BERT-based cross-lingual models for zero pronoun resolution in Arabic and Chinese.

Aloraini et al (2020) developed an Arabic neural coreference system, and showed that data processing and mention detection improve the performance by about 7.8 F1 points over the pure neural coreference system, resulting in 63.9 F1 that is higher than previous approaches but lower than ours (Table 3). Our systems are pure neural systems and we focus on a different problem (bilingual transfer learning). Our approaches and Aloraini et al (2020) are complementary, so it is possible that combining ours and Aloraini et al (2020) can achieve further improvements. We leave this for future work.

Pre-trained transformers: Pre-trained transformer based language models such as BERT has been shown to be effective for many NLP tasks. ARABERT (Antoun et al., 2020) is a BERT-like model trained with Arabic text. To enable cross-lingual transfer learning, multilingual pre-trained transformers such as MBERT (Devlin et al., 2019) are trained with large corpora with many languages to encode similar words (words with similar meanings) from different languages into nearby high-dimensional vector spaces. GIGABERT (Lan et al., 2020) is an Arabic-English bilingual language model trained with Arabic and English text.

3 Neural Coreference Models for Arabic

Our coreference resolution model is based on an end-to-end neural model BERT-COREF (Joshi et al., 2019b), which is built on top of E2E-COREF (Lee et al., 2018). Below we give a brief overview of BERT-COREF , and then describe our extensions to this model for Arabic coreference resolution.

3.1 Overview of BERT-COREF

BERT-COREF is an neural model that performs span extraction and coreference relation classification in a single end-to-end model. It first enumerates mention spans, and then for pairs of mention spans, scores their likelihoods of referring to the same entity. The training signal is back-propagated to allow the model to learn to perform span extraction and coreference resolution simultaneously, leading to impressive performance on the English coreference resolution task on the OntoNotes dataset (Pradhan et al., 2012).

For each mentions span x, BERT-COREF learns a distribution P over possible antecedent spans Y:

$$P(y) = \frac{e^{s(x,y)}}{\sum_{y' \in Y} e^{s(x,y')}}$$

The scoring function $s(x, y)$ between spans x and y uses span representations $\mathbf{g}_x$ and $\mathbf{g}_y$ to represent its inputs. The span representation are generated with BERT (Devlin et al., 2019). The model computes $s(x, y)$ as the sum of mention scores $s_m(x)$ and $s_m(y)$ for x and y respectively, and a compatibility score $s_c(x, y)$ of x and y that indicates how likely the two spans refer to the same entity:

$$s(x, y) = s_m(x) + s_m(y) + s_c(x, y)$$

$$s_m(x) = \text{FF}_m(\mathbf{g}_x)$$

$$s_c(x, y) = \text{FF}_c(\mathbf{g}_x, \mathbf{g}_y, \phi(x, y))$$

where FF represents a feed-forward (FF) network and $\phi(x, y)$ represents additional features such as speakers and metadata.

For more details, we refer readers to Lee et al. (2018) and Joshi et al. (2019b).

3.2 Arabic Coreference Resolution with Pre-Trained Transformers

We use BERT-COREF to train end-to-end neural coreference models. To encode Arabic text, we replace the English-only BERT text encoder with pre-trained transformers that are trained with Arabic corpora or multilingual corpora including Arabic.

Table 1 summarizes the configurations of the following three pre-trained transformers that we use to replace BERT to encode words in Arabic (and also English words for MBERT and GIGABERT):

Model	Training source	Training tokens (all/en/ar)	# Model parameters
ARABERT	newswire	2.5B/ – /2.5B	136M
MBERT	Wikipedia	21.9B/2.5B/153M	172M
GIGABERT	Gigaword, Wikipedia, Oscar	10.4B/6.1B/4.3B	125M

Table 1: Model configurations for the pre-trained transformers ARABERT (Antoun et al., 2020), MBERT (Devlin et al., 2019), and GIGABERT (Lan et al., 2020). Wikipedia refers to the English and Arabic portions of the Wikipedia. en and ar refers to English and Arabic respectively.

	Train	Development	Test
English	2,802	343	348
Arabic	359	44	44

Table 2: Number of documents in the *train*, *dev* and *test* sections of the English and Arabic OntoNotes datasets.

- ARABERT: An Arabic BERT-based model trained from 2.5 billion words of publicly available Arabic corpora, including El-khair (2016) that includes more than 5 million articles from ten major news sources covering 8 countries and the Open Source International Arabic News Corpus (Zeroual et al., 2019) that consists of 3.5 million articles from 31 news sources in 24 Arab countries.

- MBERT: Multilingual BERT is a multilingual BERT model that was trained with the Wikipedia dump for the top 104 languages with the largest Wikipedias.

- GIGABERT: an English-Arabic bilingual language model pre-trained from the fifth edition of English and Arabic Gigaword corpora [1] which consists of 13 million news articles, English and Arabic portions of Wikipedia [2], and the Arabic section of the Oscar corpus (Ortiz Suárez et al., 2019), a large-scale multilingual dataset filtered from the Common Crawl.

Table 1 summarizes training data and model configurations for the three models above.

3.3 Bilingual Transfer Learning

Pires et al. (2019) show that MBERT is surprisingly good at cross-lingual transfer learning for several NLP tasks, in which the task-specific training data in one language is used to fine-tune the model and then evaluate in a zero-shot setting in a different language. However, its effectiveness in Arabic coreference resolution has not been studied.

Inspired by the prior work, we developed two approaches for bilingual transfer learning to leverage OntoNotes' English coreference resolution annotation to improve Arabic coreference resolution:

Pre-training on English + fine-tuning on Arabic: We pre-train BERT-COREF for m epochs with the English training dataset, and then fine-tune it with n epochs using the Arabic training dataset. We replace the BERT encoder with MBERT or GIGABERT to allow cross-lingual transfer learning. We call this the PIPELINE approach for bilingual transfer learning (or PIPELINE for short).

Joint training on English and Arabic: We combine the English and Arabic training dataset to jointly train the BERT-COREF model. Similarly, the model uses MBERT or GIGABERT instead of the monolingual BERT as the text encoder. For each epoch, we shuffle the combined set of English and Arabic documents and perform stochastic gradient descent (SGD) on the randomized mixture of mini-batches from both English and Arabic. We call this approach the JOINT training approach for bilingual transfer learning (or JOINT for short).

4 Experiments

We evaluate the models on OntoNotes 5.0 (Pradhan et al., 2012), which is widely used as a benchmark dataset for coreference resolution. OntoNotes also contains both Arabic and English documents annotated with coreference, which makes bilingual transfer learning (Section 3.3) experiments feasible. Table 2 shows the numbers of English and Arabic documents in OntoNotes. To not overwhelm the much smaller Arabic dataset with the English dataset, we replicate the Arabic dataset $k = 6$ times [3] so that the amount of English and Arabic data is similar. We use the official *train/dev/test* split from the CoNLL 2012 shared task on multi-

[1] https://catalog.ldc.upenn.edu/LDC2011T07 and https://catalog.ldc.upenn.edu/LDC2011T11

[2] https://www.wikipedia.org/

[3] We found that $k = 6$ produces the best result on the *dev* dataset.

Model	MUC			B³			CEAF			
	P	R	F1	P	R	F1	P	R	F1	Avg. F1
(1) Coreference resolution models trained with Arabic data										
MBERT	61.71	43.81	51.24	56.72	36.34	44.3	53.79	38.48	44.86	46.8 (47.44)
ARABERT	70.07	51.61	59.44	65.87	45.32	53.69	64.5	49.62	56.09	56.41 (56.74)
GIGABERT	73.08	59.24	65.44	69.49	52.63	59.9	64.9	57.42	60.93	62.09 (61.91)
(2) Coreference resolution models trained with both English and Arabic data										
MBERT-PIPELINE	61.2	48.2	53.93	56.35	40.84	47.36	53.52	43.8	48.17	49.82 (49.79)
MBERT-JOINT	58.83	46.07	51.67	54.11	39.59	45.73	52.86	43.05	47.45	48.28 (49.13)
GIGABERT-PIPELINE	71.46	63.19	67.07	66.93	57.62	61.92	65	61.48	63.19	64.06 (64.72)
GIGABERT-JOINT	73.63	61.81	**67.21**	70.74	55.92	**62.46**	66.07	62.03	**63.99**	**64.55** (64.67)

Table 3: Performance of the models on OntoNotes Arabic *test* set. For validation, we additionally show the Avg. F1 scores on the OnteNotes Arabic *dev* set in the parentheses in the last column.

lingual coreference (Pradhan et al., 2012).

We use BERT-COREF as the end-to-end neural coreference model and then replace the BERT encoder with other encoders. We implemented three models: MBERT, ARABERT, and GIGABERT, named after the coresponding pre-trained tranformers that are used as the text encoder. We train each model with only the Arabic training data. Results are shown in Table 3 (1).

To leverage English annotation in bilingual transfer learning, we also implemented the following models (shown in Table 3 (2)) that are trained with both Arabic and English training data.

- MBERT-PIPELINE: We use MBERT as the text encoder. We train the model with the PIPELINE approach (Section 3.3). We set the number of pre-training epochs $m = 20$ and the number of fine-tuning epochs $n = 20$.
- GIGABERT-PIPELINE: Same as above except that we use GIGABERT as the text encoder.
- MBERT-JOINT: We use MBERT as the text encoder. We train the model with the JOINT approach (Section 3.3).
- GIGABERT-JOINT: Same as MBERT-JOINT except that GIGABERT is used as the encoder.

For all models, we set the pre-trained transformers' learning rate to $1e-5$, the task learning rate to $2e-4$, the number of epochs to 30 except for the PIPELINE models, and use the default values for the remaining parameters. We use the performance on the *dev* set to choose the best hyperparameter for all models, and use early stopping to prevent overfitting. All models are trained with an NVIDIA QUADRO RTX 8000 GPU. Each model trains for 3 to 12 hours depending on the size of the data (Arabic or the combined set).

Table 3 shows the performance numbers reported by the CoNLL 2012 scorer. GIGABERT-JOINT achieves the highest performance with an average F1 of 64.55. establishing a new state-of-the-art model for Arabic coreference resolution.

On pre-trained tranformers for Arabic: Comparing MBERT, ARABERT and GIGABERT, Table 3 (1) shows a stunning difference in their performance in Arabic coreference resolution. GIGABERT shows the best F1 at 62.09, ARABERT comes second at 56.41 F1, and MBERT performs the worst at 46.8 F1. There are two important factors that contribute to the difference:

First, the size of Arabic text used for pre-training significantly affects the pre-trained transformer' ability to encode text for Arabic coreference resolution. As shown in Table 1, MBERT, ARABERT and GIGABERT use drastically different amounts of Arabic training tokens (153M, 2.5B and 4.3B for MBERT, ARABERT and GIGABERT, respectively). The more data that the transformer is pre-trained on, the higher the performance.

Second, ARABERT and GIGABERT are trained specifically for Arabic, while MBERT is trained for 104 languages and has not been tuned for Arabic. The language-specific training makes ARABERT and GIGABERT models specialized to capture the intricacies of Arabic, leading to better performance.

On bilingual transfer learning: Comparing the bilingual transfer learning models (Table3 (2)) to the Arabic-only models (Table3 (1)), we observe 3 and 2.5 average F1 improvements when using MBERT and GIGABERT respectively. This shows the effectiveness of the bilingual transfer learning. The PIPELINE and JOINT approach shows similar gains. This indicates that it is the additional training data rather than the learning model that leads to the gain. Interestingly, using MBERT and GIGA-BERT gives similar gains, which shows that the transferability of the these two models in English to Arabic is about the same (though with MBERT lagging in baseline Arabic performance by 15.29 F1). It is surprising given that GIGABERT is a bilingual model trained specifically for English-Arabic. We plan to investigate this as an immediate next step.

5 Conclusion

We present bilingual tranfer learning for Arabic coreference resolution, that achieved new state-of-the-art performance as evaluated on OntoNotes.

Acknowledgments

This research is based upon work supported in part by the Office of the Director of National Intelligence (ODNI), Intelligence Advanced Research Projects Activity (IARPA), via Contract No. 2019-19051600006 under the IARPA BETTER program. The views and conclusions contained herein are those of the authors and should not be interpreted as necessarily representing the official policies, either expressed or implied, of ODNI, IARPA, or the U.S. Government. The U.S. Government is authorized to reproduce and distribute reprints for governmental purposes not withstanding any copyright annotation therein.

References

Abdulrahman Aloraini and Massimo Poesio. 2020. Cross-lingual Zero Pronoun Resolution. In *Proceedings of LREC 2020.*

Abdulrahman Aloraini, Juntao Yu, and Massimo Poesio. 2020. Neural coreference resolution for Arabic. In *Proceedings of the Third Workshop on Computational Models of Reference, Anaphora and Coreference*, pages 99–110, Barcelona, Spain (online). Association for Computational Linguistics.

Wissam Antoun, Fady Baly, and Hazem Hajj. 2020. AraBERT: Transformer-based model for Arabic language understanding. In *Proceedings of the 4th Workshop on Open-Source Arabic Corpora and Processing Tools, with a Shared Task on Offensive Language Detection*, pages 9–15, Marseille, France. European Language Resource Association.

Anders Björkelund and Jonas Kuhn. 2014. Learning Structured Perceptrons for Coreference Resolution with Latent Antecedents and Non-local Features. pages 47–57.

Chen Chen and Vincent Ng. 2012. Combining the Best of Two Worlds: A Hybrid Approach to Multilingual Coreference Resolution. In *Proceedings of the Joint Conference on EMNLP and CoNLL - Shared Task.*

Jacob Devlin, Ming-Wei Chang, Kenton Lee, and Kristina Toutanova. 2019. BERT: Pre-training of deep bidirectional transformers for language understanding. In *Proceedings of the 2019 Conference of the North American Chapter of the Association for Computational Linguistics: Human Language Technologies, Volume 1 (Long and Short Papers)*, pages 4171–4186, Minneapolis, Minnesota. Association for Computational Linguistics.

Ibrahim Abu El-khair. 2016. 1.5 billion words arabic corpus.

Eraldo Fernandes, Cícero dos Santos, and Ruy Milidiú. 2012. Latent Structure Perceptron with Feature Induction for Unrestricted Coreference Resolution. In *Proceedings of the Joint Conference on EMNLP and CoNLL - Shared Task.*

Iryna Haponchyk and Alessandro Moschitti. 2017. Don't understand a measure? learn it: Structured prediction for coreference resolution optimizing its measures. In *Proceedings of the 55th Annual Meeting of the Association for Computational Linguistics (Volume 1: Long Papers)*, pages 1018–1028, Vancouver, Canada. Association for Computational Linguistics.

Mandar Joshi, Danqi Chen, Yinhan Liu, Daniel S. Weld, Luke Zettlemoyer, and Omer Levy. 2020. SpanBERT: Improving pre-training by representing and predicting spans. *Transactions of the Association for Computational Linguistics*, 8:64–77.

Mandar Joshi, Omer Levy, Daniel S Weld, and Luke Zettlemoyer. 2019a. BERT for Coreference Resolution: Baselines and Analysis. In *Proceedings of the 2019 Conference on Empirical Methods in Natural Language Processing and the 9th International Joint Conference on Natural Language Processing (EMNLP-IJCNLP)*, arXiv.

Mandar Joshi, Omer Levy, Luke Zettlemoyer, and Daniel Weld. 2019b. BERT for coreference resolution: Baselines and analysis. In *Proceedings of the 2019 Conference on Empirical Methods in Natural Language Processing and the 9th International Joint Conference on Natural Language Processing (EMNLP-IJCNLP)*, pages 5803–5808, Hong Kong, China. Association for Computational Linguistics.

Wuwei Lan, Yang Chen, Wei Xu, and Alan Ritter. 2020. An Empirical Study of Pre-trained Transformers for Arabic Information Extraction. In *Proceedings of the 2020 Conference on Empirical Methods in Natural Language Processing (EMNLP)*, arXiv.

Kenton Lee, Luheng He, and Luke Zettlemoyer. 2018. Higher-order coreference resolution with coarse-to-fine inference. In *Proceedings of the 2018 Confer-*

ence of the North American Chapter of the Association for Computational Linguistics: Human Language Technologies, Volume 2 (Short Papers), pages 687–692, New Orleans, Louisiana. Association for Computational Linguistics.

Vincent Ng. 2010. Supervised noun phrase coreference research: The first fifteen years. In *Proceedings of the 48th Annual Meeting of the Association for Computational Linguistics*, pages 1396–1411, Uppsala, Sweden. Association for Computational Linguistics.

Pedro Javier Ortiz Suárez, Benoît Sagot, and Laurent Romary. 2019. Asynchronous Pipeline for Processing Huge Corpora on Medium to Low Resource Infrastructures. In *7th Workshop on the Challenges in the Management of Large Corpora (CMLC-7)*, Cardiff, United Kingdom. Leibniz-Institut für Deutsche Sprache.

Telmo Pires, Eva Schlinger, and Dan Garrette. 2019. How multilingual is multilingual BERT? In *Proceedings of the 57th Annual Meeting of the Association for Computational Linguistics*, pages 4996–5001, Florence, Italy. Association for Computational Linguistics.

Sameer Pradhan, Alessandro Moschitti, Nianwen Xue, Olga Uryupina, and Yuchen Zhang. 2012. CoNLL-2012 shared task: Modeling multilingual unrestricted coreference in OntoNotes. In *Joint Conference on EMNLP and CoNLL - Shared Task*, pages 1–40, Jeju Island, Korea. Association for Computational Linguistics.

Marcus Stamborg, Dennis Medved, Peter Exner, and Pierre Nugues. 2012. Using Syntactic Dependencies to Solve Coreferences. In *Proceedings of the Joint Conference on EMNLP and CoNLL - Shared Task*.

Olga Uryupina and Alessandro Moschitti. 2013. Multilingual mention detection for coreference resolution. In *Proceedings of the Sixth International Joint Conference on Natural Language Processing*, pages 100–108, Nagoya, Japan. Asian Federation of Natural Language Processing.

Wei Wu, Fei Wang, Arianna Yuan, Fei Wu, and Jiwei Li. 2020. CorefQA: Coreference resolution as query-based span prediction. In *Proceedings of the 58th Annual Meeting of the Association for Computational Linguistics*, pages 6953–6963, Online. Association for Computational Linguistics.

Hao Xiong and Qun Liu. 2012. ICT: System Description for CoNLL-2012. In *Proceedings of the Joint Conference on EMNLP and CoNLL - Shared Task*.

Imad Zeroual, Dirk Goldhahn, Thomas Eckart, and Abdelhak Lakhouaja. 2019. OSIAN: Open source international Arabic news corpus - preparation and integration into the CLARIN-infrastructure. In *Proceedings of the Fourth Arabic Natural Language Processing Workshop*, pages 175–182, Florence, Italy. Association for Computational Linguistics.

Desislava Zhekova, Sandra Kübler, Joshua Bonner, Marwa Ragheb, and Yu-Yin Hsu. 2012. UBIU for Multilingual Coreference Resolution in OntoNotes. In *Proceedings of the Joint Conference on EMNLP and CoNLL - Shared Task*.

Event and Entity Coreference using Trees to Encode Uncertainty in Joint Decisions

Nishant Yadav, Nicholas Monath, Rico Angell, and Andrew McCallum
College of Information and Computer Sciences
University of Massachusetts Amherst
{nishantyadav,nmonath,rangell,mccallum}@cs.umass.edu

Abstract

Coreference decisions among event mentions and among co-occurring entity mentions are highly interdependent, thus motivating joint inference. Capturing the uncertainty over each variable can be crucial for inference among multiple dependent variables. Previous work on joint coreference employs heuristic approaches, lacking well-defined objectives, and lacking modeling of uncertainty on each side of the joint problem. We present a new approach of joint coreference, including (1) a formal cost function inspired by Dasgupta's cost for hierarchical clustering, and (2) a representation for uncertainty of clustering of event and entity mentions, again based on a hierarchical structure. We describe an alternating optimization method for inference that when clustering event mentions, considers the uncertainty of the clustering of entity mentions and vice-versa. We show that our proposed joint model provides empirical advantages over state-of-the-art independent and joint models.

1 Introduction

Coreference resolution refers to the task of detecting mentions of various entities and events and identifying groups of mentions referring to the same real-world entity or event. It is a fundamental NLP task that has several downstream applications such as question answering (Chen et al., 2019; Bhattacharjee et al., 2020), textual entailment (Mitkov et al., 2012), building and maintaining KBs (Angeli et al., 2015; Angell et al., 2021), and multi-document summarization (Falke et al., 2017; Huang and Kurohashi, 2021). Often these downstream applications consume a set of documents, and thus require detection of coreference relations between event and entity mentions spread across documents such as multiple news articles.

Event and entity coreference decisions often have rich dependencies on each other. Consider the example in Figure 1 where a system performing

1.) [HP]$_{e1}$ **lands**$_{v1}$ green datacenter consultant [EYP]$_{e2}$.
2.) [HP]$_{e3}$ **acquires**$_{v2}$ [EYP Mission Critical Facilities]$_{e4}$.
3.) [Hewlett-Packard]$_{e5}$ will **acquire**$_{v3}$ [Electronic Data Systems]$_{e6}$ for about \$ 13 billion.

Figure 1: Example sentences from ECB+ corpus with event mentions and their argument entity mentions. Color indicate ground-truth coreference clusters.

event coreference independently of entity coreference may erroneously conclude that lands (v1) and acquires (v2) are not coreferent while acquires (v2) and acquire (v3) are coreferent. A joint model that leverages coreference decisions of these events' arguments can help avoid such errors. For instance, coreference relationships between arguments of v1, v2, and v3 could provide crucial evidence in support of v1 and v2 being coreferent, and v2 and v3 being not coreferent.

Previous work that exploits the argument-predicate structure either rely on lexical similarity between arguments while resolving related event mentions (Yang et al., 2015; Choubey and Huang, 2017; Yu et al., 2020, inter alia), or is limited to algorithmic approaches without an explicitly defined cost function (He, 2007; Lee et al., 2012; Barhom et al., 2019). Moreover, these approaches do not capture the uncertainty in coreference decisions during the inference as they represent jointness only at a flat clustering level.

In this work, we present a cost function that captures both the dependency between coreference decisions of event and entity mentions as well as the uncertainty of these decisions. Our proposed cost extends Dasgupta's cost function for hierarchical (tree-structured) clustering (Dasgupta, 2016), generalizing it to model the dependencies between two separate clustering problems of event and entity coreference. To optimize this cost, we describe an efficient inference procedure, which is based on iterated conditional modes. Our inference algorithm captures the uncertainty over clustering decisions of events and entities using the hierar-

Proceedings of the 4th Workshop on Computational Models of Reference, Anaphora and Coreference (CRAC 2021), pages 100–110
Punta Cana, Dominican Republic, November 10–11, 2021.

chical clusterings or cluster trees over event and entity mentions. The algorithm proceeds by building cluster trees over event and entity mentions, independently. We then alternate between building over event mentions conditioned on the cluster tree over entity mentions, and building cluster trees over entity mentions given the cluster tree over event mentions, until convergence.

Our proposed joint clustering model offers up to 2 CONLL-F_1 points improvement over resolving event and entity mentions independently, and up to 0.75 CONLL-F_1 points improvement over greedy iterative-merge clustering used in prior work.

2 Related Work

Entity coreference resolution, especially in the within-document setting has seen a tremendous amount of improvement over recent years. Early work on entity coreference used hand-crafted syntactic and semantic features (Ng and Cardie, 2002; Daumé III and Marcu, 2005; Durrett and Klein, 2013) while recent top-performing models are neural models that perform mention detection, followed by mention clustering in an end-to-end fashion (Lee et al., 2017, 2018; Meged et al., 2020; Joshi et al., 2020). Event coreference has also seen similar trends with early work using lexical features such as Wordnet synsets, head lemma of the verb (Chen and Ji, 2009; Bejan and Harabagiu, 2010) while more recent work uses event embeddings from pre-trained word embeddings or pretrained language models (Lu and Ng, 2018; Kenyon-Dean et al., 2018; Cattan et al., 2020; Yu et al., 2020). While the majority of the work on event or entity coreference attempts to solve the tasks separately, some prior work does exploit the argument-predicate structure to derive additional features for enriching entity/event representations. In this work, we go a step further and perform joint clustering of event and entity mentions instead of merely using event or entity mentions to derive additional lexical features.

Prior work that jointly predicts event and entity coreference decisions does so at a flat clustering level (Lee et al., 2012; Barhom et al., 2019). The joint clustering method incrementally merges entity or event clusters, and computes merge score between a pair of entity (or event) clusters based on a learned similarity function that incorporates features from the involved mentions as well as clusters of related event (or entity) mentions. However, they use flat clustering of mentions at the given time step to compute merge scores in the next time step. In this work, instead of using an incrementally built flat clustering, we use cluster trees over entity and event mentions that help encode uncertainty over coreference decisions as part of our joint inference.

3 Joint Coreference Model

Problem Definition The task of coreference resolution is a clustering problem where data points are textual spans of event (or entity) mentions and clusters refer to the real-world events (or entities). In this work, we focus on cross-document coreference[1] in which the entity and event mentions participating in the clustering problem come from a corpus of documents. Let $\mathcal{D} = \{D_1, \ldots, D_{n_d}\}$ be a set of n_d documents containing a set of event mentions M_v and a set of entity mentions M_e with ground-truth flat clustering $\mathcal{E}_v^*$ and $\mathcal{E}_e^*$ respectively. Given the documents and set of event and entity mentions as input, the task is to output flat clusterings $\hat{\mathcal{E}}_v$ and $\hat{\mathcal{E}}_e$ of M_v and M_e respectively.

Our approach for joint event and entity coreference uses dependencies between event and entity mentions (§ 3.2). We formalize a cost function that uses an independently trained pairwise similarity (§ 3.4) along with relational similarity (§ 3.5) defined using these dependencies in a way that captures uncertainty over coreference decisions. Finally, we describe our joint inference procedure to optimize the proposed cost function in § 3.7.

3.1 Cluster Trees

We will use a hierarchical clustering or *cluster tree*, denoted $\mathcal{T}$, to represent the uncertainty of coreference decisions. A cluster tree inherently represents multiple alternative flat clusterings, any of which can be selected as the predicted coreference of mentions. These tree structures are a popular choice among cross-document coreference models, and are typically built using hierarchical agglomerative clustering (Green et al., 2012; Kenyon-Dean et al., 2018; Cattan et al., 2020, inter alia).

A cluster tree has mentions as its leaves. For instance, a cluster tree over event mentions would have M_v as its set of leaves. Each internal node represents the cluster of its descendant leaves. An internal node with children x and y is associated with a score from a linkage function, $\mathcal{S}_{x,y}$ which measures similarity between clusters associated with x and y. A canonical way, as used by Cattan

[1]Distinct from the with-in document setting where each document is treated as a separate clustering problem.

et al. (2020) and others, to select a flat clustering from the cluster tree is to use a threshold τ on the linkage score and select the fewest number of clusters possible with linkage greater than τ. In this way, functions of their lowest common ancestor in the tree structure, such as the linkage score, can be informative of the likelihood of two mentions being in the same predicted flat cluster.

3.2 Relational Dependency Edges

Consider the decision of whether two events are coreferent. If the entities involved in the two events are coreferent, we might be more inclined to believe that the two events are coreferent. Similarly, we might be more inclined to believe two entity mentions are coreferent if they participate in the same real-world event. We formalize this intuition by using semantic roles (Carreras and Màrquez, 2005) for modeling dependencies between event mentions and entity mentions.

For each event, we identify entity mentions occurring in specific semantic roles. In this work, we use four semantic role labels – `ARG0`, `ARG1`, `ARG-LOC` and `ARG-TMP`, and collect a set of **relational dependency edges** between entity mentions and event mentions. In particular, we use $\arg_{\mathtt{r}}(m_i)$ to denote the entity mention in the semantic role $\mathtt{r}$ for event mention m_i, and $\arg_{\mathtt{r}}^{-1}(m_i)$ to denote the event mention for which the entity mention m_i occurs in role $\mathtt{r}$. In case an event mention m_i does not have an argument in a semantic role $\mathtt{r}$, $\arg_{\mathtt{r}}(m_i) = \epsilon$. Similarly, $\arg_{\mathtt{r}}^{-1}(m_i) = \epsilon$ if an entity mention m_i does not occur in role $\mathtt{r}$ for any event mention. Consider the example in Figure 1 where $\arg_{\mathtt{ARG0}}$(lands) = HP, $\arg_{\mathtt{ARG1}}$(lands) = EYP, and $\arg_{\mathtt{ARG1}}^{-1}$(EYP) = lands.

3.3 Joint Cost Function

We will be building two cluster trees– one for event mentions and the other for entity mentions. We formalize a cost function that assigns a cost to the pair of cluster trees considering both mention similarities as well as the dependency edges between event and entity mentions.

We begin by defining a cost for a single tree that does not include dependency edges using Dasgupta's cost (Dasgupta, 2016) for hierarchical clustering. Let $\mathcal{T}_v$ be a cluster tree over event mentions, and $\mathtt{LLCA}_{i,j}^{(v)}$ be the number of leaves under the lowest common ancestor (LCA) of event mentions m_i and m_j, and $f_{\text{ind}}^{(v)}$ be pairwise mention similarity function over event mentions computed *independently* of entity mentions. Dasgupta's cost of $\mathcal{T}_v$ is given by

$$J_{\text{ind}}(\mathcal{T}_v) = \sum_{m_i, m_j \in M_v} f_{\text{ind}}^{(v)}(m_i, m_j)\mathtt{LLCA}_{i,j}^{(v)}$$

We similarly define cost $J_{\text{ind}}(\mathcal{T}_e)$ for tree $\mathcal{T}_e$ over entity mentions. In words, each pair of mentions pays a cost that is its similarity $f_{\text{ind}}^{(v)}(m_i, m_j)$ times number of leaves under their lowest common ancestor. Intuitively, in order to minimize the cost, a pair of mentions m_i, m_j, that has high pairwise similarity should be merged near the leaf level of the tree (i.e., more likely to be in the same flat cluster) so that they have a small value of $\mathtt{LLCA}_{i,j}^{(v)}$ while pairs of mentions with low similarity could be placed thus far apart in the tree e.g., potentially with the tree root as the lowest common ancestor.

To capture information from our relational dependency edges, we introduce a relational similarity term $f_{\text{rel}}^{(v)}$. For a pair of event mentions, $f_{\text{rel}}^{(v)}$ estimates event similarity by using the cluster-assignments of the entity mentions involved in dependency edges with the two event mentions. We propose several ways to define $f_{\text{rel}}^{(v)}$ in §3.5. We define the cost of a cluster tree over event mentions ($\mathcal{T}_v$) given a cluster tree over entity mentions ($\mathcal{T}_e$) as follows:

$$J_{\text{rel}}(\mathcal{T}_v|\mathcal{T}_e) = \sum_{m_i, m_j \in M_v} f_{\text{rel}}^{(v)}(m_i, m_j)\mathtt{LLCA}_{i,j}^{(v)}$$

A pair of event mentions has high relational similarity if their arguments are present in the same flat clustering or present close to each other in their cluster tree. And, the cost function $J_{\text{rel}}(\mathcal{T}_v|\mathcal{T}_e)$ is minimized when pairs of event mentions with high relational similarity are placed close in the cluster tree, thus increasing their likelihood of being in the same inferred flat clustering. This is desired behavior based on the assumption that coreferring arguments increase the likelihood of two events being coreferent and vice-versa. We define the joint cost as a weighted combination of the independent and relational costs as follows:

$$\begin{aligned} J_{\text{joint}}(\mathcal{T}_v, \mathcal{T}_e) = \alpha_{\text{ind}}^{(v)} J_{\text{ind}}(\mathcal{T}_v) + \alpha_{\text{ind}}^{(e)} J_{\text{ind}}(\mathcal{T}_e) + \\ \beta_{\text{rel}}^{(v)} J_{\text{rel}}(\mathcal{T}_v|\mathcal{T}_e) + \beta_{\text{rel}}^{(e)} J_{\text{rel}}(\mathcal{T}_e|\mathcal{T}_v) \quad (1) \end{aligned}$$

where $\alpha_{\text{ind}}^{(t)}, \beta_{\text{rel}}^{(t)} \in \mathbb{R}, t \in \{\text{entity}, \text{event}\}$.

We can re-write the joint cost as a function of mention pairs by substituting expressions for each

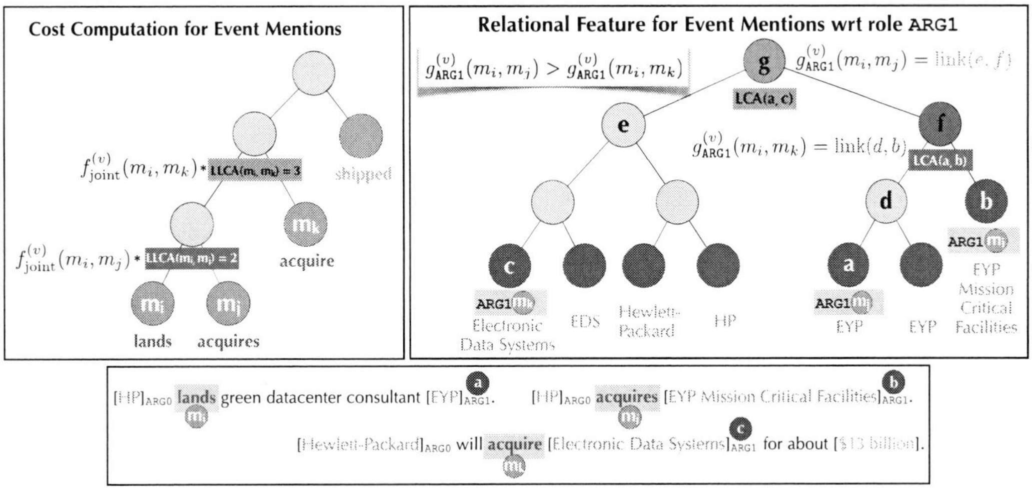

Figure 2: Illustration of the cost function and the joint relational dependence model using the tree structure. Three sentences from the corpus are shown in the lower pane. We focus on a pair of event mentions "lands" and "acquires" from the example in Figure 1. In the upper left pane, we show the computation of two terms in the cost for m_i & m_j and m_i & m_k, which involves the product of their similarities (using the joint model) and the number of leaves of their lowest common ancestors (LCA). In the upper right pane, we show the computation of the LINKAGE-SCORE relational similarity feature ($g^{(v)}_{\text{ARG1}}$) wrt ARG1 of these event mentions using linkage score of their LCA. Observe how this relational feature uses the LCA in a different way than the cost function. Here we use the linkage score at the LCA to define relational feature $g^{(v)}_{\text{ARG1}}$.

term in the cost function as follows:

$$J_{\text{joint}}(\mathcal{T}_v, \mathcal{T}_e) = \underbrace{\sum_{m_i, m_j \in M_v} f^{(v)}_{\text{joint}}(m_i, m_j)\text{LLCA}^{(v)}_{i,j}}_{1} + \underbrace{\sum_{m_i, m_j \in M_e} f^{(e)}_{\text{joint}}(m_i, m_j)\text{LLCA}^{(e)}_{i,j}}_{2} \quad (2)$$

where, for $t \in \{\text{entity, event}\}$

$$f^{(t)}_{\text{joint}}(m_i, m_j) = \alpha^{(t)}_{\text{ind}} f^{(t)}_{\text{ind}}(m_i, m_j) + \beta^{(t)}_{\text{rel}} f^{(t)}_{\text{rel}}(m_i, m_j), \quad (3)$$

Figure 2 shows example computation of the first term in Eq 2. In the following sections, we describe how we train and compute different components of the joint similarity function.

3.4 Pairwise Mention Scorer ($f^{(t)}_{\text{ind}}$)

We use the recently proposed state-of-the-art independent coreference model proposed by Cattan et al. (2020) as our pairwise mention scorers $f^{(v)}_{\text{ind}}, f^{(e)}_{\text{ind}}$ for event and entity mentions respectively. This model encodes event (or entity) mentions in context using RoBERTa (Liu et al., 2019). The mention embeddings and their element-wise product of their embeddings are concatenated to create a mention-pair representation which is then passed through an MLP to return a similarity score for the given pair of mentions. Following Cattan et al. (2020), we freeze RoBERTa parameters and only train parameter of the MLP using binary cross-entropy loss over all pairs of mentions.

3.5 Relational Similarity ($f^{(t)}_{\text{rel}}$)

The core of our joint approach is in the way relational dependency edges between events and entities contribute to the cost function. These relational edges will contribute to the relational similarity $f^{(v)}_{\text{rel}}(m_i, m_j)$ (and thereby to the cost function through the joint similarity). The relational similarities we propose will use the tree structure to represent uncertainty over the final flat clustering assignment of mentions to clusters.

Let's begin by considering the definition of relational similarity for event mentions (the similarity for entity mentions is defined analogously). Given a pair of event mentions m_i, m_j, relational similarity $f^{(v)}_{\text{rel}}(m_i, m_j)$ is computed using their semantic role arguments. Specifically, we define a relational feature $g^{(v)}_{\text{r}}(m_i, m_j)$ using similarity $f^{(e)}_{\text{sim}}$ between entity mentions which are arguments of event mentions m_i, m_j in semantic role $\texttt{r}$ as:

$$g_{\texttt{r}}^{(v)}(m_i, m_j) = f_{\text{sim}}^{(e)}(\text{arg}_{\texttt{r}}(m_i), \text{arg}_{\texttt{r}}(m_j)) \quad (4)$$

Relational similarity $f_{\text{rel}}^{(v)}(m_i, m_j)$ is then computed using weights $\phi^{(v)}$ over these features as:

$$\begin{aligned} f_{\text{rel}}^{(v)}(m_i, m_j) &= \sum_{r} \phi_r^{(v)} g_{\texttt{r}}^{(v)}(m_i, m_j) \\ &= \sum_{r} \phi_r^{(v)} f_{\text{sim}}^{(e)}(\text{arg}_{\texttt{r}}(m_i), \text{arg}_{\texttt{r}}(m_j)) \end{aligned}$$

The similarity $f_{\text{sim}}^{(e)}$ will be based on the coreference decision of the pair of entity arguments. Most simply, one could use hard assignments of entity mentions to flat clusters, such as:

- FLAT-CLUST: $f_{\text{sim}}^{(e)}(m_i, m_j) = 1$ if m_i & m_j belong to the same cluster, and 0 otherwise.

However, we would like to capture the uncertainty over (hard) flat cluster assignments using the tree-structured clustering. To do this, we define $f_{\text{sim}}^{(e)}$ as a function of $\text{LCA}_{i,j}$, the lowest common ancestor of mentions m_i, m_j in $\mathcal{T}_e$ as follows:

- LINKAGE-SCORE: $f_{\text{sim}}^{(e)}(m_i, m_j) = -\mathcal{S}_{i,j}$ where $\mathcal{S}_{i,j}$ gives the linkage score between the left and right child nodes of $\text{LCA}_{i,j}$ in $\mathcal{T}_e$.
- NODE-ORDER: $f_{\text{sim}}^{(e)}(m_i, m_j) = -\mathcal{O}_{i,j}$, where $\mathcal{O}_{i,j}$ is the position of $\text{LCA}_{i,j}$ in the array of internal nodes of $\mathcal{T}_e$, sorted in increasing order of their linkage scores.

Figure 2 shows computation of relational feature ($g_{\texttt{ARG1}}^{(v)}$) for pairs of event mentions using LINKAGE-SCORE method. Analogous similarity functions are defined for entity mentions, except in terms of the inverse relational dependencies, i.e.:

$$\begin{aligned} f_{\text{rel}}^{(e)}(m_i, m_j) &= \sum_{r} \phi_r^{(e)} g_{\texttt{r}}^{(e)}(m_i, m_j) \\ &= \sum_{r} \phi_r^{(e)} f_{\text{sim}}^{(v)}(\text{arg}_{\texttt{r}}^{-1}(m_i), \text{arg}_{\texttt{r}}^{-1}(m_j)) \end{aligned}$$

We also experiment with relational similarity features $g_{\texttt{r}}^{(v)}$ for a pair of event mentions computed using $f_{\text{sim}}^{(e)} = f_{\text{ind}}^{(e)}$ instead of defining $f_{\text{sim}}^{(e)}$ using a (hierarchical) clustering of entity mentions. Additionally, we experiment with relational similarity features computed using $f_{\text{sim}}^{(e)}$ defined using clustering of entity mentions as well as using $f_{\text{sim}}^{(e)} = f_{\text{ind}}^{(e)}$. We define relational features analogously for entity mentions as well.

3.6 Joint-Mention Pair Scorer

In order to compute joint mention-pair similarity score for mentions of type $t \in \{\text{entity}, \text{event}\}$, we first compute a joint mention-pair feature vector using the *trained* pairwise similarity $f_{\text{ind}}^{(t)}$, and relational similarity features ($g_{\texttt{r}}^{(t)}$) based on the four semantic roles- ARG0, ARG1, ARG-LOC and ARG-TMP. However, in order to compute these relational features for event (or entity) mentions, we would need a clustering over entity (or event) mentions to begin with. Thus, in order to bootstrap the process, we initially cluster entity (or event) mentions only using scores from $f_{\text{ind}}^{(e)}$ (or $f_{\text{ind}}^{(v)}$). We then compute relational similarity feature values using the cluster trees or the flat clusterings over event and entity mentions.

We finally train a linear classifier on top of this joint feature vector to generate final joint pairwise similarity as shown in Figure 3. The linear classifier is trained using binary cross-entropy loss to classify a given pair of mentions as coreferent or not.

3.7 Inference

Given trained pairwise mention similarity functions ($f_{\text{ind}}^{(v)}, f_{\text{ind}}^{(e)}$) and trained joint mention-pair scorers ($f_{\text{joint}}^{(v)}, f_{\text{joint}}^{(e)}$), our joint inference procedure starts by clustering event mentions and entity mentions independently using $f_{\text{ind}}^{(v)}$ and $f_{\text{ind}}^{(e)}$ respectively, with average linkage hierarchical agglomerative clustering (Johnson, 1967). We then alternate between rebuilding the cluster tree over event mentions and the cluster tree over entity mentions. Given a cluster tree over entity mentions, we first compute the joint pairwise feature vector, then compute the joint-pairwise similarity ($f_{\text{joint}}^{(v)}$), and use it to compute hierarchical clustering over event mentions. We similarly update clustering over entity mentions given the updated tree over event mentions and alternate until the cost function in Eq 2 has converged.

We use hierarchical agglomerative clustering (HAC) to build cluster trees as it allows use of an arbitrary pairwise scoring function and is widely used for coreference resolution in prior work (Lee et al., 2012; Clark and Manning, 2016; Barhom et al., 2019; Cattan et al., 2020, inter-alia). Moreover, average-linkage HAC provides a 2-approximation to a dissimilarity-based version of Dasgupta's cost function (Cohen-Addad et al., 2019). Our proposed inference alternates between optimizing the first and the second term in Eq 2. Clustering event men-

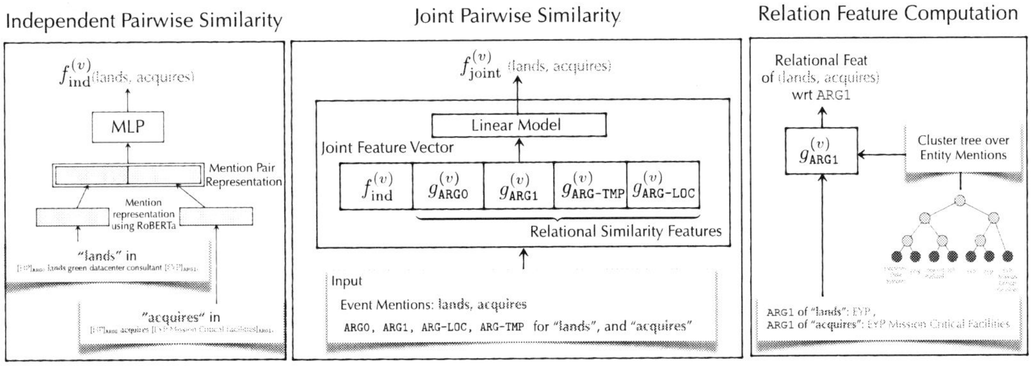

Figure 3: Illustration of joint similarity computation for a pair of event mentions "lands" and "acquires" from the example in Figure 1. Left panel in the figure shows computation of pairwise mention scorer $f_{\text{ind}}^{(v)}$ and the right panel shows computation of relational similarity feature for the two event mentions using entity mentions in semantic role ARG1, and the cluster tree over entity mentions. The central panel shows the joint feature vector computed using pairwise mention score from $f_{\text{ind}}^{(v)}$ and relational similarity features $(g_{\text{ARG0}}^{(v)}, g_{\text{ARG1}}^{(v)}, g_{\text{ARG-LOC}}^{(v)}, g_{\text{ARG-TMP}}^{(v)})$ is fed into a linear model to produce final joint pairwise similarity.

tions given a cluster tree over entity mentions using the joint similarity function $f_{\text{joint}}^{(v)}$ optimizes the first term in Eq. 2 while clustering entity mentions given event mentions using the joint similarity function $f_{\text{joint}}^{(e)}$ optimizes the second term in Eq. 2. Finally, on convergences, we use a threshold to pick a flat clustering over event and entity mentions given their cluster trees. At test time, we use threshold values picked using dev data.

4 Experiments

Dataset We run experiments on the ECB+ corpus which consists of both within- and cross-document coreference resolution for *both* entity and event mentions. ECB+ corpus consists of a set of news articles, grouped under topics. Each topic consists of two sub-topics containing articles about two different real-world events which use similar vocabulary, thus posing a challenge for coreference systems. For example, the first two sentences in Figure 1 are from the same subtopic containing documents of HP's acquisition of EYP while the third sentence comes from a document from a different subtopic which talks about HP's acquisition of EDS. This presents a challenging setting when evaluating cross-document coreference at the topic level as there are instances of coreferent event and entity mentions with divergent surfaces forms as well as mentions of different real-world events and entities with similar surface forms. We show statistics on ECB+ in Table 1.

	Train	Dev	Test	Total
# Topics	25	8	10	43
# Documents	574	196	206	976
# Event Mentions	3808	1245	1780	6833
# Event Clusters	1527	409	805	2741
# Entity Mentions	4758	1476	2055	8289
# Entity Clusters	1286	330	608	2224

Table 1: Statistics on the standard train/dev/test split of ECB+ dataset (Cybulska and Vossen, 2014).

Evaluation Metrics and Setup We use the official CoNLL scorer (Pradhan et al., 2014) and report coreference resolution metrics like MUC (Vilain et al., 1995), B^3 (Bagga and Baldwin, 1998), $CEAF_e$ (Luo, 2005) and the average of these three metric, the CONLL-F_1 metric. We follow the evaluation setup of (Cybulska and Vossen, 2014), also used in other recent work (Kenyon-Dean et al., 2018; Barhom et al., 2019; Cattan et al., 2020). Following the precedent set by recent work, we remove singletons from both gold as well as predicted clusters during evaluation. We use gold event and entity mentions, evaluate coreference performance at topic level with gold topics, and finally compute a micro average of the metrics across all topics.

4.1 Implementation Details and Baselines

Proposed Models Recall that our joint clustering model requires a similarity measure $f_{\text{sim}}^{(t)}, t \in \{\text{event}, \text{entity}\}$ between mentions to compute relational similarity features which are then use to compute the joint pairwise similarity as described in § 3.5 and § 3.6. We experiment with four different choices for this similarity measure: JOINTINF-PW uses independent pairwise mention similarity $f_{\text{ind}}^{(t)}$, JOINTINF-PF uses similarity computed using predicted flat clusterings in addition to $f_{\text{ind}}^{(t)}$, and JOINTINF-NO and JOINTINF-LS use cluster tree based similarity computed using NODE-ORDER and LINKAGE-SCORE methods respectively in addition to $f_{\text{ind}}^{(t)}$.

Baselines We compare our proposed joint clustering model with the following baselines:

- IND: Compute clustering of event and entity mentions *independently* using $f_{\text{ind}}^{(t)}, t \in$ {event, entity}. This corresponds to results[2] for models proposed in Cattan et al. (2020).
- GREEDY-MERGE:This refers to the inference procedure used by Lee et al. (2012); Barhom et al. (2019) with the features proposed in this paper. It starts with event and entity mentions in singleton clusters. At each time step, it computes the joint pairwise event (entity) mention similarity using the flat clustering of entity (event) mentions at the given time step, updates the linkage score between every pair of clusters, and finally greedily merges the pair of event or entity mention clusters with the highest linkage score. Like our proposed models, it uses $f_{\text{ind}}^{(t)}$ in addition to similarity computed using predicted flat clusterings for joint similarity computation.

Previous work on joint event and entity clustering (Lee et al., 2012; Barhom et al., 2019) uses different mention encoders and features, and/or different evaluation setting. For this reason, our results are not directly comparable with those. GREEDY-MERGE baseline uses a clustering algorithm similar to that used in previous work, on top of the mention encoder and features used in this work.

Note that, JOINTINF-PF and GREEDY-MERGE are similar in that they both use a flat clustering in the joint similarity computation with one important difference – JOINTINF-PF predicts a flat clustering over *all* event (entity) mentions *before* using updating clustering of entity (event) mentions while GREEDY-MERGE starts with a flat clustering with all singletons, and the flat clustering over event and entity mentions used in joint similarity calculations is updated after every cluster merge. We present further implementation details in Appendix A.

4.2 Results

Tables 2a and 2b show performance of our proposed clustering model and baselines for event and entity mentions respectively in ECB+ test corpus. Our joint clustering provides 1.97 and 1.18 points improvement in CONLL-F_1 over clustering entity and event mentions independently. Our joint clustering model outperforms the GREEDY-MERGE, the widely used joint clustering mechanism in previous work by up to 0.75 CONLL-F_1, thus indicating the importance of encoding uncertainty in clustering decisions as well as the efficacy of our methods in doing so. JOINTINF-NO and JOINTINF-LS which use cluster trees to compute relational similarity does better than JOINTINF-PF indicating that encoding uncertainty over coreference decisions using trees performs better than using a single predicted flat clustering. Finally, we note that JOINTINF-PW, which uses the trained pairwise similarity $f_{\text{ind}}^{(t)}$ instead of clustering-based similarity for computing relational similarity provides improvement over IND baseline, but it is outperformed by methods like JOINTINF-LS, and JOINTINF-NO which use cluster trees to compute relational similarity.

Furthermore, since GREEDY-MERGE recomputes pairwise features and scores after *each* merger of a pair of clusters during hierarchical clustering, it does not yield a time-efficient implementation. In contrast, our proposed inference methods compute joint pairwise scores only at the beginning of each round of inference and can thus leverage existing efficient hierarchical clustering libraries. We observed our proposed inference to converge in up to three rounds thus yielding a time-efficient joint inference procedure.

Figure 4 shows CONLL-F_1 scores for IND, GREEDY-MERGE and JOINTINF-LS for each topic in ECB+ test data. It shows that although joint inference methods such as GREEDY-MERGE and JOINTINF-LS offer performance improvement over IND baseline for majority of the topics, they do not offer improvement on a few topics such as topic 36, and 45 for event coreference.

We further analyze the performance of these models at the level of pairwise coreference decisions. We report a few examples in Table 3 where the joint inference method JOINTINF-LS

[2]IND baseline results differ slightly from those reported in Cattan et al. (2020) as we use a threshold chosen exhaustively on dev set while Cattan et al. (2020) chose a threshold from a heuristically fixed set of threshold values of {0.5, 0.55, 0.6, 0.65, 0.7}.

Clustering Model	MUC			B³			CEAF$_e$			CONLL-F$_1$
	P	R	F$_1$	P	R	F$_1$	P	R	F$_1$	
Baselines										
IND	74.03	84.20	78.79	48.82	69.01	57.18	43.28	54.46	48.23	61.40
GREEDY-MERGE	77.14	78.25	77.69	56.33	59.66	57.95	44.31	56.98	49.85	61.83 (+0.43)
Proposed Joint Models										
JOINTINF-PW	77.19	79.48	78.32	55.37	62.32	58.64	44.97	57.33	50.41	62.46 (+1.06)
JOINTINF-PF	77.21	78.56	77.88	56.48	60.10	58.23	44.61	56.62	49.90	62.00 (+0.60)
JOINTINF-NO	76.36	80.20	78.23	54.03	63.40	58.35	44.54	56.78	49.92	62.17 (+0.77)
JOINTINF-LS	76.57	82.15	79.26	52.65	65.90	58.53	44.57	56.82	49.96	**62.58 (+1.18)**

(a) Event Coreference

Clustering Model	MUC			B³			CEAF$_e$			CONLL-F$_1$
	P	R	F$_1$	P	R	F$_1$	P	R	F$_1$	
Baselines										
IND	77.46	89.05	82.86	49.37	72.29	58.67	48.06	50.73	49.36	63.63
GREEDY-MERGE	79.60	88.64	83.87	52.84	71.78	60.87	48.22	52.60	50.32	65.02 (+1.39)
Proposed Joint Models										
JOINTINF-PW	78.73	89.47	83.76	50.39	73.35	59.74	49.28	49.28	49.28	64.26 (+0.63)
JOINTINF-PF	78.97	90.02	84.14	50.25	74.12	59.89	50.54	49.26	49.89	64.64 (+1.01)
JOINTINF-NO	79.33	87.46	83.20	55.32	70.83	62.12	48.58	54.72	51.47	**65.60 (+1.97)**
JOINTINF-LS	80.02	87.67	83.67	55.07	69.14	61.30	46.16	53.15	49.41	64.79 (+1.16)

(b) Entity Coreference

Table 2: Precision/Recall/F$_1$ scores for Event and Entity coreference on ECB+ test set over gold mentions spans. Relative improvements in CONLL-F$_1$ over IND baseline are shown in parenthesis.

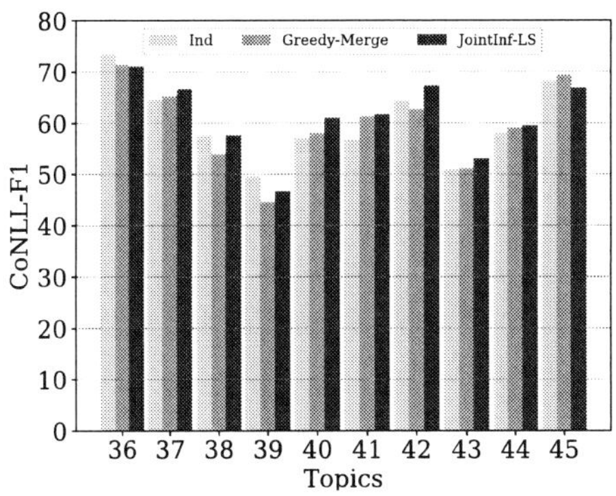

(a) Event Mentions

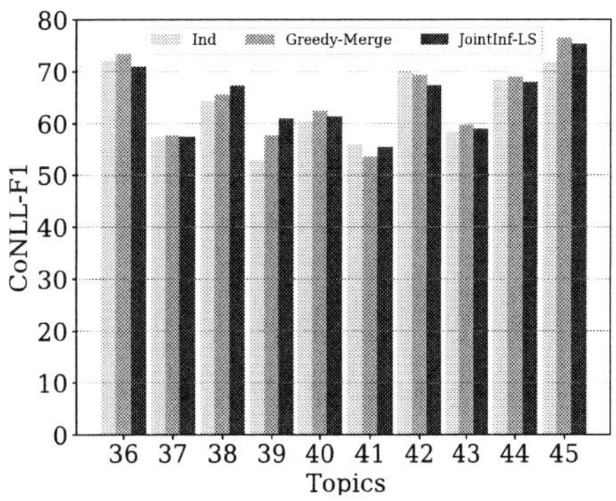

(b) Entity Mentions

Figure 4: Performance of IND, GREEDY-MERGE, and JOINTINF-LS on each test topic.

makes correct coreference decisions but IND fails, along with a potential explanation for the correct/incorrect decision made by each model. We also include a similar analysis to show where our joint inference method produces incorrect coreference decisions in Table 4. We would like to note that it is not always possible to provide an explanation for an incorrect coreference decision made by the inference algorithm as there could be multiple sources of error. An incorrect coreference decision could be a result of an incorrect value of pairwise similarity from a deep neural network such as the one used for $f_{\text{ind}}^{(v)}$ and $f_{\text{ind}}^{(e)}$, an incorrectly chosen threshold to obtain flat clustering, or errors due to non-local decisions made by the clustering algorithm which override the mention pairwise similarities amongst other potential reasons.

5 Conclusion

In this paper, we present a joint entity and event coreference model, which formally defines a cost function that extends Dasgupta's cost for hierarchical clustering and represents the uncertainty of coreference decisions along with entity-event dependencies. We present an efficient inference procedure for this cost function and empirically val-

	Event Examples
1a	[Hewlett - Packard]$_{\text{ARG0}}$ to **[buy]**$_{\text{V}}$ consulting [firm EYP Mission Critical Facilities]$_{\text{ARG1}}$.
1b	[HP]$_{\text{ARG0}}$ **[lands]**$_{\text{V}}$ green datacenter consultant [EYP]$_{\text{ARG1}}$ *Explanation*: The two event mentions "buy" and "lands" refer to the same event but have different surface forms. IND fails to cluster them while JOINTINF-LS correctly clusters them together as these two events have coreferent arguments.
2a	[HP]$_{\text{ARG0}}$ **[acquires]**$_{\text{V}}$ [EYP Mission Critical Facilities]$_{\text{ARG1}}$.
2b	[Hewlett-Packard]$_{\text{ARG0}}$ will **[acquire]**$_{\text{V}}$ [Electronic Data Systems]$_{\text{ARG0}}$ for about \$ 13 billion. *Explanation*: The two event mentions "acquire" and "acquires" refer to two different real world events but have the same surface form. IND model incorrectly predicts that these two mentions are coreferent while the joint model correctly predicts them as non-coreferent, apparently due to different arguments in ARG1 semantic role.
	Entity Examples
1a	UNHCR condemns [air attack]$_{\text{V}}$ **[on refugee camp in South Sudan]**$_{\text{ARG1}}$.
1b	South Sudan accuses Sudan of [air strike]$_{\text{V}}$ **[on refugee camp]**$_{\text{ARG1}}$. *Explanation*: The two entity mentions refer to the same entity. JOINTINF-LS correctly predicts them as coreferent, apparently because both the entity mentions appear as ARG1 for a coreferent pair of event mentions. IND model incorrectly predicts them as non-coreferent.
2a	The **[UN refugee agency]**$_{\text{ARG0}}$ on Friday strongly [condemned]$_{\text{V}}$ the aerial bombing ...
2b	The mortar strike in Jabaliya was the second attack on a school [run]$_{\text{V}}$ by the **[UN Relief and Works Agency]**$_{\text{ARG0}}$ *Explanation*: The two entity mentions refer to different entities but have some surface form similarity. JOINTINF-LS correctly predicts them as non-coreferent apparently because they appear as ARG0 of two different events but IND model incorrectly predicts them as coreferent.

Table 3: Examples of entity and events pairs (in bold face) from test data where the joint model (JOINTINF-LS) is able to correctly predict coreference decisions and the IND model fails.

	Event Examples
1a	[Apple CEO Tim Cook]$_{\text{ARG0}}$ took the stage in San Francisco to welcome developers and **[announce]**$_{\text{V}}$ new [stuff]$_{\text{ARG1}}$.
1b	Apple has chosen WWDC [week]$_{\text{ARG0}}$ to **[announce]**$_{\text{V}}$ an update to its MacBook Air line. *Explanation*: The two event mentions refer to the same event and have the same surface form. IND model correctly clusters them together while JOINTINF-LS predicts them as being non-coreferent apparently due to mismatch between their ARG0 event mentions. Note that "week" is *incorrectly* identified as ARG0 of "announce" event mention.
2a	[Matt Smith], 26, will make [his]$_{\text{ARG0}}$ **[debut]**$_{\text{V}}$ [in 2010]$_{\text{ARG1}}$, replacing David Tennant ...
2b	Peter Capaldi is officially set to replace **[exiting]**$_{\text{V}}$ [star Matt Smith]$_{\text{ARG0}}$ as the TARDIS leader. *Explanation*: The two event mentions "debut" and "exiting" are not coreferent and have different surface forms. IND model makes a correct prediction while JOINTINF-LS clusters them together as the ARG0 entity mentions refer to the same entity.
	Entity Examples
1a	**[Apple Inc]**$_{\text{ARG0}}$ on Tuesday (Jan 6) [introduced]$_{\text{V}}$ what it claims to ...
1b	**[Apple]**$_{\text{ARG0}}$ [unveils]$_{\text{V}}$ new MacBook Pro with Ivy Bridge at WWDC. *Explanation*: The two event mentions refer to the same entity and have similar surface form. IND model correctly predicts them as coreferent but JOINTINF-LS model makes an incorrect prediction, apparently because the entity mentions appear as ARGO of two distinct events.
2a	4.6-magnitude earthquake [shakes]$_{\text{V}}$ **[Lake County]**$_{\text{ARG1}}$.
2b	Lake County earthquake [shakes]$_{\text{V}}$ **[Napa]**$_{\text{ARG1}}$. *Explanation*: The two event mentions refer to two different entities and have very different surface forms. For this reason, IND model correctly predicts them as being non-coreferent but JOINTINF-LS clusters them together, apparently because the two entity mentions appear as ARG1 for mentions of the same event.

Table 4: Examples of entity and events pairs (in boldface) from test data where the joint model (JOINTINF-LS) fails but IND is able to correctly predict coreference decisions

idate the model by demonstrating state-of-the-art results on the ECB+ dataset, outperforming both independent as well as joint coreference approaches proposed in prior work.

Acknowledgements

We thank Ari Kobren, Akshay Krishnamurthy and members of UMass IESL for helpful discussions and feedback. We would also like to thank Arie Cattan for providing pretrained event and entity coreference models. This work was supported in part by the Center for Data Science and the Center for Intelligent Information Retrieval, in part by the National Science Foundation under Grant No. NSF-1763618, in part by the Chan Zuckerberg Initiative under the project "Scientific Knowledge Base Construction", in part by International Business Machines Corporation Cognitive Horizons Network agreement number W1668553, and in part using high performance computing equipment obtained under a grant from the Collaborative R&D Fund managed by the Massachusetts Technology Collaborative. Rico Angell is supported by the National Science Foundation Graduate Research Fellowship under Grant No. 1938059. Any opinions, findings and conclusions or recommendations expressed in this material are those of the authors and do not necessarily reflect those of the sponsor.

References

Gabor Angeli, Melvin Jose Johnson Premkumar, and Christopher D. Manning. 2015. Leveraging linguistic structure for open domain information extraction. In *Proceedings of the 53rd Annual Meeting of the Association for Computational Linguistics and the 7th International Joint Conference on Natural Language Processing (Volume 1: Long Papers)*, pages 344–354.

Rico Angell, Nicholas Monath, Sunil Mohan, Nishant Yadav, and Andrew McCallum. 2021. Clustering-based inference for biomedical entity linking. In *Proceedings of the 2021 Conference of the North American Chapter of the Association for Computational Linguistics: Human Language Technologies*, pages 2598–2608.

Amit Bagga and Breck Baldwin. 1998. Algorithms for scoring coreference chains. In *The first international conference on language resources and evaluation workshop on linguistics coreference*, volume 1, pages 563–566. Citeseer.

Shany Barhom, Vered Shwartz, Alon Eirew, Michael

Bugert, Nils Reimers, and Ido Dagan. 2019. Revisiting joint modeling of cross-document entity and event coreference resolution. In *Proceedings of the 57th Annual Meeting of the Association for Computational Linguistics*, pages 4179–4189.

Cosmin Bejan and Sanda Harabagiu. 2010. Unsupervised event coreference resolution with rich linguistic features. In *Proceedings of the 48th Annual Meeting of the Association for Computational Linguistics*, pages 1412–1422.

Santanu Bhattacharjee, Rejwanul Haque, Gideon Maillette de Buy Wenniger, and Andy Way. 2020. Investigating query expansion and coreference resolution in question answering on bert. In *International Conference on Applications of Natural Language to Information Systems*, pages 47–59. Springer.

Xavier Carreras and Lluís Màrquez. 2005. Introduction to the CoNLL-2005 shared task: Semantic role labeling. In *Proceedings of the Ninth Conference on Computational Natural Language Learning (CoNLL-2005)*, pages 152–164.

Arie Cattan, Alon Eirew, Gabriel Stanovsky, Mandar Joshi, and Ido Dagan. 2020. Streamlining cross-document coreference resolution: Evaluation and modeling. *arXiv preprint arXiv:2009.11032*.

Jifan Chen, Shih-ting Lin, and Greg Durrett. 2019. Multi-hop question answering via reasoning chains. *arXiv preprint arXiv:1910.02610*.

Zheng Chen and Heng Ji. 2009. Graph-based event coreference resolution. In *Proceedings of the 2009 Workshop on Graph-based Methods for Natural Language Processing (TextGraphs-4)*, pages 54–57.

Prafulla Kumar Choubey and Ruihong Huang. 2017. Event coreference resolution by iteratively unfolding inter-dependencies among events. In *Proceedings of the 2017 Conference on Empirical Methods in Natural Language Processing*, pages 2124–2133.

Kevin Clark and Christopher D. Manning. 2016. Improving coreference resolution by learning entity-level distributed representations. In *Proceedings of the 54th Annual Meeting of the Association for Computational Linguistics (Volume 1: Long Papers)*, pages 643–653.

Vincent Cohen-Addad, Varun Kanade, Frederik Mallmann-Trenn, and Claire Mathieu. 2019. Hierarchical clustering: Objective functions and algorithms. *Journal of the ACM (JACM)*, 66(4):1–42.

Agata Cybulska and Piek Vossen. 2014. Using a sledgehammer to crack a nut? lexical diversity and event coreference resolution. In *Proceedings of the Ninth International Conference on Language Resources and Evaluation (LREC'14)*, pages 4545–4552.

Sanjoy Dasgupta. 2016. A cost function for similarity-based hierarchical clustering. In *Proceedings of the forty-eighth annual ACM symposium on Theory of Computing*, pages 118–127.

Hal Daumé III and Daniel Marcu. 2005. A large-scale exploration of effective global features for a joint entity detection and tracking model. In *Proceedings of Human Language Technology Conference and Conference on Empirical Methods in Natural Language Processing*, pages 97–104.

Greg Durrett and Dan Klein. 2013. Easy victories and uphill battles in coreference resolution. In *Proceedings of the 2013 Conference on Empirical Methods in Natural Language Processing*, pages 1971–1982.

Tobias Falke, Christian M. Meyer, and Iryna Gurevych. 2017. Concept-map-based multi-document summarization using concept coreference resolution and global importance optimization. In *Proceedings of the Eighth International Joint Conference on Natural Language Processing (Volume 1: Long Papers)*, pages 801–811.

Spence Green, Nicholas Andrews, Matthew R. Gormley, Mark Dredze, and Christopher D. Manning. 2012. Entity clustering across languages. In *Proceedings of the 2012 Conference of the North American Chapter of the Association for Computational Linguistics: Human Language Technologies*, pages 60–69.

Tian Ye He. 2007. *Coreference resolution on entities and events for hospital discharge summaries*. Ph.D. thesis, Massachusetts Institute of Technology.

Yin Jou Huang and Sadao Kurohashi. 2021. Extractive summarization considering discourse and coreference relations based on heterogeneous graph. In *Proceedings of the 16th Conference of the European Chapter of the Association for Computational Linguistics: Main Volume*, pages 3046–3052.

Stephen C Johnson. 1967. Hierarchical clustering schemes. *Psychometrika*, 32(3):241–254.

Mandar Joshi, Danqi Chen, Yinhan Liu, Daniel S. Weld, Luke Zettlemoyer, and Omer Levy. 2020. SpanBERT: Improving pre-training by representing and predicting spans. *Transactions of the Association for Computational Linguistics*, 8:64–77.

Kian Kenyon-Dean, Jackie Chi Kit Cheung, and Doina Precup. 2018. Resolving event coreference with supervised representation learning and clustering-oriented regularization. In *Proceedings of the Seventh Joint Conference on Lexical and Computational Semantics*, pages 1–10.

Heeyoung Lee, Marta Recasens, Angel Chang, Mihai Surdeanu, and Dan Jurafsky. 2012. Joint entity and event coreference resolution across documents. In *Proceedings of the 2012 Joint Conference on Empirical Methods in Natural Language Processing and Computational Natural Language Learning*, pages 489–500.

Kenton Lee, Luheng He, Mike Lewis, and Luke Zettlemoyer. 2017. End-to-end neural coreference resolution. In *Proceedings of the 2017 Conference on Empirical Methods in Natural Language Processing*, pages 188–197.

Kenton Lee, Luheng He, and Luke Zettlemoyer. 2018. Higher-order coreference resolution with coarse-to-fine inference. In *Proceedings of the 2018 Conference of the North American Chapter of the Association for Computational Linguistics: Human Language Technologies, Volume 2 (Short Papers)*, pages 687–692.

Yinhan Liu, Myle Ott, Naman Goyal, Jingfei Du, Mandar Joshi, Danqi Chen, Omer Levy, Mike Lewis, Luke Zettlemoyer, and Veselin Stoyanov. 2019. Roberta: A robustly optimized bert pretraining approach. *arXiv preprint arXiv:1907.11692*.

Jing Lu and Vincent Ng. 2018. Event coreference resolution: A survey of two decades of research. In *Proceedings of the Twenty-Seventh International Joint Conference on Artificial Intelligence, IJCAI-18*, pages 5479–5486.

Xiaoqiang Luo. 2005. On coreference resolution performance metrics. In *Proceedings of Human Language Technology Conference and Conference on Empirical Methods in Natural Language Processing*, pages 25–32.

Yehudit Meged, Avi Caciularu, Vered Shwartz, and Ido Dagan. 2020. Paraphrasing vs coreferring: Two sides of the same coin. In *Findings of the Association for Computational Linguistics: EMNLP 2020*, pages 4897–4907.

Ruslan Mitkov, Richard Evans, Constantin Orăsan, Iustin Dornescu, and Miguel Rios. 2012. Coreference resolution: To what extent does it help nlp applications? In *International Conference on Text, Speech and Dialogue*, pages 16–27. Springer.

Vincent Ng and Claire Cardie. 2002. Identifying anaphoric and non-anaphoric noun phrases to improve coreference resolution. In *COLING 2002: The 19th International Conference on Computational Linguistics*.

F. Pedregosa, G. Varoquaux, A. Gramfort, V. Michel, B. Thirion, O. Grisel, M. Blondel, P. Prettenhofer, R. Weiss, V. Dubourg, J. Vanderplas, A. Passos, D. Cournapeau, M. Brucher, M. Perrot, and E. Duchesnay. 2011. Scikit-learn: Machine learning in Python. *Journal of Machine Learning Research*, 12:2825–2830.

Sameer Pradhan, Xiaoqiang Luo, Marta Recasens, Eduard Hovy, Vincent Ng, and Michael Strube. 2014. Scoring coreference partitions of predicted mentions: A reference implementation. In *Proceedings of the 52nd Annual Meeting of the Association for Computational Linguistics (Volume 2: Short Papers)*, pages 30–35.

Peng Shi and Jimmy Lin. 2019. Simple bert models for relation extraction and semantic role labeling. *arXiv preprint arXiv:1904.05255*.

Marc Vilain, John D Burger, John Aberdeen, Dennis Connolly, and Lynette Hirschman. 1995. A model-theoretic coreference scoring scheme. In *Sixth Message Understanding Conference (MUC-6): Proceedings of a Conference Held in Columbia, Maryland, November 6-8, 1995*.

Bishan Yang, Claire Cardie, and Peter Frazier. 2015. A hierarchical distance-dependent bayesian model for event coreference resolution. *Transactions of the Association for Computational Linguistics*, pages 517–528.

Xiaodong Yu, Wenpeng Yin, and Dan Roth. 2020. Paired representation learning for event and entity coreference. *arXiv preprint arXiv:2010.12808*.

A Model and Implementation Details

Implementation Details We train $f_{\text{ind}}^{(t)}$ on training data using code and hyper-parameters from Cattan et al. (2020), and train joint similarity function using sk-learn (Pedregosa et al., 2011) on dev data. We use gold mention spans and document topics during training as well as during inference.

We use a SoTA pre-trained SRL model (Shi and Lin, 2019) to generate semantic role labels for event and entity mention pairs [3]. Since the SRL system used is an end-to-end system and works on top of predicted mention spans, we align the predicted event and entity mentions with gold event and entity mentions. In case a gold event mention span is not detected by the SRL system, we heuristically assign closest left and right occurring entity mention as its `ARG0` and `ARG1` respectively.

[3]Pre-trained model downloaded from `https://demo.allennlp.org/semantic-role-labeling`

On Generalization in Coreference Resolution

Shubham Toshniwal[1]*, Patrick Xia[2]*, Sam Wiseman[3], Karen Livescu[1], Kevin Gimpel[1]
[1]Toyota Technological Institute at Chicago
[2]Johns Hopkins University
[3]Duke University

{shtoshni, klivescu, kgimpel}@ttic.edu, paxia@cs.jhu.edu, swiseman@cs.duke.edu

Abstract

While coreference resolution is defined independently of dataset domain, most models for performing coreference resolution do not transfer well to unseen domains. We consolidate a set of 8 coreference resolution datasets targeting different domains to evaluate the off-the-shelf performance of models. We then mix three datasets for training; even though their domain, annotation guidelines, and metadata differ, we propose a method for jointly training a single model on this heterogeneous data mixture by using data augmentation to account for annotation differences and sampling to balance the data quantities. We find that in a zero-shot setting, models trained on a single dataset transfer poorly while joint training yields improved overall performance, leading to better generalization in coreference resolution models. This work contributes a new benchmark for robust coreference resolution and multiple new state-of-the-art results.[1]

1 Introduction

Coreference resolution is a core component of the NLP pipeline, as determining which mentions in text refer to the same entity is used for a wide variety of downstream tasks like knowledge extraction (Li et al., 2020), question answering (Dhingra et al., 2018), and dialog systems (Gao et al., 2019). As these tasks span many domains, we need coreference models to generalize well.

Meanwhile, models for coreference resolution have improved due to neural architectures with millions of parameters and the emergence of pretrained encoders. However, model generalization across domains has always been a challenge (Yang et al., 2012; Zhao and Ng, 2014; Poot and van Cranenburgh, 2020; Aktaş et al., 2020). Since these models are usually engineered for a single dataset, they capture idiosyncrasies inherent in that dataset. As an example, OntoNotes (Weischedel et al., 2013), a widely-used general-purpose dataset, provides metadata, like the document genre and speaker information. However, this assumption cannot be made more broadly, especially if the input is raw text (Wiseman et al., 2016).

Furthermore, while there are datasets aimed at capturing a broad set of genres (Weischedel et al., 2013; Poesio et al., 2018; Zhu et al., 2021), they are not mutually compatible due to differences in annotation guidelines. For example, some datasets do not annotate singleton clusters (clusters with a single mention). Ideally, we would like a coreference model to be robust to all the standard datasets. In this work, we consolidate 8 datasets spanning multiple domains, document lengths, and annotation guidelines. We use them to evaluate the off-the-shelf performance of models trained on a single dataset. While they perform well within-domain (e.g., a new state-of-the-art of 79.3 F1 on LitBank), they still perform poorly out-of-domain.

To address poor out-of-domain performance, we propose joint training for coreference resolution, which is challenging due to the incompatible training procedues for different datasets. Among other things, we need to address (unannotated) singleton clusters, as OntoNotes does not include singleton annotations. We propose a data augmentation process to add predicted singletons, or *pseudo-singletons*, into the training data to match the other datasets which have gold singleton annotations.

Concretely, we contribute a benchmark for coreference to highlight the disparity in model performance and track generalization. We find joint training highly effective and show that including more datasets is almost "free", as performance on any single dataset is only minimally affected by joint training. We find that our data augmentation method of adding pseudo-singletons is also effective. With all of these extensions, we increase the macro average

*Equal Contribution

[1]Code available at `https://github.com/shtoshni92/fast-coref`

Proceedings of the 4th Workshop on Computational Models of Reference, Anaphora and Coreference (CRAC 2021), pages 111–120
Punta Cana, Dominican Republic, November 10–11, 2021.

Dataset	Num. Docs Train	Dev.	Test	Words/ Doc	Mentions/ Doc	Mention length	Cluster size	% of singleton mentions
OntoNotes	2802	343	348	467	56	2.3	4.4	0.0
LitBank^{k}	80	10	10	2105	291	2.0	3.7	19.8
PreCo	36120	500	500	337	105	2.7	1.6	52.0
Character Identification	987	122	192	262	36	1.0	5.1	6.4
WikiCoref	0	0	30	1996	230	2.6	5.0	0.0
Quiz Bowl Coreference^{k}	0	0	400	126	24	2.7	2.0	26.0
Gendered Ambiguous Pronouns^{p}	2000	400	2000	95	3	2.0	-	-
Winograd Schema Challenge^{p}	0	0	271	16	3	1.5	-	-

Table 1: Statistics of datasets. Datasets with ^{k} indicate that prior work uses k-fold cross-validation; we record the splits used in this work. Datasets with ^{p} are partially annotated, so we do not include cluster details.

F_1 across all datasets by 9.5 points and achieve a new state-of-the-art on LitBank and WikiCoref.

2 Datasets

We organize our datasets into three types. Training datasets (Sec. 2.1) are large in terms of number of tokens and clusters and more suitable for training. Evaluation datasets (Sec. 2.2) are out-of-domain compared to our training sets and are entirely held out. Analysis datasets (Sec. 2.3) contain annotations aimed at probing specific phenomena. Table 1 lists the full statistics.

2.1 Training Datasets

OntoNotes 5.0 (ON) (Weischedel et al., 2013) is a collection of news-like, web, and religious texts spanning seven distinct genres. Some genres are transcripts (phone conversations and news). As the primary training and evaluation set for developing coreference resolution models, many features specific to this corpus are tightly integrated into publicly released models. For example, the metadata includes information on the document genre and the speaker of every token (for spoken transcripts). Notably, it does not contain singleton annotations.

LitBank (LB) (Bamman et al., 2020) is a set of public domain works of literature drawn from Project Gutenberg. On average, coreference in the first 2,000 tokens of each work is fully annotated for six entity types.[2] We only use the first cross-validation fold of LitBank, which we call LB_0.

PreCo (PC) (Chen et al., 2018) contains documents from reading comprehension examinations, each fully annotated for coreference resolution. Notably, the corpus is the largest such dataset released.

2.2 Evaluation Datasets

Character Identification (CI) (Zhou and Choi, 2018) has multiparty conversations derived from TV show transcripts. Each scene in an episode is considered a separate document. This character-centric dataset only annotates mentions of people.

WikiCoref (WC) (Ghaddar and Langlais, 2016) contains documents from English Wikipedia. This corpus contains sampled and annotated documents of different lengths, from 209 to 9,869 tokens.

Quiz Bowl Coreference (QBC) (Guha et al., 2015) contains questions from Quiz Bowl, a trivia competition. These paragraph-long questions are dense with entities. Only certain entity types (titles, authors, characters, and answers) are annotated.

2.3 Analysis Datasets

Gendered Ambiguous Pronouns (GAP) (Webster et al., 2018) is a corpus of ambiguous pronoun-name pairs derived from Wikipedia. While only pronoun-name pairs are annotated, they are provided alongside their full-document context. This corpus has been previously used to study gender bias in coreference resolution systems.

Winograd Schema Challenge (WSC) (Levesque et al., 2012) is a challenge dataset for measuring common sense in AI systems.[3] Unlike the other datasets, each document contains one or two sentences with a multiple-choice question. We manually align the multiple choices to the text and remove 2 of the 273 examples due to plurals.

[2] They are people, facilities, locations, geopolitical entities, organizations, and vehicles.

[3] `https://cs.nyu.edu/~davise/papers/WinogradSchemas/WSCollection.html`

Model	Training	ON	LB_0	PC	CI	WC	QBC	GAP	WSC	Macro Avg.
longdoc	ON	79.0	54.8	44.3	49.8	59.6	36.8	88.9	59.8	59.1
longdoc ^{S}	ON	79.6	54.6	44.0	58.7	60.1	36.4	**89.8**	59.4	60.3
longdoc ^{S,G}	ON	79.5	54.7	44.5	59.5	59.9	37.0	89.0	58.7	60.3
longdoc ^{S}	ON + PS 60K	**80.6**	56.6	49.1	55.6	62.1	40.1	89.3	61.3	**61.8**
longdoc	LB_0	56.6	77.2	46.8	53.3	47.5	**50.5**	85.3	32.8	56.3
longdoc	PC	58.8	50.3	**87.8**	39.5	50.7	46.5	87.3	**62.7**	60.5
longdoc ^{S}	Joint	79.2	**78.2**	87.6	59.4	60.3	42.9	88.6	60.1	69.5
longdoc ^{S}	Joint + PS 30K	79.6	**78.2**	87.5	58.4	**62.5**	45.5	88.7	59.4	**70.0**

Table 2: Performance of each model on 8 datasets measured by CoNLL F_1 (Pradhan et al., 2012), except for GAP (F_1) and WSC (accuracy). Some models use speaker (^{S}) features, genre (^{G}) features, or pseudo-singletons (PS).

3 Models

3.1 Baselines

We first evaluate a recent system (Xu and Choi, 2020) which extends a mention-ranking model (Lee et al., 2018) by making modifications in the decoding step. We find disappointing out-of-domain performance and difficulties with longer documents present in LB_0 and WC (Appendix B.1). To overcome this issue, we study the *longdoc* model by Toshniwal et al. (2020), which is an entity-ranking model designed for long documents that reported strong results on both OntoNotes and LitBank.

The original longdoc model uses a pretrained SpanBERT (Joshi et al., 2020) encoder which we replace with Longformer-large (Beltagy et al., 2020) as it can incorporate longer context. We retrain the longdoc model and finetune the Longformer encoder for each dataset, which proves to be competitive for coreference.[4] For OntoNotes we train with and without the metadata of: (a) genre embedding, and (b) speaker identity which is introduced as part of the text as in Wu et al. (2020).

3.2 Joint Training

With copious amounts of text in OntoNotes, PreCo, and LitBank, we can train a joint model on the combined dataset. However, this is impractical as the annotation guidelines between the datasets are misaligned (OntoNotes does not annotate singletons and uses metadata) and because there are substantially more documents in PreCo.

Augmenting Singletons Since OntoNotes does not annotate for singletons, our training objective for OntoNotes is different from that of PreCo and LitBank. To address this, we introduce *pseudo-singletons* that are *silver* mentions derived from first training a mention detector on OntoNotes and selecting the top-scoring mentions outside the gold mentions.[5] We experiment with adding 30K, 60K, and 90K pseudo-singletons (in total, there are 156K gold mentions). We find adding 60K to be the best fit for OntoNotes-only training, and 30K is the best for joint training (Appendix B.3).

Data Imbalance PreCo has 36K training documents, compared to 2.8K and 80 training documents for OntoNotes and LitBank respectively. A naive dataset-agnostic sampling strategy would mostly sample PreCo documents. To address this issue, we downsample OntoNotes and PreCo to 1K documents per epoch. Downsampling to 0.5K documents per epoch led to slightly worse performance (Appendix B.4).

Metadata Embeddings For the joint model to be applicable to unknown domains, we avoid using any domain or dataset-identity embeddings, including the OntoNotes genre embedding. We do make use of speaker identity in the joint model because: (a) this is possible to obtain in conversational and dialog data, and (b) it does not affect other datasets that are known to be single-speaker at test time.

4 Results

Table 2 shows the results for all our models on all 8 datasets. We report each dataset's associated metric (e.g., CoNLL F_1) and a macro average across all eight datasets to compare generalizability.

Among the longdoc baseline models trained on one of OntoNotes, PreCo, or LitBank, we observe a sharp drop in out-of-domain evaluations. The LitBank model is generally substantially worse than the models trained on OntoNotes and PreCo, likely

[4]The model scores 79.5 on OntoNotes and achieves state-of-the-art on LitBank with 79.3. Details are in Appendix B.2.

[5]This mention detector is architecturally the first half of the longdoc model.

Dataset	Instance
(1) QBC	(**This poem**) is often considered the counterpart of another poem . . . name this poem about a creature "burning bright, in the forests of the night," . . .
(2) QBC	This author's non fiction works . . . another work , a plague strikes secluded valley where teenage boys have been evacuated . . . name this author of Nip the Buds, Shoot the Kids . . .
(3) QBC	This poet of "(**I**) felt a Funeral in (**my**) Brain" and "I'm Nobody, Who are you?" wrote about a speaker who hears a Blue, uncertain, stumbling buzz before expiring in "(**I**) heard a fly buzz when (**I**) died". For 10 points, name this female American poet of Because (**I**) could not stop for Death.
(4) CI	*Chandler Bing:* Okay, I don't sound like that. (**That**) is so not true. (**That**) is so not ... (**That**) is so not ... That ... Oh , shut up !

Table 3: Joint + PS 30K error analysis for zero-shot evaluation sets. Each row highlights one cluster where spans in parenthesis are predicted by the model while the blue-colored spans represent ground truth annotations. Thus, in (2) the model misses out on the ground truth cluster entirely while in (3) and (4) the model predicts an additional cluster.

due to both a smaller training set and a larger domain shift. Interestingly, the LitBank model performs the best among all models on QBC, which can be attributed to both LB and QBC being restricted to a similar set of markable entity types. Meanwhile, all OntoNotes-only models perform well on WC and GAP, possibly due to the more diverse set of genres within ON and because WC also does not contain singletons.

For models trained on OntoNotes, we find that the addition of speaker tokens leads to an almost 9 point increase on CI, which is a conversational dataset, but has little impact for non-conversational evaluations. Surprisingly, the addition of genre embeddings has almost no impact on the overall evaluation.[6] Finally, the addition of pseudo-singletons leads to consistent significant gains across almost all the evaluations, including OntoNotes.

The joint models, which are trained on a combination of OntoNotes, LitBank, and PreCo, suffer only a small drop in performance on OntoNotes and PreCo, and achieve the best performance for LitBank. Like the results observed when training with only OntoNotes, we see a significant performance gain with pseudo-singletons in joint training as well, which justifies our intuition that they can bridge the annotation gap. The "Joint + PS 30K" model also achieves the state of the art for WC.

[6]In fact, we find that for the model trained with genre embeddings, modifying the genre value during inference has almost no impact on the final performance.

5 Analysis

Impact of Singletons Singletons are known to artificially boost the coreference metrics (Kübler and Zhekova, 2011), and their utility for downstream applications is arguable. To determine the impact of singletons on final scores, we present separate results for singleton and non-singleton clusters in QBC in Table 4. For non-singleton clusters we use the standard CoNLL F_1 but for singleton clusters the CoNLL score is undefined, and hence, we use the vanilla F_1-score.

The poor performance of ON models for singletons is expected, as singletons are not seen during training. Adding pseudo-singletons improves the performance of both the ON and the Joint model for singletons. Interestingly, adding pseudo-singletons also leads to a small improvement for non-singleton clusters.

The PC model has the best performance for non-singleton clusters while the LB_0 model, which performs the best in the overall evaluation, has the worst performance for non-singleton clusters. This means that the gains for the LB_0 model can be all but attributed to the superior mention detection performance which can be explained by the fact that both LB and QBC are restricted to a similar set of markable entity types.

Impact of Domain Shift Table 3 presents instances where the Joint + PS 30K model makes mistakes. In examples (1) and (2), the model misses out on mentions referring to literary works which

Data	Singleton	Non-singleton	Overall
ON	0.4	43.9	36.4
ON + PS 60K	14.4	44.4	40.1
LB_0	**44.9**	41.2	**50.5**
PC	28.8	**50.3**	46.5
Joint	21.7	47.3	42.9
Joint + PS 30K	26.7	48.6	45.5

Table 4: Performance on singleton and non-singleton clusters for QBC. ON=longdoc^S and PS=pseudo-singletons.

is because references to literary texts are rare in the joint training data. Example (2) also requires world knowledge to make a connection between the description of the work and its title. In example (3) the model introduces an extraneous cluster consisting of first person pronouns mentioned in titles of different works. The model lacks the domain knowledge that narrators across different works are not necessarily related. Apart from the language shift, there are annotation differences across datasets as well. For example (4) drawn from CI, the model predicts a valid cluster (for Chandler Bing's speaking style) according to the ON annotation guidelines but the CI dataset doesn't annotate such clusters.

6 Related work

Joint training is commonly used in NLP for training robust models, usually aided by learning dataset, language, or domain embeddings (e.g., (Stymne et al., 2018) for parsing; (Kobus et al., 2017; Tan et al., 2019) for machine translation). This is essentially what models for OntoNotes already do with genre embeddings (Lee et al., 2017). Unlike prior work, our test domains are unseen, so we cannot learn test-domain embeddings.

For coreference resolution, Aralikatte et al. (2019) augment annotations using relation extraction systems to better incorporate world knowledge, a step towards generalization. Subramanian and Roth (2019) use adversarial training to target names, with improvements on GAP. Moosavi and Strube (2018) incorporate linguistic features to improve generalization to WC. Recently, Zhu et al. (2021) proposed the OntoGUM dataset which consists of multiple genres. However, compared to the datasets used in our work, OntoGUM is much smaller, and is also restricted to a single annotation scheme. To the best of our knowledge, our work is the first to evaluate generalization at scale.

Missing singletons in OntoNotes has been previously addressed through new data annotations, leading to the creation of the ARRAU (Poesio et al., 2018) and PreCo (Chen et al., 2018) corpora. While we include PreCo in this work, ARRAU contains additional challenges, like split-antecedents, that further increase the heterogeneity, and its domain overlaps with OntoNotes. Pipeline models for coreference resolution that first detect mentions naturally leave behind unclustered mentions as singletons, although understanding singletons can also improve performance (Recasens et al., 2013).

Recent end-to-end neural models have been evaluated on OntoNotes, and therefore conflate "not a mention" with "is a singleton" (Lee et al., 2017, 2018; Kantor and Globerson, 2019; Wu et al., 2020). For datasets with singletons, this has been addressed explicitly through a cluster-based model (Toshniwal et al., 2020; Yu et al., 2020). For those without, they can be implicitly accounted for with auxiliary objectives (Zhang et al., 2018; Swayamdipta et al., 2018). We go one step further by augmenting with *pseudo-singletons*, so that the training objective is identical regardless of whether the training set contains annotated singletons.

7 Conclusion

Our eight-dataset benchmark highlights disparities in coreference resolution model performance and tracks cross-domain generalization. Our work begins to address cross-domain gaps, first by handling differences in singleton annotation via data augmentation with pseudo-singletons, and second by training a single model jointly on multiple datasets. This approach produces promising improvements in generalization, as well as new state-of-the-art results on multiple datasets. We hope that future work will continue to use this benchmark to measure progress towards truly general-purpose coreference resolution.

Acknowledgements

This material is based upon work supported by the National Science Foundation under Award No. 1941178.

References

Berfin Aktaş, Veronika Solopova, Annalena Kohnert, and Manfred Stede. 2020. Adapting Coreference Resolution to Twitter Conversations. In *Findings of EMNLP*.

Rahul Aralikatte, Heather Lent, Ana Valeria Gonzalez, Daniel Herschcovich, Chen Qiu, Anders Sandholm, Michael Ringaard, and Anders Søgaard. 2019. Rewarding Coreference Resolvers for Being Consistent with World Knowledge. In *EMNLP-IJCNLP*.

David Bamman, Olivia Lewke, and Anya Mansoor. 2020. An Annotated Dataset of Coreference in English Literature. In *LREC*.

Iz Beltagy, Matthew E. Peters, and Arman Cohan. 2020. Longformer: The Long-Document Transformer. *arXiv:2004.05150*.

Hong Chen, Zhenhua Fan, Hao Lu, Alan Yuille, and Shu Rong. 2018. PreCo: A Large-scale Dataset in Preschool Vocabulary for Coreference Resolution. In *EMNLP*.

Bhuwan Dhingra, Qiao Jin, Zhilin Yang, William Cohen, and Ruslan Salakhutdinov. 2018. Neural Models for Reasoning over Multiple Mentions Using Coreference. In *NAACL-HLT*.

Yifan Gao, Piji Li, Irwin King, and Michael R. Lyu. 2019. Interconnected Question Generation with Coreference Alignment and Conversation Flow Modeling. In *ACL*.

Abbas Ghaddar and Phillippe Langlais. 2016. Wiki-Coref: An English Coreference-annotated Corpus of Wikipedia Articles. In *LREC*.

Anupam Guha, Mohit Iyyer, Danny Bouman, and Jordan Boyd-Graber. 2015. Removing the Training Wheels: A Coreference Dataset that Entertains Humans and Challenges Computers. In *NAACL-HLT*.

Mandar Joshi, Danqi Chen, Yinhan Liu, Daniel S. Weld, Luke Zettlemoyer, and Omer Levy. 2020. SpanBERT: Improving Pre-training by Representing and Predicting Spans. *TACL*, 8.

Ben Kantor and Amir Globerson. 2019. Coreference Resolution with Entity Equalization. In *ACL*.

Catherine Kobus, Josep Crego, and Jean Senellart. 2017. Domain Control for Neural Machine Translation. In *RANLP*.

Sandra Kübler and Desislava Zhekova. 2011. Singletons and Coreference Resolution Evaluation. In *Proceedings of the International Conference Recent Advances in Natural Language Processing 2011*.

Kenton Lee, Luheng He, Mike Lewis, and Luke Zettlemoyer. 2017. End-to-end Neural Coreference Resolution. In *EMNLP*.

Kenton Lee, Luheng He, and Luke Zettlemoyer. 2018. Higher-Order Coreference Resolution with Coarse-to-Fine Inference. In *NAACL-HLT*.

Hector J. Levesque, Ernest Davis, and Leora Morgenstern. 2012. The Winograd Schema Challenge. In *Proceedings of the Thirteenth International Conference on Principles of Knowledge Representation and Reasoning*.

Manling Li, Alireza Zareian, Ying Lin, Xiaoman Pan, Spencer Whitehead, Brian Chen, Bo Wu, Heng Ji, Shih-Fu Chang, Clare Voss, Daniel Napierski, and Marjorie Freedman. 2020. GAIA: A Fine-grained Multimedia Knowledge Extraction System. In *ACL: System Demonstrations*.

Nafise Sadat Moosavi and Michael Strube. 2018. Using Linguistic Features to Improve the Generalization Capability of Neural Coreference Resolvers. In *EMNLP*.

Massimo Poesio, Yulia Grishina, Varada Kolhatkar, Nafise Moosavi, Ina Roesiger, Adam Roussel, Fabian Simonjetz, Alexandra Uma, Olga Uryupina, Juntao Yu, and Heike Zinsmeister. 2018. Anaphora Resolution with the ARRAU Corpus. In *Proceedings of the First Workshop on Computational Models of Reference, Anaphora and Coreference*.

Corbèn Poot and Andreas van Cranenburgh. 2020. A Benchmark of Rule-Based and Neural Coreference Resolution in Dutch Novels and News. In *CRAC*.

Sameer Pradhan, Alessandro Moschitti, Nianwen Xue, Olga Uryupina, and Yuchen Zhang. 2012. CoNLL-2012 Shared Task: Modeling Multilingual Unrestricted Coreference in OntoNotes. In *Joint Conference on EMNLP and CoNLL - Shared Task*.

Marta Recasens, Marie-Catherine de Marneffe, and Christopher Potts. 2013. The Life and Death of Discourse Entities: Identifying Singleton Mentions. In *NAACL-HLT*.

Sara Stymne, Miryam de Lhoneux, Aaron Smith, and Joakim Nivre. 2018. Parser Training with Heterogeneous Treebanks. In *ACL*.

Sanjay Subramanian and Dan Roth. 2019. Improving Generalization in Coreference Resolution via Adversarial Training. In *Proceedings of the Eighth Joint Conference on Lexical and Computational Semantics*.

Swabha Swayamdipta, Sam Thomson, Kenton Lee, Luke Zettlemoyer, Chris Dyer, and Noah A. Smith. 2018. Syntactic Scaffolds for Semantic Structures. In *EMNLP*.

Xu Tan, Jiale Chen, Di He, Yingce Xia, Tao Qin, and Tie-Yan Liu. 2019. Multilingual Neural Machine Translation with Language Clustering. In *EMNLP-IJCNLP*.

Shubham Toshniwal, Sam Wiseman, Allyson Ettinger, Karen Livescu, and Kevin Gimpel. 2020. Learning to Ignore: Long Document Coreference with Bounded Memory Neural Networks. In *EMNLP*.

Kellie Webster, Marta Recasens, Vera Axelrod, and Jason Baldridge. 2018. Mind the GAP: A Balanced Corpus of Gendered Ambiguous Pronouns. *TACL*, 6.

Ralph Weischedel, Martha Palmer, Mitchell Marcus, Eduard Hovy, Sameer Pradhan, Lance Ramshaw, Nianwen Xue, Ann Taylor, Jeff Kaufman, Michelle Franchini, et al. 2013. OntoNotes Release 5.0. *Linguistic Data Consortium*.

Sam Wiseman, Alexander M. Rush, and Stuart Shieber. 2016. Antecedent Prediction Without a Pipeline. In *Proceedings of the Workshop on Coreference Resolution Beyond OntoNotes (CORBON)*.

Wei Wu, Fei Wang, Arianna Yuan, Fei Wu, and Jiwei Li. 2020. CorefQA: Coreference Resolution as Query-based Span Prediction. In *ACL*.

Patrick Xia, João Sedoc, and Benjamin Van Durme. 2020. Incremental Neural Coreference Resolution in Constant Memory. In *EMNLP*.

Liyan Xu and Jinho D. Choi. 2020. Revealing the Myth of Higher-Order Inference in Coreference Resolution. In *EMNLP*.

Jian Bo Yang, Qi Mao, Qiao Liang Xiang, Ivor Wai-Hung Tsang, Kian Ming Adam Chai, and Hai Leong Chieu. 2012. Domain Adaptation for Coreference Resolution: An Adaptive Ensemble Approach. In *EMNLP*.

Juntao Yu, Alexandra Uma, and Massimo Poesio. 2020. A Cluster Ranking Model for Full Anaphora Resolution. In *LREC*.

Rui Zhang, Cícero Nogueira dos Santos, Michihiro Yasunaga, Bing Xiang, and Dragomir Radev. 2018. Neural Coreference Resolution with Deep Biaffine Attention by Joint Mention Detection and Mention Clustering. In *ACL*.

Shanheng Zhao and Hwee Tou Ng. 2014. Domain Adaptation with Active Learning for Coreference Resolution. In *Proceedings of the 5th International Workshop on Health Text Mining and Information Analysis (Louhi)*.

Ethan Zhou and Jinho D. Choi. 2018. They Exist! Introducing Plural Mentions to Coreference Resolution and Entity Linking. In *Proceedings of the 27th International Conference on Computational Linguistics*.

Yilun Zhu, Sameer Pradhan, and Amir Zeldes. 2021. OntoGUM: Evaluating Contextualized SOTA Coreference Resolution on 12 More Genres. In *ACL*.

A Model and Training Details

A.1 Model

Our model follows the typical coreference pipeline of encoding the document, followed by mention proposal, and finally mention clustering. The model is architecturally the same as Toshniwal et al. (2020), and so we re-present their formulation throughout this section. However, we use the Longformer encoder as it accommodates longer documents. Otherwise, the model is identical to Toshniwal et al. (2020) in terms of model size and weight dimensions. We next explain the mention proposal and mention clustering stages briefly.

Mention Proposal Given a document $\mathcal{D}$, we score all mentions of length $\leq$ 20 subword tokens and choose the $K = 0.4 \times |\mathcal{D}|$ top spans among them. This is an initial pruning step that speeds up the model and reduces memory usage. Let $X(K) = \{(x_i)_{i=1}^{K}\}$ represent the top-K candidate mention spans and $s_m(x_i)$ be a learned scoring function for span x_i, which represents how likely a span is an entity mention. s_m is trained to assign positive score to gold mentions (any mention in a gold cluster), and negative score otherwise. The training objective only uses spans in $X(K)$, i.e. loss is computed after pruning. During inference, we can therefore further prune down to $\{x_i : x_i \in X(K), s_m(x_i) \geq 0\}$, which we then pass into the clustering step. During training, we use teacher forcing and only pass gold mentions among the top-K mentions to the clustering step.

Mention Clustering The entity-based model tracks M entities (initially $M = 0$). Let $E = (e_m)_{m=1}^{M}$ represent the M entities. For ease of notation, we will overload the terms x_i and e_j to also correspond to their respective representations.

The model decides whether the span x_i refers to any of the entities in E as follows:

$$s_c(x_i, e_j) = f_c([x_i; e_j; x_i \odot e_j; g(x_i, e_j)])$$
$$s_c^{top} = \max_{j=1...M} s_c(x_i, e_j)$$
$$e^{top} = \arg\max_{j=1...M} s_c(x_i, e_j)$$

where $\odot$ represents the element-wise product, and $f_c(\cdot)$ corresponds to a learned feedforward neural network. The term $g(x_i, e_j)$ corresponds to a concatenation of feature embeddings that includes embeddings for (a) number of mentions in e_j, and (b) number of tokens between x_i and last mention of e_j. If $s_c^{top} > 0$ then x_i is considered to refer to e^{top}, and e^{top} is updated accordingly.[7] Otherwise, we initiate a new cluster: $E = E \cup x_i$. During training, we use teacher-forcing i.e. the clustering decisions are based on ground truth.

A.2 Training

We train all the models for 100K gradient steps with a batch size of 1 document. Only the LB-only models are trained for 8K gradient steps which corresponds to 100 epochs for LB. The models are evaluated a total of 20 times (every 5K training steps) for all models except the LB-only models which are evaluated every 400 steps. We use early stopping and a patience of 5 i.e. training stops if the validation performance doesn't improve for 5 consecutive evaluations.

We use the full context size of 4096 tokens for Longformer-large. All training documents used in this work except 1 ON document fit in a single context window. For optimizer, we use AdamW with a weight decay of 0.01 and initial learning rate of 1e-5 for the Longformer encoder, and Adam with an initial rate of 3e-4 for the rest of the model parameters. The learning rate is linearly decayed throughout the training.

B Other Results

B.1 Xu and Choi (2020) Baselines

We run the off-the-shelf model on the test sets of ON, LB_0, PC, and QBC. LB_0 requires a 24GB GPU, while WC runs out of memory even on that hardware. The model shows strong in-domain performance with 80.2 on ON. However, out-of-domain performance is weak: 57.2 on LB_0, 49.3 on PC, and 37.6 on QBC. These are roughly on par with the ON longdoc models.

B.2 LitBank Cross-Validation Results

Table 7 presents the results for all the cross-validation splits of LitBank. The overall performance of 79.3 CoNLL F1 is state of the art for LitBank, outperforming the previous state of the art of 76.5 by Toshniwal et al. (2020). Note that in this work, the joint model outperformed (78.2 vs. 77.2) this baseline model on split 0 (LB_0). However, training 10 joint models contradicts the purpose of this work, which is to create a single, generaliz-

[7]We use weighted averaging where the weight for e^{top} corresponds to the number of previous mentions seen for e^{top}.

Training			Evaluation				
Num ON	Num PC	Num PS	ON	LB	PC	WC	QB
500	500	0	79.4	78.8	85.0	60.8	45.3
500	500	30K	79.4	79.5	84.8	61.2	47.7
1000	1000	0	79.7	79.4	85.1	60.3	42.9
1000	1000	30K	79.5	78.7	85.1	62.5	45.5
1000	1000	60K	78.9	77.4	85.1	61.3	46.6
1000	1000	90K	78.5	77.7	85.1	60.7	47.4

Table 5: Validation set scores of datasets when downsampling OntoNotes (ON) and PreCo (PC) in joint training.

	Training	ON	LB	PC	CI	WC	QBC	Macro Avg.
longdoc	ON	88.8	62.8	42.6	65.7	72.1	53.1	64.2
longdoc ^{S}	ON	89.2	61.7	41.8	75.5	69.9	52.5	65.1
longdoc ^{S,G}	ON	89.4	62.8	42.7	77.0	72.5	52.9	66.2
longdoc ^{S}	ON + PS 60K	87.7	81.5	81.0	76.1	71.6	70.4	78.0
longdoc	LB_0	77.6	85.8	81.4	67.6	69.8	70.2	75.4
longdoc	PC	76.8	81.1	93.6	66.5	67.0	77.3	77.0
longdoc ^{S}	Joint	90.9	86.9	93.4	77.2	76.6	68.7	82.3
longdoc ^{S}	Joint + PS 30K	89.4	87.1	93.3	77.3	74.6	71.7	82.2

Table 6: Result of all the models with gold mentions. Some models use speaker (^{s}) features, genre (^{g}) features, or pseudo-singletons (PS). The metric for the training and evaluation datasets is CoNLL F-score. We skip the analysis datasets because they lack the set of true gold mentions.

Cross-val split	Dev	Test
0	78.8	77.2
1	78.6	80.3
2	81.1	78.7
3	79.0	79.1
4	80.0	78.7
5	79.7	78.7
6	77.7	80.7
7	81.9	79.1
8	78.0	80.8
9	81.8	78.7
Total	79.7	79.3

Table 7: LitBank cross-validation results.

able model. Realistically, we recommend jointly training with the entirely of LitBank.

B.3 Singleton Results for OntoNotes

For ON-only models, we tune over the number of pseudo-singletons sampled among {30K, 60K, 90K}. Table 8 shows that 60K pseudo-singletons is the best choice based on validation set results on ON.

B.4 Downsampling and Singleton Results for Joint

In preliminary experiments, we sample 500 docs from ON and PC. Table 5 shows the results, confirming that 1K is slightly better than 500. Using more examples (e.g. 5K PC) begins to hurt performance on LB, likely due to data imbalance.

For the 1K downsampling setting, we tune over the number of pseudo-singletons sampled among {30K, 60K, 90K}. We find 30K to be the best choice based on validation set results.

Num PS	Val.	Test
0	79.9	79.6
30K	79.9	80.5
60K	**80.0**	**80.6**
90K	79.9	80.0

Table 8: Validation and Test results for ON-only model trained on different amount of pseduo-singletons (PS).

B.5 Results with Gold Mentions

In Table 6, we report the results with gold mentions for the training and evaluation sets. The analysis sets are skipped as they are partially annotated. We find that joint training is also helpful in this setting, as results mirror findings with predicted mentions. In particular, this shows that it is not just a failure to predict mentions that is preventing ON from performing well on LB, PC, and QBC.

C Compute Resources

Given that we are finetuning the Longformer model and using a maximum context size of 4096 tokens, the memory requirements of the model are quite large even though the cluster-ranking paradigm is considered memory efficient (Xia et al., 2020). We were able to train the PreCo-only model on a 12 GB GPU in 20 hrs (even the longest PreCo documents are shorter than 2048 tokens with the Longformer tokenization). All other models were trained over GPUs with memory 24GB or higher (Titan RTX and A6000). On an A6000, the LB-only models can be trained within 4 hrs, the ON-only models within 16 hrs, and the joint models within 20 hrs.

Improving Span Representation for Domain-adapted Coreference Resolution

Nupoor Gandhi[†], **Anjalie Field**[†], **Yulia Tsvetkov** [§]
Carnegie Mellon University [†], University of Washington [§]
{nmgandhi,anjalief}@cs.cmu.edu,yuliats@cs.washington.edu

Abstract

Recent work has shown fine-tuning neural coreference models can produce strong performance when adapting to different domains. However, at the same time, this can require a large amount of annotated target examples. In this work, we focus on supervised domain adaptation for clinical notes, proposing the use of concept knowledge to more efficiently adapt coreference models to a new domain. We develop methods to improve the span representations via (1) a retrofitting loss to incentivize span representations to satisfy a knowledge-based distance function and (2) a scaffolding loss to guide the recovery of knowledge from the span representation. By integrating these losses, our model is able to improve our baseline precision and F-1 score. In particular, we show that incorporating knowledge with end-to-end coreference models results in better performance on the most challenging, domain-specific spans[1].

1 Introduction

Recent work has achieved high performance on coreference resolution in standard benchmark datasets like OntoNotes (Kirstain et al., 2021; Joshi et al., 2020; Weischedel et al., 2013). However, in many real world settings where coreference resolution would be valuable, text differs greatly from these standard datasets. For example, coreference resolution over clinical notes can enable tracking a patient's progress and treatment history. However, clinical notes contain acronyms and medical terminology. Annotating new training data for every domain of interest is expensive and time-consuming, and coreference models trained on existing benchmark datasets perform worse on other domains (Srivastava et al., 2020; Xu and Choi, 2020; Joshi et al., 2020). In this work, we develop a domain-adaptation model for coreference resolution that requires only a small number of target training examples and target domain knowledge.

Our primary approach involves incorporating domain-knowledge into the *span representations* learned by an end-to-end neural system (Lee et al., 2017). A span representation is a vector representation of a contiguous set of tokens. When determining if a given mention refers to an antecedent, span representations are used by the model to (1.) select a set of candidate mentions and (2.) select an antecedent from the candidates for the given mention. Thus, a high-quality span representation encodes the semantic meaning of the span tokens and their local context. Joshi et al. (2020) introduced SpanBERT, a pre-training method extending BERT, designed to improve performance on span-selection tasks that involves masking contiguous spans rather than tokens. Span representations are derived by concatenating the pre-trained transformer outputs at the boundary tokens with an attention-weighted vector over the span tokens. These representations are fed into a coreference resolution model, thus integrating SpanBERT into an end-to-end coreference resolution system.

SpanBERT is able to capture coreference structure implicitly in rich span representations. The expressiveness of the SpanBERT representation is apparent from extrinsic coreference performance, but also through probing tasks that have shown that span representations can capture headedness, coreference arcs, and other linguistic features of coreference (Kahardipraja et al., 2020). The best coreference performance and span representations are obtained by training the end-to-end model with SpanBERT using labeled coreference data.

When adapting a coreference model to a new domain, fine-tuning or continued training can greatly improve performance, but this approach can be computationally expensive and requires a large amount of labelled documents from the target domain (Gururangan et al., 2020; Xia and Van Durme,

[1]Code publicly available at https://github.com/nupoorgandhi/i2b2-coref-public

Proceedings of the 4th Workshop on Computational Models of Reference, Anaphora and Coreference (CRAC 2021), pages 121–131
Punta Cana, Dominican Republic, November 10–11, 2021. ©2021 Association for Computational Linguistics

2021). Neural models have also been criticized for largely relying on shallow heuristics in the text, suggesting this data-driven learning method requires many target examples to learn a new target distribution (Lu and Ng, 2020; Rosenman et al., 2020).

The presence of out-of-vocabulary words in a new domain can create additional challenges. SpanBERT uses wordpiece tokenization, which can lead to misleading meaning representation for spans when a single wordpiece belongs to spans with different meanings (Joshi et al., 2020; Poerner et al., 2020b). Consider for example, the spans *euthmyia* and *dementia*, both of which are common medical terminology but out-of-vocabulary words for SpanBERT, which tokenizes them to contain a common wordpiece: "##ia". As described by Poerner et al. (2020b), this can lead to a coreference model incorrectly predicting the spans coreferent, since the suffix "##ia" is commonly associated with diseases. A coreference model could correct this by learning a more meaningful representation for the prefix tokens and downweighting the suffix "##ia" token, but this would take many target domain training examples.

Instead, we propose a more efficient method for integrating domain-specific knowledge into SpanBERT-based span representations, which requires only a small number of target training samples and leverages domain-specific concept knowledge.

We take a set of spans with some similarity in meaning to be a concept, and we use concepts of varying granularity (e.g., *problem, headache*).

First, we introduce a *retrofitting loss* (§2.4) which guides the representation learning of span pairs to satisfy a knowledge-based distance function. This distance function reflects pairwise span relationships from our concept knowledge. As a result, we are able to align the target domain coreference structure encoded in the span representation with the global meanings of the spans. This allows the end-to-end model to more efficiently build more meaningful span representations for the target domain.

We also introduce an auxiliary *scaffolding loss* (§2.5) for a concept prediction task in order to ensure that knowledge relevant to the coreference task can be recovered from the span representation. This usage of an auxiliary task to produce a useful inductive bias was introduced in Swayamdipta et al. (2018) to add a syntactic labeling loss for coreference resolution since syntactic constituents are often coreferent. Spans belonging to the same concept within our concept knowledge usually corefer, so we generalize this technique to a broad, knowledge-based lexicon in our domain adaptation setting. While our retrofitting loss integrates relative knowledge into the span representation, we are able to supplement the span representation with global meaning using the scaffolding loss.

To evaluate our models, we take OntoNotes as our source domain and the i2b2/VA corpus of clinical notes as our target domain. We train our model on the source domain and 200 examples from the target domain, we evaluate model performance on the target domain. Our knowledge concepts are from the i2b2/VA dataset and the UMLS Metathesaurus.

First, we describe our methodology and introduce our retrofitting and scaffolding loss functions in §2. Then, we describe our experiments to quantify model performance on our target domain in §3, and finally we demonstrate the performance improvement over our baseline and on rare/OOV spans §4.

The main contribution of this work is in developing methods to integrate concept knowledge into coreference resolution systems to improve domain adaptation. We outperform our baseline primarily by improving precision, and in doing so, we demonstrate the utility of a set of knowledge concepts for adapting span representations to a new domain. We show that our model's performance does not deteriorate on highly domain-specific spans containing OOD frequently subdivided vocabulary.

2 Model

The objective of coreference resolution is to identify a set of coreference clusters from a document containing entities, where each coreference cluster contains mentions referencing a single entity. The set of mention candidates are referred to as *spans*, where a span is any contiguous set of tokens in the document. We can use the coreference clusters $\{C_1, C_2, \ldots, C_m\}$ to define an unconnected graph where the set of spans are the vertices $V = \{s_1, s_2, \ldots, s_n\}$, and there are edges only between spans that belong to the same cluster. First, we describe the basic model setup for a neural coreference resolution system, and we then describe our proposed approach, that involves two new losses.

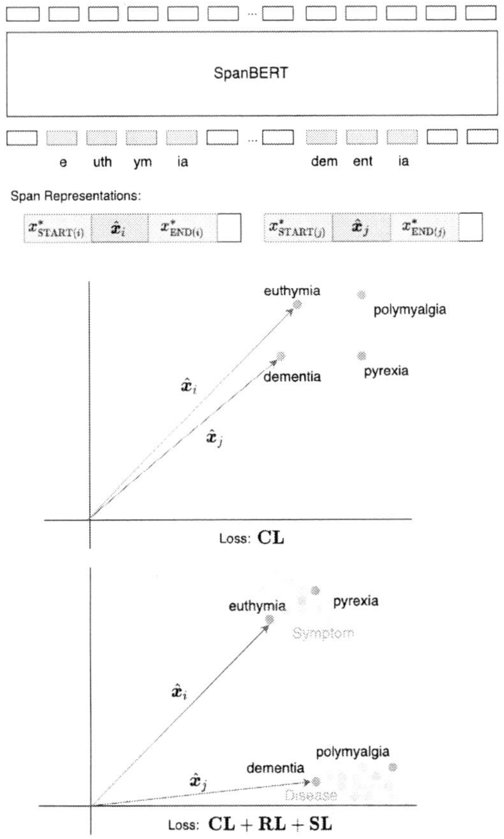

Figure 1: Span representations produced by SpanBERT for mentions "euthymia" and "dementia" are fed into a co-reference resolution model. The baseline (Joshi et al., 2020), which uses a single coreference loss, **CL**, produces similar span representations for "euthymia" and "dementia" (top). When we incorporate knowledge concepts, $C_1^k = \{\text{euthymia, pyrexia}, \ldots\}, C_2^k = \{\text{dementia, polymyalgia}\}, \ldots$, into the span representation using our proposed losses **SL** and **RL**, the span representations for "euthmyia" and "dementia" are further apart (bottom), accurately reflecting that "euthmyia" is a symptom, while "dementia"is a disease, even though they share a wordpiece "ia".

2.1 End-to-end Coreference Model

For the set of possible spans, we first produce span representations. The span representation is learned as a part of the neural end-to-end framework introduced in Lee et al. (2017). Given span representations, each span representation $\boldsymbol{h}_i$ is assigned a unary mention score. The mention score reflects the likelihood that a given span is in fact a mention. This score is used to obtain a set of candidate mentions. Each span pair $\boldsymbol{h}_i, \boldsymbol{h}_j$ is assigned a pairwise antecedent score reflecting the likelihood that $\boldsymbol{h}_i$ is the antecedent of $\boldsymbol{h}_j$. For an arbitrary span pair, the overall score is composed of the antecedent score and the mention scores for each span. The scoring functions are learned using standard feed-forward neural networks, allowing us to derive a distribution over all possible antecedents for a given span x.

$$P(y) = \frac{e^{s(x,y)}}{\sum_{y' \in Y} e^{s(x,y')}}$$

where s is the scoring function as defined in Joshi et al. (2020). We maximize the likelihood of the correct antecedents from the set of gold mentions, giving us a coreference loss (**CL**):

$$\mathbf{CL} = \log \prod_{i=1}^{N} \sum_{\hat{y} \in \mathcal{Y}(i) \cap \text{GOLD}(i)} P(\hat{y})$$

GOLD(i) denotes the set of spans in the gold cluster containing span i. Our baseline span representation is produced using SpanBERT with the single objective of minimizing the coreference loss (**CL**).

2.2 SpanBERT representation

SpanBERT is a pre-training method extending BERT that masks contiguous spans and also trains the span boundary representations to predict the masked span. The span representation $\boldsymbol{h}_i$ is the concatenation of the two SpanBERT transformer states of the span endpoints (first and last word pieces) $\mathbf{x}_{\text{START(i)}}, \mathbf{x}_{\text{END(i)}}$ and an attention vector $\hat{\mathbf{x}}_\mathbf{i}$ computed over all the word pieces in the span (Joshi et al., 2019, 2020).

$$\boldsymbol{h}_i = [\mathbf{x}_{\text{START(i)}}, \mathbf{x}_{\text{END(i)}}, \hat{\mathbf{x}}_\mathbf{i}, \phi(\mathbf{i})]$$

The attention vector $\hat{\mathbf{x}}_\mathbf{i}$ is intended to best represent the internal span itself (e.g. head word), whereas the endpoints better represent the context (Lee et al., 2017). This suggests that the $\hat{\mathbf{x}}_\mathbf{i}$ component of the overall span representation is the most natural part of the span to align with global, non-contextual knowledge.

2.3 Integrating Knowledge into Span Representation

We aim to create a span representation such that knowledge can be easily aligned with the coreference structure. Then, we can learn a span representation geometry such that connected spans are close and disconnected spans are far. In constructing such a vector space, we gain some flexibility to integrate any type of knowledge that shares the same structure as the coreference clusters. We can represent knowledge sources with concept clusters

$\{C_1^k, C_2^k, \ldots C_m^k\}$ to resemble coreference clusters, so that we can impose that the coreference cluster graph is consistent with the concept cluster graph via two additional losses.

We propose two complementary approaches to integrating knowledge. A pairwise retrofitting loss is intended to encode relative knowledge and a unary "scaffold" loss is intended to encode global knowledge into the span representation.

2.4 Retrofitting with Concept Knowledge

We want the span representation $\hat{\mathbf{x}}_\mathbf{i}$ to be close to coreferring spans $\hat{\mathbf{x}}_\mathbf{j}$. Similarly span representations belonging to the same cluster should be close. Similar to Faruqui et al. (2015), we enforce this objective by defining a custom distance function. But unlike Faruqui et al. (2015), our custom distance function is task specific and instead of using a lexicon, we are using broad concepts.

Concept Knowledge Distance metric We define our distance function to be composed of two elements: coreference information and concept knowledge.

$$d_T(s_i, s_j) = \alpha_c d_c(s_i, s_j) + \alpha_k d_k(s_i, s_j)$$

Variables α_c, α_k each denote weights that we tune, and T references the document from which valid span pairs are passed into the function.

Coreference information To capture the coreference graph, we recreate the distance between span pairs that do not corefer (d_c). Note that this distance does not discriminate between span pairs that belong to separate coreference clusters and span pairs where one span does not belong to any coreference cluster at all. We define $d_c(s_i, s_j) = 1$ if the spans do not corefer, otherwise 0.

Knowledge From our knowledge, we can obtain *concepts*, or sets of spans with some level of similarity of non-contextual meaning: $\{C_1^k, C_2^k, \ldots, C_m^k\}$. Coreferent spans refer to the same entity, and as a result, the concept type (e.g. person) must be consistent for any pair of coreferent spans. Thus, given a set of concepts, we want spans belonging to the same concept to have similar representations. Accordingly, we define $d_k(s_i, s_j) = 0$ if both spans belong to the same concept type, otherwise 1.

Retrofitting Loss (RL) We want to create a span representation with a geometry defined by our custom distance function. We can optimize the end-to-end model to satisfy a loss applied to the $\hat{\mathbf{x}}_\mathbf{i}$ component of the span representation:

$$\mathbf{RL} = \sum_{\ell} \frac{1}{|r^\ell|} \sum_{i,j} |d_{T^\ell}(s_i^\ell, s_j^\ell) - d(\hat{\boldsymbol{x}}_i^\ell, \hat{\boldsymbol{x}}_j^\ell)|$$

Here $|r^\ell|$ denotes the number of span pairs internal to one document, which we use to normalize, ℓ identifies the document that span s_i, s_j belongs to, and the function d is cosine distance.

2.5 Concept Identification as an Auxiliary Task

We introduce a concept identification auxiliary task to guide the model to construct a span representation from which the concept can be recovered. Swayamdipta et al. (2018) introduces the notion of a "scaffold" or auxiliary supervised loss function that is related to the primary task. Since coreferring spans nearly always belong to the same concept in our concept knowledge, concepts are a good choice for a scaffold. By sharing SpanBERT parameters optimizing for the scaffold loss and the overall coreference loss, we are able to encode the concept type in the span representation.

Auxiliary Scaffolding Loss (SL) Following from Swayamdipta et al. (2018), we assign a distribution over the set of concepts

$$p(s_i \in C \mid \hat{\mathbf{x}}_\mathbf{i}) = \text{softmax}_\mathbf{c} \mathbf{w_c} \cdot \hat{\mathbf{x}}_\mathbf{i}$$

where $\boldsymbol{w}_c$ is a parameter vector associated with a concept C. This gives us the loss:

$$\mathbf{SL} = \sum_{\ell} \frac{1}{|r^\ell|} \sum_{i} \log p\left(c_i^k \mid \hat{\mathbf{x}}_\mathbf{i}\right)$$

where c_i^k is the concept associated with span s_i.

Finally, we optimize a summation of these losses, weighting each loss with a hyperparameter that we tune.

$$\mathcal{L} = \beta_1 \mathbf{CL} + \beta_2 \mathbf{RL} + \beta_3 \mathbf{SL}$$

3 Experiments

3.1 Datasets

Our target corpus is a medical notes dataset, released as a part of the i2b2/VA Shared-Task and Workshop in 2011 (Uzuner et al., 2011). The dataset contains 251 train documents, 51 of which we have randomly selected for development and 173 test documents. Our dev set is used to select some model parameters (e.g., loss function weights

$\beta_1, \beta_2, \beta_3$). The average length of these documents is 962.62 tokens with average coreference chain containing 4.48 spans. For our source domain corpus, we use OntoNotes, with documents on average half as long as the clinical notes and similar average chain length 4.21.

3.1.1 Knowledge Lexicons

i2b2 Concepts (i2b2): In addition to coreference chains, the i2b2/VA dataset includes broad concept labels for spans. We focus on four concepts: *person* (e.g. the patient, Dr. X), *treatment* (e.g. abdominal hysterectomy, the procedure), *problem* (e.g. coronary artery disease, slurred speech), *test* (e.g. MRI, echocardiogram). The i2b2 dataset annotates coreference chains s.t. corefering spans must belong to the same concept. In Table 1, we report how these i2b2 concepts are distributed among the coreference chains.

i2b2 Concept	Avg. Chain length		# of Chains	
	Train	Test	Train	Test
Problem	2.96	2.9	1704	1186
Test	2.31	2.51	568	360
Person	14.16	12.54	754	571
Treatment	2.66	2.63	1262	1063

Table 1: Breakdown of i2b2 concepts in coreference chains

Unified Medical Language System Concepts (UMLS): The Unified Medical Language System (UMLS) defines concept unique identifier (CUI) codes in the UMLS Metathesuarus tool (Bodenreider, 2004). Each UMLS concept links synonymous spans, so the UMLS concepts are much more fine-grained than those defined in the i2b2 dataset. For example, a CUI for *headache* would map to {headaches, cranial pain, head pain cephalgia}. We used string match to assign a UMLS concept to spans in the training set. This resulted in the identification of 3,500 unique CUI's for the spans. We also experimented with using a partial string match to assign UMLS concepts to spans which we refer to as "UMLS overlap".

3.2 Baseline

For our supervised domain adaptation approach, we use a familiar approach of training a model on a source domain and tuning this model on a target domain. We take the current state of the art end-to-end coreference model from Joshi et al. (2020) for our baseline.

First, we train this SpanBERT-based end-to-end model on OntoNotes using the hyperparameters from Joshi et al. (2020). Then, we continue training this model using the target i2b2 training dataset. Continued training has been shown to be effective for coreference resolution in out-of-domain settings (Xia and Van Durme, 2021).

3.3 Model Setup

In order to improve the SpanBERT-based span representation, we introduce the i2b2 and UMLS concept knowledge in two ways: we retrofit the span representation to the concept knowledge (§2.4) and introduce an auxiliary task of concept identification as a scaffold (§2.5).

In our implementation, we add the corresponding retrofitting loss (**RL**) and scaffolding loss (**SL**) from these two objectives to the coreference loss (**CL**) to produce an overall loss which we optimize for. Aside from the difference in the loss function, the training process for our model resembles that of our baseline. We train our model first with the source domain OntoNotes and then continue training on the i2b2 dataset.

For the retrofitting loss, we experiment with the knowledge lexicons i2b2 and UMLS individually and together. Recall that the knowledge lexicon distance metric relies on two main components: coreference clusters $C_1, C_2, \ldots$ and knowledge clusters $C_1^k, C_2^k, \ldots$. When using i2b2 or UMLS knowledge concepts individually, we experiment with α_k, α_c values between $(0, 1]$ at intervals of .1, and we found that $\alpha_k = .2$ and $\alpha_c = 1.0$ performs best over the dev set. When using i2b2 and UMLS concepts together, we found that assigning more weight ($\alpha_k = .5$) to the broader i2b2 concepts than the UMLS concepts ($\alpha_k = .2$) performs best over the dev set. When training our model on OntoNotes, we do not have the same knowledge lexicon available, so effectively, we have $\alpha_k = 0$ until we begin training on the i2b2 data.

For the concept identification auxiliary task, we use only i2b2 concepts for our knowledge lexicon, since using the fine-grained UMLS concepts would induce 3,500 class labels. Additionally, since the i2b2 knowledge lexicon is not available for OntoNotes, we ignore **SL** ($\beta_3 = 0$).

For our model, we choose max_seq_length of 512, BERT learning rate of $2e-5$, and task specific learning rates of $1e-4$. Similar to Joshi et al. (2020), we fine-tune 20 epochs for OntoNotes and the i2b2 training examples.

4 Results

For successful domain adaptation, our model aims to demonstrate the value of incorporating concept knowledge. We evaluate overall coreference performance improvement as a result of the span retrofitting and auxiliary concept identification task in §4.1. Then, we inspect whether representations for highly domain-specific spans are better for the coreference resolution task in our model than in the baseline (§4.2).

4.1 Coreference Performance

In Table 2, we see that combining both of the losses we introduce in this work (**CL + RL + SL**) improves the model precision by 2.23% resulting in a .8% improvement in the F-1 score.

Combining the retrofitting loss and the auxiliary scaffolding loss performs better than using each individually. It is possible that adding the scaffolding loss alone is not as helpful because it does not contain the UMLS knowledge.

While our model does improve precision and the overall F-1 score, recall largely remains constant. The retrofitting loss pushes unrelated spans belonging to different concepts further apart, and consequently we penalize the detection of any valid mention that does not appear in our concept knowledge. Incompleteness of our concept knowledge may be a contributing factor to the lack of recall improvement.

It is expected that precision should be affected most by the additional losses **SL** and **RL**, since both are designed to integrate knowledge in the pairwise relationships between spans.

The scaffolding loss guides the model to be able to distinguish spans belonging to different concepts from the span representation, and the retrofitting loss enforces a knowledge-based distance function between spans. Model recall is partly determined by a unary mention score used to identify candidate mentions from spans in our model. This mention score is impacted by our losses, since span representation is taken as input to the scoring function. However, the pairwise knowledge integrated into the span representation is much more useful for selecting an antecedent among a set of candidates for a given span. Consequently, since our loss functions have a bigger impact on the antecedent scoring function, then they will also have a bigger impact on model precision.

4.2 Performance on Domain-specific Spans

In addition to overall performance, we are interested in comparing performance on rare spans that do not occur or occur infrequently in the source domain. Specifically, we are interested in addressing performance degradation that can occur as a result of wordpiece tokenization.

For example, consider a coreference cluster containing spans that are on average subdivided many times. This is an indication that the vocabulary of spans in the cluster is out of domain. The attention weighted vector over the tokens in the spans may be a misleading representation since the token embeddings correspond to shorter, less meaningful subwords. We report in Table 6 some examples of span pairs that the baseline model incorrectly predicts as coreferent.

Consider the spans "open laparoscopy" and "exploratory laporotomy". Their tokenizations would include the subwords ["lap", "##aro", "##tom", "##y"] and ["lap", "##aro", "##sco", "##py"]. This overlap of the first few subwords might lead the baseline to conclude that the spans are similar in non-contextual meaning and consequently coreferent. From our fine-grained UMLS knowledge, we know that laparoscopy and laparotomy belong to distinct concepts. Our loss functions **RL**, **SL** guide the model to produce disparate span representations since the spans map to distinct concepts. Our model uses knowledge to learn to upweight the wordpieces that are meaningful in context of the target domain (e.g., the suffix tokens in this example). We report examples of challenging span pairs that our model identifies and the baseline fails to identify in Table 5.

To collect quantitative evidence for our model's performance on the most challenging spans, we evaluate how model performance changes as the average number of wordpieces per span increases in Table 4. We can observe that as the average number of wordpieces per span increases beyond 3.4, we start to see an increasing F-1 performance over the baseline. Similar to the overall results for the entire test set, we see that performance improvements in precision are largely responsible.

Beyond average number of wordpieces per span, we can also use the concept labels annotated in the i2b2 dataset to verify the performance of our model on domain-specific spans. We verified that concepts *person* and *treatment* are respectively dominated by spans like "doctor", "patient" "surgery",

Model Losses	Knowledge	Model Performance											
		MUC			B-cubed			CEAFE			averages		
		R	P	F-1	R	P	F-1	R	P	F-1	R	P	F-1
Baseline (**CL**)	NA	70.93	72.51	71.71	64.91	66.48	65.69	54.57	58.44	56.44	63.47	65.81	64.61
CL + **RL** + **SL**	i2b2, UMLS	71.15	73.64	**72.37**	65.03	67.59	**66.28**	54.77	60.64	**57.56**	63.65	68.04	**65.41**
CL + **RL**	i2b2, UMLS	70.66	73.88	72.23	64.36	67.89	66.06	54.39	60.38	57.22	63.14	67.28	65.17
CL + **SL**	i2b2	70.28	74.14	72.16	64.22	68.27	66.18	54.69	60.43	57.41	63.43	67.17	65.24

Table 2: Overall coreference performance for various combinations of loss functions and knowledge resources. Our model surpasses our Baseline (**CL**) largely as a result of an improvement in precision (scores averaged over 6 random seed initializations).

Model Losses	Metric	i2b2 Concepts			
		Person	Problem	Treatment	Test
Baseline (**CL**)	Avg. R	63.47	50.92	54.85	48.08
	Avg. P	83.76	79.98	82.98	84.43
	Avg. F-1	69.92	58.0	**62.24**	54.74
CL + **RL** + **SL**	Avg. R	62.66	51.98	53.17	48.67
	Avg. P	86.23	83.20	86.22	86.67
	Avg. F-1	**69.98**	**59.56**	61.84	**55.62**

Table 3: Performance on coreference chains belonging to a specific concept. Our model outperforms the baseline on more domain-specific spans indicating our model improves domain adaptation *problem* and *test* coreference clusters

and "procedure", which are more likely to appear in the source domain than spans like "afebrile", "basal cell carcinoma", "asculation" from the *problem* and *test* concepts. Therefore, the performance improvement in Table 3 for concepts *problem* and *test* suggests that our model can outperform the baseline on domain-specific spans.

4.3 Visualization

We want to visualize how the span representation captures the mention-antecedent relationship for different types of concepts – specifically how consistently information is extracted from the mention span representation to arrive at a predicted antecedent. We randomly select 200 span pairs with a mention-antecedent relationship. For each span pair, we extract the attention weighted vector over the span tokens, which is the same piece of the span used to compute **SL**, **RL**. For these 768-dimensional vectors, we take the projection vectors from the mention to the antecedent vector. Then, in Figure 2 we transform these projections into a 2-dimensional space using PCA and plot them in $\mathbb{R}^2$ similar to Faruqui et al. (2015).

For the baseline model (top), most of the mention-antecedent vectors share a similar direction regardless of concept type. However, for the **CF** + **RL** + **SL** model (bottom), there is a clear distinction in mention-antecedent vectors for each concept. This suggests that our model is able to construct a span representation that can capture the mention-antecedent relationship in a way that is (1) specific to the concept (2) consistent across all mention-antecedent pairs belonging to the concept.

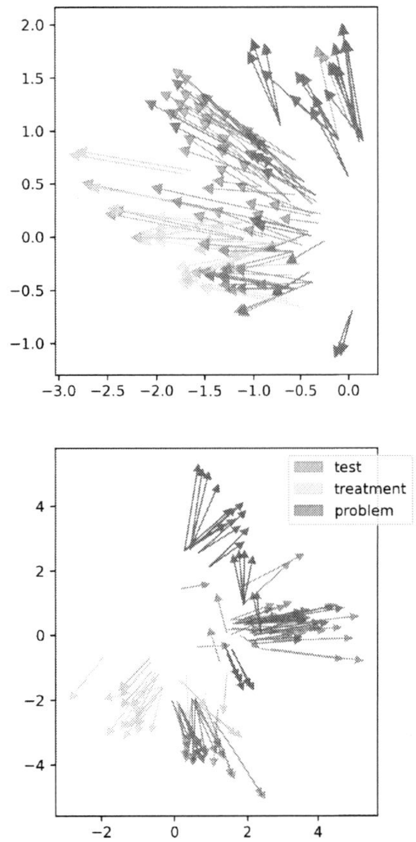

Figure 2: Two-dimensional PCA projections of attention-weighted span tokens for vector pairs holding the mention-antecedent relation for the baseline (top) and our model **CL** + **SL** + **RL** (bottom). Our model uses concept knowledge to construct a span representation that more consistently captures the mention-antecedent relationship specific to each concept.

5 Related Work

Prior to the introduction of end-to-end neural models in Lee et al. (2017), coreference resolution for the clinical domain used pipelined approaches, allowing for the propagation of errors from other core NLU tasks and relying on hand-crafted rules for

Model Losses	Metric	Avg. # of wordpieces/span range				
		[0.0,1.7)	[1.7,3.4)	[3.4,5.1)	[5.1,6.8)	[6.8,8.5)
Baseline (**CL**)	Avg. R	47.19	31.46	35.33	27.77	26.49
	Avg. P	79.94	64.55	60.63	54.32	49.28
	Avg. F-1	54.64	**38.40**	41.16	35.10	29.81
CL + **RL** + **SL**	Avg. R	47.18	29.41	36.88	30.76	27.93
	Avg. P	83.04	67.42	65.31	54.74	60.17
	Avg. F-1	55.19	37.39	**43.57**	**37.28**	33.78
CL + **RL** + **SL** (Overlap UMLS)	Avg. R	48.68	31.73	38.03	31.73	29.59
	Avg. P	79.22	63.06	57.89	52.26	51.65
	Avg. F-1	**55.50**	38.25	41.86	37.22	33.103
CL + **RL** (Overlap UMLS)	Avg. R	47.32	29.71	34.67	29.74	36.82
	Avg. P	80.63	64.58	65.58	55.67	56.89
	Avg. F-1	54.92	37.03	42.03	37.07	**38.11**

Table 4: We take the set of coreference chains s.t. the average number of wordpieces per span falls withing the range, and evaluate model of the subset. We observe that our model outperforms the baseline coreference chains with spans that are subdivided more frequently

TP Coreferent Span Pair Examples
Hereafter, wife noted development of left sided weakness, facial droop, slurring of speech ... with past medical history of atrial fibrillation on coumadin, coronary artery disease, hyperlipidemia, dementia with sudden onset left sided weakness, dysarthria
evaluation and treatment of adenocarcinoma involving the transverse colon and gallbladder ... DISCHARGE DIAGNOSIS: 1. Metastatic gallbladder cancer
He is status post a hemiarthroplasty on 10/17/97 ... decreased hematocrit prior to his humeral fixation surgery
An angiogram was done which disclosed possible subsegmental pulmonary emboli of the upper lobes as well ... patient was bolused with intravenous heparin due to concern for pulmonary embolism

Table 5: Examples of coreferent span pairs missed by Baseline (**CL**), identified by our model (**CL** + **RL** + **SL**). In these cases, we can see that wordpiece tokenization is likely misleading the baseline model, since the spans in each pair have few wordpieces in common.

FP Non-coreferent Span Pair Examples
She underwent an open laparoscopy ... The patient is now admitted for exploratory laparotomy
Right heart catheterization and coronary angiography on October 15 ... urgently transferred by Dr. Lenni Factor for possible angioplasty
78-yo male with atrial fibrillation... Mechanical mitral valve: Anticoagulation was reversed
He had a cardiac catheterization performed which revealed ... management after this hospitalization and has done very well

Table 6: Examples of non-coreferent span pairs correctly missed our model (**CL** + **RL** + **SL**), but identified by Baseline (**CL**). In these cases, we can see that wordpiece tokenization is likely misleading the baseline model, since the spans in each pair have wordpieces in common.

resolving each type of entity in the domain (Jindal et al., 2014). Feature-based methods like (Jindal et al., 2014) using knowledge in the coreference model rely on the availability of knowledge at test time. We are focused instead on the case where there may be no concept knowledge available when our model is deployed.

There has been some limited work in domain adaptation for coreference resolution. Yang et al. (2012) adapts a model trained on the MUC-6 and ACE 2005 datasets to the biomedical domain using an active learning approach, applying data augmentation and pruning techniques. Zhao and Ng (2014) propose a feature-based active learning method to learn cross-domain knowledge. Unlike these works, we take advantage of the modern expressive power of the SpanBERT representation. With the introduction of SpanBERT, there was a marked performance improvement for several NLU tasks including coreference resolution. Joshi et al. (2020) showed that SpanBERT could be fine-tuned to perform well on several datasets, e.g., GLU and ACE (Wang et al., 2018; Doddington et al., 2004).

However, Lu and Ng (2020) found that SpanBERT coreference resolvers generally rely more on mentions than context, so they are susceptible to small perturbations (e.g., changing all the names/nominal mentions in the test set). More generally, for NLU tasks several studies have found that neural models rely heavily on shallow heuristics in the text rather than learning the underlying structure of the linguistic phenomenon (Peng et al., 2020; Rosenman et al., 2020), leading to the misinterpretation of context (Alt et al., 2020).

This poses a challenge for adapting a coreference model to noisy domains like clinical text and mostly OOD spans. With the recent success of fine-tuning for domain adaptation, a natural approach would be to fine-tune the SpanBERT representation, the coreference model, or both (Gururangan et al., 2020). Fine-tuning the pretrained SpanBERT method alone can be expensive – Gururangan et al. (2020) showed that the best performing scheme requires 180K documents. In settings where there are fewer documents available in the target domain, it is still possible to fine-tune a coreference model with SpanBERT (Joshi et al., 2020).

However, a persisting challenge with adapting the span representation is associated with the wordpiece tokenization employed by SpanBERT. For highly technical domain-specific language, it is natural that there is a higher average number of subwords per span, since it is unlikely that many spans or spans split only once belong to the limited 300,000 word SpanBERT vocabulary. Poerner et al. (2020a) show that wordpiece tokenization in the biomedical domain can lead to misleading span representations. Purely fine-tuning approaches fail to address this issue, since the SpanBERT vocabulary is constant.

At the same time, SpanBERT implicitly learns a geometry that encodes rich information related to the coreference task. Hewitt and Manning (2019) show that it is possible to learn a linear projection space from BERT embeddings to capture linguistic phenomena like syntactic dependencies. In Kahardipraja et al. (2020), the authors use a Feedforward Neural Network (FFNN) to probe for properties of coreference structure, finding evidence that the SpanBERT representation can be used to predict coreference arcs and the head word of the span with >90% F1. Therefore, it is likely that overall performance greatly depends on the quality of span representation.

In our work, we develop multiple techniques to adapt the span representation to a new domain with concept knowledge, allowing the model to be fine-tuned with fewer target domain examples and perform better on highly domain-specific entities. In particular, by incorporating knowledge into the span representation, we are able to restore a global, non-contextual meaning to excessively subtokenized spans.

6 Conclusion

We present methods to efficiently adapt coreference resolution models to a new domain using domain-specific concept knowledge. We demonstrate that we can integrate knowledge into the span representation using two losses to (1) retrofit the span representation to the concept knowledge and (2) ensure that knowledge can be recovered from the span representation using an auxiliary concept identification task. Using these methods, we are able to improve the performance of our baseline, especially for highly domain-specific spans.

Acknowledgements

Thanks to Alex Chouldechova, Amanda Coston, David Steier, and the Allegheny County Department of Human Services for valuable feedback on this work. This work is supported by the Block Center for Technology and Innovation, and A.F. is supported by a Google PhD Fellowship.

References

Christoph Alt, Aleksandra Gabryszak, and Leonhard Hennig. 2020. Probing linguistic features of sentence-level representations in neural relation extraction. In *Proceedings of the 58th Annual Meeting of the Association for Computational Linguistics*, pages 1534–1545, Online. Association for Computational Linguistics.

Olivier Bodenreider. 2004. The unified medical language system (umls): integrating biomedical terminology. *Nucleic acids research*, 32(suppl_1):D267–D270.

George R Doddington, Alexis Mitchell, Mark A Przybocki, Lance A Ramshaw, Stephanie M Strassel, and Ralph M Weischedel. 2004. The automatic content extraction (ace) program-tasks, data, and evaluation. In *Lrec*, volume 2, pages 837–840. Lisbon.

Manaal Faruqui, Jesse Dodge, Sujay Kumar Jauhar, Chris Dyer, Eduard Hovy, and Noah A. Smith. 2015. Retrofitting word vectors to semantic lexicons. In *Proceedings of the 2015 Conference of the North American Chapter of the Association for Computational Linguistics: Human Language Technologies*, pages 1606–1615, Denver, Colorado. Association for Computational Linguistics.

Suchin Gururangan, Ana Marasović, Swabha Swayamdipta, Kyle Lo, Iz Beltagy, Doug Downey, and Noah A. Smith. 2020. Don't stop pretraining: Adapt language models to domains and tasks. In *Proceedings of the 58th Annual Meeting of the Association for Computational Linguistics*, pages 8342–8360, Online. Association for Computational Linguistics.

John Hewitt and Christopher D Manning. 2019. A structural probe for finding syntax in word representations. In *Proceedings of the 2019 Conference of the North American Chapter of the Association for Computational Linguistics: Human Language Technologies, Volume 1 (Long and Short Papers)*, pages 4129–4138.

Prateek Jindal, Dan Roth, and Carl A Gunter. 2014. Joint inference for end-to-end coreference resolution for clinical notes. In *Proceedings of the 5th ACM Conference on Bioinformatics, Computational Biology, and Health Informatics*, pages 192–201.

Mandar Joshi, Danqi Chen, Yinhan Liu, Daniel S Weld, Luke Zettlemoyer, and Omer Levy. 2020. Spanbert: Improving pre-training by representing and predicting spans. *Transactions of the Association for Computational Linguistics*, 8:64–77.

Mandar Joshi, Omer Levy, Luke Zettlemoyer, and Daniel Weld. 2019. BERT for coreference resolution: Baselines and analysis. In *Proceedings of the 2019 Conference on Empirical Methods in Natural Language Processing and the 9th International Joint Conference on Natural Language Processing (EMNLP-IJCNLP)*, pages 5803–5808, Hong Kong, China. Association for Computational Linguistics.

Patrick Kahardipraja, Olena Vyshnevska, and Sharid Loáiciga. 2020. Exploring span representations in neural coreference resolution. In *Proceedings of the First Workshop on Computational Approaches to Discourse*, pages 32–41.

Yuval Kirstain, Ori Ram, and Omer Levy. 2021. Coreference resolution without span representations. In *Proceedings of the 59th Annual Meeting of the Association for Computational Linguistics and the 11th International Joint Conference on Natural Language Processing (Volume 2: Short Papers)*, pages 14–19, Online. Association for Computational Linguistics.

Kenton Lee, Luheng He, Mike Lewis, and Luke Zettlemoyer. 2017. End-to-end neural coreference resolution. In *Proceedings of the 2017 Conference on Empirical Methods in Natural Language Processing*, pages 188–197, Copenhagen, Denmark. Association for Computational Linguistics.

Jing Lu and Vincent Ng. 2020. Conundrums in entity reference resolution. In *Proceedings of the 2020 Conference on Empirical Methods in Natural Language Processing (EMNLP)*, pages 6620–6631.

Hao Peng, Tianyu Gao, Xu Han, Yankai Lin, Peng Li, Zhiyuan Liu, Maosong Sun, and Jie Zhou. 2020. Learning from Context or Names? An Empirical Study on Neural Relation Extraction. In *Proceedings of the 2020 Conference on Empirical Methods in Natural Language Processing (EMNLP)*, pages 3661–3672, Online. Association for Computational Linguistics.

Nina Poerner, Ulli Waltinger, and Hinrich Schütze. 2020a. E-BERT: Efficient-yet-effective entity embeddings for BERT. In *Findings of the Association for Computational Linguistics: EMNLP 2020*, pages 803–818, Online. Association for Computational Linguistics.

Nina Poerner, Ulli Waltinger, and Hinrich Schütze. 2020b. Inexpensive domain adaptation of pretrained language models: Case studies on biomedical NER and covid-19 QA. In *Findings of the Association for Computational Linguistics: EMNLP 2020*, pages 1482–1490, Online. Association for Computational Linguistics.

Shachar Rosenman, Alon Jacovi, and Yoav Goldberg. 2020. Exposing Shallow Heuristics of Relation Extraction Models with Challenge Data. In *Proceedings of the 2020 Conference on Empirical Methods in Natural Language Processing (EMNLP)*, pages 3702–3710, Online. Association for Computational Linguistics.

Ankit Srivastava, Piyush Makhija, and Anuj Gupta. 2020. Noisy text data: Achilles' heel of bert. In *Proceedings of the Sixth Workshop on Noisy User-generated Text (W-NUT 2020)*, pages 16–21.

Swabha Swayamdipta, Sam Thomson, Kenton Lee, Luke Zettlemoyer, Chris Dyer, and Noah A. Smith. 2018. Syntactic scaffolds for semantic structures. In *Proceedings of the 2018 Conference on Empirical Methods in Natural Language Processing*, pages 3772–3782, Brussels, Belgium. Association for Computational Linguistics.

Özlem Uzuner, Brett R South, Shuying Shen, and Scott L DuVall. 2011. 2010 i2b2/va challenge on concepts, assertions, and relations in clinical text. *Journal of the American Medical Informatics Association*, 18(5):552–556.

Alex Wang, Amanpreet Singh, Julian Michael, Felix Hill, Omer Levy, and Samuel Bowman. 2018. GLUE: A multi-task benchmark and analysis platform for natural language understanding. In *Proceedings of the 2018 EMNLP Workshop BlackboxNLP: Analyzing and Interpreting Neural Networks for NLP*, pages 353–355, Brussels, Belgium. Association for Computational Linguistics.

Ralph Weischedel, Martha Palmer, Mitchell Marcus, Eduard Hovy, Sameer Pradhan, Lance Ramshaw, Nianwen Xue, Ann Taylor, Jeff Kaufman, Michelle Franchini, Mohammed El-Bachouti, Robert Belvin, and Ann Houston. 2013. OntoNotes Release 5.0.

Patrick Xia and Benjamin Van Durme. 2021. Moving on from ontonotes: Coreference resolution model transfer. *arXiv preprint arXiv:2104.08457*.

Liyan Xu and Jinho D. Choi. 2020. Revealing the myth of higher-order inference in coreference resolution. In *Proceedings of the 2020 Conference on Empirical Methods in Natural Language Processing (EMNLP)*, pages 8527–8533, Online. Association for Computational Linguistics.

Jian Bo Yang, Qi Mao, Qiao Liang Xiang, Ivor Wai-Hung Tsang, Kian Ming A Chai, and Hai Leong Chieu. 2012. Domain adaptation for coreference resolution: An adaptive ensemble approach. In *Proceedings of the 2012 Joint Conference on Empirical*

Methods in Natural Language Processing and Computational Natural Language Learning, pages 744–753.

Shanheng Zhao and Hwee Tou Ng. 2014. Domain adaptation with active learning for coreference resolution. In *Proceedings of the 5th International Workshop on Health Text Mining and Information Analysis (Louhi)*, pages 21–29.

Coreference by Appearance: Visually Grounded Event Coreference Resolution

Liming Wang[1], Shengyu Feng[1], Xudong Lin[2], Manling Li[1], Heng Ji[1], Shih-Fu Chang[2]
[1]University of Illinois at Urbana-Champaign, [2]Columbia University

Abstract

Event coreference resolution is critical to understand events in growing number of online news with multiple modalities including text, video, speech, etc. However, the events and entities depicting in different modalities may not be perfectly aligned and can be difficult to annotate, which makes the task especially challenging with little supervision available. To address the above issues, we propose a supervised model based on attention mechanism and an unsupervised model based on statistical machine translation, capable of learning the relative importance of modalities for event coreference resolution. Experiments on a video multimedia event dataset show that our multimodal models outperform text-only systems in the event coreference resolution task. A careful analysis reveals that the performance gain of the multimodal model especially under the unsupervised setting comes from better learning of visually salient events.

1 Introduction

With the advance of Internet, news articles nowadays are becoming increasingly multimodal. For example, news about a recent launch of a SpaceX rocket may contain the traditional text article, a drone video of the launch and a narration from the talking head or reporter. Such a diverse source of information provides us a multi-faceted understanding of the newsworthy event, and helps us better follow the content of the article. Event coreference resolution, the task of resolving whether two words or phrases called *mentions* in the article refer to the same real-world event or not, is the first step toward such an understanding.

While human can efficiently and accurately identify the coreference relations when reading an article, this task has shown to be quite challenging to machines. The state-of-the-art coreference resolution system not only accepts textual input, but typically requires over 4000 annotated articles with more than 400 words fully annotated with mention span and coreference relation to train (Lee et al., 2018). Further, since event coreference resolution requires careful reading and deep understanding of the text, it becomes prohibitively expensive to annotate for low-resource languages.

Another issue with the current system is that the model lacks a way to incorporate real-world knowledge typically required for coreference. One potential way to incorporate such knowledge is to consider an alternative modality – videos. A fascinating aspect of multimodal event coreference resolution is that the correlation between the visual modality and the text can be quite weak, and the text tends to contain most of the information for resolving coreference. Nevertheless, the meanings of the event triggers often require additional information sources to resolve. For example, we never know an "attack" is a physical one or verbal one without seeing or imagining a particular scene based on additional contextual constraints, or it is hard to know whether "chant" and "protest" co-refer without knowing the event in the text is a demonstration. But if a video of the relevant events is played, we can immediately understand the relations between the trigger words. In this paper, we answer the following research question: How to leverage weakly aligned multimodal data for event coreference resolution system, especially in an unsupervised setting?

2 Approach

2.1 Notations and Definitions

A *multimodal document* $S = (M, V)$ is defined as the tuple of two sequences: the sequence of *textual event mentions* $M = (m_0, \cdots, m_I)$, including the artificial root mention m_0, and the sequence of *visual event mentions* $V = (v_1, \cdots, v_J)$, i.e., event-level segments from the related video. Each text mention is represented as a span of con-

Proceedings of the 4th Workshop on Computational Models of Reference, Anaphora and Coreference (CRAC 2021), pages 132–140
Punta Cana, Dominican Republic, November 10–11, 2021.

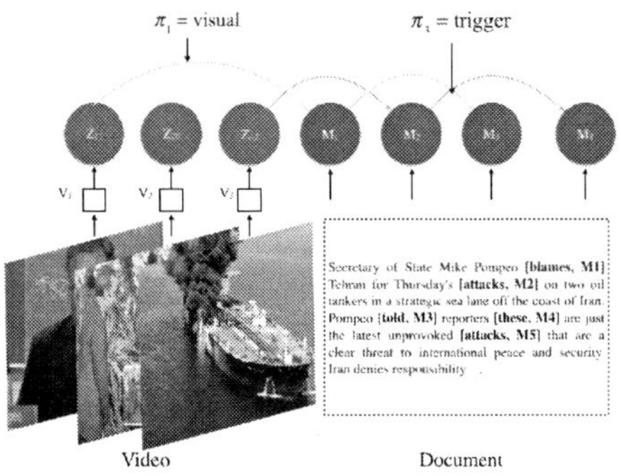

Figure 1: The proposed unsupervised multimodal coreference resolution model. The bubbles represent the random variables involved in the generative process, the squares represent raw feature inputs and arcs represent the values taken by the antecedent variables

secutive word tokens $(x_{\text{start}(i)}, \cdots, x_{\text{end}(i)})$, where $\text{start}(i)$ and $\text{end}(i)$ are the indices of the start and end token of the span. The mention spans can be extracted either using a binary classifier as done in previous works (Lee et al., 2017, 2018) or by an end-to-end event extraction system such as OneIE (Lin et al., 2020) as in this work. Similarly, each visual mention is a span of consecutive embeddings of video frames $(y_{\text{start}(j)}, \cdots, y_{\text{end}(j)})$ extracted by human annotators. Inspired by (Ma et al., 2016), the coreference relations between events can be represented by a sequence of latent *antecedent variables* $C = (c_1, \cdots, c_I)$ associated with each event mentions, where $c_i = j$ means that mention i is the parent of (textual or visual) mention j in the tree formed by mentions that are coreferent. For within-text coreference, $c_i \in \{0, \cdots, i-1\}$ and for crossmedia coreference, $c_i \in \{1, \cdots, J\}$.

2.2 Supervised model for end-to-end event coreference resolution

In the setting of supervised coreference resolution, the model tries to learn the coreference relation between textual mention pairs $(m_i, m_{i'})$ from labeled mention pairs $\{(m_i, m_{i'}), y^c_{ii'}\}$, where $y^c_{ii'} = 1$ if m_i and $m_{i'}$ are coreferent and 0 otherwise. In the multimodal setting, we allow the model to observe *crossmedia coreference labels* y^v_{ij}'s, where $y^v_{ij} = 1$ if textual mention m_i and visual mention v_j are coreferent.

Our end-to-end model consists of two main components: a crossmedia coreference resolver and a text-only coreference resolver. For both resolver, embeddings from the RoBERTa-large (Liu

Name	Definition
x_n	n-th token in a document
f_t	t-th frame in a video
m_i	i-th text event mention in a document
v_j	j-th visual event mention in a video
c_i	the position of antecedent for text mention i
MLP	Multi-layer perecptron
$F_v(m_i, v_j)$	Crossmedia coreference score between textual mention m_i and visual mention v_j
$F_c(m_i, m_{i'})$	Textual context score between textual mention m_i and $m_{i'}$
$F_{cv}(m_i, m_{i'})$	Visual context score between textual mention m_i and $m_{i'}$
π_i	mode of i-th text event mention
μ_k	the centroid of k-th visual cluster
$p(m_i \vert m_j, \pi_i)$	probability of features used in mode π_i for m_i given mention m_j is its antecedent
$q(c_i \vert i)$	probability that the antecedent of mention i is at position c_i in attribute mode

Table 1: Definitions of key notations

et al., 2019) transformer is used as input to the textual mention encoder, and embeddings from the penultimate layer of the TSN action recognition model (Contributors, 2020) is used as input to the visual mention encoder. The transformer is frozen during training. To represent the text mentions, instead of concatenating start token, end token and head word token embeddings as in (Lee et al., 2017, 2018), the textual encoder forms the mention embedding by averaging the embeddings within its span:

$$m_i = \frac{\sum_{n=\text{start}(i)}^{\text{end}(i)} x_n}{\text{end}(i) - \text{start}(i)} \tag{1}$$

Similarly, the visual mention encoder compute a fixed-dimensional embedding for each visual mention by averaging over its frame embeddings f_t's:

$$v_j = \frac{\sum_{t=\text{start}(j)}^{\text{end}(j)} f_t}{\text{end}(j) - \text{start}(j)}. \tag{2}$$

This saves memory without losing significant amount of information since most of the triggers consist of only one token.

To compute the probability that a visual mention and a textual mention are coreferent, the crossmedia resolver first encodes each textual and visual mention pair (m_i, v_j) into the common embedding space as $(m^{\mathbb{C}}_i, v^{\mathbb{C}}_j)$. This is done by two three-layer bidirectional LSTMs (Hochreiter and Schmidhuber, 1997) (BiLSTMs) as visual and textual crossmedia encoder:

$$m_i^{\mathbb{C}} = \text{BiLSTM}_i(M) \quad (3)$$
$$v_j^{\mathbb{C}} = \text{BiLSTM}_j(V). \quad (4)$$

The crossmedia coreference score is then simply the dot-product similarity between the embeddings:

$$F_v(m, v) = m^{\mathbb{C}\top} v^{\mathbb{C}} \quad (5)$$

To compute the probability that two textual mentions are coreferent, we first computed the text-only coreference score using a multilayer perceptron (MLP):

$$F_c(m, m') = \text{MLP}_c([m, m', m \odot m']). \quad (6)$$

To fuse visual and linguistic information, we use a special attention mechanism (Bahdanau et al., 2015) similar to the one proposed in (Yu et al., 2019). In particular, the model attends over the visual mention embedding to create a contextualized embedding as additional feature for each textual mention:

$$\alpha_{m_i, v_j} = \frac{\exp(F_v(m_i, v_j))}{\sum_v \exp(F_v(m_i, v))} \quad (7)$$

The text resolver then utilizes the contextualized embeddings as additional cues to resolve coreference between the mention pairs:

$$\beta_{m_i} = \max_j \alpha_{m_i, v_j} \quad (8)$$
$$\beta_{m_i, m_{i'}} = \max_j \alpha_{m_i, v_j} \alpha_{m_{i'}, v_j} \quad (9)$$
$$F_{cv}(m_i, m_{i'}) = \text{MLP}_{cv}([\beta_{m_i}; \beta_{m_{i'}}; \beta_{m_i, m_{i'}}]). \quad (10)$$

Intuitively, the value of β_{m_i}'s scores how "visual" a particular mention is and $\beta_{m_i, m_{i'}}$ scores how likely the two mentions refer to the same visual event. The final text coreference score is then the weighted sum of the textual and viusal context score:

$$F(m_i, m_{i'}) = \lambda_v \cdot F_{cv}(m_i, m_{i'}) + (1 - \lambda_v) \cdot F_c(m_i, m_{i'}). \quad (11)$$

The score can be then interpreted as the logit of the probability $p(y_{ii'}^c | m_i, m_{i'})$ and learned by maximizing the standard binary cross-entropy loss. We will refer to this later as the *weight fusion* model.

2.3 Amodal SMT: Unsupervised model for multimodal event coreference resolution

The supervised multimodal model requires a large amount of labeled training data, which makes it unsuitable for real-world multimodal documents where coreference labels are mostly unavailable. Therefore, it is desirable to design an unsupervised coreference resolution algorithm to learn coreference relations without of the need of such labels. Instead of maximizing the likelihood of the coreference labels as in the supervised case, our unsupervised multimodal coreference resolution model instead tries to maximize the conditional likelihood $p(M|V)$, with independence assumptions based on (Ma et al., 2016):

$$p(M|V) = \prod_{i=1}^{I} p(\pi_i|i) p(c_i|i, \pi_i) \cdot p(m_i|v_{c_i}, m_{c_i}, \pi_i), \quad (12)$$

where $\Pi = (\pi_1, \cdots, \pi_I)$ are discrete variables called *mode* variables. This likelihood resembles that of the classical statistical machine translation (SMT) model (Brown et al., 1993) where the text mentions form the source language sentence the entire multimoal document is the target language sentence. Therefore, we call the model *amodal SMT*. In each mode, the model will resolve the current mention with a different subset of linguistic features. This is motivated by the observation that while resolving proper-nominal mention pairs such as "the Great War" and "World War I" mostly requires semantic features such as embedding similarity, resolving pronoun-nominal mention pairs such as "the Great War" and "it" relies more on syntactic and discourse features such as part-of-speech tags, parse trees and sentence distance. The need of distinct features for different coreferent types is also demonstrated in previous works (Haghighi and Klein, 2009; Ratinov and Roth, 2012; Lee et al., 2013; Ma et al., 2016).

The overview of our unsupervised model is shown in Fig. 1. Our unsupervised model has three modes, one *visual* mode and two *textual* modes, one called *trigger*-matching mode and the other called *attribute*-matching mode. In visual mode, π_i = visual, the antecedent of mention i is restricted to only visual event mentions. In textual modes, the antecedent of event mention i is restricted to only previous textual event mentions as in (Ma et al., 2016). Further, in trigger-matching

Mode	Feature	Description
trigger	Head Lemma	lemmatized head word extracted using NLTK and AllenNLP
	Number	consider only mention pairs with the same number
	Event Type	consider only mention pairs with different types
	GloVe	consider only mention pairs with cosine similarity ≥ 0.5
	String Match	consider mention pair if normalized edit distance ≥ 0.5
attribute	Mention Type	same as in (Ma et al., 2016)
	Number	same as in (Ma et al., 2016)
	Event Type	same as in trigger mode
	Arguments	consider only events with non-overlapping argument entity types or sharing argument of the same type
	Sentence distance	same as in (Ma et al., 2016)
visual	Head Lemma	same as in trigger mode
	Number	consider only pairs with the same number
	Event Type	consider only mention pairs with different types
	Is Visual	consider mention whose type of event appears in at least one video

Table 2: Features for different modes of amodal SMT

mode with π_i = trigger, the model will use primarily semantic features such as the embedding of the trigger. Finally, in attribute-matching mode with π_i = attribute, it will use mostly syntactic and discourse features. More details about the features can be found in Table. 2. Therefore, we have:

$$p(m_i|v_{c_i}, m_{c_i}, \pi_i) =: \begin{cases} p(m_i|m_{c_i}, \pi_i), \text{ if } \pi_i \in \{\text{trigger, attribute}\} \\ p(m_i|v_{c_i}), \text{ if } \pi_i = \text{visual} \end{cases} \tag{13}$$

In textual mode, two textual event mentions $(m_i, m_{i'})$ are *coreferent* if they belong to the same text coreference chain specified by the antecedent variables c_i's; in visual mode, however, they are coreferent only if they refer to the same visual mention, i.e., $c_i = c_{i'}$. Further, the modes are assumed to be equally likely and the prior of antecedent is learnable in the attribute-matching mode to model the discourse structure of the document:

$$p(c_i|i, \pi_i) = \begin{cases} q(c_i|i), \text{ if } \pi_i = \text{attribute}, \\ \frac{1}{i}, \text{ if } \pi_i = \text{trigger}, \\ \frac{1}{J}, \text{ if } \pi_i = \text{visual} \end{cases} \tag{14}$$

Since the representation of a visual event is continuous, we assume that the visual features of similar events tend to cluster together and can be well modeled by a Gaussian distribution with mean μ_k and variance σ_k for each event type k. However, the type of a visual event mention is ambiguous given the visual feature alone because events like "attack" and "protest" tend to co-occur in the video, leading to overlapping visual mentions and similar visual features. To model this, we allow each visual mention j to represent a *different* event type for each text mention i it refers to with cluster variables $z_{ji}, i = 1, \cdots, I, j = 1, \cdots, J$. With such a multi-label assumption, the probabilities $p(m_i|v_j)$ become:

$$p(m_i|v_j) = \sum_{z_{ji}=1}^{K} p(z_{ji}|v_j)p(m_i|z_{ji}, \pi_i) \tag{15}$$

$$p(z_{ji} = s|v_j) := \frac{\exp(\frac{-\|v_j - \mu_s\|^2}{2\sigma_s^2})}{\sum_{k=1}^{K} \exp(\frac{-\|v_j-\mu_k\|^2}{2\sigma_k^2})} \tag{16}$$

2.4 Antecedent prediction

We can use the maximum a posteriori (MAP) estimator to find the optimal antecedent for each mention separately as:

$$\arg\max_{c_i} q(c_i|i)p(m_i|m_{c_i}, v_{c_i}, \pi_i). \tag{17}$$

This approach, however, is less robust when the visual event boundaries are noisy or overlapping, as in our case. Therefore, we instead *marginalize* out all possible alignments for each mention pairs to obtain the pairwise score as in the textual mode:

$$\arg\max_j p(c_i = c_j|m_i, m_j, V, \pi_i = \text{visual}) = \arg\max_j \sum_{c=1}^{J} p(m_i|v_c)p(m_j|v_c) \tag{18}$$

2.5 Training

The whole model can be trained using EM algorithm (Dempster et al., 1977) with more details in Algorithm 1. We initialized the visual centroids using K-means algorithm and the other parameters uniformly on their supports. The model is then trained for 10 EM iterations. We experimented with various number of visual clusters, and the result is shown in Figure 2. The subsequent results are all obtained with 15 clusters.

3 Experiments and Results

3.1 Data and Experiments Setup

The video M2E2 dataset (Anonymous, 2021), inspired by the image M2E2 dataset (Li et al., 2020),

Algorithm 1: Learning with EM

Initialization: initialize $t_0, q_0, \mathbf{M}_0$

for $\tau = 1$ **to** T **do**

  for *each document D* **do**

    for $i = 1$ **to** I **do**

      Update counts for $p(m'|m, \pi)$ and $q(c|i)$ as in (Ma et al., 2016);

      for $c = 1$ **to** J **do**

        $L_{icz} = \frac{p(z_{ci}|v_c)p(m_i|z_{ci})}{\sum_j p(z_{ji}|v_j)p(m_i|z_{ji})}$

        $c(m_i, z) += \sum_{c=1}^{J} L_{icz}$

        $\Delta\mu_z += (L_{icz} - p(z_{ci}|v_c))\frac{v_c - \mu_z}{\sigma_z}$

    Update $p(m'|m, \pi)$ and $q(c|i)$ parameters as in (Ma et al., 2016);

    $\mu_z = \mu_z + \eta\Delta\mu_z$

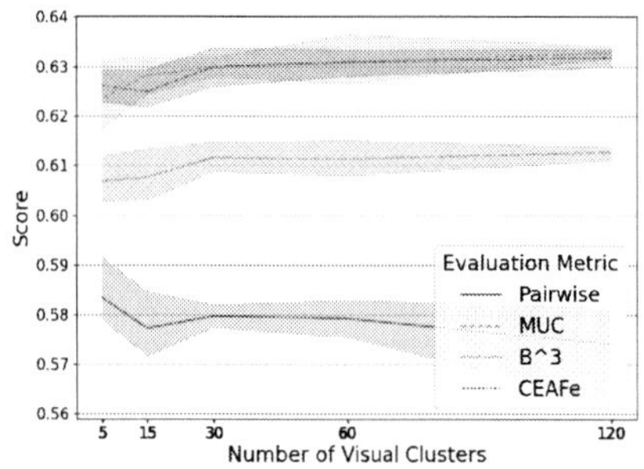

Figure 2: Coreference scores vs. number of visual clusters used by amodal SMT

consists of 860 manually annotated documents, each paired with a 1-2 minutes video released by authentic news outlets such as British Broadcasting Company (BBC), Voice of American (VoA) and Reuters. The videos are found from Youtube channel with event types as searching keywords such as "attack" and "elect". The textual coreference labels are annotated by two annotators with three rounds of adjudication using the Brat interface (Stenetorp et al., 2011) following ACE2005 guideline. More details about this dataset are available in Table 3 as well as (Anonymous, 2021). We follow the 3:1 random split of training/test sets by (Anonymous, 2021). Three standard metrics for coreference resolution are used to evaluate the models at the cluster level: the MUC (Vilain et al., 1995), B^3 (Bagga and Baldwin, 1998), Entity-based CEAFe (Luo, 2005).

	Video M2E2
# Train/Test	645/215
# Event mentions	4158
# Event clusters	647

Table 3: Dataset statistics. Only non-singleton clusters are counted

The CoNLL score is calculated as the average of these three scores and we used the CoNLL 2012 scorer (Pradhan et al., 2014). We also used the more straightforward pairwise F1 score and mean average precision (mAP) score, which score the overlap between the set of predicted coreference links and the gold links.

3.2 Baselines

We used the following supervised coreference resolution model as baseline, namely,

- **Text-only model**: an implementation of the state-of-the-art neural coreference resolution model (Lee et al., 2018) by (Cattan et al., 2020), which uses RoBERTa (Liu et al., 2019) to extract contextualized word embeddings. All parameter and optimization settings are made the same as the multimodal supervised model described in Section 2.2. We used ground truth mention spans and within-document antecedent prediction instead of using their cross-document hierarchical clustering algorithm.

In addition, we used the following unsupervised models as baselines, including

- **HDP-LF**: re-implementation of (Bejan and Harabagiu, 2010) with a rich set of semantic and syntactic features;

- **DD-CRP**: re-implementation of (Yang et al., 2015) with additional pairwise features compared to HDP-LF;

- **Text-only SMT**: proposed in (Ma et al., 2016) with features adapted to event coreference resolution for each textual mode described in Section 2.

3.3 Results

The overall results on video M2E2 are shown in Table. 4 respectively. We make the following claims:

Video M2E2	Pairwise F1	MUC	B^3	CEAFe
(Cattan et al., 2020)	61.0±0.7	66.4±1.0	63.6±0.9	64.3±0.8
Weight Fusion (Ours)	**61.6**±0.5	**67.0**±1.0	**64.4**±1.2	**64.7**±1.8
HDP-LF	51.9±0.0	55.2±0.0	53.7±0.0	54.2±0.0
DD-CRP	56.4±1.7	62.3±0.6	60.7±0.8	**63.3**±1.2
Text-only SMT	54.1±0.0	60.3±0.0	58.7±0.0	59.8±0.0
Amodal SMT (Ours)	**57.7**±0.7	**62.8**±0.4	**60.8**±0.5	62.5±0.4

Table 4: Event coreference resolution performance of all systems on the video M2E2 dataset. Models above the line are supervised models while models below are unsupervised. All results are averages of 4 runs. Note that the confidence interval of text-only SMT is 0.0 since the model is initialized and trained deterministically.

Effect of Visual Supervision The supervised multimodal model outperforms the text-only model by 2% in pairwise F1 and 3% in CoNLL (average of the last three metrics), demonstrating the effectiveness of multimodal data for coreference resolution. Further, amodal SMT achieves 3.5% and 2.4% improvement in pairwise and CoNLL score respectively over its text-only counterpart, 5.8% and 7.7% improvement over the HDP-LF method, indicating that video features contain additional information to the text features and can benefit unsupervised coreference resolution. Further, the amodal SMT also outperforms the text-only supervised baselines, though with the help of event type information. However, it does not outperform the DD-CRP approach, possibly due to the lack of global clustering mechanism. A breakdown of pairwise coreference scores across event types is shown in Table 6. We found that the amodal SMT performs significantly better than the text-only approach in visually salient event types such as Demonstrate, TransportPerson and Meet, but perform worse on rare events such as ArrestJail and ReleaseParole or non-visual events such as Die. The amodal SMT also performs worse in visual event such as Attack and Broadcast, probably because the model is confused its visual representation with those of other event types such as Demonstrate as the two events often co-occur in the video. Although the amodal SMT approach underperforms in 7 out of 10 most frequent event types, we found its overall performance superior to the text-only approach because the large improvement in events such as Demonstrate, TransportPerson and Meet (about 18% absolute in average) outweighs the performance drop. On the other hand, for the supervised event coreference, we found a reverse trend that the multimodal model performs superior to the text-only model in 7 out of the 10 most frequent event types, though the improvements are minor for types such as Attack and Broadcast. Furthermore, all the improved event types in the unsupervised setting suffer from performance drop in the supervised setting except Meet event, and all events except Elect that suffer from performance drop in the supervised setting enjoy a performance gain in the supervised setting. This suggests that different aspects of the visual feature is used for the two settings.

Effect of Multi-mode mechanism From Table 4 and Table 5, removing any mode leads to degradation to the model, suggesting the importance of using multi-mode mechanism. In particular, the most performance degradation results from removing trigger mode, followed by removing both textual modes, then by removing visual mode and finally by removing attribute mode. This suggests that semantic information in video is less important than semantic information in text, but more important than discourse information. We also found that HDP does not perform as well as the text and amodal SMTs on video M2E2, probably because of the lack of multi-mode mechanism in the model.

Qualitative analysis To better understand the performance gain of using videos, we look at two typical examples in Fig. 3. we can see that the text-only SMT fails to cluster the trigger word "blew out" with the word "explosion" and "blast", probably because the word embeddings of multi-phrase expressions such as "blew out" and of"explosion" are quite different. However, thanks to the context provided by the video, the amodal SMT is able to identify the two triggers as coreferent, improving the recall of the system. Similarly, we found that while "killed" and "assassination" have similar meaning, the similarity score of their word embeddings is below the threshold we use (0.5), resulting in a miss detection of the coreferent pair. However, with the help of video, the amodal SMT is able to resolve the coreference using their correlations with similar type of videos in the visual mode. Nevertheless, we observe that introducing the visual mode can sometimes lead to false positives.

4 Related Work

Motivated by event coreference resolution for low-resource languages, unsupervised event coreference resolution algorithms have been proposed (Haghighi and Klein, 2007, 2010; Bejan

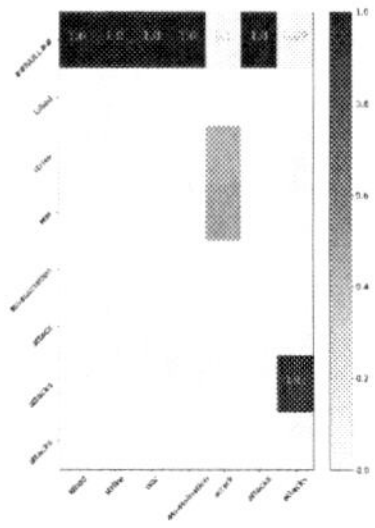

(a) Text SMT

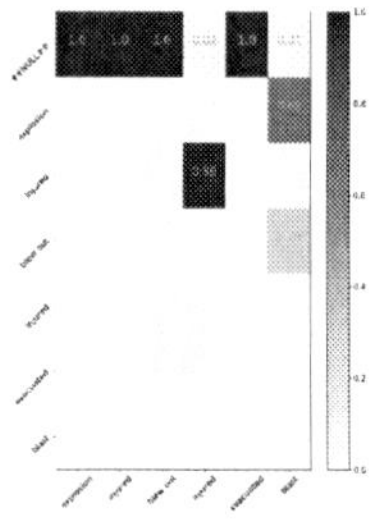

(b) Text SMT

Document	
A powerful **explosion** and fire apparently caused by a gas leak at a Paris bakery Saturday injured several people , **blew out** windows and overturned cars ... Witnesses described the overwhelmingly sound of the **blast** and people trapped inside nearby buildings.	
Text SMT	(explosion, blast)
Amodal SMT	(explosion, blew out, blast)

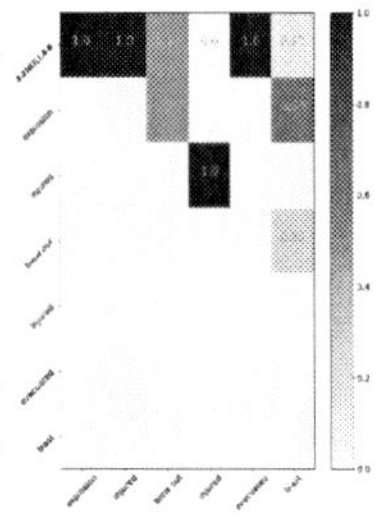

(c) Amodal SMT

Document	
Hundreds of thousands of mourners have turned out in Iran to receive home the remains of Qasem Soleimani, the general **killed** by a US drone strike in Iraq ... His **assassination** marked a significant escalation between Iran and the US. Iran 's Supreme Leader Ayatollah Khamenei, ...	
Text SMT	()
Amodal SMT	(killed, assassination)

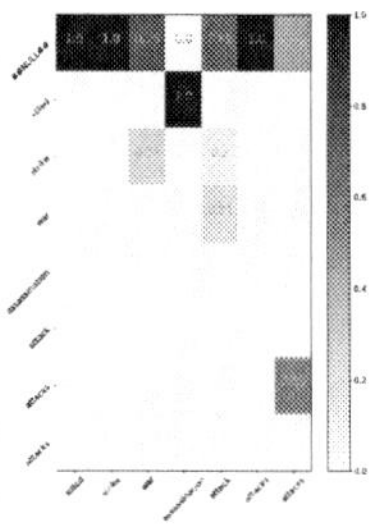

(d) Amodal SMT

Figure 3: Coreference examples when adding a video as an additional modality helps. Only relevant event of the video is shown. Green color denotes true positives detected by the amodal SMT but not by the text-only SMT. The grid plots shows the posterior distribution $p(c_i|M, V), i = 1, \cdots, I$, where the x-axis are the text mentions and y-axis are their antecedent candidates.

Video M2E2	Pairwise F1	MUC	B^3	CEAFe
Full model	**57.7**±0.7	**62.8**±0.4	**60.8**±0.5	**62.5**±0.4
-textual mode	50.7±0.2	53.0±0.2	54.0±0.1	55.2±0.1
Δ	-7.0	-9.8	-6.8	-7.3
-trigger mode	47.7±1.5	53.4±0.8	51.5±0.7	53.0±0.8
Δ	-10.0	-9.4	-9.3	-9.5
-attribute mode	55.1±0.4	61.3±0.3	59.5±0.4	61.7±0.3
Δ	-2.6	-1.5	-1.3	-0.8

Table 5: Ablation study on the effect of removing different modes on amodal SMT. "-textual" means using visual mode only

Event type	Frequency	Text SMT	Amodal SMT	Supervised (Text Only)	Supervised (Multimodal)
Attack	2389	59.0±0.0	58.1±1.3	65.3±1.1	[illegible]±1.0
Die	1148	39.3±0.0	37.6±1.4	39.9±3.8	[illegible]±4.2
Demonstrate	874	55.0±0.0	[illegible]±0.2	69.8±2.1	69.5±2.2
Injure	348	75.0±0.0	70.6±0.0	35.3±11.2	[illegible]±17.3
TransportPerson	325	32.4±0.0	[illegible]±1.6	30.7±4.8	25.4±4.5
Broadcast	319	46.2±0.0	43.5±2.4	18.2±0.6	[illegible]±1.1
Elect	238	50.0±0.0	7.9±0.3	46.4±1.7	45.5±7.6
Meet	214	27.3±0.0	[illegible]±3.9	21.1±2.4	[illegible]±2.1
ArrestJail	165	80.0±0.0	38.5±5.2	0.0±0.0	0.0±0.0
ReleaseParole	139	100.0±0.0	66.7±0.0	25.0±0.0	[illegible]±15.2

Table 6: Pairwise F1 breakdown across the 10 most frequent event types for the text and amodal models. Numbers colored in green denote improvement over the text-only baseline and those in red denote degradation. Frequency for each event type is the number of distinct mention pairs that have at least one of the mention belonging to that event type.

and Harabagiu, 2010; Yang et al., 2015; Ma et al., 2016). Notably, (Bejan and Harabagiu, 2010) proposed a hierarchical Dirichlet process (HDP) to capture recurring surface patterns on the global cluster level such as matching trigger lemma, arguments, neighboring events, etc, with a rich-get-richer mechanism. (Yang et al., 2015) developed a probabilistic model to combine global features with rich pairwise features by learning a distance metric between mentions. (Ma et al., 2016) reformulated text-only coreference resolution as a translation process from each mention to its antecedent with different resolution modes. Previous works on multimodal event coreference resolution focus on the supervised setting with specialized datasets. (Zhang et al., 2015) proposed a pipeline approach based on a pretrained text-only coreference system with additional aligned videos for each event and their visual similarity as visual features for cross-document coreference. However, their cross-document model is not applicable to our within-document coreference setting. (Yu et al., 2019) proposed a supervised end-to-end model to resolve pronouns in short conversational texts, which uses an attention mechanism (Bahdanau et al., 2015) to control the tradeoff between cross-modal and within-modal coreference resolution. Instead of directly applying their model, which is tailored to entity pronoun resolution with images and dialogues and may not be applicable to event coreference resolution with weakly correlated news articles and videos, we adapt their attention mechanism and use crossmedia coreference instead of object detection result as additional supervision. (Li et al., 2020) employed an multimoda event extraction system to perform cross-modal coreference.

5 Conclusions

In this work, we proposed one supervised and one unsupervised model for multimodal event coreference resolution, which outperform the text-only baselines on a realistic multimedia event dataset.

References

Anonymous. 2021. Joint multimedia event extraction from video and article. *Under review*.

Amit Bagga and Breck Baldwin. 1998. Algorithms for scoring coreference chains. In *In The First International Conference on Language Resources and Evaluation Workshop on Linguistics Coreference*, pages 563–566.

Dzmitry Bahdanau, Kyunghyun Cho, and Yoshua Bengio. 2015. Neural machine translation by jointly learning to align and translate. In *ICLR*.

Cosmin Bejan and Sanda Harabagiu. 2010. Unsupervised event coreference resolution with rich linguistic features. In *Proceedings of the 48th Annual Meeting of the Association for Computational Linguistics*, pages 1412–1422, Uppsala, Sweden. Association for Computational Linguistics.

Peter F. Brown, Vincent J. Della Pietra, Stephen A. Della Pietra, and Robert L. Mercer. 1993. The mathematics of statistical machine translation: parameter estimation. *Computational Linguistics*, 19(2):263 – 311.

Arie Cattan, Alon Eirew, Gabriel Stanovsky, Mandar Joshi, and I. Dagan. 2020. Streamlining cross-document coreference resolution: Evaluation and modeling. *ArXiv*, abs/2009.11032.

MMAction2 Contributors. 2020. Openmmlab's next generation video understanding toolbox and benchmark. `https://github.com/open-mmlab/mmaction2`.

Arthur Dempster, Nan Laird, and Donald Rubin. 1977. Maximum likelihood from incomplete data via the EM algorithm. *Journal of the Royal Statistical Society*, 39:1–38.

Aria Haghighi and Dan Klein. 2007. Unsupervised coreference resolution in a nonparametric Bayesian model. In *Proceedings of the 45th Annual Meeting of the Association of Computational Linguistics*, pages 848–855, Prague, Czech Republic. Association for Computational Linguistics.

Aria Haghighi and Dan Klein. 2009. Simple coreference resolution with rich syntactic and semantic features. In *Proceedings of the 2009 Conference on Empirical Methods in Natural Language Processing*, pages 1152–1161, Singapore. Association for Computational Linguistics.

Aria Haghighi and Dan Klein. 2010. Coreference resolution in a modular, entity-centered model. In *Human Language Technologies: The 2010 Annual Conference of the North American Chapter of the Association for Computational Linguistics*, pages 385–393, Los Angeles, California. Association for Computational Linguistics.

Sepp Hochreiter and Jurgen Schmidhuber. 1997. Long short-term memory. *Neural Computation*, 9:1735–1780.

Heeyoung Lee, Angel Chang, Yves Peirsman, Nathanael Chambers, Mihai Surdeanu, and Dan Jurafsky. 2013. Deterministic coreference resolution based on entity-centric, precision-ranked rules. *Computational Linguistics*, 39(4):885–916.

Kenton Lee, Luheng He, Mike Lewis, and Luke Zettlemoyer. 2017. End-to-end neural coreference resolution. In *Proceedings of the 2017 Conference on Empirical Methods in Natural Language Processing*, pages 188–197, Copenhagen, Denmark. Association for Computational Linguistics.

Kenton Lee, Luheng He, and Luke Zettlemoyer. 2018. Higher-order coreference resolution with coarse-to-fine inference. In *Proceedings of the 2018 Conference of the North American Chapter of the Association for Computational Linguistics: Human Language Technologies, Volume 2 (Short Papers)*, pages 687–692, New Orleans, Louisiana. Association for Computational Linguistics.

Manling Li, Alireza Zareian, Qi Zeng, Spencer Whitehead, Di Lu, Heng Ji, and Shih-Fu Chang. 2020. Cross-media structured common space for multimedia event extraction. In *Proceedings of the Annual Meeting of the Association for Computational Linguistics*.

Ying Lin, Heng Ji, Fei Huang, and Lingfei Wu. 2020. A joint neural model for information extraction with global features. In *Proceedings of The 58th Annual Meeting of the Association for Computational Linguistics*.

Yinhan Liu, Myle Ott, Naman Goyal, Jingfei Du, Mandar Joshi, Danqi Chen, Omer Levy, Mike Lewis, Luke Zettlemoyer, and Veselin Stoyanov. 2019. Roberta: A robustly optimized bert pretraining approach. *arXiv preprint arXiv:1907.11692*.

Xiaoqiang Luo. 2005. On coreference resolution performance metrics. In *Proceedings of Human Language Technology Conference and Conference on Empirical Methods in Natural Language Processing*, pages 25–32, Vancouver, British Columbia, Canada. Association for Computational Linguistics.

Xuezhe Ma, Zhengzhong Liu, and Eduard Hovy. 2016. Unsupervised ranking model for entity coreference resolution. In *Proceedings of the 2016 Conference of the North American Chapter of the Association for Computational Linguistics: Human Language Technologies*, pages 1012–1018, San Diego, California. Association for Computational Linguistics.

Sameer Pradhan, Xiaoqiang Luo, Marta Recasens, Eduard Hovy, Vincent Ng, and Michael Strube. 2014. Scoring coreference partitions of predicted mentions: A reference implementation. In *Proceedings of the 52nd Annual Meeting of the Association for Computational Linguistics (Volume 2: Short Papers)*, pages 30–35, Baltimore, Maryland. Association for Computational Linguistics.

Lev Ratinov and Dan Roth. 2012. Learning-based multi-sieve co-reference resolution with knowledge. In *Proceedings of the 2012 Joint Conference on Empirical Methods in Natural Language Processing and Computational Natural Language Learning*, pages 1234–1244, Jeju Island, Korea. Association for Computational Linguistics.

Pontus Stenetorp, Goran Topić, Sampo Pyysalo, Tomoko Ohta, Jin-Dong Kim, and Jun'ichi Tsujii. 2011. Bionlp shared task 2011: Supporting resources. In *Proceedings of BioNLP Shared Task 2011 Workshop*, pages 112–120, Portland, Oregon, USA. Association for Computational Linguistics.

Marc Vilain, John Burger, John Aberdeen, Dennis Connolly, and Lynette Hirschman. 1995. A model-theoretic coreference scoring scheme. In *Proceedings of the 6th conference on Message understanding*.

Bishan Yang, Claire Cardie, and Peter Frazier. 2015. A hierarchical distance-dependent Bayesian model for event coreference resolution. *Transactions of the Association for Computational Linguistics*, 3:517–528.

Xintong Yu, Hongming Zhang, Yangqiu Song, Yan Song, and Changshui Zhang. 2019. What you see is what you get: Visual pronoun coreference resolution in dialogues. In *Proceedings of the 2019 Conference on Empirical Methods in Natural Language Processing and the 9th International Joint Conference on Natural Language Processing (EMNLP-IJCNLP)*, pages 5123–5132, Hong Kong, China. Association for Computational Linguistics.

Tongtao Zhang, Hongzhi Li, Heng Ji, and Shih-Fu Chang. 2015. Cross-document event coreference resolution based on cross-media features. In *Proceedings of the 2015 Conference on Empirical Methods in Natural Language Processing*, pages 201–206, Lisbon, Portugal. Association for Computational Linguistics.

Anatomy of OntoGUM—Adapting GUM to the OntoNotes Scheme to Evaluate Robustness of SOTA Coreference Algorithms

Yilun Zhu[1], **Sameer Pradhan**[2,3], and **Amir Zeldes**[1]

[1]Department of Linguistics, Georgetown University
[2]Linguistic Data Consortium, University of Pennsylvania
[3]cemantix.org

yz565@georgetown.edu, pradhan@cemantix.org, Amir.Zeldes@georgetown.edu

Abstract

SOTA coreference resolution produces increasingly impressive scores on the OntoNotes benchmark. However lack of comparable data following the same scheme for more genres makes it difficult to evaluate generalizability to open domain data. Zhu et al. (2021) introduced the creation of the OntoGUM corpus for evaluating geralizability of the latest neural LM-based end-to-end systems. This paper covers details of the mapping process which is a set of deterministic rules applied to the rich syntactic and discourse annotations manually annotated in the GUM corpus. Out-of-domain evaluation across 12 genres shows nearly 15-20% degradation for both deterministic and deep learning systems, indicating a lack of generalizability or covert overfitting in existing coreference resolution models.

1 Introduction

Coreference resolution is the task of grouping referring expressions that point to the same entity, such as noun phrases and the pronouns that refer to them. The task entails detecting correct mention or 'markable' boundaries and creating a link with previous mentions, or antecedents. A coreference chain is a series of decisions which groups the markables into clusters. As a key component in Natural Language Understanding (NLU), the task can benefit a series of downstream applications such as Entity Linking, Dialogue Systems, Machine Translation, Summarization, and more (Poesio et al., 2016).

In recent years, deep learning models have achieved high scores in coreference resolution. The end-to-end approach (Lee et al., 2017, 2018) jointly scoring mention detection and coreference resolution currently not only beats earlier rule-based and statistical methods but also outperforms other deep learning approaches (Wiseman et al., 2016; Clark and Manning, 2016a,b). Additionally, language models trained on billions of words significantly improve performance by providing rich word and context-level information for classifiers (Lee et al., 2018; Joshi et al., 2019a,b).

However, scores on the identity coreference layer of the benchmark OntoNotes dataset (Pradhan et al., 2013) do not reflect the generalizability of these systems. Moosavi and Strube (2017) pointed out that lexicalized coreference resolution models, including neural models using word embeddings, face a covert overfitting problem because of a large overlap between the vocabulary of coreferring mentions in the OntoNotes training and evaluation sets. This suggests that higher scores on OntoNotes-test may not indicate a better solution to the coreference resolution task.

To investigate the generalization problem of neural models, several projects have tested other datasets consistent with the OntoNotes scheme. Moosavi and Strube (2018) conducted out-of-domain evaluation on WikiCoref (Ghaddar and Langlais, 2016), a small dataset employing the same coreference definitions. Results showed that neural models (with fixed embeddings) do not achieve comparable performance (16.8% degradation in score) to scores on OntoNotes. More recently, the e2e model using BERT (Joshi et al., 2019b) showed gains on the GAP corpus (Webster et al., 2018) using contextualized embeddings; however GAP only contains name-pronoun coreference, a very specific subset of coreference, and is limited in domain to the same single source – Wikipedia.

Though previous work has already identified the overfitting problem, it has three main shortcomings. First, the scale of out-of-domain evaluation has been small and homogeneous: WikiCoref only contains 30 documents with ~60K tokens, much smaller than the OntoNotes test set, and the single genre Wiki domain in both WikiCoref and GAP is arguably not very far from some OntoNotes materials. Second, pretrained LMs, e.g. BERT (Devlin

Proceedings of the 4th Workshop on Computational Models of Reference, Anaphora and Coreference (CRAC 2021), pages 141–149
Punta Cana, Dominican Republic, November 10–11, 2021.

Genre	Documents	Tokens	Mentions	Proper	Pron.	Other	Clusters
academic	16	15,112	1,232	283	262	687	421
bio	20	17,963	2,312	934	796	582	487
conversation	5	5,701	1,027	40	728	259	176
fiction	18	16,312	2,740	259	1,700	781	469
interview	19	18,060	2,622	501	1,223	898	608
news	21	14,094	1,803	796	340	667	477
reddit	18	16,286	2,297	117	1,336	844	578
speech	5	4,834	601	171	245	185	134
textbook	5	5,379	466	108	165	193	133
vlog	5	5,189	882	22	600	260	149
voyage	17	14,967	1,339	564	300	475	348
whow	19	16,927	2,057	53	1,001	1,003	491
Total	168	150,824	19,378	3,848	8,696	68,34	4,471

Table 1: Genre-breakdown Statistics of OntoGUM.

et al., 2019), popularized after the WikiCoref paper, can learn better representations of markables and surrounding sentences. Aside from GAP, which targets a highly specific subtask, no study has investigated whether contextualized embeddings encounter the same overfitting problem identified by Moosavi and Strube. Third, previous work may underestimate the performance degradation on WikiCoref in particular due to bias: In Moosavi and Strube (2018), embeddings were also trained on Wikipedia themselves, potentially making it easier for the model to learn coreference relations in Wikipedia text, despite limitations in other genres.

In this paper, we explore the generalizability of existing coreference models on a new benchmark dataset, which we make freely available. Compared with work using WikiCoref and GAP, our contributions can be summarized as follows:

- We propose OntoGUM, the largest open, gold standard dataset consistent with OntoNotes, with 168 documents (~150K tokens, 19,378 mentions, 4,471 coref chains) in 12 genres,[1] including conversational genres, which complement OntoNotes for training and evaluation.
- We show that the SOTA neural model with contextualized embeddings encounters nearly 15% performance degradation on OntoGUM, showing that the overfitting problem is not overcome by contextualized language models.
- We give a genre-by-genre analysis for two popular systems, revealing relative strengths and weaknesses of current approaches and the range of easier/more difficult targets for coreference resolution.

2 Related Work

OntoNotes and similar corpora OntoNotes is a human-annotated corpus with documents annotated with multiple layers of linguistic information including syntax, propositions, named entities, word senses, and within-document coreference (Weischedel et al., 2011; Pradhan et al., 2013). It covers three languages—English, Chinese and Arabic. The English subcorpus has 3,493 documents and ~1.6 million words annotated for coreference. WikiCoref, which is annotated for anaphoric relations, has 30 documents from English Wikipedia (Ghaddar and Langlais, 2016), containing 7,955 mentions in 1,785 chains, following OntoNotes guidelines.

GUM The Georgetown University Multilayer (GUM) corpus (Zeldes, 2017) is an open-source corpus of richly annotated texts from 12 genres, including 168 documents and over 150K tokens. Though it originally contains more coreference phenomena than OntoNotes using more exhaustive guidelines, it also contains rich syntactic, semantic and discourse annotations which allow us to create the OntoGUM dataset described below. The syntactic annotations, which consist of manually annotated Universal Dependencies trees (de Marneffe et al., 2021), are particularly useful in analyzing and converting the GUM corpus. We also note that due to its smaller size (currently about 10% the size of the OntoNotes coreference dataset), it is not possible to train SOTA neural approaches directly on this dataset while maintaining strong performance.

Other corpora As mentioned above, GAP is a gender-balanced labeled corpus of ambiguous

[1]**Written:** News/Fiction/Bio/Academic/Forum/Travel/How-to/Textbook; **Spoken:** Interview/Political/Vlog/Conversation.

pronoun-name pairs, used for out-of-domain evaluation but limited in coreferent types and genre. Several other comprehensive coreference datasets exist as well, such as ARRAU (Poesio et al., 2018) and PreCo (Chen et al., 2018), but these corpora cannot be used for out-of-domain evaluation because they do not follow the OntoNotes scheme. Their conversion has not been attempted to date.

Coreference resolution systems Prior to the introduction of deep learning systems, the coreference task was approached using deterministic linguistic rules (Lee et al., 2013; Recasens et al., 2013) and statistical approaches (Durrett and Klein, 2013, 2014). More recently, three neural models achieved SOTA performance on this task: 1) ranking the candidate mention pairs (Wiseman et al., 2015; Clark and Manning, 2016a), 2) modeling global features of entity clusters (Clark and Manning, 2015, 2016b; Wiseman et al., 2016), and 3) end-to-end (e2e) approaches with joint loss for mention detection and coreferent pair scoring (Lee et al., 2017, 2018; Fei et al., 2019). The e2e method has become the dominant one, gaining the best scores on OntoNotes. To investigate differences between deterministic and deep learning models on unseen data, we evaluate the two approaches on OntoGUM.

3 Dataset Conversion

GUM's annotation scheme subsumes all markables and coreference chains annotated in OntoNotes, meaning we do not need human annotation to recognize additional mentions in the conversion process, though mention boundaries differ subtly (e.g. for appositions and verbal mentions). Since GUM has gold syntax trees, we were able to process the entire conversion automatically. Additionally, most coreference evaluations use gold speaker information in OntoNotes, which is available in GUM (for *fiction*, *reddit* and spoken data) and could be assembled automatically as well.

The conversion is divided into two parts: removing coreference relations not included in the OntoNotes scheme, and removing or adjusting markables. For coreference relation deletion, we cut chains by removing expletive cataphora, and identifying the definiteness of nominal markables, since indefinites cannot be anaphors in OntoNotes - this was done based on the lemma of determiners attached to the head token of the span (or lack of a determiner) and the POS tag of the head. In addition to modifying existing mention clusters, we also remove particular coreference relations and mention spans, such as Noun-Noun compounding (only included in OntoNotes for proper-name modifiers), bridging anaphora, copula predicates, nested entities ('i-within-i'= single mentions containing coreferring pronouns), and singletons, i.e. mentions that are not referred to again (all not included in OntoNotes). We note that singletons are removed as the final step, in order to catch singletons generated during the conversion process. We also contract verbal markable spans to their head verb, and merge appositive constructions, which are explicitly marked in GUM, into single mentions, following the OntoNotes guidelines. The order of conversion steps are shown in Table 2.

Order of conversion steps
`> Remove bridging & cataphora`
`> Contract verbal spans`
`> Merge appositions`
`> Remove NN compounding`
`> Remove copula`
`> Remove nested entities`
`> Adjust chains by definiteness`
`> Remove singletons`

Table 2: The order of the steps in the dataset conversion from GUM to OntoNotes scheme.

3.1 Coreference relations

Cataphora Cataphora encompasses pronominal elements, including demonstratives, e.g. *those*, which precede an occurrence of a non-pronominal element that occurs within the same utterance and resolves their discourse referent. GUM specifies cataphora in the coreference annotation while OntoNotes only annotates pronominal markables and discards the resolved non-pronominal elements.

Unlike other relations, cataphora 'points forward', i.e. it is resolved by finding a subsequent lexical phrase corresponding to an earlier underspecified pronoun. As in (1), the pronoun *it* (bolded in the box) is resolved by the subsequent markable within the same utterance.

(1) *Before:* [**it**] 's good [to be able to do well at the World Cup , to be placed] , but [it] also means that you get a really good opportunity to know where you 're at in that two year gap between the Paralympics .

(2) *After:* [it] 's good [to be able to do well

at the World Cup , to be placed , but it also means that you get a really good opportunity to know where you 're at in that two year gap between the Paralympics .

Because GUM annotates coreference types for each relation, We create a heuristic algorithm to process cataphora. As in (2), the expletive pronoun (dashed box) is removed from the cluster it originally belongs to, leaving it as a singleton. Other coreference relations remain the same in that cluster.

Definiteness A definite marker indicates the referent is identifiable in a given context while indefinite markers often function to introduce new entities not mentioned before. Following these tendencies, OntoNotes does not allow coreference relations between an indefinite nominal and any kind of antecedents. GUM, however, only considers whether the markables refer to the same entity or not. For example, the indefinite noun phrase *a farm several miles outside of town* in (3) can occur in the middle of the coreferring chain.

(3) *Before:* Rachel Rook took Carroll home to meet her parents two months after she first slept with him ... her parents lived on a farm several miles outside of town ... He knew that they never left the farm ...

(4) *After:* Rachel Rook took Carroll home to meet her parents two months after she first slept with him ... her parents lived on a farm several miles outside of town ... He knew that they never left the farm ...

We use the POS tags, dependency labels, and lemmas to distinguish definite and indefinite markables. A definite nominal markable satisfies one of the following cases: (1) it is a pronoun; (2) the head noun is possessed; (3) it is a proper noun; and (4) anything which has the dependency relation DET with a definite determiner lemma such as *the*, *that*, etc. The converted document looks like (4), where the indefinite nominal phrase and its original antecedent (dashed box) fall in different clusters and the indefinite markable is the first mention in the new cluster[2].

[2]If the markable *home* also has an antecedent, the coreference relation is not affected by the chain-breaking operation.

3.2 Markables

Noun-Noun compounding In Universal Dependencies (UD), a noun compound is a relation that connects common noun modifiers. GUM marks the noun compounding span in coreference annotations while OntoNotes annotation guidelines do not permit any common noun compound modifiers. As in (5), the two compounds are marked in one coreference chain.

(5) *Before:* Allergan Inc. said it received approval to sell the PhacoFlex intraocular lens, the first foldable silicone lens available for cataract surgery . The lens' foldability enables it to be inserted in smaller incisions than are now possible for cataract surgery .

(6) *After:* ... available for cataract surgery ... possible for cataract surgery .

To convert the dataset, the conversion program recursively removes the compounding construction from a coreference chain and create a singleton span for that compound, as the two dashed markable spans in (6).

Bridging and split antecedents Bridging coreference occurs when two entities do not corefer exactly, but the basis for the identifiability of one referent is the previous mention of one or more previous referents. Particularly, in GUM, an anaphor may have multiple antecedents and each antecedent creates a part-whole relationship with the referent (split antecedent). This part-whole relation, however, is not a valid coreference relation in OntoNotes because two nominal mentions are not semantically identical.

(7) *Before:* Claire Bailey-Ross ... Andrew Beresford ... Daniel Smith ... In this paper, we report upon the novel insights ... We will discuss the potential implications ...

bridge:aggr

... Claire Bailey-Ross ... we

(8) *After:* Claire Bailey-Ross ... Andrew Beresford ... Daniel Smith ... In this paper, we report upon the novel insights ... We will discuss the potential implications ...

As in the example (7), the three proper nouns link to the collective nominal *we*. With the rich coreference annotation in GUM, all coreference relations identified as BRIDGE, including both split antecedent and other types of bridging anaphora, are removed, possibly leaving the nominals with the original bridging relations as singletons. The example (8) shows the coreference relations after the conversion process. The proper names are unlinked (dashed boxes) from the original cluster while the pronouns are not affected.

Copula Copula predicates are annotated in GUM while are not markables in OntoNotes. If two markables are coreferred, the conversion process utilizes the UD annotations to identify whether or not a copula construction is between the two mention spans. If the ROOT is within the second span and it is the head of COP, we decide to remove the second span from the coreference chain.

(9) *Before:* [The viewing experience of art] is [a complex one] ... The time [it] takes ...

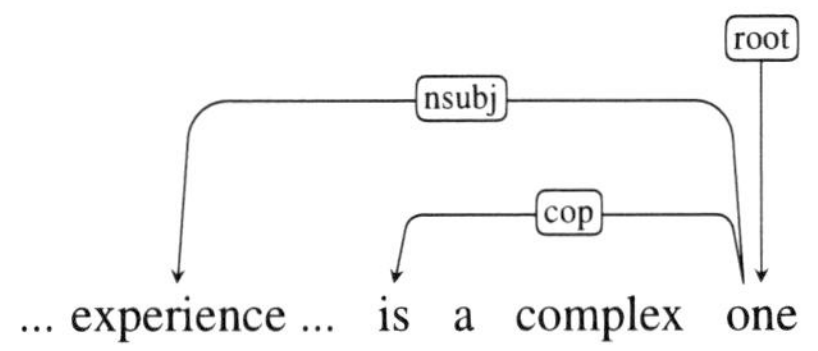

(10) *After:* [The viewing experience of art] is [a complex one] ... The time [it] takes ...

For example, in (9), the head noun *one* in the second span *a complex one* is the ROOT and the head of the copula *is*. Additionally, it corefers with a markable that is the subject of the copula construction. Therefore, we unlink the second span from the cluster and connect the first span with the markable that the second span refers to. The post-conversion annotations are marked in (10).

Nested entity A proper noun may be included in a larger proper noun mention span, as in the nested proper noun *America* within the span *Bank of America*. In OntoNotes, all proper names are considered to be atomic, so that *America* will not be annotated in the above example. Differently from OntoNotes, GUM allows all nested entities to be considered as valid referents. Because a nominal mention is a candidate referent, its possessive modifier, which is also considered as a candidate referent, should be removed from the coreference relation.

(11) *Before:* I 'm about to go visit and would like to know [the best way to communicate with her if [it] 's helpful] .

(12) *After:* I 'm about to go visit and would like to know [the best way to communicate with her if [it] 's helpful] .

For example, in (11), *it* and *the best way to communicate with her if it's helpful* refer to the same entity, while the pronoun is within the span of the noun phrase, so we remove *it* as in (12). In general, the conversion process removes the nested entity when it is included by its antecedent.

Singletons Singletons are markables that are not referred to by other mentions in a document. GUM explicitly annotates all nominal spans while OntoNotes only considers co-referring noun phrases as valid mention spans. Exemplified in (13), the dashed box indicates that the span is not referred to in the context.

(13) *Before:* a unique collection of [17th Century] Zurbarán paintings

The singleton removal process is the last layer for the conversion because previous steps may delete coreference relations and create new markables that are not referred to again.

3.3 Agreement study

To evaluate conversion accuracy, three annotators, including an original OntoNotes project member, conducted an agreement study on 3 documents, containing 2,500 tokens and 371 output mentions. Re-annotating from scratch based on OntoNotes guidelines, the conversion achieves a span detection score of ~96 and CoNLL coreference score of ~92, approximately the same as human agreement scores on OntoNotes. After adjudication, the conversion was found to make only 8/371 errors, in addition to 2 errors due to mistakes in the original GUM data, meaning that degradation due to conversion errors is marginal, and consistency should be close to the variability in OntoNotes itself.

Genre	MUC			B^3			$CEAF_{\phi 4}$				Mention Detection		
	P	R	F1	P	R	F1	P	R	F1	Avg. F1	P	R	F1
	dcoref												
academic	35.1	37.5	36.2	32.6	34.4	33.5	35.7	37.5	36.6	35.4	48.3	51.3	49.8
bio	58.0	61.6	59.8	36.8	43.6	39.9	32.1	33.5	32.8	44.1	58.9	62.3	60.6
conversation	62.2	52.9	57.1	40.5	36.7	38.5	37.1	38.2	37.6	44.4	76.6	67.8	72.0
fiction	57.7	43.9	49.9	50.4	33.2	40.0	37.1	**49.0**	**42.2**	44.0	68.2	59.0	63.3
interview	57.3	53.3	55.2	29.3	21.6	24.8	22.4	24.6	23.5	27.6	64.3	60.3	62.2
news	57.6	55.2	56.4	45.7	42.3	44.0	39.6	32.5	35.7	45.3	44.0	50.2	46.9
reddit	59.6	65.1	62.3	38.3	53.5	44.6	32.9	34.0	33.5	46.8	60.5	64.6	62.5
speech	50.6	56.2	53.2	40.1	43.9	41.9	**46.5**	38.6	**42.2**	45.8	63.5	64.2	63.9
textbook	36.0	34.2	35.1	32.7	31.0	31.9	23.9	39.9	29.9	32.3	18.1	45.8	26.0
vlog	**63.6**	**69.4**	**66.4**	**56.4**	**60.8**	**58.5**	31.4	36.2	33.6	**52.8**	76.4	76.8	76.6
voyage	34.7	37.1	35.9	30.7	28.7	29.7	29.7	35.8	32.5	32.7	46.6	62.4	53.3
whow	35.8	24.2	28.9	30.0	24.5	27.0	29.9	34.0	31.8	29.2	50.0	42.9	46.2
All OntoGUM	45.7	47.0	46.3	17.1	38.1	37.6	33.4	37.3	35.3	39.7	56.2	59.1	57.6
OntoNotes	57.5	61.8	59.6	68.2	68.4	68.3	47.7	43.4	45.5	57.8	66.8	75.1	70.7
	Joshi et al. (2019a)												
academic	84.5	53.0	65.1	83.3	48.5	61.3	**83.2**	47.0	60.1	62.2	91.0	55.2	68.7
bio	85.8	74.7	79.8	61.4	64.3	62.8	65.4	49.9	56.6	66.4	87.7	74.5	80.5
conversation	85.0	73.4	78.7	67.9	64.5	66.2	70.2	51.1	59.1	68.0	93.0	77.9	84.8
fiction	**87.0**	62.5	73.0	78.8	54.1	64.1	62.5	53.1	57.4	64.8	91.1	67.7	77.7
interview	83.9	71.8	77.4	76.1	60.4	67.3	72.9	50.6	59.7	68.2	85.9	70.4	77.3
news	65.3	65.8	65.5	60.1	59.6	59.9	58.9	54.3	56.5	60.6	71.9	70.5	71.2
reddit	76.7	67.4	71.7	67.5	60.3	63.7	69.5	40.5	51.1	61.7	85.3	68.1	75.8
speech	83.3	63.4	72.0	71.2	56.6	63.1	77.3	57.3	**65.8**	67.0	91.9	69.4	79.0
textbook	50.0	66.6	57.1	45.2	65.7	53.6	55.6	55.6	55.6	55.5	60.0	72.2	65.5
vlog	**86.1**	**86.1**	**86.1**	78.4	**79.8**	**79.1**	63.6	47.7	54.5	**73.3**	89.4	85.4	87.4
voyage	69.0	70.4	69.7	52.7	64.1	57.9	65.9	53.0	58.8	62.1	78.9	75.5	77.2
whow	84.8	40.9	55.2	**83.4**	39.2	53.3	71.4	**57.4**	63.6	57.4	93.2	52.4	67.1
All OntoGUM	79.7	66.3	72.4	69.5	58.58	63.7	67.7	50.7	58.0	64.6	85.4	69.2	76.5
OntoNotes	85.8	84.8	85.3	78.3	77.9	78.1	76.4	74.2	75.3	79.6	89.1	86.5	87.8

Table 3: Results on the OntoGUM's test dataset with the deterministic coref model (top) and the SOTA coreference model (bottom). The underlined text is the lowest score across 12 genres and bold text is the highest.

4 Experiments

We evaluate two systems on the 12 OntoGUM genres, using the official CoNLL-2012 scorer (Pradhan et al., 2012, 2014). The primary score is the average F1 of three metrics – MUC, B^3, and $CEAF_{\phi 4}$.

Deterministic coreference model We first run the deterministic system (dcoref, part of Stanford CoreNLP, Manning et al. 2014) on the OntoGUM benchmark, as it remains a popular option for off-the-shelf coreference resolution. As a rule-based system, it does not require training data, so we directly test it on OntoGUM's test set. However, POS tags, lemmas, and named-entity (NER) information are predicted by CoreNLP, which does have a domain bias favoring newswire. The system's multi-sieve structure and token-level features such as gender and number remain unchanged. We expect that the linguistic rules will function similarly across datasets and genres, notwithstanding biases of the tools providing input features to those rules.

SOTA neural model Combining the e2e approach with a contextualized LM and span masking is the current SOTA on OntoNotes. The system utilizes the pretrained SpanBERT-large model, fine-tuned on the OntoNotes training set. Hyperparameters are identical to the evaluation of OntoNotes test to ensure comparable results between the benchmarks. We note that while we choose the SOTA system as a 'best case scenario', most off-the-shelf neural NLP toolkits (e.g. spaCy) actually use somewhat simpler e2e models than SpanBERT-large, due to memory/performance constraints.

5 Results

OntoGUM vs. OntoNotes The last rows in each half of Table 3 give overall results for the systems on each benchmark. e2e+SpanBERT encounters a substantial degradation of 15 points (19%) on OntoGUM, likely due to lower test set lexical and stylistic overlap, including novel mention pairs. We note that its average score of 64.6 is somewhat optimistic, especially given that the system receives access to gold speaker information wherever avail-

Genres	PRON (R)	Other (R)	Total	CoNLL	Span
vlog	600 (.66)	309 (.34)	909	1	1
interview	1223 (.45)	1485 (.55)	2708	2	6
conversation	729 (.61)	323 (.39)	1052	3	2
speech	245 (.40)	364 (.60)	609	4	4
bio	796 (.34)	1529 (.66)	2325	5	3
fiction	1700 (.61)	1091 (.39)	2791	6	5
academic	262 (.21)	997 (.79)	1259	7	10
voyage	300 (.22)	1053 (.78)	1353	8	7
reddit	1337 (.55)	1077 (.45)	2414	9	8
news	340 (.19)	1483 (.81)	1823	10	9
whow	1001 (.47)	1129 (.53)	2130	11	11
textbook	165 (.34)	315 (.66)	480	12	12

Table 4: Mention-type counts (ratios) & ranks of SOTA scores by genre (CoNLL score + span detection).

able (including in *fiction*, *conversation* and *interview*, some of the better scoring genres), which is usually unrealistic. dcoref, assumed to be more stable across genres, also sees losses on OntoGUM of over 18 points (30%). We believe at least part of the degradation may be due to mention detection, which is trained on different domains for both systems (see the last three columns in the table). These results suggest that input data from CoreNLP degrades substantially on OntoGUM, or that some types of coreferent expressions in OntoGUM are linguistically distinct from those in OntoNotes, or both, making OntoGUM a challenging benchmark for systems developed using OntoNotes.

Comparing genres Both systems degrade more on specific genres. For example, while *vlog* (with gold speaker information) fares well for both systems, neither does well on *textbook*, and even the SOTA system falls well below (or around) 60s for the *news*, *whow* and *textbook* genres. This might be surprising for *vlog*, which contains transcripts of spontaneous unedited speech from YouTube Creative Commons vlogs quite unlike OntoNotes data; conversely the result is less expected for carefully edited texts which are somewhat similar to data in OntoNotes: OntoNotes contains roughly 30% newswire text, and it is not immediately clear that GUM's *news* section, which comes from recent Wikinews articles, differs much in genre. Examples (14)–(15) illustrate incorrectly predicted coreference chains from both sources and the type of language they contain.

(14) *I've been here just crushing ultrasounds ... I've been like crushing [these] all day today ... I got sick when I was on Croatia for vacation. I have no idea what it says, but I think [they] 're cough drops.* (example from a radiologist's vlog, incorrect: ultrasounds ≠ cough drops)

(15) *[The report] has prompted calls for all edible salt to be iodised ... Tasmania was excluded from [the study - where a voluntary iodine fortification program using iodised salt in bread], is ongoing* (newswire example, incorrect span and coref: [the study - where a voluntary...])

These examples show that errors occur readily even in quite characteristic news writing, while genre disparity by itself does not guarantee low performance, as in the case of the vlogs whose lanugage is markedly different. In sum, these observations suggest that accurate coreference for downstream applications cannot be expected in some common well edited genres, despite the prevalence of news data in OntoNotes (albeit specifically from the Wall Street Journal, around 1990). This motivates the use of OntoGUM as a test set for future benchmarking, in order to give the NLP community a realistic idea of the range of performance we may see on contemporary data 'in the wild'.

We also suspect that prevalence of pronouns and gold speaker information produce better scores in the results. Table 4 ranks genres by their e2e CoNLL score, and gives the proportions of pronouns, as well as score rankings for span detection. Because pronouns are usually easier to detect and pair than nouns (Durrett and Klein, 2013), more pronouns usually means higher scores. On genres with more than 50% pronouns and gold speakers (*vlog*, *interview*, *conversation*, *speech*, *fiction*) e2e gets much higher results, while genres with few pronouns (<30%) have lower scores (*academic*, *voyage*, *news*). This diversity over 12 genres supports the usefulness of OntoGUM, which can evaluate the genrealizability of coreference systems.

6 Conclusion

This paper presented the mechanics of the conversion of the GUM corpus to the OntoGUM version using the OntoNotes coreference scheme, creating the largest open, gold standard coreference dataset following the OntoNotes scheme, which adds several new genres (including more spoken data) to the OntoNotes family. The corpus is automatically converted from GUM by modifying the existing markable spans and coreference relations using multi-layer annotations, such as dependency trees. Results showed a lack of generalizability of existing systems, especially in genres low in pronouns and lacking speaker information. We suspect that at least part of the success of SOTA approaches is due to correct mention detection and high matching scores in genres rich in pronouns, and more so with gold speaker information. Success for other types of mentions in OntoNotes data appears to be much more sensitive to lexical features, performing well on the benchmark test set with high lexical overlap to the training data, but degrading very substantially outside of it, even on newswire texts from our OntoGUM data. This supports use of this challenging dataset for future work, which we hope will benefit evaluations of systems targeting the OntoNotes standard.

References

Hong Chen, Zhenhua Fan, Hao Lu, Alan Yuille, and Shu Rong. 2018. PreCo: A large-scale dataset in preschool vocabulary for coreference resolution. In *Proceedings of EMNLP 2018*, pages 172–181, Brussels.

Kevin Clark and Christopher D. Manning. 2015. Entity-centric coreference resolution with model stacking. In *Proceedings of ACL-IJCNLP 2015, Long Papers*, pages 1405–1415, Beijing, China.

Kevin Clark and Christopher D. Manning. 2016a. Deep reinforcement learning for mention-ranking coreference models. In *Proceedings of the 2016 Conference on Empirical Methods in Natural Language Processing*, pages 2256–2262, Austin, Texas.

Kevin Clark and Christopher D. Manning. 2016b. Improving coreference resolution by learning entity-level distributed representations. In *Proceedings of ACL 2016, Long Papers*, pages 643–653, Berlin.

Marie-Catherine de Marneffe, Christopher D. Manning, Joakim Nivre, and Daniel Zeman. 2021. Universal Dependencies. *Computational Linguistics*, 47(2):255–308.

Jacob Devlin, Ming-Wei Chang, Kenton Lee, and Kristina Toutanova. 2019. BERT: Pre-training of deep bidirectional transformers for language understanding. In *Proceedings of NAACL 2019*, pages 4171–4186, Minneapolis, MN.

Greg Durrett and Dan Klein. 2013. Easy victories and uphill battles in coreference resolution. In *Proceedings of EMNLP 2013*, pages 1971–1982, Seattle, WA.

Greg Durrett and Dan Klein. 2014. A joint model for entity analysis: Coreference, typing, and linking. *TACL*, 2:477–490.

Hongliang Fei, Xu Li, Dingcheng Li, and Ping Li. 2019. End-to-end deep reinforcement learning based coreference resolution. In *Proceedings of ACL 2019*, pages 660–665, Florence, Italy.

Abbas Ghaddar and Phillippe Langlais. 2016. Wiki-Coref: An English coreference-annotated corpus of Wikipedia articles. In *Proceedings of LREC 2016)*, pages 136–142, Portorož, Slovenia.

Mandar Joshi, Danqi Chen, Yinhan Liu, Daniel S. Weld, Luke Zettlemoyer, and Omer Levy. 2019a. SpanBERT: Improving pre-training by representing and predicting spans. *CoRR*, abs/1907.10529.

Mandar Joshi, Omer Levy, Daniel S. Weld, and Luke Zettlemoyer. 2019b. BERT for coreference resolution: Baselines and analysis. In *Proceedings of EMNLP-IJCNLP 2019*, pages 5803–5808, Hong Kong, China.

Heeyoung Lee, Angel Chang, Yves Peirsman, Nathanael Chambers, Mihai Surdeanu, and Dan Jurafsky. 2013. Deterministic coreference resolution based on entity-centric, precision-ranked rules. *Computational Linguistics*, 39(4):885–916.

Kenton Lee, Luheng He, Mike Lewis, and Luke Zettlemoyer. 2017. End-to-end neural coreference resolution. In *Proceedings of EMNLP 2017*, pages 188–197, Copenhagen, Denmark.

Kenton Lee, Luheng He, and Luke Zettlemoyer. 2018. Higher-order coreference resolution with coarse-to-fine inference. In *Proceedings of NAACL 2018, Short Papers*, pages 687–692, New Orleans, LA.

Christopher D. Manning, Mihai Surdeanu, John Bauer, Jenny Finkel, Steven J. Bethard, and David McClosky. 2014. The Stanford CoreNLP natural language processing toolkit. In *ACL 2014 System Demonstrations*, pages 55–60.

Nafise Sadat Moosavi and Michael Strube. 2017. Lexical features in coreference resolution: To be used with caution. In *Proceedings of ACL 2017, Short Papers*, pages 14–19, Vancouver, Canada.

Nafise Sadat Moosavi and Michael Strube. 2018. Using linguistic features to improve the generalization capability of neural coreference resolvers. In *Proceedings of EMNLP 2018*, pages 193–203, Brussels.

Massimo Poesio, Yulia Grishina, Varada Kolhatkar, Nafise Moosavi, Ina Roesiger, Adam Roussel, Fabian Simonjetz, Alexandra Uma, Olga Uryupina, Juntao Yu, and Heike Zinsmeister. 2018. Anaphora resolution with the ARRAU corpus. In *Proceedings of CRAC 2018*, pages 11–22, New Orleans, LA.

Massimo Poesio, Roland Stuckardt, and Yannick Versley. 2016. *Anaphora resolution*. Springer.

Sameer Pradhan, Xiaoqiang Luo, Marta Recasens, Eduard Hovy, Vincent Ng, and Michael Strube. 2014. Scoring coreference partitions of predicted mentions: A reference implementation. In *Proceedings of ACL 2014*, pages 30–35, Baltimore, MD.

Sameer Pradhan, Alessandro Moschitti, Nianwen Xue, Hwee Tou Ng, Anders Björkelund, Olga Uryupina, Yuchen Zhang, and Zhi Zhong. 2013. Towards robust linguistic analysis using OntoNotes. In *Proceedings of CoNLL 2013*, pages 143–152, Sofia.

Sameer Pradhan, Alessandro Moschitti, Nianwen Xue, Olga Uryupina, and Yuchen Zhang. 2012. CoNLL-2012 shared task: Modeling multilingual unrestricted coreference in OntoNotes. In *Joint Conference on EMNLP and CoNLL - Shared Task*, pages 1–40, Jeju Island, Korea.

Marta Recasens, Marie-Catherine de Marneffe, and Christopher Potts. 2013. The life and death of discourse entities: Identifying singleton mentions. In *Proceedings of NAACL 2013*, pages 627–633, Atlanta, Georgia.

Kellie Webster, Marta Recasens, Vera Axelrod, and Jason Baldridge. 2018. Mind the GAP: A balanced corpus of gendered ambiguous pronouns. *TACL*, pages 605–617.

Ralph Weischedel, Eduard Hovy, Mitchell Marcus, Martha Palmer, Robert Belvin, Sameer Pradhan, Lance Ramshaw, and Nianwen Xue. 2011. OntoNotes: A large training corpus for enhanced processing. In Joseph Olive, Caitlin Christianson, and John McCary, editors, *Handbook of Natural Language Processing and Machine Translation: DARPA Global Autonomous Language Exploitation*. Springer.

Sam Wiseman, Alexander M. Rush, Stuart Shieber, and Jason Weston. 2015. Learning anaphoricity and antecedent ranking features for coreference resolution. In *Proceedings of ACL-IJCNLP 2015, Long Papers*, pages 1416–1426, Beijing, China.

Sam Wiseman, Alexander M. Rush, and Stuart M. Shieber. 2016. Learning global features for coreference resolution. In *Proceedings of NAACL 2016*, pages 994–1004, San Diego, CA.

Amir Zeldes. 2017. The GUM corpus: Creating multilayer resources in the classroom. *Language Resources and Evaluation*, 51(3):581–612.

Yilun Zhu, Sameer Pradhan, and Amir Zeldes. 2021. OntoGUM: Evaluating contextualized SOTA coreference resolution on 12 more genres. In *Proceedings of the 59th Annual Meeting of the Association for Computational Linguistics and the 11th International Joint Conference on Natural Language Processing (Volume 2: Short Papers)*, pages 461–467, Online. Association for Computational Linguistics.

Understanding Mention Detector-Linker Interaction in Neural Coreference Resolution

Zhaofeng Wu
Paul G. Allen School of CSE
University of Washington
zfw7@cs.washington.edu

Matt Gardner
Allen Institute for AI
mattg@allenai.org

Abstract

Despite significant recent progress in coreference resolution, the quality of current state-of-the-art systems still considerably trails behind human-level performance. Using the CoNLL-2012 and PreCo datasets, we dissect the best instantiation of the mainstream end-to-end coreference resolution model that underlies most current best-performing coreference systems, and empirically analyze the behavior of its two components: mention detector and mention linker. While the detector traditionally focuses heavily on recall as a design decision, we demonstrate the importance of precision, calling for their balance. However, we point out the difficulty in building a precise detector due to its inability to make important anaphoricity decisions. We also highlight the enormous room for improving the linker and show that the rest of its errors mainly involve pronoun resolution. We propose promising next steps and hope our findings will help future research in coreference resolution.

1 Introduction

Coreference resolution identifies mentions in a document that co-refer to the same entity. It is an important task facilitating many applications such as reading comprehension (Dasigi et al., 2019) and text summarization (Azzam et al., 1999).

Lee et al. (2017) proposed the first neural end-to-end architecture for coreference resolution. Most recent systems use it as a backbone and employ better scoring functions (Zhang et al., 2018), pruning procedures (Lee et al., 2018), or token representations (Joshi et al., 2019, 2020).[1] Despite this usage, little in-depth analysis has been done to better understand the inner workings of such an influential system. Xu and Choi (2020) analyzed the effect of the high-order inference, while Subramanian and Roth (2019) and Zhao et al. (2018) respectively examined its generalizability and gender bias. Few work has inspected the interaction between its components. Lu and Ng (2020) conducted oracle experiments that are related to ours, but without fine-grained control over confounding factors affecting oracle mentions. Such an understanding is important: for example, Kummerfeld and Klein (2013)'s dissection of the then-best classical coreference systems inspired many important follow-up works (Peng et al., 2015; Martschat and Strube, 2015; Wiseman et al., 2016, *inter alia*). However, it is unknown if observations on such classical feature-based and often pipelined systems extend to current neural end-to-end models.

We consider the best instantiation of this model family, SpanBERT (Joshi et al., 2020) + c2f-coref (Lee et al., 2018), and investigate the interaction between its two components: mention detector and mention linker. We study how their errors independently or jointly affect the final clustering.

Using the CoNLL-2012 (Pradhan et al., 2012) and PreCo (Chen et al., 2018) datasets, we highlight the low-precision, high-recall nature of the detector. While traditionally only recall is emphasized for the detector as a design decision (Lee et al., 2011; Lee et al., 2017), we show huge degradation from noisy mentions and, perhaps surprisingly, increasing the number of candidates considered by the baseline linker only deteriorates the performance. While some classical coreference pipelines focused on detector precision (Uryupina, 2009), it is rarely emphasized for current end-to-end systems. We hence stress the importance of a precision-recall balance for the detector and demonstrate how pruning hyperparameters, in addition to reducing computational complexity, control this trade-off. However, we show the difficulty of obtaining a precise detector by demonstrating the importance of anaphoricity decisions and the inability of the detector to make them. Finally, we highlight the high potential of the linker and that the

[1] Except Wu et al. (2020) which has not seen wide adoption.

Proceedings of the 4th Workshop on Computational Models of Reference, Anaphora and Coreference (CRAC 2021), pages 150–157
Punta Cana, Dominican Republic, November 10–11, 2021.

remaining errors mainly involve pronoun resolution. We hope this work sheds light on the internals of the mainstream coreference system and, with our proposed next steps, catalyze future research. We believe some of our findings may also transfer to other tasks with a similar joint span detection and span (pair) classification architecture, such as SRL (He et al., 2018), IE (Luan et al., 2019), and entity linking (Kolitsas et al., 2018). See Jiang et al. (2020) which subsumes many other tasks under such a span-based framework.

2 Background

Model We study the coarse-to-fine coreference system (c2f-coref; Lee et al. 2018). It assigns an antecedent for every span in a document of length T, including a dummy that indicates non-mentions or non-anaphoric mentions. The final clustering is the transitive closure of connected spans. The system consists of a mention detector and a mention linker. The detector scores all $O(T^2)$ spans up to length L and outputs the λT highest-scoring spans as possibly anaphoric mentions. The linker links each mention candidate with the highest-scoring antecedent among K ones. Hyperparameters L, λ, and K control the number of considered spans and antecedents, reducing computational complexity.

Data CoNLL-2012 is the most common dataset to test coreference models. However, it lacks singleton mention annotation (Pradhan et al., 2012).

Singleton, or non-anaphoric, mentions do not co-refer with other spans, e.g. "The dog" in "[The dog] barks." However, they may become anaphoric in another context, e.g. "[The dog] barks at [itself]." Being a mention is a span's inherent property, while anaphoricity, whether or not a mention co-refers, is context-dependent. We use "all mentions" to refer to the union of singleton and anaphoric mentions.

To understand the effect of singleton mentions, we heuristically generate all mentions for CoNLL-12 (§B) for relevant experiments. We also experiment with PreCo, a coreference dataset with annotated singleton mentions. We do all analyses on development sets and report dataset statistics in §A.

3 Experiments

Settings We embed tokens with SpanBERT-large, a pre-trained transformer (Vaswani et al., 2017) with state-of-the-art performance in coreference resolution. We choose $L = 30, \lambda = 0.4, K =$ 50. We only keep the first 110 sentences per document during training. To reduce confounding factors, we do not use speaker and genre metadata.

	CoNLL-12	PreCo
Coref F_1	79.17	85.04
ANA. P	28.37	39.23
ANA. R	96.42	98.40
ALL P	82.04	76.55
ALL R	57.35	95.98

Table 1: Original system coreference F_1 and precision / recall for anaphoric mentions (ANA.) and all mentions (ALL) on CoNLL-12 and PreCo development sets.

"Original" System refers to a standard SpanBERT + c2f-coref trained baseline. Its F_1 score[2] is reported in Table 1, similar to the results in Joshi et al. (2020) considering we disregard metadata.

Oracles We build oracle detectors where, starting from the original system's mention candidates (its detector output), we either remove all non-gold mentions (prefect precision), add all missing gold mentions (perfect recall), or both (perfect precision & recall). We give the altered, rather than the original, mention candidates to the linker. We consider both anaphoric mentions and all mentions as gold mentions and modify either in a post-hoc manner or re-train the system with the altered candidates. To control for a non-trainable detector, we train only a linker reusing the original system's mention candidates, dubbed **Fixed Detector**. We consider this baseline as the comparison target for the oracles. Besides oracle detectors, we also build an oracle linker that assigns the correct antecedent (including dummy) to each of the λT mention candidates.

4 Precision-Recall Trade-Off for the Mention Detector

Traditionally, coreference systems heavily favor recall over precision for the detector (Lee et al., 2011) as the linker cannot recover missed mentions. Similarly, our c2f-coref system gets >96% anaphoric mention recall yet only <40% precision (Table 1). We therefore explore if detector recall is always more important than its precision. If more spans are considered by increasing the max span width L or the number of spans considered per word λ, will the system performance necessarily improve? In the extreme case, if we hypothetically

[2]We use coreference F_1 to refer to the average F_1 of MUC, B^3, and $CEAF_{\phi_4}$, the most common coreference metric.

		Span Error	Conflated Entities	Extra Mention	Extra Entity	Divided Entity	Missing Mention	Missing Entity
Original		1.6	3.1	1.3	3.1	2.6	2.1	4.5
Fixed Detector		1.7	3.1	1.7	3.3	2.8	2.1	4.7
ANA.	Perfect P	0.0	2.4	0.0	0.0	2.0	2.6	5.7
Post-hoc	Perfect R	1.6	3.1	1.4	3.1	2.6	2.0	4.4
Oracle	Perfect P&R	0.0	2.3	0.0	0.0	1.9	2.5	5.5
ANA.	Perfect P	0.0	3.4	0.0	0.0	0.9	1.5	1.4
Re-train	Perfect R	0.7	3.1	2.0	3.4	2.6	1.5	4.4
Oracle	Perfect P&R	0.0	3.0	0.0	0.0	1.0	0.4	0.3

Table 2: The F_1 score improvement after fixing different types of errors on the CoNLL-12 development set. The errors are independently fixed after span errors are fixed. The categorization is from Kummerfeld and Klein (2013).

		CoNLL-12	PreCo
Fixed Detector		78.28	84.64
ANA.	Perfect P	86.02	90.31
Post-hoc	Perfect R	79.37	85.17
Oracle	Perfect P&R	86.28	90.45
ANA.	Perfect P	89.98	95.09
Re-train	Perfect R	79.65	85.22
Oracle	Perfect P&R	92.39	96.50
ALL	Perfect P	79.48	88.37
Re-train	Perfect R	78.52	85.23
Oracle	Perfect P&R	80.05	89.13
Oracle Linker		97.07	98.69

Table 3: Baseline and oracle coreference F_1 for anaphoric mentions (ANA.) and all mentions (ALL) on CoNLL-12 and PreCo development sets. "Fixed Detector" is the baseline with a non-trainable detector. The middle three sections are oracle detectors with perfect candidate precision/recall. The last row is an oracle linker that always makes correct antecedent decisions.

had enough compute that allows the linker to consider all $O(T^4)$ span-antecedent pairs, should we simply remove the pruning in the detector?

The Aggregated Importance of Precision For all oracles in Table 3, fixing precision yields a larger improvement than recall, especially with anaphoric mentions. This highlights the importance of detector precision and the extent to which the linker suffers from noisy mention candidates. In Table 2, we present the F_1 improvement after independently fixing categorized errors following Kummerfeld and Klein (2013).[3] Noisy candidates result in extra mention and extra entity errors, fixing which accounts for more than half of the $\approx$8 F_1 gap between the post-hoc perfect precision oracle and the baseline for CoNLL-12 (Table 3). Furthermore, re-training the system to leverage the distributional shift of the absence of noise leads to another $\approx$4 and 5 F_1 increase (CoNLL-12/PreCo).

To analyze how higher detector precision helps the linker, we examine the coreference score the linker assigns to every span-antecedent pair. The anaphoric mention re-trained perfect precision oracle has an average score of –13.0 on CoNLL-12, higher than –15.1 with perfect recall. Among only correct span-antecedent pairs, these scores are 11.7 and 7.1, with the same pattern. This indicates that the noise with perfect recall prevents the linker from reliably assigning high coreference scores, even for correct links. The effect of higher coreference scores also shows in that, compared with perfect recall, the perfect precision oracle produces on average larger (4.44 vs. 4.26 entities) and longer-distance (154 vs. 152 tokens spanned) clusters.

We also see this effect by examining the amount of improvement with reduced noise in Table 2. In the anaphoric mention post-hoc oracles, as expected, fixing precision results in fewer extra mention/entity errors and more missing errors, while the perfect recall oracle behaves conversely. However, when re-trained, the perfect precision oracle has much fewer missing entities, even fewer than with perfect recall. This is surprising as the latter considers more candidates. The reason is likely that the linker learns to leverage the absence of noise and reliably assigns high coreference scores. Despite some incorrect links leading to more conflated entities, the many correct ones drastically reduce missing mention/entity errors. On the other hand, the noise in the perfect recall or the original system prevents consistent high scores, resulting in more missing mentions and entities. Hence, the improvement with perfect precision partly stems

[3] Span (boundary) errors are fixed before independently fixing all others. The numbers do not add up to the performance gap due to error type interactions.

	CoNLL-12		PreCo	
	# Op	Op effect	# Op	Op effect
ANA.; P	135.9	0.086	79.2	0.132
ANA.; R	1.9	**0.715**	0.8	**0.709**
ALL; P	34.1	**0.035**	30.6	0.122
ALL; R	115.3	0.002	4.1	**0.143**

Table 4: The number of addition/removal operations needed for the oracle candidates, and the oracle performance increase, in F_1, amortized over each operation. Boldface indicates the higher per-operation effect between perfect precision and recall in each category.

L	30	32	34	36	38	40
F_1	**79.17**	78.76	78.86	79.03	78.88	78.85
λ	0.4	0.45	0.5	0.55	0.6	0.65
F_1	**79.17**	78.99	79.15	78.35	79.05	78.85

Table 5: CoNLL-12 development F_1 with increased max span width L or the number of spans considered per word λ. The first column is the original setting. Boldface indicates the best performance.

from the linker's increased confidence in assigning coreference scores when *not* tasked with ignoring non-mentions (and singletons) in noisy candidates.

The Average Importance of Recall The large improvement from fixing precision may be due to its larger original headroom than recall (Table 1). We compute the number of operations (span addition/removal) needed for each oracle and the average F_1 improvement per operation in Table 4. For anaphoric mentions, recall has 5-8$\times$ the average effect of precision.[4] If we control the number of operations by re-training an anaphoric mention (semi-)perfect precision oracle removing only as many top-scoring extra spans as the number of missing correct spans (rather than removing all extra spans), it gets 79.08 and 85.01 F_1 on CoNLL-12 and PreCo, lower than the perfect recall oracle with 79.65 and 85.22. It is therefore only due to the low-precision high-recall nature of the original detector that precision is more important in aggregate.

Precision-Recall Trade-Off We return to the original question: if we had more compute, is it always beneficial to consider more spans in the detector? From our results, while recall is important, an imprecise detector has substantial adverse effects by increasing the linker's learning burden. Indeed, Table 5 shows that increasing the max span width by up to 33% or the spans considered per word by up to 38% only degrades the performance. As the extra low-scoring spans are mostly noise, we slightly increase recall but more heavily decrease precision, causing more harm than benefit. Hence, besides saving computation, these hyperparameters also balance the precision-recall trade-off. Future work should hence put more emphasis on precision which is often overlooked in end-to-end systems.

5 Difficulties Facing Each Component

5.1 The Detector's Difficulty With Anaphoricity Decisions

Despite its large aggregated improvement, i.e. $\approx$11.7 and 10.5 F_1 for CoNLL-12 and PreCo, perfect anaphoric mention precision requires perfectly distinguishing anaphoric from singleton mentions. These anaphoricity decisions in fact account for most of the improvement, $\approx$10.5 and 6.7 F_1 (Table 3, anaphoric v.s. all mentions perfect precision).[5] However, the detector, as a span classifier, does not explicitly model inter-span anaphoric relationships. To test this architecture's ability to distinguish anaphoric from singleton mentions, we build two span classifiers with the same structure as the detector, supervised with sigmoid loss, that recognize all mentions and anaphoric mentions in PreCo. The former achieves 79.89 classification F_1 while the latter only 54.32, showing the inability of a span classifier to make anaphoricity decisions.

To better understand this difficulty, we define a confusion index as singleton recall divided by anaphoric mention recall. It correlates with the classifier's inability to identify anaphoricity. Ideally, this value should be close to 0, recalling more anaphoric mentions and fewer singletons. A random classifier incapable of distinguishing between the two has an expected confusion index of 1.

The anaphoric mention classifier above has a confusion index of 0.81, showing its inability to make anaphoricity decisions even when explicitly trained with the signal. If we only consider text appearing as both singleton and anaphoric mentions in the same document, demanding contextual reasoning by disregarding obvious anaphoric mentions such as pronouns, the confusion index degrades to 0.997. Hence, the classifier is poor at leveraging self-attentive contextual cues to make anaphoric-

[4] CoNLL-12 with all mentions has a different pattern as we noisily generated singletons in a recall-oriented way.

[5] Chen et al. (2018) observed a similar pattern on an LSTM architecture that less directly receives global information which is important for anaphoricity decisions. We confirm that this still holds on transformers with a larger receptive field.

Error Type (#)	Example
Pronoun (109)	... a cross-sea bridge connecting **Hong Kong, Zhuhai, and Macao** .
	... after **their** return, Macao, and Hong Kong, the two special administrative regions ...
Exact Match (6)	The most important thing about **Disney** is that it is a global brand .
	The subway to **Disney** has already been constructed .
Head Match (11)	**Ten landmark buildings located on Hong Kong Island** reveal themselves ...
	... **those private , er , buildings** , that is , the business community , ah , is willing to ...
Other Match (7)	And **Dr. Andy Henry** notices something else
	Dr. Mann says they 've narrowed it down ...
Semantic Proximity (12)	... **Hong Kong cinema** has nurtured many internationally renowned directors ...
	... memorializing **Hong Kong 's 100 - year film history** .
Others (5)	But [**Paul Kelly**] [**Steve Sodbury**] and Mel Anderson ... had no idea ...

Table 6: Examples of categorized conflated entity errors in the CoNLL-12 development set with a perfect detector. Following past studies (Kummerfeld and Klein, 2013; Joshi et al., 2019), we consider all deictic terms as pronouns. Each example contains two incorrectly linked entities in bold. Square brackets are added to separate mentions.

ity decisions without explicit inter-span relational modeling. In §C we also show the degradation of the confusion index with shorter spans.

Given the importance of anaphoric mention precision (§4), more research in improving anaphoricity decisions in the detector would be fruitful, for example, by more explicitly attending to neighboring spans. Alternatively, as Zhong and Chen (2021) showed the benefit of disentangling the span representations for entity detection and relation extraction in information extraction based on the intuition that they are disparate tasks, one may split the task of anaphoricity decision from mention linking and introduce a separately parameterized anaphoricity module, similarly considering the discrepancy between the two tasks. Recasens et al. (2013); Moosavi and Strube (2016); *inter alia* have pursued similar ideas in the pre-neural era, but it has still not yet been explored with deep models.

5.2 The Linker's Errors

While the detector struggles with anaphoricity decisions, the linker explicitly models anaphoricity by assigning the dummy to extra mentions. It is hence also viable to determine anaphoricity in the linker. Indeed, the current detector would suffice with a stronger linker: in Table 3, the oracle linker gets near-perfect scores with the original mentions (not perfect since the candidates are not gold).[6]

To analyze the remaining non-anaphoricity linker errors, we assume a perfect anaphoric mention detector. Here, conflated entities is the single major error source (last row of Table 2). Table 6 shows 150 manually categorized conflated entities in the CoNLL-12 development set.[7] Suboptimal pronoun resolution is the biggest issue, and the linker also tends to link spans with various degrees of text match or semantic proximity. Within pronoun errors, the most common case is a pronoun linked to an incorrect nominal (in Table 6), occurring 43 times. Sometimes two pronouns, often identical, are incorrectly linked, a case that necessitates better higher-order inference. Third person pronouns with different referents are conflated 29 times. Errors with first or second person pronouns occur 37 times, usually due to speaker switching.

Similar to §5.1, separately parameterizing the linker's encoder may help reduce conflation: intuitively, the span representation for mention detection may promote homogeneity. Meanwhile, the lack of discerning span-internal content for certain error types including pronoun resolution and exact match, combined with current systems' trend to rely on such cues (Lu and Ng, 2020), calls for more focus on improving their contextual reasoning.

6 Conclusion

We analyzed the complex interaction between the mention detector and linker in the mainstream coarse-to-fine coreference system. Using oracle experiments, we showed that, while detector recall is important, higher anaphoric mention precision would lead to dramatically better linker performance, though achieving this is difficult. We also demonstrated that the oracle linker performance is near perfect and that the vast majority of remaining linker errors besides anaphoricity decisions are about pronoun resolution. We hope these discoveries will help future coreference research.

[6] A modified oracle linker that only considers coarse-pruned antecedents (Lee et al., 2018) still gets 96.61 and 98.65 F_1 on CoNLL-12 and PreCo. The small difference compared to considering all antecedents also shows that, with a strong linker, coarse-to-fine pruning has only negligible performance impact while substantially reducing the decision space.

[7] Joshi et al. (2019) and Lu and Ng (2020) conducted similar analyses but we study in a more controlled setting by excluding detector errors and focusing on entity conflation, the largest remaining error source.

References

Saliha Azzam, Kevin Humphreys, and Robert Gaizauskas. 1999. Using coreference chains for text summarization. In *Coreference and Its Applications*.

Hong Chen, Zhenhua Fan, Hao Lu, Alan Yuille, and Shu Rong. 2018. PreCo: A large-scale dataset in preschool vocabulary for coreference resolution. In *Proceedings of the 2018 Conference on Empirical Methods in Natural Language Processing*, pages 172–181, Brussels, Belgium. Association for Computational Linguistics. Downloaded from `https://preschool-lab.github.io/PreCo`.

Pradeep Dasigi, Nelson F. Liu, Ana Marasović, Noah A. Smith, and Matt Gardner. 2019. Quoref: A reading comprehension dataset with questions requiring coreferential reasoning. In *Proceedings of the 2019 Conference on Empirical Methods in Natural Language Processing and the 9th International Joint Conference on Natural Language Processing (EMNLP-IJCNLP)*, pages 5925–5932, Hong Kong, China. Association for Computational Linguistics.

Luheng He, Kenton Lee, Omer Levy, and Luke Zettlemoyer. 2018. Jointly predicting predicates and arguments in neural semantic role labeling. In *Proceedings of the 56th Annual Meeting of the Association for Computational Linguistics (Volume 2: Short Papers)*, pages 364–369, Melbourne, Australia. Association for Computational Linguistics.

Zhengbao Jiang, Wei Xu, Jun Araki, and Graham Neubig. 2020. Generalizing natural language analysis through span-relation representations. In *Proceedings of the 58th Annual Meeting of the Association for Computational Linguistics*, pages 2120–2133, Online. Association for Computational Linguistics.

Mandar Joshi, Danqi Chen, Yinhan Liu, Daniel S Weld, Luke Zettlemoyer, and Omer Levy. 2020. Spanbert: Improving pre-training by representing and predicting spans. *Transactions of the Association for Computational Linguistics*, 8:64–77.

Mandar Joshi, Omer Levy, Luke Zettlemoyer, and Daniel Weld. 2019. BERT for coreference resolution: Baselines and analysis. In *Proceedings of the 2019 Conference on Empirical Methods in Natural Language Processing and the 9th International Joint Conference on Natural Language Processing (EMNLP-IJCNLP)*, pages 5803–5808, Hong Kong, China. Association for Computational Linguistics.

Nikolaos Kolitsas, Octavian-Eugen Ganea, and Thomas Hofmann. 2018. End-to-end neural entity linking. In *Proceedings of the 22nd Conference on Computational Natural Language Learning*, pages 519–529, Brussels, Belgium. Association for Computational Linguistics.

Jonathan K. Kummerfeld and Dan Klein. 2013. Error-driven analysis of challenges in coreference resolution. In *Proceedings of the 2013 Conference on Empirical Methods in Natural Language Processing*, pages 265–277, Seattle, Washington, USA. Association for Computational Linguistics.

Heeyoung Lee, Yves Peirsman, Angel Chang, Nathanael Chambers, Mihai Surdeanu, and Dan Jurafsky. 2011. Stanford's multi-pass sieve coreference resolution system at the conll-2011 shared task. In *Proceedings of the fifteenth conference on computational natural language learning: Shared task*, pages 28–34. Association for Computational Linguistics.

Kenton Lee, Luheng He, Mike Lewis, and Luke Zettlemoyer. 2017. End-to-end neural coreference resolution. In *Proceedings of the 2017 Conference on Empirical Methods in Natural Language Processing*, pages 188–197, Copenhagen, Denmark. Association for Computational Linguistics.

Kenton Lee, Luheng He, and Luke Zettlemoyer. 2018. Higher-order coreference resolution with coarse-to-fine inference. In *Proceedings of the 2018 Conference of the North American Chapter of the Association for Computational Linguistics: Human Language Technologies, Volume 2 (Short Papers)*, pages 687–692, New Orleans, Louisiana. Association for Computational Linguistics.

Jing Lu and Vincent Ng. 2020. Conundrums in entity coreference resolution: Making sense of the state of the art. In *Proceedings of the 2020 Conference on Empirical Methods in Natural Language Processing (EMNLP)*, pages 6620–6631, Online. Association for Computational Linguistics.

Yi Luan, Dave Wadden, Luheng He, Amy Shah, Mari Ostendorf, and Hannaneh Hajishirzi. 2019. A general framework for information extraction using dynamic span graphs. In *Proceedings of the 2019 Conference of the North American Chapter of the Association for Computational Linguistics: Human Language Technologies, Volume 1 (Long and Short Papers)*, pages 3036–3046, Minneapolis, Minnesota. Association for Computational Linguistics.

Sebastian Martschat and Michael Strube. 2015. Latent structures for coreference resolution. *Transactions of the Association for Computational Linguistics*, 3:405–418.

Nafise Sadat Moosavi and Michael Strube. 2016. Search space pruning: A simple solution for better coreference resolvers. In *Proceedings of the 2016 Conference of the North American Chapter of the Association for Computational Linguistics: Human Language Technologies*, pages 1005–1011, San Diego, California. Association for Computational Linguistics.

Haoruo Peng, Daniel Khashabi, and Dan Roth. 2015. Solving hard coreference problems. In *Proceedings of the 2015 Conference of the North American Chapter of the Association for Computational Linguistics: Human Language Technologies*, pages 809–

819, Denver, Colorado. Association for Computational Linguistics.

Sameer Pradhan, Alessandro Moschitti, Nianwen Xue, Olga Uryupina, and Yuchen Zhang. 2012. Conll-2012 shared task: Modeling multilingual unrestricted coreference in ontonotes. In *Joint Conference on EMNLP and CoNLL-Shared Task*, pages 1–40. Association for Computational Linguistics.

Marta Recasens, Marie-Catherine de Marneffe, and Christopher Potts. 2013. The life and death of discourse entities: Identifying singleton mentions. In *Proceedings of the 2013 Conference of the North American Chapter of the Association for Computational Linguistics: Human Language Technologies*, pages 627–633, Atlanta, Georgia. Association for Computational Linguistics.

Sanjay Subramanian and Dan Roth. 2019. Improving generalization in coreference resolution via adversarial training. In *Proceedings of the Eighth Joint Conference on Lexical and Computational Semantics (*SEM 2019)*, pages 192–197, Minneapolis, Minnesota. Association for Computational Linguistics.

Olga Uryupina. 2009. Detecting anaphoricity and antecedenthood for coreference resolution. *Procesamiento del Lenguaje Natural*, 42.

Ashish Vaswani, Noam Shazeer, Niki Parmar, Jakob Uszkoreit, Llion Jones, Aidan N Gomez, Łukasz Kaiser, and Illia Polosukhin. 2017. Attention is all you need. In *Advances in neural information processing systems*, pages 5998–6008.

Sam Wiseman, Alexander M. Rush, and Stuart M. Shieber. 2016. Learning global features for coreference resolution. In *Proceedings of the 2016 Conference of the North American Chapter of the Association for Computational Linguistics: Human Language Technologies*, pages 994–1004, San Diego, California. Association for Computational Linguistics.

Wei Wu, Fei Wang, Arianna Yuan, Fei Wu, and Jiwei Li. 2020. CorefQA: Coreference resolution as query-based span prediction. In *Proceedings of the 58th Annual Meeting of the Association for Computational Linguistics*, pages 6953–6963, Online. Association for Computational Linguistics.

Liyan Xu and Jinho D. Choi. 2020. Revealing the myth of higher-order inference in coreference resolution. In *Proceedings of the 2020 Conference on Empirical Methods in Natural Language Processing (EMNLP)*, pages 8527–8533, Online. Association for Computational Linguistics.

Rui Zhang, Cícero Nogueira dos Santos, Michihiro Yasunaga, Bing Xiang, and Dragomir Radev. 2018. Neural coreference resolution with deep biaffine attention by joint mention detection and mention clustering. In *Proceedings of the 56th Annual Meeting of the Association for Computational Linguistics (Volume 2: Short Papers)*, pages 102–107, Melbourne, Australia. Association for Computational Linguistics.

Jieyu Zhao, Tianlu Wang, Mark Yatskar, Vicente Ordonez, and Kai-Wei Chang. 2018. Gender bias in coreference resolution: Evaluation and debiasing methods. In *Proceedings of the 2018 Conference of the North American Chapter of the Association for Computational Linguistics: Human Language Technologies, Volume 2 (Short Papers)*, pages 15–20, New Orleans, Louisiana. Association for Computational Linguistics.

Zexuan Zhong and Danqi Chen. 2021. A frustratingly easy approach for entity and relation extraction. In *Proceedings of the 2021 Conference of the North American Chapter of the Association for Computational Linguistics: Human Language Technologies*, pages 50–61, Online. Association for Computational Linguistics.

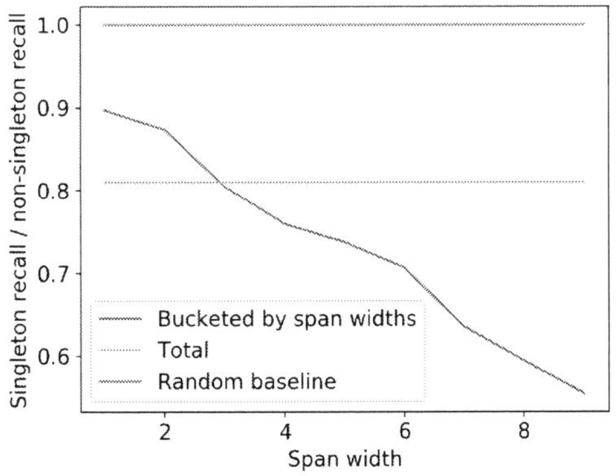

Figure 1: The PreCo anaphoric mention classifier confusion index (§5.1) on spans with different widths.

A Dataset Statistics

We use the English portion of the CoNLL-12 shared task (Pradhan et al., 2012) and the PreCo (Chen et al., 2018) dataset. The former contains 2,802/343/348 training/development/testing documents and the latter has 36.6K training documents and 500 each for development and testing.

B Heuristically Generated CoNLL-12 All Mentions

We heuristically generate the set of all mentions for CoNLL-12 in a recall-oriented manner. We use the gold syntactic information as a proxy and consider the union of all phrases tagged with NP or NML and all words tagged with PRP, PRP$, WP, WDT, WRB, NNP, VB, VBD, VBN, VBG, VBZ, or VBP. This set includes 99.63% anaphoric mentions which constitute 20.89% of this set. We obtain the set of all mentions by merging this set with the non-singleton mentions to ensure all mentions are a superset of anaphoric mentions.

C The Confusion Index's Variation With Span Width

In Figure 1, we plot how the confusion index of the PreCo anaphoric mention classifier (§5.1) changes with span widths. The classifier's inability to make anaphoricity decisions is the most pronounced for short phrases, possibly because these phrases are also more likely to appear as both singleton and anaphoric mentions whose anaphoricity status is especially hard to determine, discussed in §5.1.

Association for Computational Linguistics
209 N. Eighth Street
Stroudsburg, Pennsylvania 18360

CURRAN ASSOCIATES INC.
proceedings.com

ISBN 978-1-7138-9176-5

3rd Workshop on Knowledge Augmented Methods for NLP (KnowledgeNLP 2024)

Bangkok, Thailand
16 August 2024